Eighteenth-Century
English Literature

MODERN ESSAYS IN CRITICISM

Eighteenth-Century English Literature

MODERN ESSAYS IN CRITICISM

Edited by JAMES L. CLIFFORD

A GALAXY BOOK

New York OXFORD UNIVERSITY PRESS 1959

CONTENTS

INTRODUCTION   *vii*
JAMES L. CLIFFORD

THE GLOOM OF THE TORY SATIRISTS   3
LOUIS I. BREDVOLD

'WIT AND POETRY AND POPE':
SOME OBSERVATIONS ON HIS IMAGERY   21
MAYNARD MACK

POPE ON WIT: THE *ESSAY ON CRITICISM*   42
EDWARD NILES HOOKER

POPE SEEN THROUGH HIS LETTERS   62
JOHN BUTT

THE BACKGROUND OF THE ATTACK ON
SCIENCE IN THE AGE OF POPE   68
R. F. JONES

THE CONCISENESS OF SWIFT   84
HERBERT DAVIS

A MODEST PROPOSAL AND POPULOUSNESS   102
LOUIS A. LANDA

THE PRIDE OF LEMUEL GULLIVER   112
SAMUEL HOLT MONK

JOHN GAY   130
JAMES SUTHERLAND

ADDISON   144
C. S. LEWIS

ROBINSON CRUSOE AS A MYTH   158
    IAN WATT

THOMSON AND BURNS   180
    D. NICHOL SMITH

AESTHETIC IMPLICATIONS OF
NEWTON'S *OPTICKS*   194
    MARJORIE HOPE NICOLSON

EIGHTEENTH-CENTURY POETIC DICTION   212
    GEOFFREY TILLOTSON

THE POETRY OF THOMAS GRAY   233
    LORD DAVID CECIL

FIELDING'S SOCIAL OUTLOOK   251
    GEORGE SHERBURN

LAURENCE STERNE, APOSTLE OF
LAUGHTER   274
    RUFUS D. S. PUTNEY

THE DOUBLE TRADITION OF DR. JOHNSON   285
    BERTRAND H. BRONSON

JOHNSON'S CRITICISM OF
THE METAPHYSICAL POETS   300
    WILLIAM R. KEAST

TOWARDS DEFINING AN AGE OF
SENSIBILITY   311
    NORTHROP FRYE

OPTIMISM AND ROMANTICISM   319
    ARTHUR O. LOVEJOY

SELECTIVE INDEX   345

INTRODUCTION

In this volume there are twenty-one critical and scholarly selections which concentrate on the literature of eighteenth-century England. In one way or another, each challenges some deep-rooted false impression or oversimplified generalization, or provides a fresh interpretation of a major author or literary masterpiece. Complexity and richness are stressed, rather than superficial syntheses.

Too often in the past this period has been characterized by facile, broad labels. As a so-called 'Neoclassic Age,' it has been described as formal, bound by rules, illiberal, shallow, and uninspired. Its chief poet, Alexander Pope, has been called essentially a prose writer and not a true poet at all. As an era of enlightenment, when reason was pre-eminent, it is supposed to have held the imagination under such strict control as to inhibit genuine creativity. Completely lost, it seems, was man's sense of wonder. With optimism and placid confidence the accepted norm, life is reputed to have been pleasant and comfortable. Even George Saintsbury could write about 'The Peace of the Augustans' as a 'place of rest and refreshment.'

Yet every such attempt at generalization runs into inconsistencies and difficulties. If this was a time of complacence, what about Swift, Johnson, and *The Dunciad*? If this was a time of straightforward and uninspired writing, what about the many levels of meaning in *Gulliver's Travels* and the complicated artistry of Pope? For a supposed 'Age of Reason' there was a remarkable number of writers who were constantly puncturing man's pride in his own intelligence.

The plain fact is that no modern century has ever achieved unity of belief and expression. 'Neoclassic,' 'Augustan,' 'Reactionary'—'The Enlightenment,' 'The Age of Skepticism,' 'The Age of Reason,' 'The Age of Prose'—each describes only one aspect. To use Burke's phrase, one cannot with a single term draw up an indictment against a whole century.

As an alternative, it has been suggested that we should think of the period as divided into three successive parts, with the neoclassic concentration coming in the late seventeenth century, when there was more insistence on the rules and classical standards and a cynical disregard of romantic idealism. During the reigns of Queen Anne and the first two Georges, on the other hand, there emerged what might better be called 'The Age of Common Sense.' Indeed, rigid concentration on older authority was fading by the time of Addison and Pope. If there was still a search for rules, it was not because of over-dependence on ancient precedents, but because of a settled conviction that there must be some order in the universe. Although lip-service was still paid to the classics, a sturdy feeling of independence was developing, which found its most eloquent advocate in Samuel Johnson. It was every man's reliance on common sense which counted most. Then, in the latter half of the century, there followed a time of aesthetic uncertainty, of increasingly subjective sensibility, which heralded the coming romantic revival.

But even with such a useful triple division, the fact still remains that it is futile to expect homogeneity, no matter how restricted the period. If Shaftesburian benevolism is stressed, one tends to forget the savage pessimism and gloom of the satirists. If enlightened skepticism, then one must ignore the simple piety of Watts, Law, Wesley, Smart, and Cowper. Against any attempt to make a single attribute the norm, there will always be scores of conflicting elements. We are told, for example, that the Lisbon earthquake in 1755, together with Voltaire's bitter commentary, 'killed optimism.' The world, it is asserted, had been blandly confident; now it was rudely awakened by this definite evidence of the cruelty of Nature and the injustice of Providence. But who among the major English writers before 1755 had been supinely optimistic? Swift, Dryden, Pope, Johnson?

The fault has been in not keeping ever before our eyes the many deep cleavages of the time—between those who clung to the wisdom of the past, and the reckless innovators—between the tradition of nobility, and that of a down-to-earth realism—the aristocratic versus the commercial— between the land-conscious countryfolk, and the new industrialists. Moreover, two great streams of thought were struggling desperately for supremacy: the pessimistic orthodox belief in the natural depravity of man, exemplified in the Tory satirists; and the new Whig optimistic acceptance of progress and the perfectibility of human institutions, with its accompanying benevolent spirit and liberalism. There was a basic disagreement between those who attacked man's essential constitution, and those who merely expressed disapproval of his manners and everyday morals. As Louis I. Bredvold so ably points out in the first essay in this volume, there were the tough-minded and the tender-minded, and their disagreement was basic and irreconcilable. Extending more widely than in religion and philosophy, the split was also implicit in theories of art and literary style.

To be sure, the use of political labels to differentiate the two positions is dangerous. To speak of 'Tory satirists' and 'Whig perfectibilitarians and benevolists' is certain to produce some wrong impressions for modern students, since party principles have changed with the centuries, and the dichotomy was not always openly connected with politics. But whatever terms are used, the antagonism between the two fundamental positions cannot be ignored. By the mid-eighteenth century it was obvious which side had won. Indeed, even as early as the reign of Queen Anne (so C. S. Lewis suggests) the Tories sensed that they were inevitably to be the losers, and this heightened the bitterness of their attacks. Conversely, the Whigs, as certain victors, could afford to be light and amiable. Increasingly throughout the period, any stress on the brutish, depraved nature of man was certain to be resented on all sides as a libel on essential human goodness. Yet even in a time of softened sensibility there were men like Johnson who refused to accept the verdict.

All this is merely to stress the fact that the eighteenth century was complex, and that it is a mistake to attempt to impose simple patterns on its conflicts. The same is true in the matter of literary forms. It was the conviction of many nineteenth-century critics that the couplet seriously shackled poetic creativity. There were constant references to the 'jog trot' rhythms, the 'monotony of versification' of neoclassic verses. This, coupled with slurs on their 'want of originality of thought' produced by too slavish following of older genres, was enough to render obvious to every student that artistically the period was an arid desert. Although nobody today denies the depth and submerged passion in Purcell's lament of Dido, or in any of the compositions of Mozart, despite the fact that they too worked within the strict confines of classical forms, there has been a disinclination to extend the same acceptance to neoclassical poets. Yet a glance at the discussions which follow by Maynard Mack and the late Edward Hooker should be enough to dispel any lingering notions that Pope was facile, shallow, and monotonous.

Let us admit at once that to understand properly the writing of the period requires study and help. It is not easy to grasp immediately the intricacy and the allusiveness of its metaphoric structure. Moreover, there is required a genuine willingness to free oneself, for a time at least, from instinctive romantic convictions. The contents of this volume should provide stimulus and aid in such an attempt.

Obviously a collection such as this can present only a sampling of the more significant publications of recent years. Regretfully, many eminent scholars have not been included, either because of the decision to concentrate on works applicable to classroom discussion, or because the writings of these men are already easily obtainable in inexpensive reprintings. Ronald S. Crane's critical essays, W. K. Wimsatt, Jr.'s discussions of Pope's versification, Cleanth Brooks's analysis of *The Rape of the Lock,* to name only a few, are all available in paperback editions. Furthermore, the recent books by Meyer H. Abrams, Walter Jackson Bate, Ian Jack, René Wellek, and Aubrey Williams, invaluable for any understanding of the critical cross-currents of the time, are not difficult to procure. Our purpose has been to bring together essays which cannot easily be purchased, or even be found in small libraries.

There are further omissions, much to be lamented, but forced by lack of space. Those eager to carry their investigations farther afield should consult the important scholarly works of such authorities as Sir Harold Williams and Ricardo Quintana on Swift, A. D. McKillop on Thomson and the novelists, John Robert Moore on Defoe, Ernest Mossner on Hume, and Frederick A. Pottle on Boswell. Stimulating, too, are the critical evaluations of T. S. Eliot, F. R. Leavis, Allen Tate, William Empson, Austin Warren, Bonamy Dobrée, and Donald Davie, all of whom have written specifically about the period.

Rather than a balanced history of the literature of the eighteenth century, this book must be thought of merely as a series of individual explorations. There are gaps, and many of the more important figures are not discussed at all. As will be obvious, concentration is heavy on the writers of the strong Augustan tradition, rather than on the so-called pre-romantic dissidents, who have perhaps in the past received a disproportionate amount of attention. Yet there has been no attempt to impose any single unifying theme. Each contributor speaks for himself about some topic which interests him. The basis for choice has been a usefulness in stimulating further argument and detailed study.

Inclusion, it might be added, does not necessarily imply complete agreement with the position taken by each individual author. Some of the pieces are conservative, some openly provocative. A few are rigorously historical in approach; others are suggestive and interpretive in the new critical manner. Some are broadly discursive; others are careful explications of a single work. They are as different in tone and concept as can be, representing almost every modern technique.

In point of time the selections range from 1927, with one of Arthur

O. Lovejoy's epoch-making essays in the history of ideas, to a B.B.C. broadcast in 1957. All have been in print before—as public addresses or as contributions to scholarly or popular periodicals; as part of special volumes honoring D. Nichol Smith, George Sherburn, and Chauncey B. Tinker; or as sections of other scholarly works. Because some were originally published in England and others in the United States, there is a discrepancy in superficial matters of spelling, punctuation, and usage. No attempt has been made to achieve complete uniformity of style. Except for the use of single quotation marks throughout, the shift of footnotes to the end of each article for reasons of economy, and a few authorial revisions, the essays are here reproduced substantially in their original form. Indication of source, with acknowledgment of permission, appears with each article.

It is hoped that this volume will make clearer to many readers the aims and literary achievements of a complex century.

New York City
July 1958
James L. Clifford

Eighteenth-Century
English Literature

MODERN ESSAYS IN CRITICISM

remark, not to be matched elsewhere in biography; it could have appeared only in a life of Pope), 'but few biographies give a more striking proof that the loving discharge of a common duty may give a charm to a whole character. It is melancholy to add that we often have to appeal to this part of his story, to assure ourselves that Pope was really deserving of some affection.'[2] Such an admission that some human qualities, at once heavily discounted, may be discovered in a venomous creature lays bare the whole mental process of denigration in a passage which its author probably did not intend to be harsh.

It would seem, too, that too much has been made of the impairing influence on Swift and Pope of their 'crazy constitutions,' as if their satire were a phase of their medical history. There has grown up around them a kind of cult of the satiric genius as a tortured mind inhabiting a tortured body. Pope's deformity and weakness seem to add an appropriate grotesqueness to a sinister character. Swift's final insanity, which, so far as modern medical authorities can determine, was most likely the last stage of a life-long disease of the inner ear and which was therefore unrelated to his satire either as cause or effect, is raised to a more than medical significance as the fitting conclusion of the career of a bitter satirist, the awful disintegration of a great mad genius in self-devouring rage. And his remark that he would die like the tree, first at the top, is repeated with all the solemnity of an oracular doom in Greek tragedy, whereas common sense tells us that, within the limits of Swift's medical knowledge, it could only have been the apprehension of a sufferer from chronic headaches. Had Swift not lived beyond the scriptural age of three score and ten, his biographies would not have been overcharged with these dramatic themes of premonition and fate. We should still have had the 'mad parson,' but we might have had fewer intimations that his satire verges on madness, in quite another sense.

As for the diseases of the mind, the heaviest charge against Pope and Swift is a negativeness of spirit which depresses the worth and dignity of human life. But pessimism is a concept so vague and broad that it often leads to erroneous inferences and interpretations. The Tory satirists, the group gathered about Pope and Swift, did not suffer from philosophical or religious pessimism, or from anything that can be called *Weltschmerz*. There is no spiritual *malaise* in them; their gloom is not an enervating apathy. They seem generally to have had firm faith in the ultimate right order of things, and we must avoid carrying back to them such more recent philosophies of despair as are familiar in our post-Schopenhauer era. We do not even find in them that melancholy brooding over the destiny of man which in their century oppressed

Johnson and Gray. The Christian resignation of Johnson to a world in which there is little to be enjoyed and much to be endured would have fitted well with their satire—as it did with Johnson's—but it is not an attitude characteristic of Swift or Pope. Nor were they steeped, as Gray was, in the melancholy wisdom of the Greeks, which in its sobriety and humility was so nearly allied to the sadness of Johnson. Gray's *Ode on a Distant Prospect of Eton College* with its motto from Menander, and his *Hymn to Adversity* with a similar motto from Aeschylus, all admonish us that an enduring heart is the gift the gods have fittingly bestowed on the sons of men.

Such views of human fate touch issues above and beyond the reach of satire, and it was not any such cosmic gloom which hung over the Tory satirists, but a mundane darkness conjured up by human folly and knavery. The satirists were much more attentive to the problems of the world of men than to ultimate questions of philosophy and religion. Even Pope's *Essay on Man* (radiating optimism, not gloom), which seems to have come as a surprise to Swift ('I confess I did never imagine you were so deep in morals'),[3] and Bolingbroke's philosophical excursions, were speculations of a kind not common among them, and certainly did not constitute any bond of union. Prior rebuked the system-building pretensions of the human reason in both *Alma* and *Solomon*. Swift habitually ridiculed those philosophers who deal in cosmic explanations, and in *A Tale of a Tub* (Section ix) attributed their 'innovations' to madness. The learning of the Brobdingnagians 'is very defective,' reports Gulliver, 'consisting only in morality, history, poetry, and mathematics, wherein they must be allowed to excel. But the last of these is wholly applied to what may be useful in life, to the improvement of agriculture, and all mechanical arts; so that among us it would be little esteemed. And as to ideas, entities, abstractions, and transcendentals, I could never drive the least conception into their heads.' Stella, indeed, 'understood the Platonic and Epicurean philosophy, and judged very well of the defects of the latter,' as Swift recorded in his memoir of her, and her programme of studies, we may be sure, reflected the intellectual character of her friend and tutor, who never in his writings alluded to Socrates or Plato except with respect. But we know that Swift valued the Socratic dialogues, not for any 'abstractions and transcendentals,' but for their ethical and political wisdom. Gulliver's master among the Houyhnhnms laughed 'that a creature pretending to reason should value itself upon the knowledge of other people's conjectures, and in things where that knowledge, if it were certain, could be of no use. Wherein he agreed entirely with the sentiments of Socrates, as Plato delivers them; which I mention as the highest honour I can do that prince of philosophers.' Moral and political wisdom occupies a level a little lower than metaphysics, and doubtless a little lower also than the greatest poetry. But Swift's genius moved in this middle flight, and here his massive common sense and his satiric gift had their full opportunity. The moment we try to read more into Swift than he read in Socrates, we misinterpret him. In one of his greatest passages he praised credulity as 'a more peaceful possession of the mind than curiosity,' and laid down the proposition 'that wisdom, which converses about the surface,' is therefore preferable 'to that pretended philosophy, which enters into the depth of things, and then comes gravely back with information and discoveries, that in the inside they are good for nothing,'[4] Anyone who has had experience in reading this passage with modern young people can testify that it is more often than not taken as the language of philosophical nihilism. But Swift was not thinking in metaphysical terms about appearance and reality. He was letting his irony play over the repugnance some people feel for satire, for 'the art of exposing weak sides, and publishing infirmities.' It was in 'most corporeal beings,' that is, human beings, such as the flayed woman and the stripped carcass of the beau, that 'the outside hath been infinitely preferable to the in.' The 'serene, peaceful state, of being a fool among knaves' is a moral condition which we may choose, but for which we must ourselves accept the responsibility.

In this exposure of the insides of human nature, in stripping the human carcass, the satirists were united, but again only on the level of practical common sense; they were observers, not spinners of theory. They naturally ignored the cynical materialistic psychology of Hobbes and Mandeville, which was completely alien to their spirit. But it is significant that they could not agree even on the system of La Rochefoucauld. When Pope wrote Swift in October 1725 that he was busy with 'a set of maxims in opposition to all Rochefoucauld's principles,' he drew from Swift the celebrated confession that La Rochefoucauld 'is my favourite, because I found my whole character in him. However I will read him again, because it is possible I may have since undergone some alterations.'[5] Bolingbroke promptly dissociated himself from 'the founder of your sect, that noble original whom you think it so great an honour to resemble.'[6] From Gay and Arbuthnot we have no comment on the matter. Swift therefore stands alone among these men as a professed disciple of the author of the *Maxims*.

But we must not take this profession too literally, as Professor Quintana has already warned us.[7] The famous system of reducing every virtue to a form of disguised selfishness, though far from being the whole of the *Maxims,* is nevertheless their conspicuous and distinguishing feature. With a finesse far beyond the capacity of either Hobbes or Mandeville, whose systems at some points paralleled his, La Roche-foucauld exposed certain kinds of deception which human nature prac-tises on itself. He applied his method with brilliant virtuosity, but it must be admitted that his commentary on human nature is rather specialized and iterative. One can learn and practise the trick of it. To turn from the *Maxims* to the works of Swift is like passing from a narrow room into the great world. Swift also probed the deceitfulness of the human heart, but his *art de connaître les hommes* is not reducible to rule or system. In both originality of thought and fertility of wit Swift was the greater man, and the philosophy of the *Maxims* could have filled only one corner of his capacious mind. When Swift remarks that 'complainers never succeed at Court, though railers do,'[8] we note his characteristic qualities in the brief pronouncement; the startling, amus-ingly cynical paradox mellows, as we linger over it, into an utterance of shrewdness and practical wisdom.

Swift habitually wrote with the purpose of imparting wisdom, and his satire is therefore quite different in tone and temper from that of La Rochefoucauld. The latter composed his observations in the period after his retirement from active life, when he could assume the vantage of a seigniorial detachment; he played the roles of spectator, psycholo-gist, and stylist. For the author of the *Maxims* a fault in mankind was something to be disdainfully indicated and wittily exposed; but for Swift it was also something to be judged, castigated, and corrected. Swift wrote, not from a position of detachment, but in the stream of events. Aside from his *bagatelles,* he was normally a publicist, a man of action, by every instinct a manager of affairs. From his retreat at Letcombe in the fateful month of July 1714 he truly described himself to Arbuthnot: 'I could never let people run mad without telling and warning them sufficiently.' His whole biography is a continuous record of his attempts to patch up differences, guide the choice of policies, abolish abuses, manage the presentation of new political and ecclesiasti-cal measures, and in general serve as counsellor to anyone and everyone with whom business or friendship brought him into contact. His interest in history, which Professor Nichol Smith has noted,[9] is another aspect of his eminently practical cast of mind. His satire is so largely occasional and journalistic because of this innate urge for action, and it can be fully understood only as a part of the history of his time.

As these practical urges of Swift's nature differentiate his satire on the one hand from the amused detachment of La Rochefoucauld, so on the other they distinguish it from the depressive melancholy that feeds on stagnant brooding. The satire of Swift, even at its bitterest, never depends for its intensity on any sense of frustration; it has the force of intellectual statement—often mock-scientific in tone—and has the effect of arousing in the reader, by means of the *vis comica* and indignation, a will to action which is sympathetic with Swift's own character. Even the darkest page of Swift leaves us with this feeling of soundness at the core, with a firm conviction of our moral competence and responsibility. It is the expression of a bitter but not a sick mind, and has the invigorating power of a call to action.

This firm grip on actualities is characteristic also of the satire of the other members of Swift's brotherhood, Arbuthnot, Gay, and Pope. They were as ready as Swift, whose genius towered among them, to aline themselves in political struggles, even though political parties were still thought undesirable in principle. A political party—that is, the party one was opposed to—was a faction seeking to disrupt the national unity. To give up one's neutrality and become a party man, even with the right party, was in a sense a sacrifice of moral position and justifiable only because the nation was in danger. In an age when each party maintained that it was the voice of the nation and the other was a faction, it was natural that imputations of political and moral turpitude should be freely exchanged in the controversy on the real issues. Friendships across the political line were chilled by suspicion and could be maintained only by cautious and magnanimous demeanour on both sides. Hence the peculiarly bitter asperities of both Whig and Tory satirists and their tendency to resort to the lampoon, the popular weapon of all parties in all the controversies of the age, literary as well as political. Hence also the practical intent of so much of the Tory satire. For better as well as for worse, the Tory satirists were in the mêlée, not above it, and they wrote with the conviction that they were dealing battle-blows to save from extinction the virtue and glory of England.

Wit and politics drew them together before the end of Queen Anne's reign into a literary collaboration symbolized by the Scriblerus Club, which diverted itself by ridiculing pedantry rather than political iniquity. But the inclusion in this brotherhood of Oxford and Bolingbroke indicates that the Tory complexion of the group was as openly professed as the Whiggism of Button's Coffee House. Arbuthnot, the universally beloved physician to the Queen, had already ventured into Tory journalism and thus discovered that vein of satire which 'lay like a Mine in the Earth, which the Owner for a long time never knew of.'[10]

In a companionship so intimate and so congenial it is difficult to divine what each individual contributed to the other; but in the free give and take many a suggestion thrown out by one man in a convivial hour was later developed by another into a major literary work. Henceforth the members of the Scriblerus Club constituted a defensive and offensive alliance; they freely exchanged confidences; they distrusted the same men and the same measures; above all they were agreed on the unreliability of the nature of that animal called man.

The sincerity of their professions was immediately put to the severest test by the disintegration of the ministry of Oxford and Bolingbroke. In the sequence of events leading up to the final catastrophe they had an opportunity to observe how precariously the welfare of the whole nation, present and future, depended on traits of human character. In bitterness they had to admit to themselves and to one another that England was, from their point of view, being betrayed by their own friends, Oxford and Bolingbroke, not to mention the indecisive poor sick queen. Swift indicated publicly his own forecast of the disaster that was coming by withdrawing early in the summer to Letcombe, whence he refused angrily all solicitations to return to the scene where the drama was playing itself out. He was 'weary to death of Courts and Ministers and business and politics. . . . I shall say no more but that I care not to live in storms when I can no longer do service in the ship and am able to get out of it.'[11] He was, however, busy writing something that he thought would 'vex' the great ministers; it was the pamphlet, *Some Free Thoughts upon the Present State of Affairs*, in which he set forth how, with other policies, and more wisdom, and less foolish dissension among the ministers, the 'present state of affairs' might have been far different. 'It may serve for a great lesson of humiliation to mankind,' Swift was writing in the rectory at Letcombe, 'to behold the habits and passions of men otherwise highly accomplished, triumphing over interest, friendship, honour, and their own personal safety, as well as that of their country, and probably of a most gracious princess, who hath entrusted it to them.'[12] Such were the reflections Swift intended to publish to the nation as the crisis was approaching. The pamphlet was a castigating sermon to his friends, the Tory ministers, who had been measured by the moral test and found wanting. They had also failed by the test of common sense, from first to last so important in the eyes of Swift; their 'mystical manner of proceeding' baffled and galled him:

I have been frequently assured by great ministers, that politics were nothing but common sense; which, as it was the only thing they spoke,

9

so it was the only thing they could have wished I should not believe. God hath given the bulk of mankind a capacity to understand reason when it is fairly offered; and by reason they would easily be governed, if it were left to their choice. Those princes in all ages who were most distinguished for their mysterious skill in government, found by the event, that they had ill consulted their own quiet, or the ease and happiness of their people.[13]

Swift's bitter anger at Oxford and Bolingbroke in 1714 reappeared years later as the contempt of the King of Brobdingnag for 'all *mystery, refinement,* and *intrigue,* either in a prince or a minister.' The lovable Arbuthnot was, if anything, more severe even than Swift:

I have an opportunity calmly and philosophically to consider that treasure of vileness and baseness, that I always believed to be in the heart of man; and to behold them exert their insolence and baseness; every new instance, instead of surprising and grieving me, as it does some of my friends, really diverts me, and in a manner improves my theory.[14]

That is a satirist's view of human nature, but Swift and Arbuthnot were not at this time engaging in satire; they were assessing in all seriousness the moral meaning of the Tory collapse. Their intellectual honesty and resolute clear-sightedness in this episode vouches for their integrity when they turn to satire.

In spite of these strains the personal friendships between wits and ministers held fast, not least perhaps because of the candour and sincerity in which Swift set an example. 'In your public capacity,' Swift told Oxford, 'you have often angered me to the heart, but, as a private man, never.'[15] The threats of danger which for a time hung over Oxford, Bolingbroke, Ormond, and Prior naturally only strengthened the loyalties of the whole group. However, defeated and dispersed as they were, they hardly ventured into politics for a dozen years. Swift won a heartening victory in the early twenties with his *Drapier's Letters,* but it was only towards 1726, when Swift first dared to return to London, carrying with him the completed manuscript of *Gulliver's Travels,* that the survivors of the Scriblerus Club (Oxford and Parnell and Prior had died) resumed their old intimacy and gathered their forces for their great campaign. Bolingbroke had returned from France and rejoined Pope. Letters to and from Swift became more frequent and in 1725 contained suggestions that he might risk a visit to England. On 15 October Pope expressed a hope that 'you are coming towards us, and that you incline more and more to your old friends in proportion as you draw nearer to them; in short that you are getting into our vortex.' Two days later Arbuthnot added his plea: 'I cannot help imagining some of our old club met together like mariners after a storm.' It was as mariners after a storm that they met again the following summer.

But new storms had been brewing, and, with their sense of solidarity renewed, they were soon to be engaged in a prolonged satirical crusade against the degeneracy of the times. Even their ridicule of pedantry, dullness, and bad taste now assumed a larger social significance, as related to their general attack on moral and political corruption. Dr. Johnson, whose misfortune it was never to understand Swift, thought they were all guilty of self-righteousness:

> From the letters that pass between him [Swift] and Pope it might be inferred that they, with Arbuthnot and Gay, had engrossed all the understanding and virtue of mankind, that their merits filled the world; or that there was no hope of more. They shew the age involved in darkness, and shade the picture with sullen emulation.[16]

The satirist is perforce a judge, and he is nothing unless he can speak with the voice of righteousness. The darkness of his gloom is the measure of the depth of his indignation, and a sense of isolation is inevitable in his calling. Johnson had himself in his younger days joined forces with the Tories against the corruption of the Walpole era, and his satire in *London* is as gloomy and scornful as any. The warm friendship and mutual confidence which Pope and Swift and their friends so constantly reaffirmed in their letters was the obverse of their common bitterness over the decay of the nation. It is possible to agree in substance with the somewhat sentimental comment of Richter, with which Birkbeck Hill annotated the passage just quoted from Johnson:

> Have not many others felt themselves, like me, warmed and encouraged by the touching quiet love of these manly hearts, which, though cold, cutting, and sharp to the outer world, yet laboured and throbbed in their common inner world warmly and tenderly for one another?[17]

Good satire may be withering, it may be dark anger, it may be painfully bitter; but it cannot be great satire without having at its core a moral idealism expressing itself in righteous indignation. The *saeva indignatio* which Swift suffered from is radically different in quality from a morbid *Schadenfreude*. Once that distinction is admitted we have the essential justification for our pleasure in satire, as well as an understanding of the fellow feeling with which the satirists sustained one another.

In the declining moral tone of England under Walpole they now professed to see the extinction of the best elements of English life. Under the circumstances it was inevitable that they should turn their satire on the political situation. The leaders of the Opposition to Walpole and the Court were mostly veteran Tories, old friends of Swift and Pope, and there was Bolingbroke operating without much disguise in the background. The satirists had a score to settle with the Whigs in general, but Walpole provided them with special opportunities for the exercise of their talent, which they were not backward to improve. John Gay was able, by adding some political touches to his ballad operas, to raise an ominous political storm, accompanied by a minor social disturbance at Court; the inoffensive Gay, as Arbuthnot wrote Swift, became 'one of the obstructions to the peace of Europe,' and 'if he should travel about the country he would have hecatombs of roasted oxen sacrificed to him.' Swift, from Dublin, congratulated Gay on 'the felicity of thriving by the displeasure of Courts and Ministers.'[18] The political strains and tensions of the time became increasingly apparent in the life and work of Pope, now entering upon the period of his greatest poetic achievement. It was therefore only to be expected that, in spite of his professed resolution to avoid party, he should find that his satire involved him in attacks on the corruption emanating from high places. In the final *Dunciad* the celebration of the Greater Mysteries of the Goddess of Dullness is opened by a wizard who represents the Court influence and who is therefore assumed to stand for Walpole himself:

> With that, a Wizard old his Cup extends;
> Which whoso tastes, forgets his former friends,
> Sire, Ancestors, Himself. One casts his eyes
> Up to a Star, and like Endymion dies:
> A Feather, shooting from another's head,
> Extracts his brain; and Principle is fled;
> Lost is his God, his Country, every thing:
> And nothing left but Homage to a King!
> The vulgar herd turn off to roll with Hogs,
> To run with Horses, or to hunt with Dogs;
> But, sad example! never to escape
> Their Infamy, still keep the human shape.[19]

The Mysteries which are thus happily initiated under the highest auspices lead directly to the final triumph of Chaos and Universal Darkness in those concluding lines which Dr. Johnson always praised as noble, and which bring to a climax and conclusion the satirical career of Pope in all its aspects. After that pronouncement of doom there was nothing more to be said.

But Pope and his friends, apostles of disenchantment, were by no means alone in their apprehensions for England. Walpole enjoys a bad pre-eminence among English statesmen for drawing upon himself the hostility of writers of all parties and shades of party, men representing the best elements in the nation. Poets and satirists alike show the age involved in darkness. The old Tories associated amicably with the younger Whigs, the Boy Patriots. By 1735 Pope was on the friendliest terms with the future Earl of Chatham, whose letters and speeches at this time abounded with such expressions as 'this gloomy scene' and 'this disgraced country.' This was the age that we know from Hogarth's pictures, from Fielding's political farces and *Jonathan Wild*. The literature of protest was copious, and Warton's list of some of the notable contributions will indicate its great variety of source and nature:

> About this time a great spirit of liberty was prevalent. All the men of wit and genius joined in increasing it. Glover wrote his *Leonidas*; Nugent his *Odes to Mankind* and *to Mr. Pulteney*; King his *Miltonis Epistola* and *Templum Libertatis*; Thomson his *Brittania*, his *Liberty*, and his *Agamemnon*; Mallet his *Mustapha*; Brooke his *Gustavus Vasa*; Pope his *Imitations* and these two *Dialogues* [the *Epilogue to the Satires*]; and Johnson his *London*.[20]

In his poem Johnson described the metropolis of those 'degenerate days' in these terms:

> Here let those reign, whom pensions can incite
> To vote a patriot black, a courtier white;
> Explain their country's dear-bought rights away,
> And plead for pirates in the face of day;
> With slavish tenets taint our poison'd youth,
> And lend a lie the confidence of truth.[21]

This gloomy theme of the decadence of England continued to occupy English writers as long as English politics remained in the doldrums, even after Walpole was gone. The sentimentalists echoed its phrases, especially in their eulogies of the life of primitive man; Joseph Warton, in *The Enthusiast* (1744), wished to escape to a life among the simple Indian swains of the New World, 'since Virtue leaves our wretched land.' John Brown summed up the whole case thoroughly and elaborately when he published in 1757 his famous *Estimate of the Manners and*

Principles of the Times. The 'ruling character' of the times he asserted to be 'a vain, luxurious, and selfish effeminacy.' He laid the blame impartially at the door of every portion of the public; but the political significance of his indictment is evident from his characterization of Walpole 'in these few words, that while he seemed to *strengthen* the *Superstructure,* he *weakened* the *Foundations* of our Constitution.'[22]

But Brown's sensational book, after being the town talk for a season, lapsed thereafter into an obscurity from which even modern scholars have been reluctant to rescue it. It happened to come out in the very year when Pitt began the great administration which was to win England glorious victories abroad and restore her morale at home. The grim predictions of Brown were made to seem spectral and unreal by the splendours of Pitt's leadership, and therefore, as Lecky long ago pointed out, it is difficult even for us to do full justice to the *Estimate.*[23] The Tory satirists of course suffered a similar loss of credit. When Dr. Johnson in his old age was writing the *Lives of the Poets* he had only words of disparagement for the 'long course of opposition to Sir Robert Walpole,' the opposition to which he had in 1739 contributed *Marmor Norfolciense,* but which he now said 'had filled the nation with clamours for liberty, of which no man felt the want, and with care for liberty, which was not in danger.'[24] About the same time Joseph Warton expressed a similar judgement in his commentary on Pope's two *Dialogues* of 1738:

> The satire in these pieces is of the strongest kind; sometimes, direct and declamatory, at others, ironical and oblique. It must be owned to be carried to excess. Our country is represented as totally ruined, and overwhelmed with dissipation, depravity, and corruption. Yet this very country, so emasculated and debased by every species of folly and wickedness, in about twenty years afterwards, carried its triumphs over all its enemies, through all the quarters of the world, and astonished the most distant nations with a display of uncommon efforts, abilities, and virtues. So vain and groundless are the prognostications of poets, as well as politicians.[25]

It was the fate of all the literature of the Opposition to Walpole to appear excessive as it receded into the past. All the Cassandra prophecies of doom, the bitter diatribes of the satirists, the patriotic appeals of the poets, even the jeremiads of Pitt himself, faded into historical documents. Henceforth, to recapture their original appeal, and even to understand what they contributed to the regenerative forces aroused by Pitt, has required the exercise of the historical imagination.

On the whole, these historical considerations seem favourable to the satirists and a justification of their indignation. Literal accuracy is not, of course, to be expected in satire, which, like caricature, presents a truth by means of a distortion. In satire, as in any art which aims to imitate nature under ideal conditions, the general ideas and qualities of mind of the artist command our real attention and determine our response. The mass of contemporaneous references in the work of the Tory satirists, with the subsidiary question of their faithfulness to fact, must not be allowed to obscure the permanent values enveloped in the tissue of particulars. The satire of this group, taken as a whole, reflects the general views of life held by all its members. They were not content with attacking moral and political corruption merely on the superficial level of fashions or manners or passing social conditions. They would not 'sodder and patch up the flaws and imperfections of nature.' Basically, they were opposed to the sect, to be met with in all ages, which holds that the evil in the world is not in men, but between them. They probed for its origin in the recesses of human nature; they cut into the flesh. All their allusions to particular individuals provide so many case-histories of the baseness of man. Their work remains for all ages a painful discipline in self-examination and humiliation.

In this disillusionment, as in their politics, the satirists were old-fashioned. When they are viewed against the setting of the history of literature and thought of the whole eighteenth century, they appear as survivors of a dying era. Even as they were at work, they were challenged by what seemed a more modern spirit, a more sympathetic and comforting way of looking at human nature. The 'softness of the heart,' Steele intimated in his preface to *The Conscious Lovers* (1723), is a greater merit than the 'hardness of the head.' In the early years of the century this spirit flourished in Whig literary circles, very obvious in Steele, more subtly pervasive in Addison. As the century progressed it gradually prevailed everywhere; in spite of the declared opposition of Fielding and Johnson and Burke, the 'new sensibility' dominated in poetry, drama, and fiction. The same change was going on in France and the rest of Europe. La Rochefoucauld was replaced by Vauvenargues; Rousseau attacked Molière and drenched Europe in sentiment. Towards the end of the century the doctrine of the essential goodness of man became the basic tenet of the French revolutionary philosophers, and of William Godwin, who believed that nature never made a dunce. In our own time it serves as the indispensable assumption of those schools of political thought which attribute the evils of our human condition exclusively to environment, absolve human nature from all fault, and, as a logical consequence, outlaw genetics as an 'anti-social science.' In the present day the Tory satirists appear as old-fashioned, and to young readers as novel, as the doctrine of original sin.

The new literature of sentiment in the eighteenth century had, of course, its merits, especially as an influence in the reformation of manners, and Addison's work was highly praised for this reason by both Gay and Pope.[26] But ever since the eighteenth century the custom has obtained of pointing the praise of these merits by adding some disparagement of Pope and Swift. Joseph Warton quoted with approval James Harris, nephew and disciple of Shaftesbury: 'Whoever has been reading this unnatural Filth,' Harris wrote, referring to the fourth book of *Gulliver's Travels,* 'let him turn for a moment to a *Spectator* of Addison, and observe the Philanthropy of that Classical writer.'[27] As no one writer is adequate to all the needs of literature or life, it may be equally appropriate to recommend the satirists as a complement and correction to the literature of philanthropy.

Mandeville, a tavern character whose malice sharpened his wit, was especially qualified to expose the weaknesses of what he disliked. He disliked the *Characteristics* of the third Earl of Shaftesbury, which presented a system of ethics not only contrary to his own, but, he maintained, contrary to the teachings of 'the generality of moralists and philosophers' up to that time. Shaftesbury, he said,

> imagines that men without any trouble or violence upon themselves may be naturally virtuous. He seems to require and expect goodness in his species, as we do a sweet taste in grapes and China oranges, of which, if any of them are sour, we boldly pronounce that they are not come to that perfection their nature is capable of. . . . His notions I confess are generous and refined; they are a high compliment to human-kind, and capable by the help of a little enthusiasm of inspiring us with the most noble sentiments concerning the dignity of our exalted nature. What a pity it is that they are not true! [28]

Mandeville likewise turned his sarcasm on Steele:

> When the incomparable Sir Richard Steele, in the usual elegance of his easy style, dwells on the praises of his sublime species, and with all the embellishments of rhetoric sets forth the excellency of human nature, it is impossible not to be charmed with his happy turns of thought, and the politeness of his expresions. But tho' I have been often moved by the force of his eloquence, and ready to swallow the ingenious sophistry with pleasure, yet I could never be so serious, but reflecting on his artful

16

encomiums I thought on the tricks made use of by the women that would teach children to be mannerly.[29]

These criticisms of Shaftesbury and Steele stem from Mandeville's materialistic system, but they have a value of their own as shrewd observations. Dr. Johnson, who of course abhorred any materialistic system, could say late in his life: 'I read Mandeville forty, or, I believe, fifty years ago. He did not puzzle me; he opened my eyes into real life very much.'

All readers have, like Mandeville, been charmed by the gentleness and easy indulgence which grace the *Tatler* and the *Spectator* even in their satiric moods. But complacency is an extremely vulnerable attitude. At the end of a paper recommending the art of dancing as 'a great improvement, as well as embellishment to the theatre,' Steele observes, with perhaps a touch of humour, that 'delicacy in pleasure is the first step people of condition take in reformation from vice.'[30] A jolly way of doing the best one can with people of condition, but on second thought a most incautious remark on the part of one who professed to abhor cynicism, and most undiscriminating coming from a moral reformer. Burke, in a famous passage, said that 'vice itself lost half its evil, by losing all its grossness'; but he avoided saying that vice in this way lost its viciousness and changed into virtue. Addison charmed his friends, but he was apparently not a laughing man. He agreed with Hobbes that laughter 'is nothing else but sudden Glory arising from some sudden Conception of some Eminency in our selves, by Comparison with the Infirmity of others, or with our own formerly'; that is, laughter arises from the passion of derision and is reprehensible.[21] It is therefore not surprising that Addison 'always preferred Chearfulness to Mirth.'

> The latter I consider as an act, the former as a Habit of the Mind. Mirth is short and transient, Chearfulness fix'd and permanent. Those are often raised into the greatest Transports of Mirth, who are subject to the greatest Depressions of Melancholy: On the contrary, Chearfulness, tho' it does not give the Mind such an exquisite Gladness, prevents us from falling into any depths of Sorrow.[32]

In unperturbable serenity Addison concluded that 'there are but two things which, in my Opinion, can reasonably deprive us of this Chearfulness of Heart,' namely, Guilt and Atheism. Admitting that Addison does himself some injustice in this paper, granting that a perverse generation, perhaps of Tory fox-hunters, might really drive him at times to what Mark Twain called a state of mind bordering on impatience, the reader cannot but remark how perfectly this celebration of cheerfulness betrays Addison's limitations, his complacency, his lack of penetration. This is, indeed, the 'serene, peaceful state, of being a fool among knaves.' There is an abysmal division between men of this cast of mind and the satirists. When Thomas Tickell, Addison's friend and biographer, had newly arrived in Dublin as under-secretary and had established himself on a friendly footing with Swift, he ventured to inquire regarding the manuscript of an 'imaginary treatise' of which he had heard. But Swift declined to favour him, saying that *Gulliver's Travels* would not please Tickell, 'chiefly because they wholly disagree with your notions of persons and things.'[33]

Through all the ages there has been this opposition of the tough-minded and the tender-minded—William James's classification of philosophies and philosophers. In the eighteenth century it was the tender-minded who were gaining in popularity and were controlling the new literary modes. They were the party of the moderns, and until recently they have prescribed the tone of most of the criticism of the satirists. But the tough-minded also, in their way, have a claim to the title of friend of man. They warn against the illusions which not only end in bitterness but corrupt the heart in the process. They provide a discipline in looking steadily at the stark truth. In September 1725, shortly before Swift penned the famous letter to Pope about the philosophy of *Gulliver's Travels*, he was busy assisting and advising the mercurial Thomas Sheridan, who was in trouble over a politically imprudent sermon and had been removed from the Viceroy's list of chaplains. Swift interceded with Tickell, to whom he explained that Sheridan, 'as he is a creature without cunning, so he hath not overmuch advertency.' To the naïve Sheridan himself he gave this advice: 'You should think and deal with every man as a villain, without calling him so, or flying from him, or valuing him less. This is an old true lesson.'[34] There appears the paradox of Swift's misanthropy, and perhaps it is the paradox also of Pope's portrait of Atticus, where, to use the words of Wotton, 'grief is forced to laugh against her will.' For all his perspicacity into the nature of 'that animal called man,' Swift heartily loved individuals, and did not value them less because he had to speak to them with candour.

The tough-minded have always produced realistic literature, sometimes certainly very unpleasant. The Tory satirists shared the temper and ideals of the great French classical writers of the age of Louis XIV, who also aimed to anatomize man with complete honesty, to portray man in his true colours and lineaments. 'Rien n'est beau que le vrai,' said Boileau, their literary dictator. This very general dictum meant, among other things, that all extravagance and sentimentality, all credulous softening of the harsh truth, were to be shunned as offensive weakness. This is what the French call *le naturalisme classique*. The same spirit pervades the work of the Tory satirists—the pastorals, fables, and ballad operas of Gay, the poems, histories, and polemics of Swift, the political satires of Arbuthnot, the ethic and satiric poems of Pope. The gloom of these men is not an indulgence in lyrical melancholia, but the astringent and penetrating observation of the realist. That is why the tough-minded literature they left behind has recommended itself to generations of English-speaking readers. The popular appropriation of the figure of John Bull as representative of the English character is a tribute, not only to the genius of Arbuthnot, but in a larger way also to the spirit of the *naturalisme classique* of the whole group. If the Tory satirists are rightly called pessimists, their pessimism is of a variety both tonic and exhilarating.

NOTES

1. The need for correction in Swift's case is thoroughly shown by Louis A. Landa in an article on 'Jonathan Swift and Charity,' in the *Journal of English and Germanic Philology*, xliv (1945), 337–50.
2. *Alexander Pope* (1908), p. 100.
3. Swift to Pope, 1 Nov. 1734.
4. *A Tale of A Tub*, section lx.
5. Swift to Pope, 26 Nov. 1725.
6. Bolingbroke to Swift, 14 Dec. 1725.
7. *The Mind and Art of Jonathan Swift* (1936), pp. 159–62 and 301–2.
8. Swift to Pope, 29 Sept. 1725.
9. *Letters of Swift to Ford* (1935), Introduction, pp. xxxi ff.
10. Swift to Arbuthnot, 25 July 1714.
11. Swift to Archdeacon Walls, 11 June 1714.
12. Swift, *Prose Works*, ed. Temple Scott, v. 405.
13. Ibid. 396.
14. Arbuthnot to Swift, 12 Aug. 1714.
15. Swift to Oxford, 3 July 1714. Swift was equally frank to Bolingbroke in his letter of 7 Aug.
16. *Lives of the Poets*, ed. Birkbeck Hill, iii. 61.
17. Ibid. 62, note 1.
18. Swift to Gay, 20 Nov. 1729.
19. *Dunciad*, iv. 517–28.
20. Quoted by Birkbeck Hill in Johnson's *Lives of the Poets*, iii. 179, note 6.
21. *London*, 51–6.
22. *Estimate* (1757), p. 115.
23. Lecky, *History of England in the Eighteenth Century* (1892), ii. 91.

MAYNARD MACK

—

'Wit and Poetry and Pope':
Some Observations on his Imagery

THE point of departure of this essay is the current and useful description of Pope's kind of poetry as a poetry of statement.[1] One advantage of this description is that it is general enough to apply to other poetry as well. It asks us to bear in mind—what the temper of our present sensibility often disposes us to forget—that all poetry is in some sense poetry of statement; that without statement neither the Metaphysical kind of poem, witty, intellectual, and definitive, nor the Romantic kind, fluid and as it were infinitive (to mention only two) could be articulated at all; and accordingly, that the project of discrimination we are engaged on here is one of degree and not of kind.

Still, the real merit of the phrase is that it can apply specifically to Pope: it can set the problem. On the one hand, Pope writes a poetry with striking prose affinities. It has the Augustan virtues of perspicuity and ease which, whatever their status in poetry, are among the distinguishing attributes of prose discourse. It utilizes the denotative emphasis of Augustan diction, its precision and conciseness; the logical emphasis inherent in couplet rhetoric, its parallelism and antithesis. And it honours a whole body of reticences, reserves, restraints, exemplified perhaps best in the term 'correctness,' which tend to subdue and generalize its feeling and its wit. On the other hand, every reader of Pope is conscious of a host of qualities that look the other way. There is the kind of thing that Mr. Eliot is apparently glancing at when he says of Dryden's poetry that it states 'immensely.'[2] Or Mr. Tillotson, when he remarks in Pope a 'composite activity,' 'a combination of simultaneous

---

From *Pope and His Contemporaries: Essays Presented to George Sherburn* (Clarendon Press, 1949), 20–40. Reprinted by permission of the author.

effects.'[3] Or what Mr. Leavis and Mr. Wimsatt have pointed to in saying that Pope reconciles correctness with a subtle complexity, offsets and complicates the abstract logical patterns of his verse with counter patterns which are alogical, poetic.[4]

Facing this duality in its leading poet, the eighteenth century (if I may over-simplify to make the point) was usually able to read the terms as 'poetry is statement' and dismiss the problem: 'If Pope be not a poet, where is poetry to be found?'[5] The nineteenth century tended to re-aline the terms in an antithesis, 'poetry or statement,' and rested its case by denying Pope a poet's name: 'Dryden and Pope are not classics of our poetry, they are classics of our prose.'[6] Our own present rephrasing, in which the antithesis becomes a paradox, seems to me an improvement. It enables us to take account of both extremes; to see that if Johnson was right in his evaluation of Pope's success, Arnold was right in his perception of some of the conditions out of which the success was made. By the same token, it enables us to situate the distincive character of Pope's achievement—and hence of the critical problem he presents—in a very special kind of reconciliation between qualities of poetry and prose, a reconciliation managed even after the maximum concessions have been made to prose.

In this essay I want to discuss some of the aspects of this reconciliation that affect Pope's imagery. We regard imagery to-day, especially metaphor, as the most essential of the means by which language achieves poetic character, whether we choose to designate this character in its totality as 'iconic,' 'alogical,' 'opaque,' 'complex,' or by any other of our present set of honorific terms. If we are right in this assumption about metaphor, it implies that a poetry of statement will be signalized not by the absence of metaphorical effects but by their use in such a way that they do not disturb a logical surface of statement. And this, I think, is true in the case of Pope. In response to the sensibility of his time (and doubtless his own sensibility, too), Pope seems to me to have evolved an amazing variety of ways of obtaining the interest, richness, or tensions of metaphor while preserving, at any rate in appearance, those prose-like simplicities without which (as he probably agreed with Swift) 'no human Performance can arrive to any great Perfection.'[7] My purpose here is therefore to indicate some of the general principles that govern the effect of metaphor in Pope's poetry and then proceed to several of his characteristic methods of obtaining the benefits of metaphor without being, in any of the ordinary senses, strikingly metaphoric.

Probably the best place to begin an examination of this kind is with a passage from Pope's *Elegy on the Death of an Unfortunate Lady*, which has often been cited as evidence of his belonging to the Metaphysical 'line of wit':

> Most souls, 'tis true, but peep out once an age,
> Dull sullen pris'ners in the body's cage:
> Dim lights of life that burn a length of years,
> Useless, unseen, as lamps in sepulchres;
> Like Eastern kings a lazy state they keep,
> And close confin'd to their own palace sleep.[8]

The general affinities of these lines with Metaphysical poetry certainly need no emphasis, and the opening metaphor, at least, can be traced back through Dryden's

> imprison'd in so sweet a cage
> A soul might well be pleas'd to pass an age [9]

to Donne's

> She, whose faire body no such prison was
> But that a Soule might well be pleas'd to passe
> An age in her.[10]

Since we are looking for differences, however, we must not fail to notice that Pope rarely uses these extensive collocations of witty and ingenious images, and that when he does, it is almost always to establish something that his poems intend to disvalue—here a death-in-life theme, contrasting with a life-in-death theme built up around the lady. In consequence, only certain areas in Pope's poetry show the type of imagery that most Metaphysical poems tend to show throughout, with the result that the centre of gravity in his poetry often passes to other kinds of complication. It passes, for example, to such powerful counterpointings of tone and meaning as are obtained in the *Unfortunate Lady* by modulating from lines like those quoted to those beginning 'Yet shall thy grave with rising flow'rs be drest.' [11] The contrast in theme and feeling that these lines offer to those above is one that Donne would have elected to obtain through a conjunction of brilliant images. Pope obtains it—not only here, but habitually in his poems—through a conjunction of styles. The implied comparison usually possesses the richness and suggestiveness of a metaphor but is not, in any strict sense, metaphorical. We must notice also in the passage quoted that the images, witty and to some extent ingenious as they are, stem from comparisons that are at bottom traditional and familiar—the soul as prisoner, lamp, monarch, the body as cage, sepulchre, palace. This is Pope's normal practice. Except in comic poetry like the *Dunciad* (where, again, it is partly a matter of disvaluing) he rarely stresses heterogeneity in the objects he brings together. For this reason he has little occasion to expand or amplify his comparisons in the manner we associate with Donne. It has not been often enough remarked, I think, that the 'extended' Metaphysical image is a simple consequence of the Metaphysical discovery of 'occult resemblances in things apparently unlike.' That is to say, if one sets about comparing lovers to compasses at all, or the world to a beheaded man,[12] one is bound to specify in some detail the nature of the resemblances that make the image relevant; the value of the image is, as it were, generated in the process of constructing it. But it is also spent there. If such images seem wittier than any other kind because they display their wit at length, they also have less power in reserve. There is nothing in Donne's compass image, handsome as it is, to tempt the imagination to keep on unfolding it beyond the point at which the poet leaves it. On the other hand, Donne's gold-leaf image in the same poem has this power. It has it because it is powerfully compressed, and it can be powerfully compressed because it does not have to generate all its own potential: it is nourished at the source by normal and traditional associations. Pope's images, as suggested above, rely heavily on such associations. They take the ordinary established relationships of, say, singing and breath and soul, flesh and oblivion and marble, sepulchre and decay, finger and flute, parent and child, body and beauty, and with a delicate readjustment, freshen and fortify their implications:

> Oft as the mounting larks their notes prepare
> They fall, and leave their little lives in air.

> Tho' cold like you, unmov'd and silent grown,
> I have not yet forgot myself to stone.

> See the sad waste of all-devouring years,
> How Rome her own sad sepulchre appears.

> Such were the notes thy once-lov'd poet sung,
> Till death untimely stopp'd his tuneful tongue.[13]

> Me, let the tender Office long engage
> To rock the Cradle of reposing Age.

> Still round and round the ghosts of beauty glide,
> And haunt the places where their honour died.[14]

Finally, we must notice that the closed couplet exercises on images a peculiarly muting or subordinating influence. When we look at Dryden's lines quoted earlier, we see that, though he has taken over in large part the very words of Donne, the image in his verse has somehow become submerged. The reason, I think, is partly that Donne has sprawled the image across a weak rhyme which calls no attention to itself, whereas Dryden has suspended it within a strong rhyme which has a meaning of its own—which suggests, in fact, a correspondence between the soul's envelopment in body and its envelopment in time. Partly, also, that the movement of Donne's lines (and this is customary in his couplet poetry) exists simply to carry the image on its back; its pattern, in so far as it has any, is determined by and coextensive with the image. Dryden's couplet, on the other hand, being closed, has an assertive pattern of its own. The coiling and uncoiling rhythmical effect that comes from alternation of inverted with normal word order works with the movement of meaning to emphasize the logical stages of the soul's acceptance ('so sweet a cage'; 'might well be pleas'd'; 'pleased to pass an age') and the climactic stage is affirmed by rhyme. The closed couplet, in other words, tends to subdue images by putting them into competition with other forms of complication.

This point can be illustrated equally well from Pope. In the lines from the *Unfortunate Lady,* certainly the wittiest and boldest image is that in the third couplet. Yet here again the interest of the comparison has to compete with other interests—the strong rhyme, the parallelism, the humorously inverted syntax in both lines, which by withholding the completion of the sense units as long as possible keeps rather a lazy state itself.[15] Or take a passage in which Pope is developing one of Donne's images. This is Donne:

> Now,
> The ladies come; As Pirates, which doe know
> That there came weak ships fraught with Cutchannel
> The men board them.[16]

This is Pope:

> Painted for sight, and essenc'd for the smell,
> Like Frigates fraught with Spice and Cochine'l,

> Sail in the Ladies: How each Pyrate eyes
> So weak a Vessel, and so rich a Prize!
> Top-gallant he, and she in all her Trim,
> He boarding her, she striking sail to him.[17]

Donne is not at his best in this case, and Pope has the advantage of maturing Donne's idea at length—about as much at length as he was ever inclined to go. Still, leaving all that aside, one can see, I think, that Pope's figure, in spite of its richer elaborations, is not the primary and exclusive focus of attention that Donne's is. Donne's, as in our earlier instance, is the sole occupant of the verse rhetoric which presents it; Pope's is jostled for *Lebensraum* by many other contenders. There is, first, the drama of the ladies' arrival, which the verse itself is at some pains to enact in the first two and a half lines. Then there is the confrontation of forces in line 3, and the double assessment of the booty in line 4, both again rhetorically enacted. Finally, in line 5 comes a brilliant chiastic *rapprochement* of male and female in their bedizenment, to be followed in line 6 by an extension and also a qualification of this *rapprochement* with respect to sex (both parties are interested in the amorous duel, but their functions differ), the former carried by the metrical parallel, the latter by the antithesis in the sense. All these effects grow out of the potentialities of couplet rhetoric, not out of the image; and though they may co-operate with imagery, as here, they have a life of their own which tends to mute it.[18]

So far we have been discussing orthodox kinds of imagery in Pope's poetry, together with some of the modifications to which this imagery is subjected. It is time to turn now to some of his more reticent modes of imaging, which achieve metaphorical effect without using what it is customary to regard as metaphor. The first of these may be studied in his proper names.

Pope's names warrant an essay in themselves. With the possible exception of Milton, no poet has woven so many so happily into verse. And this is not simply because, as Pope said of himself,

> Whoe'er offends, at some unlucky Time,
> Slides into Verse, and hitches in a Rhyme,[19]

but because Pope saw, like Milton, the qualitative elements (including in Pope's case the humorous qualities) that could be extracted from proper names. For an effect of romance, sonority, and exoticism akin to Milton's, though much mitigated by the couplet, any passage of his translation of Homer's catalogue of ships will do:

> The Paphlagonians Pylaemenes rules,
> Where rich Henetia breeds her savage Mules,
> Where Erythinus' rising Clifts are seen,
> Thy Groves of Box, Cytorus! ever green;
> And where Aegyalus and Cromna lie,
> And lofty Sesamus invades the Sky;
> And where Parthenius, roll'd thro' Banks of Flow'rs,
> Reflects her bord'ring Palaces and Bow'rs.[20]

For a combination of romance and humour, this passage:

> First he relates, how sinking to the chin,
> Smit with his mien, the Mud-nymphs suck'd him in:
> How young Lutetia, softer than the down,
> Nigrina black, and Merdamante brown,
> Vy'd for his love in jetty bow'rs below,
> As Hylas fair was ravish'd long ago.[21]

And for pure humour:

> 'Twas chatt'ring, grinning, mouthing, jabb'ring all,
> And Noise and Norton, Brangling and Breval,
> Dennis and Dissonance, and captious Art,
> And Snip-snap short, and Interruption smart,
> And Demonstration thin, and Theses thick,
> And Major, Minor, and Conclusion quick.[22]

It will be observed in all these passages that as the names slide into verse they tend to take on a metaphorical colouring. Those in the first and third passages are of real places and persons, but the poetry does not require, any more than Milton's, that we identify them closely. Instead they become vehicles of an aura of associations clinging to epic warriors before Troy, or else of the vulgarity of a disputatious literature, which swallows up writers as Noise, Brangling, Dissonance swallow up Norton, Breval, and Dennis. Pope is a master of this metaphorical play with names. Sometimes the names he uses are quasi-metaphorical to begin with, like those he has invented in the Lutetia passage above. Or like those which allude—Adonis, Atossa, Shylock, Balaam, Timon, Sporus. Or those which have an allegorical cast—Uxorio, Worldly, Sir Morgan, Sir Visto, Patritio, Papillia, Hippia. Or those which personify—Avarice, Profusion, Billingsgate, Sophistry, Mathesis. Pope's habit with these classes of names is to interlayer them among his real objects and real persons, so that there results an additional and peculiarly suggestive kind of metaphorical play between concrete and abstract: allegorical Sir Morgan astride his cheese;[23] allusive Adonis driving to St. James's a whole herd of swine;[24] or personified Morality, Chicane, Casuistry, and Dulness suddenly brought into incongruous union with a judge named Page:

> Morality, by her false Guardians drawn,
> Chicane in Furs, and Casuistry in Lawn,
> Gasps, as they straiten at each end the cord,
> And dies, when Dulness gives her Page the word.[25]

Unquestionably, however, Pope's best metaphorical effects with names were obtained from specific ones, as in the lines on Dennis and Dissonance above. Did a certain duchess show an indiscriminate appetite for men? How better image it than with a nice derangement of proper names, opened with a particularly felicitous 'what':

> What has not fired her bosom or her brain?
> Caesar and Tall-boy, Charles, and Charlemagne.[26]

Did the vein of poetry in contemporary versifiers hardly weigh up to a gramme? Then doubtless it was an age when

> nine such Poets made a Tate.[27]

Why was philosophy at Oxford so backward, so ponderous? Because the Oxford logicians came riding whip and spur, through thin and thick,

> On German Crousaz and Dutch Burgersdyck.[28]

Or, since the current drama was slavishly derivative, why not let the patchwork image be projected partly with syntax and partly with names—a roll-call of stately ones, a tumbling huddle of risible ones:

> A past, vamp'd, future, old reviv'd, new piece,
> Twixt Plautus, Fletcher, Shakespeare, and Corneille
> Can make a Cibber, Tibbald, or Ozell.[29]

A second restrained mode of imaging in Pope's poetry is the allusion. Not simply the kind of descriptive allusion to persons, places, events,

and characters that all poets make continual use of, and of which I shall
say nothing here, but a kind that is specifically evaluative, constructing
its image by setting beside some present object or situation not so much
another object or situation as another dimension, a different sphere--
frequently for the purpose of diminishing what is present, but often, too,
for the purpose of enlarging or elevating it. Familiar examples of the
first use are the correspondence of Sporus to Satan in one of his more
degrading disguises—'at the Ear of *Eve,* familiar Toad';[30] or (more
humorously) of Cibber to Satan, on his exalted throne, at the opening
of *Dunciad,* ii. A less familiar example is the witty correspondence
suggested in *Dunciad,* iv between the dunces irresistibly drawn into the
gravitational field of Dulness—

> by sure Attraction led
> And strong impulsive gravity of Head—[31]

and the feeling Sin has in Milton's poem, after the Fall, of being pulled
toward earth by 'sympathy, or some connatural force,'

> Powerful at greatest distance to unite
> With secret amity things of like kind. . . .
> Nor can I miss the way, so strongly drawn
> By this new-felt attraction and instinct.[32]

As for the second use, the *Essay on Man* begins with a particularly fine
example, in the 'garden tempting with forbidden fruit';[33] while *Windsor
Forest* both begins and ends with one; the groves of Eden, which
establish the central symbol of the poem; and the dove of Noah, also
described as the dove of grace and peace, which throws around Pope's
vision of England as she comes out of her continental wars all the
seventeenth-century religious associations of covenant, happy rescue,
and divine mission.[34]

This evaluative kind of metaphor in Pope, whether diminishing or
enlarging, is usually religious, and often very powerfully so. Here are
some instances in the lighter hues (I limit myself to instances that I
think have not been recorded by Pope's editors):

> And Heav'n is won by violence of song.[35]
> And Zeal for that great House which eats him up.[36]
> Blest be the *Great!* for those they take away.[37]
> And instant, fancy feels th' imputed sense.[38]

These colours are darker:

> Each does but hate his neighbour as himself.[39]
> What Lady's Face is not a whited Wall?[40]

And this, though light in tone, carries a scathing indictment of the perversion of religious values in a money culture. Since it admirably illustrates the way allusion can construct a cogent metaphor without intruding on a casual surface and is, in fact, one of the most scarifying passages Pope ever wrote, I quote it in full:

> On some, a *Priest* succinct in Amice white,
> Attends; *all flesh is nothing in his Sight!*
> Beeves, at his touch, at once to jelly *turn,*
> And the huge Boar is shrunk into an *Urn:*
> The board with specious *miracles* he loads,
> *Turns* Hares to Larks, and Pigeons into Toads.
> Another (for in all what one can shine?)
> Explains the Seve and Verdeur of the *Vine.*
> What cannot copious *Sacrifice attone?*
> Thy Treufles, Perigord! thy Hams, Bayonne!
> With French *Libation,* and Italian Strain
> *Wash* Bladen *white,* and *expiate* Hays's stain.
> Knight lifts the head, for what are crowds undone
> To *three essential* Partridges *in one.*[41]

There are two other modes of imagery of which Pope is fond, modes that the concision of the closed couplet encourages and almost insists on, though no other writer of the couplet has perfected them to a like extent. These are pun and juxtaposition. Juxtaposition operates in Pope's poetry in several ways. One of them, as has lately been pointed out,[42] is through zeugma, which the economy of this verse form often calls for and which can itself be modulated either into metaphor—'Or stain her Honour, or her new Brocade,' or into pun—'And sometimes Counsel take—and sometimes *Tea.*'[43] (In either case, the effect is ultimately metaphorical, a correspondence being suggested between Belinda's attitudes to chastity and brocade, or between Queen Anne's, and her society's, to politics and tea.)

My own concern, however, is not with zeugma, but with the metaphorical effects that can arise from simple juxtaposition. For example, from a list of items *seriatim,* with one inharmonious term:

> Puffs, Powders, Patches, Bibles, Billet-doux.[44]

Or from a simple parallel inside the line:

> Dried Butterflies, and Tomes of Casuistry.[45]

Or from a similar parallel inside the couplet:

> Now Lapdogs give themselves the rowzing Shake,
> And sleepless Lovers, just at Twelve, awake.[46]

This is a very versatile device. In the *Rape of the Lock,* from which the above examples are taken, Pope uses it to mirror in his lines and couplets the disarray of values in the society he describes, the confounding of antithetical objects like lapdogs and lovers, bibles and *billets-doux.* On the other hand, in the *Essay on Man*, this same device, redirected by the context, can be made to mirror the 'equalizing' view of antithetical objects taken by the eye of God or by the god-like magnanimous man:

> A hero perish, or a sparrow fall.[47]
> As toys and empires, for a god-like mind.[48]

It is also a very sensitive device. The potential metaphor that every juxtaposition tends to carry in suspension requires only the slightest jostling to precipitate it out. Sometimes a well-placed alliteration will do it:

> The Mind, in Metaphysics at a Loss,
> May wander in a wilderness of Moss.[49]

Sometimes an inter-animation of words, as here between the 'smooth' eunuch and the 'eas'd' sea:

> Where, eas'd of Fleets, the Adriatic main
> Wafts the smooth Eunuch and enamour'd Swain.[50]

And sometimes a set of puns, as in this example, fusing the biologist with the object of his study:

> The most recluse, discreetly open'd, find
> Congenial matter in the Cockle-kind.[51]

Pun, of course, brings before us Pope's most prolific source of imagery in his comic and satiric poetry—which is to say, in the bulk of his work. His puns in other poems—*Windsor Forest, Eloisa,* the *Essay on Man,* the

Essay on Criticism—are deeply buried and always reticent. But in the satires and the *Dunciad,* particularly the latter, he spends them openly and recklessly, with superb effect. They cease to be in these poems ordinary puns, like those we find in Metaphysical poetry, where, because of the conceit, pun has a lesser job to do; they become instead Metaphysical conceits themselves, yoking together violently, as Mr. Leavis has noticed,[52] the most heterogeneous ideas. Moreover, when they are used together with ordinary images, the real metaphorical power is likely to be lodged in them. Thus the following figures are not especially bold themselves, but the puns inside them open out like peacocks' tails:

> Ye tinsel Insects! whom a Court maintains,
> That counts your Beauties only by your *Stains.*

> On others Int'rest her gay liv'ry flings,
> Int'rest that waves on *Party-colour'd* wings.

> At length Corruption, like a gen'ral flood,
> (So long by watchful ministers withstood)
> Shall deluge all; and Av'rice, creeping on,
> Spread like a *low-born* mist, and blot the sun.[53]

Here, then, are four classes of metaphorical effect in Pope's poetry, all of them obtained outside the normal channels of overt simile and metaphor. One of them, juxtaposition (its collateral descendant, zeugma, would make a second), stems from the structure of the closed couplet itself. Two more, allusion and pun, are encouraged to a large extent by its fixed and narrow room. And none of them, it is important to notice, calls attention to itself as metaphorical. Between them, nevertheless, without violating at all the prose conventions of the Augustan mode, they do a good deal of the work that we to-day associate with the extended metaphor and conceit.

The devices of complication touched on in the preceding sections pertain primarily to local texture: the line and couplet. I want to add to these, in conclusion, three patterns that are more pervasive; that help supply the kind of unity in Pope's poems which he is popularly not supposed to have. Actually, there is a wide variety of such patterns. There are the characteristics of the dramatic speaker of every poem, who shifts his style, manner, and quality of feeling considerably from poem to poem, as anyone will see who will compare carefully the *Essay* on *Criticism* with the *Essay on Man*, or the *Epistle to Dr. Arbuthnot* with that to *Augustus*. There is the character of the interlocutor in the poems that have dialogue, by no means a man of straw. There is the implicit theme, usually announced in a word or phrase toward the outset of the poem, and while seldom developed in recurrent imagery, as in Shakespeare, almost always developed in recurrent references and situations. There is also, often, a kind of pattern of words that reticulates through a poem, enmeshing a larger and larger field of associations—for instance, words meaning light in the *Essay on Criticism*, or the word 'head' (and, of course, all terms for darkness) in the *Dunciad*. And there are a great many more such unifying agents.

The three that I shall examine briefly here are irony, the portrait, and mock-heroic. Pope's irony, fully analysed, would require a book. The point about it that is most relevant to our present topic is that it is a mode of complication closely resembling metaphor. At its most refined, in fact, as in Swift's *Modest Proposal* or Pope's praise of George II in the *Epistle to Augustus*, it asks us to lay together not two, but three different perspectives on reality. First, the surface, and second, the intended meanings, these two corresponding roughly to vehicle and tenor in a metaphor; and then, third—to use again the Pope and Swift examples—the kind of propositions that English projectors were *usually* making about Ireland, or the poets about George II. Pervasive irony of this type—of which there is a good deal in Pope—tends to resist the presence of bold imagery, for two reasons. In the first place, because it consists already in a mutual translation, to and fro, between one kind of complex whole with all its particularities clinging to it (what is said), and a different complex whole with all its revised particularities (what is meant); a translation that profuse or striking imagery only clutters and impedes. And in the second place, because the success of the medium depends on adopting the attitudes, motives, and so far as possible even the terms of a very conventional point of view. If one is going to write an ironic love song 'in the modern taste,' one almost has to refer to 'Cupid's purple pinions'[54]; or if a panegyric on George II, to the usual terms for kingly prowess:

Your Country, chief, in Arms abroad defend.[55]

To find a more striking phrase would destroy the subtlety of the ironic comment (i.e. its resemblance to what a Cibber might have said); and would, of course, too, destroy the mutual translation between the arms of battle and those of Madame Walmoden.

33

To all this, in the *Epistle to Augustus*, is added the further layer of metaphor that results from Pope's imitation of what Horace had written about *his* Caesar. Nor is this layer confined alone to the poems which are imitations. The Roman background, it has been well observed, is a kind of universal Augustan metaphor or 'myth.'[56] It lies behind Pope's work, and much of Swift's and Fielding's, like a charged magnetic field, a reservoir of attitudes whose energy can be released into their own creations at a touch. Not through the Horatian or Virgilian or Ovidian tags; these are only its minor aspect; but through the imposed standard of a mighty and civilized tradition in arts, morals, government. At the same time, conveniently, it is a standard that can be used two ways: for a paradigm of the great and good now lost in the corruptions of the present, as in the comparison of George II with Augustus Caesar; or for the head-waters of a stream down which still flow the stable and continuing classic values:

> You show us Rome was glorious, not profuse.
> The world's just wonder, and ev'n thine, O Rome!
> Who would not weep, if Atticus were he![57]

This last example brings us to Pope's portraits. These, again, have the complicating characteristics of metaphors, without drawing attention to themselves as such. They are often erroneously called 'illustrations,' as if their content were exhausted in being identified with some abstraction implied or stated by the poem. But what abstractions will exhaust the characters of Atticus, Sporus, Atossa, Balaam, and a score of others? To instance from one of the simplest portraits, so that it may be quoted entire, here is Narcissa:

> 'Odious! in woollen! 'twould a saint provoke!'
> (Were the last words that poor Narcissa spoke):
> 'No, let a charming chintz, and Brussels lace
> Wrap my cold limbs, and shade my lifeless face:
> One would not, sure, look frightful when one's dead:
> And—Betty—give this cheek a little red.' [58]

This, to the extent that it illustrates anything, illustrates the poem's prose argument that our ruling passion continues to our last breath. But as a metaphor it explores, not without considerable profundity, through the character of one type of woman, the character of the human predicament itself. Here we have, as her name implies, the foolish self-lover; but also—in a wider, more inevitable, and uncensorable sense—the self-lover who inhabits each of us by virtue of our mortal situation, the very principle of identity refusing to be erased. Here, too, we have the foolish concern for appearances, vastly magnified by the incongruity of its occasion; but also the fundamental human clutching at the familiar and the known. And embracing it all is the central paradox of human feelings about death and life. Cold limbs don't need wrapping (the conjunction of terms itself suggests that death can be apprehended but not comprehended), nor dead faces shading; and yet, as our own death rituals show, somehow they do. The levels of feeling and experience startled into activity in this short passage can hardly be more than pointed at in the clumsiness of paraphrase. The irony of words like 'saint,' the ambiguities of 'charming' and 'shade,' the tremendous compression in 'frightful,' of 'the anguish of the marrow, The ague of the skeleton,' accumulate as one contemplates them.

All of Pope's portraits have at least the complexity of this one, and all are equally metaphorical in effect. If they do not call attention to themselves as metaphors, it is probably because in them the vehicle has largely absorbed the tenor; for metaphors in general seem to take on prominence according as both the tenor and the vehicle (viz. lovers as well as compasses) are insisted on at once. In any case, they behave like metaphors in Pope's poems, usually assuming, in addition to their functions locally, an important unifying role. Sometimes they define the entire structure of a poem, as in *Moral Essays*, ii, where they develop the easy-going aphorism of the opening—'Most women have no characters at all'—into a mature interpretation of what personality is. Sometimes they supply the central symbols, as with Timon in *Moral Essays*, iv, 'Vice' in Dialogue ii of the *Epilogue to the Satires*, or the Man of Ross and Balaam in *Moral Essays*, iii. Likewise, in *Arbuthnot*, Atticus and Sporus appear at just the crucial phases in the argument and knit up, as it were, the two essential ganglia in the sinews of the drama that the poem acts out between the poet and his adversaries. They give us, successively, the poet analytical and judicial, who can recognize the virtues of his opponents ('Blest with each Talent and each Art to please'), whose deliberation is such that he can even mirror in his language—its subjunctives, its antitheses, the way it hangs the portrait over an individual without identifying it with him—the tentative, insinuating, never-wholly-committed hollow man who is Atticus; and then the poet roused and righteous, no longer judicial but executive, touching with Ithuriel's spear the invader in the garden, spitting from his mouth (with a concentration of sibilants and labials) the withered apple-seed. Both portraits are essential to the drama that unifies the poem.

The great pervasive metaphor of Augustan literature, however, including Pope's poetry, is the metaphor of tone: the mock-heroic. It is very closely allied, of course, to the classical or Roman myth touched on earlier and is, like that, a reservoir of strength. By its means, without the use of overt imagery at all, opposite and discordant qualities may be locked together in 'a balance or reconcilement of sameness with difference, of the general with the concrete, the idea with the image, the individual with the representative, the sense of novelty and freshness with old and familiar objects'—the mock-heroic seems made on purpose to fit this definition of Coleridge's of the power of imagination. For a literature of decorums like the Augustan, it was a metaphor with every sort of value. It could be used in the large, as in *Joseph Andrews, Tom Jones*, the *Beggar's Opera*, the *Rape of the Lock*, the *Dunciad*, or in the small—the passage, the line. It could be set in motion by a passing allusion, not necessarily to the classics:

> Calm Temperance, whose blessings those partake,
> Who hunger, and who thirst, for scribling sake;

by a word:

> Glad chains, warm furs, broad banners, and broad faces;

even by a cadence:

> And the fresh vomit run for ever green.[59]

Moreover, it was a way of getting the local, the ephemeral, the pressure of life as it was lived, into poetry, and yet distancing it in amber:

> That live-long wig, which Gorgon's self might own,
> Eternal buckle takes in Parian stone.[60]

It was also a way of qualifying an attitude, of genuinely 'heroicizing' a Man of Ross, a parson Adams, a School-mistress, yet undercutting them with a more inclusive attitude:

> Rise, *honest* Muse! and sing the Man of Ross.[61]

Above all—and this, I think, was its supreme advantage for Pope—it was a metaphor that could be made to look two ways. If the heroic genre and the heroic episodes lurking behind the *Rape of the Lock* diminish many of the values of this society, they also partially throw their weight behind some others. Clarissa's speech is an excellent case in point.[62] Her words represent a sad shrinkage from the epic views of Glaucus which reverberate behind them, views involving real heroism and (to adapt Mr. Eliot's phrase) the awful daring of a real surrender. Still, the effect of the contrast is not wholly minimizing. Clarissa's vision of life, worldly as it is when seen against the heroic standard, surpasses the others in the poem and points, even if obliquely, to the tragic conflict between the human lot and the human will that is common to life at every level.

This flexibility of the mock-heroic metaphor is seen in its greatest perfection in the *Dunciad*. There are, indeed, three thicknesses of metaphor in this poem: an overall metaphor, in which the poem as a whole serves as vehicle for a tenor which is the decline of literary and human values generally; a network of local metaphor, in which this poem is especially prolific; and in between, the specifically mock-heroic metaphor which springs from holding the tone and often the circumstances of heroic poetry against the triviality of the dunces and their activities. But what is striking about this metaphor in the *Dunciad*, and indicative of its flexibility, is that it is applied quite differently from the way it is applied in the *Rape of the Lock*. There, the epic mode as vehicle either depresses the values of the actors, as with Belinda, or somewhat supports them, as with Clarissa. Here, on the contrary, one of the two lines of development (the comic) grows from allowing the actors to depress and degrade the heroic mode, its dignity and beauty. Again and again Pope builds up in the poem effects of striking epic richness, only to let them be broken down, disfigured, stained—as the word 'vomit' stains the lovely movement and suggestion of the epic line quoted above. Thus the diving and other games in Book II disfigure the idea of noble emulation and suggest the befoulment of heroic values through the befoulment of the words and activities in which these values are recorded. Thus the fop's Grand Tour in IV mutilates a classical and Renaissance ideal (cf. also Virgil's Aeneas, to whose destined wanderings toward Rome the fop's are likened) of wisdom ripened by commerce with men and cities. Indeed, the lines of the whole passage are balanced between the ideal and the fop's perversions of it:

> A dauntless infant! never scar'd with God.
> Europe he saw, and Europe saw him too.
> Judicious drank, and greatly daring dined;

or between related ideals and what has happened to them:

> To happy Convents, bosomed deep in Vines,
> Where slumber Abbots, purple as their Wines.

or between epic resonances, the epic names, and the sorry facts:

> To where the Seine, obsequious as she runs,
> Pours at great Bourbon's feet her silken sons.[63]

This is one line of development in the *Dunciad*. The other is its converse: the epic vehicle is gradually made throughout the poem to enlarge and give a status of serious menace to all this ludicrous activity. Here the epic circumstance of a presiding goddess proved invaluable. Partly ludicrous herself, she could also become the locus of inexhaustible negation behind the movements of her trivial puppets; her force could be associated humorously, but also seriously, with the powerful names of Chaos, Night, Anti-Christ, and with perversions of favourite order symbols like the sun, monarchy, and gravitation. Here, too, the epic backgrounds as supplied by Milton could be drawn in. Mr. C. S. Lewis has remarked of *Paradise Lost* that 'only those will fully understand it who see that it might have been a comic poem.'[64] The *Dunciad* is one realization of that might-have-been. Over and above the flow of Miltonic echoes and allusions, or the structural resemblances like Cibber's (or Theobald's) Pisgah-vision based on Adam's, or the clustered names of dunces like those of Milton's devils, thick as the leaves that strew bad books in Grubstreet—the *Dunciad* is a version of Milton's theme in being the story of an uncreating Logos. As the poem progresses, our sense of this increases through the calling in of more and more powerful associations by the epic vehicle. The activities of the dunces and of Dulness are more and more equated with religious anti-values, culminating in the passage on the Eucharist quoted earlier. The metaphor of the coronation of the king-dunce moves always closer to and then flows into the metaphor of the Day of the Lord, the descent of the anti-Messiah, the uncreating Word. Meantime, symbols which have formerly been ludicrous—insects, for instance, or sleep—are given by this expansion in the epic vehicle a more sombre cast. The dunces thicken and become less individual, more anonymous, expressive of blind inertia—bees in swarm, or locusts blackening the land. Sleep becomes tied up with its baser physical manifestations, with drunkenness, with deception, with ignorance, with neglect of obligation, and finally with death. This is the sleep which *is* death, we realize, a *Narren-dämmerung*, the twilight of the moral will. And yet, because of the ambivalence of the mock-heroic metaphor, Pope can keep to the end the tension between all these creatures as comic and ridiculous, and their destructive potentiality in being so. Certainly two of the finest puns in any poetry are those with which he continues to exploit this tension at the very end of the poem, when Dulness finally *yawns* and Nature *nods*.

The purpose of this essay has been to supply a few, a very few, of the materials that are requisite for giving the phrase 'poetry of state-ment' specific content. I have tried to suggest that Pope is poetic, but not in the way that the Metaphysicals are poetic, even where he is most like them; that if the prominent metaphor is the distinctive item in their practice, this has been replaced in Pope's poetry partly by devices of greater compression, like allusion and pun, partly by devices that are more distributive, like irony and mock-heroic, and of course by a multi-tude of other elements—the net effect of all these being to submerge the multiplicities of poetic language just beneath the singleness of prose. Twenty-five years ago it would have been equally important to say that Pope is not poetic as the Romantics are poetic, for in this century there has always been a tendency to subsume him as far as possible under the reigning orthodoxy. It is true that in certain areas Pope's poetry faintly resembles that of the Romantics; in certain others, that of the line of wit. But the task of criticism for the future, when we are likely to be paying more and more attention to Pope as our own poetry moves in the direction suggested by Mr. Auden, and by Mr. Eliot in his *Quartets,* is not with Pope as a pre-Romantic or a post-Metaphysical, but as an Augustan poet whose peculiar accomplishment, however we may choose to rate it on the ultimate scale of values, was the successful fusion of some of the most antithetical features of verse and prose.

NOTES

1. The phrase probably owes its present currency to Mr. Mark Van Doren's use of it in his study of *The Poetry of John Dryden* (1920; repub-lished in 1931 and 1946).

2. T. S. Eliot, 'John Dryden,' 1922 (*Selected Essays,* 1932, p. 273).

3. G. Tillotson, *On the Poetry of Pope* (1938), pp. 156, 141. Cf. also his *Essays in Criticism* (1942), p. 103.

4. F. R. Leavis. *Revaluation* (1936), p. 71; W. K. Wimsatt, 'Rhetoric and Poems: The Example of Pope' (in *English Institute Essays, 1948*, published by the Columbia University Press, 1949).

5. Johnson, 'Life of Pope' (*Lives of the Poets*, ed. G. B. Hill, iii. 251).

6. Arnold, 'The Study of Poetry,' *Essays in Criticism, Second Series* (*Wks.*, 1903, iv. 31).

7. *A Letter to a Young Clergyman*, 1721 (*Wks.*, ed. Herbert Davis, ix. 68).

8. Ll. 17–22. This passage is cited for its metaphysical character by Middleton Murry, *Countries of the Mind* (1922), p. 86; and F. R. Leavis, op. cit., pp. 70 ff.

9. *To the Duchess of Ormond*, ll. 118–19.

10. *The Second Anniversary*, ll. 221–3.

11. Ll. 63 ff.

12. For the second instance, see *The Second Anniversary*, ll. 9ff.

13. This example illustrates particularly well the way in which an unbroken logical surface can cushion and absorb a powerful or even violent image. If we were to paraphrase the image, we should have to say something like: 'Death took up the instrument of Parnell's music, and fingering (stopping) it in his own (untimely) tempo, brought the music to a premature (untimely) stop.' Yet the effect of the normal logical meaning of 'stopp'd' is to carry us smoothly across the opposites that are being yoked here.

14. The quotations are from *Windsor Forest*, ll. 133–4; *Eloisa to Abelard*, ll. 23–4; *To Mr. Addison*, ll. 1–2; *To Robert, Earl of Oxford*, ll. 1–2; *Epistle to Dr. Arbuthnot*, ll. 408–9; and *Moral Essays*, ii. 241–2.

15. This effect is easily verified by rearranging the words in normal order.

16. *Satyre IV*, ll. 187–90.

17. *The Fourth Satire of Dr. John Donne, Versifyed*, ll. 226–31.

18. See also on this point, with respect to Dryden, M. W. Prior, *The Language of Tragedy* (1947), p. 169.

19. *Imit. of Hor., Sat. II*, i, ll. 77–8.

20. *Iliad*, ii. 1034 ff.

21. *Dunciad* (1743), ii. 331–6.

22. Ibid. 237–42.

23. *Moral Essays*, iii. 61.

24. *Moral Essays*, iii. 73–4.

25. *Dunciad* (1743), iv. 27–30.

26. *Moral Essays*, ii. 78.

27. *Epistle to Dr. Arbuthnot*, l. 190.

28. *Dunciad* (1743), iv. 198.

29. Ibid. i. 284–6.

30. *Epistle to Dr. Arbuthnot*, l. 319.

31. Ll. 75–6.

32. Bk. x, ll. 244 ff.

33. Ep. i. 8.

34. Ll. 8 and 429–30.

35. *Imit. of Hor., Ep. II.* i, l. 240. Cf. Matt. xi. 12.

36. *Moral Essays*, iii. 208. Cf. Ps. lxix. 9.

37. *Epistle to Dr. Arbuthnot*, l. 225. Cf. Job i. 21.

38. *Dunciad*, ii. 200. Cf. the theological sense of 'imputed.'

39. *Moral Essays*, iii. 108. Cf. Matt. xxii. 39. I have noticed this allusion elsewhere (*College English* (1946), vii. 269).

40. *The Fourth Satire of Dr. John Donne, Versifyed*, l. 151. Cf. Matt. xxiii. 27. (The allusion is Pope's addition.)

41. *Dunciad* (1743), iv. 549–62. (Italics mine.)

42. In Mr. Wimsatt's essay cited above, p. 21, n. 1. Cf. also Austin Warren, 'The Mask of Pope' (*Rage for Order*, 1948, p. 45).

43. *Rape of the Lock*, ii. 107, iii. 8.

44. Ibid. i. 138.

45. Ibid. v. 122. A particularly graceful comparison in its suggestion of a common animation, brilliance, delicacy of movement, and perishableness in the worlds of ethics and Lepidoptera.

46. Ibid. i. 15–16.

47. Ep. i. 88.

48. Ep. iv. 180.

49. *Dunciad* (1743), iv. 449–50.

50. Ibid. 309–10.

51. *Dunciad* (1743), iv. 447–8.

52. Op. cit., p. 99.

53 From *Epil. to the Sats.*, Dial. ii. 220–1; *Dunciad* (1743), iv. 537–8; and *Moral Essays*, iii. 135–8. (Italics mine.)

54. Cf. Swift's *A Love Song, in the Modern Taste*, st. 1.

55. *Imit. of Hor., Ep. II*, i, l. 3.

56. Cf. J. C. Maxwell, 'Demigods and Pickpockets,' *Scrutiny*, xi (1942–3), 34 ff.

57. From *Moral Essays*, iv. 23; *Essay on Criticism*, l. 248; *Epistle to Dr. Arbuthnot*, l. 214.

58. *Moral Essays*, i. 246–51.

59. From *Dunciad* (1743), i. 49–50, 88; ii. 156.

60. *Moral Essays*, iii. 294–5.

61. Ibid. 250. (Italics mine.) The blend of irony and praise is carefully maintained throughout the passage.

62. Canto v, ll. 9 ff.

63. *Dunciad* (1743), iv. 284 ff.

64. *A Preface to Paradise Lost* (1942), p. 93.

EDWARD NILES HOOKER

Pope on Wit:
The *Essay on Criticism*

Since the publication of Tillotson's admirable study we have become increasingly aware of the extraordinary art of Pope's verse. That awareness, however, has not led us insistently enough to suspect that the *Essay on Criticism* has something to say, something neither trivial nor commonplace, and worthy of the artistry with which the ideas are set forth. Supposing that Pope never could make up his mind about certain crucial terms such as *wit* and *nature,* we are tempted to regard the poem as a mélange of confused and sometimes contradictory assertions or as a potpourri of Augustan clichés. Poor addled Pope (one recent editor intimates) employed the word *wit* throughout the *Essay on Criticism* in seven different senses; and we can conclude, if we like, that he knew no better.

To the acute and subtle mind of Empson we stand indebted for the explicit recognition that the *Essay* has a solid core of intelligible meaning, or perhaps a complex of meanings, coherent and applicable, and revolving around what he regards as the key word, *wit.*[1] A close reading of the poem leaves no room for doubting that Pope intended to convey what seemed to him the significant facts about the place of wit in literature, and that for some reason it struck him as particularly desirable to do so. To understand the *Essay,* therefore, we should address ourselves to three questions. Why, in an essay devoted to the principles of criticism, does Pope lavish space and attention on wit rather than on

From *The Seventeenth Century: Studies in the History of English Thought and Literature from Bacon to Pope,* by Richard Foster Jones and others writing in his honor; copyright 1951 by Stanford University Press. Reprinted by permission of the publisher and Mrs. Edward Niles Hooker.

taste? Second, what controversies being agitated at the time he was composing the poem would have led Pope to take a stand, and how is that stand established in the *Essay*? And third, what body of contemporary thought, more or less parallel to his own, was available to him as he wrote, and how can it illumine the direction and implications of his thinking?

In the first place, Pope at the start, after describing the highest form of artistic talent in the poet as true genius, and the highest gift of the critic as true taste, proceeds to the principle that the best critics are those who excel as authors (lines 15–16).[2] True taste, therefore, is best revealed in the operations of genius. That genius and taste 'have so intimate a Connection' is not an idea peculiar to Pope; as one of his contemporaries remarked, 'there are Cases where they cannot be . . . separated, without almost taking away their Functions.'[3] A discussion of the art of criticism would be idle unless it expounded taste by revealing the ways and standards of genius.

Or, since genius is distressingly rare, one may, like Pope, examine the ways of wit, that more inclusive thing, conceived of as literary talent or as the distinguishing element in literature, the breath of life informing the dull clay. As Dryden had proclaimed, 'The composition of all poems is, or ought to be, of wit. . . .'[4] He meant, not ingenuity, but a spark. The special gift of those who create literature is to 'invigorate their conceptions, and strike Life into a whole Piece'; what would otherwise remain leaden or sluggish is magically transformed by Flame and Strength of Sense.[5] Nothing could be more natural than that Homer and Virgil, authors who possessed such qualities in the highest degree, should be called 'these Two supreme Wits.'[6] Fire, invention, and imagination became inextricably associated with wit; they were the life-giving forces—so David Abercromby meant when he said that 'we never write wittily, but when our Imagination is exalted to a certain degree of heat, destructive to our cold dulness.'[7] In the words of John Oldmixon, a minor contemporary of both Dryden and Pope: 'Every Thing that pleases in Writing is with us . . . resolved into Wit, whether it be in the Thought or the Expression.'[8] When John Sheffield, Duke of Buckingham, said in his *Essay upon Poetry*, ' 'Tis Wit and Sence that is the Subject here,'[9] he had in mind much the same idea that Blackwall owned when he remarked of Horace, 'His Sprightliness of Imagination is temper'd with Judgment; and he is both a pleasant Wit, and a Man of Prudence.'[10] Sense and judgment are the solid, useful stuff with which the writer works, but wit is the magic that lifts the stuff to the plane of belle-lettres. A critic must understand wit if he is to talk of literature. And in an essay on literary criticism we should expect Pope to deal in generous measure with the problem of wit.

But in 1711 there were additional reasons why he had to confront the subject, reasons general and reasons personal. As for the general reasons, no one at the time could have forgotten that outburst of hostilities in 1698–1700, in which the righteous had beset the wits—and had driven them to cover. It is true, of course, that the attack had been directed overtly against specific forms of wit, the facetious varieties which played with sex and trifled with religion and morality. But underneath-lay an impulse more sinister, more dangerous, which denied the worth of literature itself (or what we think of as creative writing).

The psychological basis for the hostility can be found in Dryden's friend Walter Charleton, who observed that in works of wit 'Phansie ought to have the upper hand, because all Poems, of what sort soever, please chiefly by Novelty.'[11] How this remark becomes significant will appear when it is set beside Charleton's definition of Fancy as the faculty by which we conceive similarities 'in objects really unlike, and pleasantly confound them in discourse: Which by its unexpected Fineness and allusion, surprizing the Hearer, renders him less curious of the truth of what is said.'[12] In an age when the utilitarian and scientific movement had grown to giant size, an art which pleased by confounding truth and deceiving men was bound to be viewed with hostility. All wit came under attack.

The philosophic and moral basis for the hostility was well stated by Malebranche, who wrote:[13]

But that which is most opposite to the efficacy of the Grace of Christ, is that which in the Language of the World is call'd Wit; for the better the Imagination is furnish'd, the more dangerous it is; subtilty, delicacy, vivacity and spaciousness of Imagination, great qualities in the Eyes of Men, are the most prolifick and the most general causes of the blindness of the Mind and the corruption of the Heart.

Without intending to betray her own cause Margaret, Duchess of Newcastle, made this humble request:[14]

> Give me a Wit, whose Fancy's not confin'd;
> That buildeth on it self, with no Brain join'd. . . .

Exactly what many had suspected! The current prejudice against wit
was vigorously put by Ferrand Spence, who viewed it as nothing but
the froth and ferment of the soul, beclouding reason and sinking rational
pursuits into the miasma of fantasy.[15]

In the few years preceding the publication of Pope's *Essay* the
agitation concerning wit was intensified, partly because of the appearance of the *Letter concerning Enthusiasm* (1707) and *Sensus Com-
munis* (1709), both of which, by pleading for the complete freedom
of wit and raillery, even in the most serious matters, sent shivers of
horror down the spines of some English and Continental readers. Both
were speedily translated into French, and both reviewed in 1709 by
the indefatigable Jean Le Clerc, who warned concerning the former:
'*Le livre mérite d'être lû avec attention, pour ne pas lui donner un sens
et un but, qu'il n'a point.*'[16] But whether they read attentively or not,
many readers detected the sense and aim which was not really present
(to Le Clerc). There soon issued a long and bitter retort called
*Bart'lemy Fair: or, an Enquiry After Wit; In Which Due Respect Is
Had to a Letter Concerning Enthusiasm* (1709). This work takes
Shaftesbury's *Letter* to be primarily an assault on religion, and sees wit
as a mode of enquiry that would unsettle everything, morals and
government alike. Of the terrible menace lurking in wit the anonymous
author bitterly remarks: 'To be Witty, if a Man knows how, is the only
way to please. Wit is the Salt that gives a goût to any Carrion: Nothing
so Profane, or Lewd, but shall be relish'd if it pass for Wit.'[17]

Such objections are obviously directed against, not true wit, but the
abuse of it. Yet wit easily lent itself to abuse, and the contemporary
mind distrusted it as a likely enemy to all goodness. With almost uncanny prescience the learned Dr. Samuel Clarke answered part of
Shaftesbury's contentions a few years before they were printed. In a
series of sermons preached at St. Paul's in 1705, he denounced the sort
of men who pretend to seek for truth and to explode falsehood by means
of wit.:[18]

. . . whatsoever things are profane, impure, filthy, dishonourable and
absurd; these things they make it their business to represent as harmless
and indifferent, and to laugh Men out of their natural shame and abhor-
rence of them; nay, even to recommend them with their utmost Wit.
Such Men as these, are not to be argued with, till they can be persuaded
to use Arguments instead of Drollery. For Banter is not capable of being
answered by Reason: not because it has any strength in it; but because it
runs out of all the bounds of Reason and good Sense, by extravagantly
joining together such Images, as have not in themselves any manner of

Similitude or Connexion; by which means all things are alike easy to be rendered ridiculous. . . .

Wit appeared to many good men as a threat to decency because it walked regularly with irreligion and vice. Thus James Buerdsell, fellow of Brasenose College, complained in 1700 that 'the prevailing Humour of Scepticism' had become 'so extreamly Modish, that no Person can be that self-admir'd thing, a Wit, without it.'[19] In the same year young Samuel Parker, of Trinity College, Oxford, deplored the sad fact that 'Dissoluteness and Irreligion are made the Livery of Wit, and no body must be conscious of good parts, but he loses the credit of them unless he take care to finish 'em with Immoralities.'[20]

Because wit, having become fashionable, began to appear as the natural ally of the scoffer, undermining religion and morals, it seemed to constitute a menace to society—a menace that must be understood if one is to feel the force of Swift's digressions on wit in the *Tale of a Tub* (1704). The threat, obvious to large numbers of intelligent men, was aggravated by the appearance of Shaftesbury's essays, at the very time when Pope meditated on the problems of wit and criticism.

One must not forget that the publication of the *Tatler* and the *Spectator*, both by their nature and their purpose, affected the debate: by their nature, for they were seen to follow in the footsteps of Montaigne, one of the greatest of modern wits; and by their purpose, for they proposed to temper wit with morality and to enliven morality with wit. Wit *could* be made an ally of goodness, they demonstrated forcefully—and so successfully that it was possible two decades later for the author of the Preface to the *Plain Dealer* to assume general agreement when he remarked that periodical essays are composed in the finest taste

> when they cloath good Sense with Humour, and embellish good Morals with Wit; when they instruct Familiarly, and reprove Pleasantly; when they don't swell above Comprehension, nor sink below Delicacy: In short, when they adapt the Wisdom of the Antients to the Gust of the Moderns, and constrain Montaigne's Pleasantry within Bickerstaffe's Compass.

Much of the *Tatler* and *Spectator* papers was devoted to exposing false wit in social life, discrediting the antics of the unseemly biters and banterers, the scatterbrained and volatile, the uncouth leapers and slappers, the hollow laughers, the pert coxcombs. False wit in literature was attended to by Addison in the *Spectator*. Underlying these endeavors is the assumption that wit needed to be defended, and that it could be restored to its rightful place by stripping it of the gaudy and unclean adornments which thoughtless admirers had forced upon it. And at least since the time of Cowley's ode 'Of Wit,' the separation of true from false wit had been a regular mode of defending literature itself.

But besides these general reasons Pope had a personal stake in the argument over wit. The subject had interested him for years before the *Essay on Criticism* was published, as the correspondence with Walsh shows. It was in his correspondence with Wycherley, however, that the subject became crucial—and almost necessarily so. For in the late years of Dryden and the early years of Pope, Wycherley had become the very symbol of the poet of wit.

The trouble began with Wycherley's belated urge for recognition as a nondramatic poet, signalized by the publication in 1704 of his *Miscellany Poems*. Preceding the poems is a Preface that remains one of the unreadable wonders of our language. It is wit gone mad, an avalanche of simile and metaphor, a breathless flow of whim and fancy, out of which, now and then, there half emerges, here and there, a globule of meaning; after which a cloud of darkness settles, and the reader gropes his way blindly toward the poems that follow (where he is not to fare much better).

Little enthusiasm greeted the *Miscellany Poems*. But Wycherley, undaunted, commenced almost immediately to plan a new collection which should contain some unpublished verses and some revised and corrected versions of poems already printed. This time, however, he showed no unseemly haste in afflicting printer and public. Instead, he passed copies around to his friends for advice and correction. Among others so honored was Alexander Pope.

Pope, as we know, took this responsibility seriously. In Wycherley's letter dated February 5, 1705/6[21] we discover that our bold youth was already pruning excrescences from the elder bard's disorganized fancies. On April 10, Pope was explaining with admirable candor that some of the poems were so wretched that 'to render them very good, would require a great addition, and almost the entire new writing of them.' Wycherley's chaos sprang from a false conception of wit. For great wits such as John Donne, said Pope, like great merchants take least pains to set out their valuable goods, whereas the 'haberdashers of small wit' spare no decorations to present their little wares as seductively as possible.[22] As the business of lopping and grafting proceeded, Wycherley's assumed meekness wore thin, until a minor explosion occurred in 1707. Pope had set about to produce a semblance of logical order in the poem on Dullness, subjecting it to radical alterations; such amiable helpfulness provoked Wycherley to this response on November 22:[23]

> And now for the pains you have taken to recommend my Dulness, by making it more methodical, I give you a thousand thanks, since true and natural dulness is shown more by its pretence to form and method, as the sprightliness of wit by its despising both.

Here was a home-thrust, impelled by some resentment and hostility. Pope's letter, dated one week later, shows that he was aware of the resentment; nevertheless he replied patiently: 'To methodize in your case, is full as necessary as to strike out; otherwise you had better destroy the whole frame, and reduce them into single thoughts in prose, like Rochefoucauld, as I have more than once hinted to you.'[24] As for the alleged incompatibility of wit and method, Pope urged that this is true only for the trivial forms of wit embodied in fancy or conceit; but as for true wit, which is propriety, why, that requires method not only to give perspicuity and harmony of parts, but also to insure that each detail will receive its increment of meaning and beauty from the surrounding elements.

This strange contest of wills lasted from 1706 until 1710 at least. In the latter year, on April 11, Wycherley wrote to Pope in protest against the extent to which the younger man was improving his verses. By your tuning of my Welsh harp, he said, my rough sense is to become less offensive to the fastidious ears of those finicky critics who deal rather in sound than in meaning.[25] Wit shines with a native luster that defies the need of polish.

As Wycherley saw it, there was a generous, libertine spirit in wit, too free to be confined, and too noble to be sacrificed for smoothness or regularity. Taking form as a novel simile, a brilliant metaphor, a dazzling paradox, or a smart aphorism, wit is its own justification wherever it happens to appear. Some of Wycherley's contemporaries were wont to say of great wits that their 'careless, irregular and boldest Strokes are most admirable.'[26] For wit in writing is the sign of a fertility of mind, of multitudinous thoughts crowding in upon one or flying out toward the most sublime and exalted objects, of a capacity for wide-ranging speculation that soars above man's necessities and desires, of a flame and agitation of soul that little minds and men of action cannot comprehend.[27] To sacrifice such flashes of wit to an ordered design, to a carefully conceived framework, is to sacrifice poetry itself. Even the feebler manifestations of wit are sacred; we recall that Wycherley had composed a Panegyrick upon Puns.

Pope's artistic conscience told him that such scintillation, when it failed to fit into its proper place and contribute to the effect of the whole, was false wit because it was bad art. And he must have understood that such irresponsible, uncontrolled flashes, lacking any relationship with artistic purpose and solid sense, had contributed to the disrepute into which wit had fallen. As he was driven to correct and revise Wycherley's manuscripts, he was impelled to defend himself, and true wit as well, by reaching a coherent view of literature that would justify his own practice. It was a bold step for a virtually unknown young author to set himself against the most famous wit surviving from the glamorous court of Charles II. But he might draw comfort and support from the fact that a few of the distinguished men of the time had expressed concepts of wit similar to his own. Little by little his ideas take form; we can see them developing in his correspondence, especially that with Wycherley. He told Spence later that he had formulated the substance of the *Essay on Criticism* in prose before he undertook the poem.

One passage in the poem that would seem to have Wycherley in mind is that contained in lines 289–304, where he speaks of the writers addicted to conceits and glittering thoughts, specious prodigalities which are valued by their creators not because they are essential parts of the meaning or because they fit into the places where they are thrown, but because they startle and surprise or raise admiration for their makers' liveliness. These are diseases. Works so constructed are 'One glaring Chaos and wild heap of wit'—an extraordinarily apt description of Wycherley's *Miscellany Poems* of 1704.

But there is a clearer and more specific connection between the correspondence and the poem visible in the passage comprising lines 494–507. Here Pope describes the unhappiness that wit brings to those who possess it by stirring up malice and envy in the dull and ignorant. This, as we learn from a letter dated November 20, 1707,[28] was a subject which he had treated in his reorganization of Wycherley's poem on Dullness. If his distinguished correspondent failed to appreciate the addition, nothing prevented the use of it in a new poem.

By an interesting association of ideas Pope proceeds from here, through a short transitional passage (lines 508–25) dealing with the shame and disgrace that wit suffers at the hands of its friends, to the conclusion of Part II. This concluding section (lines 526–55) completes the subject of Dullness and likewise fulfills the thought developed in lines 408–51, where Pope describes two types of false wit, one caused by servile dullness and the other by modes and current folly. In the closing lines of Part II two more kinds of false wit are exposed: that which grows out of the union of dullness with bawdry, and that which springs from dullness and irreligion. The interesting feature of Pope's strategy in this passage is that these two abuses of wit are made to appear as temporary phases in a historical process, the first brought about by the dissoluteness, luxury, and idleness in the reign of Charles II, and the second, by the license and impiety allowed in the reign of William III. These particular manifestations of false wit (both of them 'modes in wit' and 'current folly') are sharply dissociated from true wit by artfully fixing them in past reigns, which Pope had no need to defend, especially as, out of the Wit's Titans who flourished in these two reigns, the last surviving member and champion was none other than William Wycherly.

It would take a monograph to show in detail how the analysis of false wit (with which Part II of the *Essay* is largely concerned) responds to particular literary developments in Pope's age, and this is not the point where such an investigation could be most profitable. We must still ask ourselves, what did Pope mean by true wit, and what Augustan writers whose thoughts were taking a similar direction can help us to comprehend the import of his view?

In the course of exposing false wit, Pope suggests two criteria by which true wit may be determined. First, it belongs not to the part but to the whole. It is the master idea which informs every portion of the body and gives life and energy; it is the joint force of all components, and not the beauty, regularity, or brilliance of any one feature. It unites the parts, and prevents undue attention from falling on any one; and no part has goodness or badness in itself except in its relation to the whole. And if the whole is properly informed with wit, it gives a generous pleasure, warming the mind with rapture so that we are delighted though we know not why, so delighted that we cannot be disturbed by trivial faults in the execution.

The second test is, that it must take its course from nature, that is, from truth. But not necessarily from the worn or commonplace; enough that we recognize, when we encounter it in art, its essential agreement with the frame of our minds, with universal human experience. So far from being commonplace, the whole piece gives the effect of boldness, not because of style or artifice but because new life, energy, and insight have been added. It comes with the graces of expression, which tend to heighten the outlines of truth rather than to disguise or conceal them.

The expression, in fact, should be as modestly plain as the subject and form permit; and sprightly wit is so far from adhering to it that the expression may rather be said to set off the wit. Nature alone is not true wit until it becomes animated and is drawn into a unity by the shaping spirit.

It is in Part I of the *Essay*, however, where we must look for a fuller account of the relationship of wit and art in the production of poetry.

Pope begins by specifying genius as the quality necessary in the poet, and taste in the critic, but notes that the two functions ideally should coincide. Genius is a synonym for wit, and after the first sixteen lines the former word is discarded in favor of the latter. Wit, then, is a quality that must be present at birth, and it is apportioned to men in varying measure and strength. If it is the genuine poetic gift, it may be fitted for only one type of poetry. Each man must discover his own special strength and cultivate only that for which he is specially fitted.

Along with genius (or taste) we can expect to find at least a rudimentary sense, or judgment, which is just as much the gift of heaven as wit. This sense needs developing; otherwise it is easily perverted, either by the formulas of academic learning or by the distortions of fashion. But nature, to protect us, herself provides the standard of good judgment: an impulse that leads us to prefer the lasting and universal over the ephemeral and local.

This thought is first suggested in lines 19–27, and is taken up again for further development in lines 68–87. Again we are assured that nature furnishes us with a just and universal standard of judgment. But nature also provides the life, force, and beauty that a work of genius requires; it is the source and end as well as the test of art. From this fund art draws its supplies, and proceeds quietly, unobtrusively, to endow all parts of the body with spirit and vigor.

At this point it is easy for the reader to become confused, for the principle of control, which at the start of the passage was called *judgment*, has now become *art*; a few lines later it appears as *wit*, and by the end of the passage it has been transformed back to *judgment* again. Perhaps the most perplexing lines are the oft-quoted:

> Some, to whom Heaven in wit has been profuse.
> Want as much more to turn it to its use. . . .

The lines lend themselves to ridicule, and Pope knew all too well that they left him open to banter. Yet, with his marvelous gift of lucidity to aid him, he left the couplet as we see it. Why? Presumably because it seemed to be the best way of putting something that was very difficult to express.

He found it difficult because it involved a question on which the credit of literature depended. For Pope's contemporaries, encouraged by Locke, were erecting a wall between wit and judgment and attempting to deposit the most valued achievements of mankind on the side of the wall occupied by judgment. This way of thinking is well described by Sir William Temple in his essay 'Of Poetry.' In the usual acceptation, he says, man's goal is taken to be profit or pleasure. The faculty of the mind conversant with profit is wisdom; that conversant with pleasure is wit (or the vein that produces poetry). To wisdom is attributed 'the Inventions or Productions of things generally esteemed the most necessary, useful, or profitable to Human Life'; and to wit, 'those Writings or Discourses which are the most Pleasing or Entertaining.'[29] Wit may borrow from wisdom, of course, but its own proper role is to dazzle the eyes and tickle the ears and cut capers; it has no insight of its own, no peculiar way of thinking, nothing to offer but toys.

Into this pitfall Pope had no desire to plunge. Nor was he tempted by the compromise that seduced many of his contemporaries: to say that the essence of poetry is fable, design, or structure (product of the faculty to which we assign reason, judgment, and wisdom).[30] If the core of literature is provided by the plain rational faculty, then it is conceivable that whatever is valuable in it could be conveyed more profitably in another way (say, in plain didactic prose), without the fuss and feathers of literary art. But apart from that, the compromise effectively disinherits most of the kinds of poetry, for only epic, tragedy, and comedy necessarily have fables.

To Pope, wit and judgment, as they operate in literature, are married. In this union, so long as they are in a healthy state, they work together as a single faculty. As for the meaning of *wit* in the perplexed couplet, we must go back to the early lines in the poem, where we are told that genius and taste must ideally coincide; or, as the thought is expanded, that wit is accompanied by a rudimentary sense, potentially excellent, which requires development by experience. However great the gifts of heaven, wit, without that development, falls short of its perfection: natural wit needs training for its proper expression in art. But such training does not propose to foster an alien power, at odds with wit. Pope tries to make himself clear in the following passage (lines 88–140). The training designed to perfect the rudimentary sense is an experience of the great wit of the past, first through a study of the rules, in which the principles underlying the mighty achievements of past art are set forth in simple abstraction; and second by a detailed study of 'each Ancient's proper character' in every page of his work. Out of such experience should come *literary* judgment, *literary* taste, which is the accomplished phase of wit; or, to put it in another way, wit in the writer is not merely the power to conceive of objects and endow them with 'Life, force, and beauty,' but also the ability to find an appropriate style and form in which to express them; the latter ability, developed by knowledge of the rules and of masterpieces of literature, serves as taste and judgment. In the writer it is also art, invisibly guiding the energy of the conception so that it permeates the form and language, and achieves its desired end. Thus, if this sense (call it taste, judgment, or art) guides the creative energy and, in a way, contains it, nature is still the test of art, for this judgment must be constructed on the foundation of a natural artistic gift. And because this gift comes originally from Heaven, or nature, it may at times conduct the creative impulse to its objective by a route not recognized by the rules and untried by past masterpieces—so snatching a grace beyond the reach of art.

The important point is that Pope believed there was a special way of thinking peculiar to literature, a way called *wit*, which possessed unique values; he saw that wit (in the narrower sense) and judgment in the artist are but two aspects of a single way of thinking, and that judgment (or art) is not a churlish, rational censor but a natural literary sense cultivated by a wide acquaintance with literary masterpieces. Literature therefore is good, not because it charms eye or ear with sparkle and melody nor because it borrows wisdom from philosophy or science, but because wit, the unique mode of the literary artist, provides an insight into nature, endows it with 'Life, force, and beauty,' and conveys it directly to our hearts, charming us as it makes us wiser.

The *Essay on Criticism*, then, had something to say. There is much more in it than we have either time or space to examine. But if we can follow what Pope says of wit, we can grasp his primary purpose. He had difficulty in expressing his ideas concerning wit because there existed no adequate critical vocabulary for him to draw upon. There did, however, exist a body of thought concerning wit, some expressions of which Pope was certainly acquainted with, and some part of which could serve to strengthen and clarify his own views. To the consideration of that body of thought it is reasonable that we proceed.

The first fact about wit that struck observers was that it made for a lively mind. Hobbes himself defined it as celerity of imagining, and thought of it as a tenuity and agility of spirits, which, as it distinguished its possessors from the dull and sluggish of soul, must to that extent have seemed to him as a virtue.[31] If wit meant nothing more than liveliness, it would have its value. Welsted, who liked to take an extreme position, remarked years later, partly out of admiration for sheer life and animation, that even the sprightly *nonsense* of wit is preferable to the dull sense of plodding, earth-bound creatures.[32]

A number of writers, however, refused to confine the liveliness of wit to sprightly nonsense. Liveliness, indeed, was the first quality that impressed the author of *Remarques on the Humours and Conversations of the Town* (1673), who described wit as 'properly the vivacity, and the agreeableness of the fancy'; nevertheless he adds immediately, 'yet there ought to belong something more to that high quality, than a little flash and quibble.'[33] 'Something more,' as he explains in the following pages, meant to him an intelligent subject, delivered 'sweet and pleasantly, in the native beauties of our Language.' In that high quality, true wit, we see, sense, liveliness, and worthy expression might coalesce. So likewise it appeared in the opinion of the great Robert Boyle, who remarked that wit, 'that nimble and acceptable Faculty of the Mind,' involves both a readiness and subtlety in conceiving things, and a quickness and neatness in rendering them[34]—a way of putting the idea that neatly anticipates Pope's phrasing in a letter to Wycherley dated December 26, 1704: true wit is 'a perfect conception, with an easy delivery.'[35]

The vivacity of wit could be valuable for one of two reasons: either because it naturally operated to charm other minds, or because it was the mark of a soul capable of unusual powers, beyond the reach of ordinary men. There is a point at which vivacity and subtlety melt into swiftness and acuity. To the soon-to-be-duncified Fleckno, wit appeared to have an extraordinary force; it was, he said, a spiritual fire that rarefies and renders everything spiritual like itself.[36] To Margaret, Duchess of Newcastle, it seemed unearthly, mysterious, 'the purest Element, and swiftest Motion of the Brain: it is the Essence of Thoughts; it incircles all things: and a true Wit is like the Elixir, that keeps Nature always fresh and young.'[37] And, lest we smile at this, let us remind ourselves that the mysterious power of wit to penetrate to the heart of darkness is attested by the greatly influential La Rochefoucauld, whose Augustan translator (perhaps Stanhope) rendered him thus:[38]

> The making a Difference between Wit and Judgment, is a Vulgar Error. Judgment is nothing else but the exceeding Brightness of Wit, which, like Light, pierces into the very Bottom of Things, observes all that ought to be observed there, and discovers what seemed to be past any

bodies finding out: From when we must conclude, that the Energy and Extension of this Light of the Wit, is the very Thing that produces all those Effects, usually ascribed to the Judgment.

The comparison between wit and light appealed strongly to a few writers of the age, who reveal something of the mystic's fervor when they address themselves to it. Thus an unknown author wrote at the turn of the century:[39]

> Wit is a Radiant Spark of Heav'nly Fire,
> Full of Delight, and worthy of Desire;
> Bright as the Ruler of the Realms of Day,
> Sun of the Soul, with in-born Beauties gay. . . .

And at the time when the ideas of the *Essay on Criticism* were beginning to take form in Pope's mind, another author, rejecting the notion that wit consists of merely exotic language, satire, floridity, quibbles or trifles, banter, or smart repartee, insisted:[40]

> No, 'tis a Thought sprung from a Ray Divine,
> Which will through Clouds of Low'ring Criticks shine:
> When in a Clear, Innubilous Serene,
> The Soul's Abstracted, Purg'd from Dross and Spleen . . . .

These mystic utterances are interesting but rather less important than the remarks of men like La Rochefoucauld, who looked upon wit as a natural instrument for probing the secrets of nature, and apparently as a mode of thinking unlike the rational method operating in mathematics. As representative of this group we may take Joseph Glanvill, who instructed his readers that true wit might be useful even in sermons:[41]

> . . . For true Wit is a perfection in our Faculties, chiefly in the Under-
> standing, and Imagination; Wit in the Understanding is a Sagacity to
> find out the Nature, Relations, and Consequences of things; Wit in
> the Imagination, is a quickness in the phancy to give things proper
> Images. . . .

And in another work he castigates those who debase wit, which is truly fitted for 'great and noble Exercises of the Mind.' It is in reality, he remarks, 'a Faculty to dive into the depth of things, to find out their Causes and Relatives, Consonancies and Disagreements, and to make fit, useful, and unobvious Applications of their respective Relations and Dependencies.'[42] The simile and metaphor of literature, therefore, *may* become, not the trifling ornaments laid upon the truth, but instruments of the profoundest thinking, the natural way of revealing the discovery of hidden relationships. A second representative of this group is Francis Atterbury, later a friend of Pope's, who discussed the subject in a sermon printed in 1708, while Pope was establishing his defenses against Wycherley. Atterbury wrote, 'Wit, indeed, as it implies a certain uncommon Reach and Vivacity of Thought, is an Excellent Talent; very fit to be employ'd in the Search of Truth, and very capable of assisting us to discern and embrace it. . . .'[43] His subsequent remarks show clearly that wit was not to be employed, as Shaftesbury proposed, in banter and raillery, to strip the mask from falsehood and thus arrive, indirectly, at truth; rather, it plunged straight to its object by virtue of its own range, acuity, and vivacity.

Even though Addison accepted Locke's definition of wit, thereby splitting off wit from judgment and demoting wit to the role of a mild spice serviceable in making morality pleasing to the palate, there were enough others who refused to be so misled. They persisted in thinking of wit as 'a high quality,' fitted for 'great and noble Exercises of the Mind,' as a special and valuable mode of apprehending nature and truth—not the plain and obvious, but the depth of things, where the complex relationships, the consonancies and disagreements, among the parts of nature lay open to wit alone. Some thought of judgment as a phase of wit; some thought of fancy as that part of wit which provided appropriate images and expression to deliver wit's discoveries. Wit and art are eternally wedded, and true wit is 'a perfection in our Faculties.'

This lofty conception of wit, making it possible to claim for literature a noble rank among human activities and a value far greater than can be granted that which merely entertains and pleases, was overshadowed in the early eighteenth century by the ideas of Locke and of men like him. And yet, sanctioned as it was by such formidable names as Robert Boyle, La Rochefoucauld, and Atterbury (some of whom were known to Pope), it offered an easily tenable position from which to defend literature from the assaults of those intent on debasing it.

There was one other type of answer to those engaged in depreciating wit, and it is worth examining because Pope was evidently attracted by it. At least from the Renaissance, men had been familiar with the idea that strangeness is an essential element in all excellent beauty. So Bacon had said. Wit and strangeness seemed inextricably connected in Davenant's mind, for he explained the wit of *Gondibert* to lie 'in bringing Truth, too often absent, home to mens bosoms, to lead her through unfrequented and new ways, and from the most remote Shades. . . .'[44]

Likewise Leonard Welsted defined wit as 'some uncommon Thought or just Observation, couch'd in Images or Allusions, which create a sudden Surprize'—a definition which admits the just Observation but stresses the uncommon and surprising.[45] In actual practice, wit became increasingly associated after 1690 with the strange, novel, and surprising.

But because novelty was so often connected with the emphemeral, with whim or fashion, and because subtle, uncommon ideas were often suspected of heresy, or the kind of enthusiasm which had led to the logic-chopping and violence of the Civil War, the charge was constantly made that wit depended on a love of quaintness and paradox, of novelty rather than truth, and was therefore offensive to the wise and good.[46] To meet this charge certain writers began to stress the sound content of the product rather than the swiftness and acuity of mind that wit signified. Thus David Abercromby in 1685 defined wit as 'either a senceful discourse, word, or Sentence, or a skilful Action.'[47] Not 'dead, and downright flat Sence' would do, but good sense properly animated. Something similar appears to have been in Boileau's mind when he remarked that 'Wit is not Wit, but as it says something every Body thought of, and that in a lively, delicate, and New Manner'[48]—an observation that probably lays more stress on style and manner than the author intended; even as Pope's

> True wit is Nature to advantage dressed,
> What oft was thought, but ne'er so well expressed . . .

is easily misinterpreted to mean that any old saw will do as wit so long as it is well groomed and elegantly turned out. Actually Pope was far from desiring to confine wit to expression. His thinking at the time was close to that of William Walsh, who observed to him in a letter dated September 9, 1706, that nature alone is to be followed, and that we must carefully eschew similes, conceits, and all kinds of 'fine things.' And as for what you remark concerning expression, said Walsh, it is truly in the same relation to wit as dress is to beauty.[49]

Certainly Pope intended to oppose any idea of wit that separated subject matter from style. It is significant that in a letter dated November 29, 1707, he defined wit, in 'the better notion of it,' as propriety.[50] This, of course, was Dryden's definition, stated as early as 1677, and rephrased as 'thoughts and words elegantly adapted to the subject.'[51] It was Dryden's idea of wit to the end of his career, a definition which, as he says, 'I imagin'd I had first found out; but since am pleasingly convinc'd, that Aristotle has made the same Definition in other Terms.'[52]

That Dryden's conception of wit interested other men than Pope at this time is strongly suggested by the *Tatler's* article from Will's Coffee-house which begins, 'This evening was spent at our table in discourse of propriety of words and thoughts, which is Mr. Dryden's definition of wit . . .'[53]

The term *propriety* conveys no very clear idea to us when it is applied to literary criticism, and for that reason Dryden's definition has been taken much less seriously by modern scholars than it was by the Augustans. It deserves to be understood. The *Tatler* supposed, incorrectly, that it involved a relationship between thoughts and words only. In reality Dryden was urging a threefold relationship, between thoughts, words, *and* subject, effected in such a way that the three elements appear to belong to one another (*propriety* conveyed the sense of *ownership*); and the words 'elegantly adapted' point to the need of an active literary intelligence to produce the work of wit.

This account of wit as propriety bears a resemblance to an Augustan theory concerning the artistic process which may help to explain it. The theory, in brief, supposed that objects produce in genius (the artistic mind raised to a high degree of emotion and sensibility) certain thoughts which, in the very instant of their generation, take on forms and expression adequate to convey them and completely appropriate to them. A form of the theory can be found in the works of Dryden's young friend, John Dennis. In the genius, says Dennis, 'as Thoughts produce the Spirit, the Spirit produces and makes the Expression; which is known by Experience to all who are Poets . . .'[54] The expression (which includes style, harmony, rhythm, etc.), then, is not the result of a separate act but exists in the most intimate and necessary relationship with the ideas, emotions, and attitudes of the artist, being engendered along with them. The thoughts do not become wit until they are animated and transfused by the shaping spirit which gives them expression—and all elements take form in perfect propriety.

To define wit, therefore, as 'What oft was thought, but ne'er so well expressed,' does not say or imply that wit is a stale or commonplace thought nicely tricked out. The definition rather supposes that the writer, starting with a common and universal experience, sees it in a new light; and his sensitive spirit, endowing it with life and fresh meaning, provides it with form, image, language, and harmony appropriate to it. It presupposes the liveliness and insight of the creative mind; and it demands propriety, the perfect agreement of words, thoughts (as reshaped by the artist), and subject. The result is nature, and it is wit.[55]

When Pope composed the *Essay on Criticism,* there was need for a defense of wit—and that is to say, of literature as well. His own circumstances, involved as he was in a controversy with the most famous writer surviving from the court of Charles II and what was understood to have been the golden age of wit, demanded that he should justify his bold and rash treatment of Wycherley. Locke's conception of wit was of no use to him; in fact, it served the enemy better. But there were other ideas available which were consistent with a conviction of the high dignity and noble function of literature. Through this maze Pope attempted to thread his way. If he was not entirely successful in conveying his meaning with utter clarity, the fault lay partly in the lack of a critical vocabulary. But he had something important to say, and there are good clues to his intention. Pope saw, thought, felt, and wrote as the complete artist. Those who would like to understand his views of the literary art (and of criticism, its complement) must read the *Essay on Criticism* with a fuller awareness of its historical setting.

NOTES

1. 'Wit in the *Essay on Criticism*,' *Hudson Review*, Vol. II, No. 4 (Winter 1950), pp. 559–77.
2. References to and quotations from the *Essay on Criticism* are based on George Sherburn's edition, *Selections from Pope* (New York: Nelson and Sons, n.d.).
3. Anon., *The Polite Arts* (1749), p. 15.
4. Preface to *Annus Mirabilis*, in *Essays of Dryden*, ed. W. P. Ker, I, 14.
5. Antony Blackwall, *An Introduction to the Classics* (6th ed., 1746), p. 12.
6. *Ibid.*, p. 18.
7. *Discourse of Wit* (1685), p. 180.
8. *Essay on Criticism* (1728), p. 44.
9. In *Critical Essays of the 17th Century*, ed. Spingarn, II, 288.
10. *Introduction to the Classics*, p. 21.
11. *Brief Discourse concerning the Different Wits of Men* (1669), p. 25.
12. *Brief Discourse*, pp. 20–21.
13. *A Treatise of Morality*, trans. James Shipton (1699), p. 114.
14. *Poems, or, Several Fancies in Verse* (3d ed., 1668), p. 224.
15. Preface to trans. of St. Évremond, *Miscellanea* (1686), *sig.* A9v–A10r.
16. *Bibliotheque Choisie*, XIX (Amsterdam, 1709), 431.
17. P. 18.
18. *Works of Samuel Clarke* (4 vols., 1738), II, 603–4.
19. *Discourses and Essays on Several Subjects* (Oxford, 1700), p. 205.
20. *Six Philosophical Essays* (1700), p. 18.
21. Pope, *Works*, ed. Elwin-Courthope, VI, 26.
22. Elwin-Courthope, VI, 28.

23. *Ibid.*, VI, 33.

24. *Ibid.*, VI, 34–35.

25. *Ibid.*, VI, 44.

26. Cf. John Dennis, *Critical Works,* II (Baltimore, 1943), 381.

27. *Ibid.*, II, 383. Thus Dennis wrote to Wycherley, knowing he was addressing a sympathetic spirit.

28. Elwin-Courthope, VI, 32.

29. In Spingarn, III, 73–74.

30. For a rather typical expression of the idea, see Mary Astell (?), *Bart'lemy Fair* (1709), p. 80: 'Colouring is the least of the Matter, both in Wit and Painting; a few bold Strokes never made an Artist; the Attitudes, Proportions, and above all the Design, shew the Masterly Genius.' Cf. also Dennis, *Critical Works,* II, 46.

31. *Leviathan,* I, viii.

32. *Epistles, Odes, &c* (1724), Dedication, p. xli.

33. P. 93.

34. *Occasional Reflections* (1665), p. 37.

35. Elwin-Courthope, VI, 16.

36. 'Of Wit,' in *A Farrago* (1666), pp. 58–59.

37. *The Worlds Olio* (2d ed., 1671), p. 11.

38. Maxim 98, in La Rochefoucauld, *The Moral Maxims and Reflections* (2d ed., 1706), as reprinted in the edition of George Powell (New York: F. A. Stokes Company, n.d.).

39. *A Satyr upon a Late Pamphlet Entitled, A Satyr Against Wit* (1700).

40. *The British Apollo,* September 1–3, 1708.

41. *Essay Concerning Preaching* (2d ed., 1703), pp. 71–72.

42. *A Whip for the Droll* (1700), pp. 4–5.

43. 'A Scorner Incapable of True Wisdom' (preached, 1694), in *Fourteen Sermons* (1708), pp. 158–59.

44. Preface to *Gondibert,* in Spingarn, II, 23.

45. *Epistles, Odes, &c* (1724), Dedication, p. lx.

46. Thus Atterbury, in *Fourteen Sermons* (1708), pp. 158–59, describing the forms most commonly taken by wit in his day, wrote: 'Men of Quick and Lively Parts are apt to give themselves a loose beyond plain Reason and Common Sense; and to say many things not exactly Right and True, in order to say somewhat New and Surprizing.' For this reason Wycherley himself remarked that wit is generally false reasoning—a remark that was pounced upon gleefully by Warburton in the *Divine Legation* (2d ed., 1738), I, xiv. The excellent author of the *Whole Duty of Man,* in *Works* (1726), Part II, pp. 47, 82, 85, 248, anticipates one of Swift's most brilliant essays in irony by observing that a great deal of wit depended on reversing universally accepted judgments on the most serious and sacred subjects and that if the Bible were taken away, the wit of many men would forthwith dry up.

47. *Discourse of Wit* (1685), p. 7.

48. *Works,* trans. Ozell (2d ed., 1736), I, iii.

49. Elwin-Courthope, VI, 55.

50. *Ibid.*, VI, 34–35.

51. *Essays of Dryden,* ed. W. P. Ker, I, 190; cf. also I, 270, and II, 9.

52. 'Life of Lucian,' in *Works of Lucian* (1711), I, 42.

53. *Tatler,* No. 62 (September 1, 1709).

54. *Advancement and Reformation of Modern Poetry* (1701), in *Critical Works*, I (Baltimore, 1939), 222.

55. The tendency to define wit in terms of the thoughts produced, or to emphasize the necessary presence in wit of common sense, is well illustrated by Bouhours, who in *Les Entretiens d'Ariste et d'Eugene* (Paris, 1737), p. 258, defined wit as: '*C'est un corps solide qui brille. . . .*' It is no accident that Bouhours, after a neglect of three decades, was becoming influential in England by 1710. Garth had recommended him to Oldmixon, as he probably had to Pope; and Addison in the *Spectator* was to proclaim him the greatest of the French critics. Although Bouhours in *La Maniere de Bien Penser* seemed to lay heavy stress on common sense and the logical element in wit, he made it clear that he was really concerned not with thought but with the turn given the thought by the ingenious mind and with the appropriateness of the style and language to that turn or attitude. Common sense did not strike him as wit until it was vivified and illuminated by the author. This much Pope and Bouhours had in common; in what remains, Pope's superior artistic sense is obvious.

JOHN BUTT

Pope Seen Through His Letters

POPE was a great poet; he was also a most enigmatic personality. It should be possible to enjoy his poetry without thinking too much about the man who wrote it; and several critics have managed to expound and assess it without sitting in judgment upon the poet's character. But there has always been a strong temptation to assume that Pope's satires must have been written by a person of peculiarly vindictive temperament. The man who held so many of his contemporaries up to ridicule must have been quick to take offence; he cannot have had many friends; and surely that deformed body was a faithful representation of the deformed mind within. This was a common view amongst the Victorians, and it is still not uncommon today. The trouble partly is that we have never had a reliable full scale life of Pope. Such a Life was indeed impossible until his correspondence was properly edited; for the evidence to correct the common view of Pope lies in his letters. Pope himself recognised that they would serve this purpose by throwing light upon his moral character, and it was partly with this object in view that he published a selection of them.

It is still unusual to publish one's private letters, and a man who does so, unless he is exceptionally conceited, may well feel that such an action is lacking in modesty, especially if the letters are mainly concerned with his private life. That was what Pope thought; but nevertheless he was determined to publish. He therefore resorted to stratagem. There was a notorious publisher called Edmund Curll, who had made a special line of scandalous biographies—a wit described them as adding a new

From a discussion of *The Correspondence of Alexander Pope*, edited by George Sherburn, originally given as a B.B.C. broadcast, and printed in *The Listener* for June 20, 1957. Reprinted by permission of the publisher and author.

terror to death. Pope had been suffering from Curll's attentions for many years. Curll had published attacks upon his character; he had also managed to get hold of some of Pope's more indiscreet verses as well as a small collection of Pope's letters, and he had had no compunction in publishing these too. He had now advertised for biographical facts and documents to be used in a life of Pope. The opportunity seemed too good to miss, and Pope sent him by some mysterious agent printed copies of his own letters, which Curll proceeded to publish. Pope was then able to declare that he was injured, and that he must preserve his reputation by publishing a correct and authentic edition.

In telling this story I have left out several involutions of Pope's complicated intrigue; and even more complicated was the intrigue by which he secured the publication of his correspondence with Swift a few years later. He has been severely censured for these equivocal dealings, and he has been equally severely condemned for tampering with the text of his letters; he can also be shown to have invented dates which are patently incorrect. But none of this is very serious. Where the originals of these letters survive, or independent transcripts of them, a comparison reveals that what he omitted were trivialities and occasional profanities, but that his principal revisions were purely stylistic. It is not too reprehensible for a man to make a poor guess at the day twenty years ago on which he wrote a letter that he forgot to date, and it is only a venial crime if you take a letter sent to one dead acquaintance and re-address it to another who had tiresomely failed to preserve the actual letters you sent him.

The publishing intrigues are more difficult to condone. Essentially what they show is a confusion between ends and means: deceits were practised in order that ends regarded as worthy might be accomplished. We can readily imagine a man recalling and publishing his private letters if they contained a record of his travels in remote parts, or of his role in some important transactions of state, or if they constituted a discussion of some matter of philosophical or scientific interest, or even if they described the social scene of fifty years ago. But Pope's letters were not like that. We catch an occasional glimpse of society, as when he describes to Martha Blount the life of a Maid of Honour at Hampton Court in 1717:

> To eat Westphalia Ham in a morning, ride over Hedges & ditches on borrowed Hacks, come home in the heat of the day with a Feavor, & what is worse a hundred times, with a red mark in the forehead from an uneasy hat; all this may qualify them to make excellent Wives for Fox-hunters,

& bear abundance of ruddy-complexion'd Children. As soon as they can wipe off the Sweat of the day, they must simper an hour, & catch cold, in the Princesses apartment; from thence (as *Shakespear* has it) *To Dinner, with what appetite they may*—And after that, till midnight, walk, work, or think, which they please? I can easily believe, no lone House in Wales, with a Mountain & a Rookery, is more contemplative than this Court; and as a proof of it I need only tell you Mrs. Lepell walk'd all alone with me three or four hours, by moonlight; and we mett no Creature of any quality, but the King, who gave audience all alone to the Vice-chamberlen, under the Garden-wall.

The merit of that passage lies as much in the comment as in the description, as it does when he bluffly condoles with the same lady twenty years later on her enforced dissipations:

To be all day, first dressing one's body, then dragging it abroad, then stuffing the guts, then washing them with Tea, then wagging one's tongue, & so to bedd; is the life of an Animal, that may for all that I know have Reason in it (as the Country Girl said a Fiddle had a Tune in it) but wanted somebody to fetch it out. And Ladies indeed do seldome learn to play this way, or show what's in them at all, till they meet with some clever Fellow, to wind them up, & frett their fiddle-strings.

He has little to say to his correspondents about the process of poetical composition, though he will occasionally comment on a poem, as when he remarks of the revised *Rape of the Lock* that

this whimsical piece of work . . . is at once the most a satire, and the most inoffensive, of anything of mine. People who would rather it were let alone laugh at it, and seem heartily merry, at the same time that they are uneasy. 'Tis a sort of writing very like tickling. I am so vain as to fancy [it] a pretty complete picture of the life of our modern ladies in this idle town.

Though the poet is sometimes found defending himself from the objections of his fellow Catholics or deferring to the criticism of his friends, he is more often discovered as a man of business, dealing with printers and publishers, collecting his subscriptions, ever warehousing copies of his books at Lord Oxford's town house, or arranging for them to be advertised, as in this passage:

I shall take it as a favour of you [he writes to the editor of the *Gazette*] to insert the inclosed advertisement both in the Gazette and Daily Courant, three times. What I particularly recommend to your care is to cause it to be distinguishd with proper dignity, & the title in Capitals, as here drawn. Also to stand at the head of the more vulgar advertisements at least rankd before Eloped wives, if not before Lost Spaniels & Strayd Geldings. Do not, I beseech you, grudge to bestow One Line at large in honour of my name, who wd bestow many to celebrate yours.

The same elegance of phrase characterises even a brief note, written in the winter before his death, which today would be replaced by a telephone message:

> If my Lord Burlington goes to Chiswick on Saturday or Sunday, & cares to be troubled with me, I will, upon his sending a warm Chariot (for I dare not go in a Chaise) put my self into his power, like a small Bird half starved, in this miserable weather.

But these qualities are not the essence of the letters. Pope had begun re-assembling them and re-reading them before he was twenty-five years old, since he recognised so early in his life that they were an important part of his literary output: perhaps some thoughts thrown out in the freedom of soul might be used as essays for *The Spectator* or *The Guardian*. But though he does not seem to have made much use of his letters that way, he was pleased to see that what he called these 'thoughts just warm from the brain without any polishing or dress, the very *déshabille* of the understanding' did record the true and undisguised state of his mind and preserve a sketch of his friendships. To the reader who is accustomed to think of Pope sitting in angry solitude, nursing his injuries and meditating his next vituperative attack, this record of his friendships will appear both varied and astonishing. Here we can see the terms on which he lived with survivors of the Restoration wits, notably Wycherley and Congreve, with his co-religionists as well as with Anglican bishops and inferior clergy, with the men of letters of his own generation like Swift, Parnell, and Gay, with the artists of the age such as Kent, Jervas, and Sir Godfrey Kneller, with great ladies like the Duchesses of Marlborough and Buckingham, and the Countess of Burlington, with politicians like Oxford and Bolingbroke, and with eminent physicians, generals, lawyers, and peers.

The course of these friendships was not always smooth. There was some coolness with Wycherley, with Ralph Allen the philanthropist (the original of Fielding's Squire Allworthy) and with Broome, one of his collaborators in translating the 'Odyssey,' though in each instance good relations were re-established. Three correspondences were abruptly terminated and never resumed, two with early friends, Cromwell and

Teresa Blount, and the third, notoriously, with Lady Mary Wortley Montagu. But for the most part the correspondences are ended only by death, and they are punctuated not merely by affectionate enquiries but by numerous acts of kindness on the poet's part.

Pope made many demands upon his friends: they ship him curious stones for his grotto and wine for his table, they handle his investments, they carry him about in their coaches, and procure subscriptions for his 'Homer'; his noble friends place rooms in their houses at his disposal, and they are so tame as to lend their names to his publishing devices, and to copy out his poems. But he on his side seemed never tired of doing good turns. He procures gardeners and designs gardens; he advises on architecture, on sculpture, and on the choice of pictures and furniture; and he presents pineapples of his own growing. If a preacher is to be elected at the Charterhouse or a Professor of Poetry at Oxford, Pope is energetic in working for his candidates. Though a Roman Catholic, he uses his influence in disposing of Anglican livings. He even arranges to supply Lord Bathurst's son with Scots cattle; and with monumental patience he reads a tragedy of Aaron Hill's four times, suggests revisions, and procures the same degree of attention from Bolingbroke. As the editor of his letters, Mr. Sherburn, remarks, 'He was always busy, even officiously busy.' Furthermore this kindliness of nature survived to the very end. An ancedote is told by his friend, Spence, of Pope's last illness, when his mind had begun to wander:

> When I was telling his Lordship that Mr. Pope on every catching & recovering of his Mind was always saying something kindly of his present and absent friends; & that this in some cases was so surprizing, that his Humanity seem'd to have outlasted his Understanding; [Lord Bolingbroke] said, 'It has so!'—& then added, 'I never knew a man, that had a tenderer heart for his particular friends; or a more general friendship, for mankind.'

Here then is evidence enough at least to modify the traditional view of Pope's character. We cannot surely believe that Pope made a lifelong habit of insincere professions of friendship, and that his intimates—the characters of a great many of whom are known independently of these letters—were so much afraid of him as to pretend a devotion that they did not feel. Lord Orrery, a close acquaintance of his later years, wrote a brief description of Pope at home, which confirms this impression of his friendliness:

> His manners were delicate, easy, and engaging; and he treated his friends with a politeness that charmed, and a generosity that was much

to his honour. Every guest was made happy within his doors. Pleasure dwelt under his roof, and elegance presided at his table.

Of course there was more than one Pope, as he himself recognised. After telling Caryll how strangely his mind is divided every hour of his life, he goes on to remark:

> Good God! What an Incongruous Animal is Man? how unsettled in his best part, his soul; and how changing and variable in his frame of body? The constancy of the one, shook by every notion, the temperament of the other, affected by every blast of wind. What an April weather in the mind! In a word, what is Man altogether, but one mighty inconsistency.

This is one of the moral truisms which shine almost as brightly in his letters as in his poetry; but it should also serve to caution us about assuming that in any career so well documented as Pope's there should be perfect congruity of action and morals. Certain episodes in his life, if judged by his own austere standards, are not altogether easy to justify: for example, the relentless vilification of Lady Mary Wortley Montagu, his equivocal treatment of his collaborator Broome in 'The Art of Sinking in Poetry' and in *The Dunciad,* and the means by which he secured the publication of his correspondence with Swift. It is possible both to wish that on those occasions Pope had acted differently and at the same time to see what the injured but forgiving Broome meant when he told Pope that

> the humane companion, the dutiful and affectionate son, the compassionate and obliging friend, appear so strongly almost in every page [of your letters] that I assure you I had rather be the owner of the writer's heart than of the head that has honoured England with Homer, his Essays, [and] Moral Epistles.

R. F. JONES

The Background of the Attack on
Science in the Age of Pope

In the three centuries or more that have elapsed since experimental science was first established in England, each period has reacted to it in ways sometimes similar but frequently different. In each there has appeared the eternal struggle between spirit and matter, man and nature, morality and naturalism—the old debate between body and soul. But in each period there have been certain local and temporal conditions that have determined attitudes peculiar to the age. Though the view of science in the nineteenth century contains elements similar to the view expressed in the seventeenth, there were some unique features of the earlier period that fostered attitudes not to be found in the later, features that history has almost forgotten. It is my purpose to analyse the unique features of the opposition to experimental science in the second half of the seventeenth century, largely for the light that may thus be thrown upon literary history, though literature is kept in the background. In the soil of this period the roots of the satire which Pope, Swift, and others directed against science are to be found.

The normal conception of the history of science views it as a record of the discoveries of the past, their significance and influence. Those who make such discoveries are the chief heroes of the narrative and monopolize most of the attention. In short, this type of history presents, for the most part, an unfolding picture of man's increasing knowledge of his natural environment. Yet if one investigates the formative period of modern experimental science in England, he will discover that those interested in science at this time were not so much concerned with great

From *Pope and His Contemporaries: Essays Presented to George Sherburn* (Clarendon Press, 1949), 96–113. Reprinted by permission of the author.

discoveries as with the stream of thought which these discoveries supported or out of which they arose. The main principles found in this thought-current were few and definite. First was the demand for a sceptical mind, freed from all preconceptions and maintaining a critical attitude toward all ideas presented to it. Second, the need of sufficient authentic data was stressed, and observation and experimentation were insisted upon as the only trustworthy means of securing these data. And third, the inductive method of reasoning was to be employed on them. Such were the central or primary ideas in this thought-movement, or, to use an expression borrowed from criticism, the timeless element, for they are as true to-day, though perhaps more generally taken for granted, as they were then. But besides these there was also the time element, or those secondary principles which came into being when the primary clashed with their age. The necessity of opposing the authority of the ancients contributed an anti-authoritarian element. But to undermine the authority of antiquity it was necessary to attack a prevailing theory of the Renaissance, which asserted that modern times represented the old age of the world and the last stages of the decay of nature, in which human powers had degenerated to a level far below that of the ancients, who lived when nature was in its prime. In order to advance new discoveries against established ideas the scientists insisted upon the principle of freedom of thought and discussion. And finally, the belief that knowledge could expand if submission to the ancients were abandoned, and the realization that some discoveries had already shown the possibility of advancement, moved those who had embraced the scientific faith to develop the idea of progress, which indeed joined hands with the opposition to the idea of nature's decay.

These values, attitudes, and ideas, together with a few others, combined to form the scientific movement, and they were expressed by an ever-increasing chorus of voices, not of authentic scientists only, or even chiefly, but of noblemen, state officials, clergymen, and even of the rabble of magicians, astrologers, graceless quacks, and other representatives of the lunatic fringe. Most thought-movements require leaders, and science furnishes no exception. During the first forty years of the seventeenth century it seemed that William Gilbert, author of *De Magnete* (1600), a thoroughly scientific work on terrestrial magnetism, would assume this position. Both by example and precept he had promoted the ideas of induction, observation, and experiment, hostility to ancient authority, and intellectual freedom, and his followers perpetuated his ideas. But when the Puritans secured political power in England, they seized with avidity upon Bacon's philosophy, and enthroned him as leader of the scientific movement, a position he maintained throughout the century. The substitution of Bacon for Gilbert was a happy and, perhaps, inevitable one. In his works Lord Verulam had expressed the idea of science much more comprehensively; some of its constituent elements were primarily due to him. But even more important, his ardent reforming spirit qualified him for leadership, and his eloquence made his leadership effective. In the many references to him during the second half of the century we easily detect the warmth of personal feeling such as the leader of any movement should and does inspire, a feeling of human discipleship.

All the principles which I have represented as constituting the idea of science find varied and eloquent expression in Bacon's works. To these we should add another conception, one peculiarly Bacon's, which, though of no significance to-day, was one of the most important factors, if not the most important, in the development of science at this time. Sir Francis believed that all the phenomena in the universe were the result of the operation of the primary laws of nature, alone and combined. He did not think that these laws were many in number, but just as out of a relatively small number of letters innumerable words may be formed, so any number of phenomena could spring from various combinations of the laws. If man could discover these primary laws, then by combining them he could produce all natural phenomena and be indeed master of nature. But to discover them, Bacon held that it was first necessary to compile a natural history which would include all the data that the earth and the fullness thereof could contribute. The absurdity of such an undertaking is quite apparent to us now, but so eloquently had he impressed upon his followers the need, and possibility, of such a history, that they accepted it with a faith which stifled all misgivings, and which made them eager to undertake an enterprise, the completion of which they could not hope to see. For Bacon had stated that the undertaking could be achieved only by the co-operative endeavours of large numbers of men extended over several ages. So scientists came together to form groups of experimenters, some of which merged to form the Royal Society. The desire to contribute to the natural history intensified their efforts and was largely responsible for the rapid spread of observing and experimenting so characteristic of this period. Again and again we find men declaring that the motive of their scientific activities is a desire to furnish data for the history. The avowed purpose of the Royal Society, the most important embodiment of the scientific movement, was not to discover natural laws, but to accumulate large stocks of data against the time when the master thinker would have sufficient material for the discovery of primary laws. Robert Boyle ascribed the same purpose to his activities. From this situation, as we shall see later, sprang an exaggerated emphasis upon mere sense-observation and a corresponding distrust of reason.

The thought-movement which I have tried to describe emerged in definite outline in the fifth and sixth decades of the century when the Puritans came into power, and as long as they remained in power they zealously supported it. By appointing Puritan experimental scientists to important positions in the universities, by the encouragement of men engaged in promoting experimentation and spreading propaganda in its behalf, and especially by numerous educational treatises, which proposed turning the universities into scientific and technological institutions, the Puritans launched the scientific movement well on its way. But the asset of Puritan support became a liability in the Restoration for obvious reasons. The strong reaction against the Puritans which followed the King's return made men quick to note the Puritan associations which clung to experimental science and thus to become hostile to science itself. In the next decade the adjective 'Oliverian' (from Oliver Cromwell) was slyly used by enemies of the new philosophy to call attention to this earlier association. The antipathy thus developed would have proved much more serious to the advancement of science had it not been for His gracious Majesty Charles II, who while in France acquired under the influence of Cartesianism an interest in the new philosophy, and who upon his return to England protected the experimenters with his patronage of the Royal Society. The favour shown the scientists by His Majesty is no inconsiderable fact in the history of science, for it discouraged the critics of Baconianism from calling attention too openly to the Puritan past of an organization now sponsored by the King. But the popular preacher Robert South dared to do so in a long oration delivered at the dedication of the Sheldonian Theatre in Oxford in 1669. Of this oration Wallis the famous Oxford mathematician says:

> The first part . . . consisted of satyrical invectives against Cromwell, fanaticks, the Royal Society, and new philosophy; the next of encomiasticks, in praise of the archbishop, the theatre, the vice-chancellor, the architect, and the painter: the last of execrations against fanaticks, conventicles, comprehension, and new philosophy; damning them *ad inferos, ad gehennam*.[1]

Though unfortunately the oration has not survived, Wallis's words make it plain that Puritanism and science were in conjunction the object of South's wrath.

There was one manifestation of the Puritans' interest in science which did more than anything else to prejudice the Restoration against it. During the period when they were in power there appeared a series of educational treatises by John Dury, John Hall, William Petty, Noah Biggs, John Webster, and others, addressed to Parliament and advocating revolutionary reforms in English universities.[2] Inspired by Bacon, though sometimes indirectly through Comenius, these advocate the most thoroughgoing changes ever proposed for the universities in the same length of time. The writers in most determined fashion urge Parliament to abolish nearly all the subjects taught there and to substitute for them the new science, both the great discoveries that had been published and also the principles embodied in the scientific movement. Even more earnestly they advocate the introduction of all kinds of technological and vocational subjects. They entertained fond hopes that great progress in this direction could be made through Baconian experimentation. They would abolish the study of syllogistic logic, ethics, metaphysics, and religion. They viewed the study of languages only as the preparation of tools whereby the knowledge contained in them might be secured. They dismissed linguistic study pursued for its own sake or for literary purposes as a vain and useless enjoyment. The disputations, declamations, and public lectures, comprising the old methods of training and instruction, were likewise reprehended. Generally speaking, in place of the traditional curriculum they advocated only useful and profitable subjects, to use their own words. First and foremost the students were to be taught the experimental philosophy of Bacon, described by one reformer as demonstration, observation, and experimental induction. Another reformer, John Webster, declares that

It cannot be expected that *Physical* Science will arrive at any wished perfection unless the ways and means, so judiciously laid down by our learned Country-man the Lord *Bacon,* be observed, and introduced into exact practice; and therefore I humbly desire, and earnestly presse, that his way and method may be imbraced, and set up for a rule and pattern: that no *Axioms* may be received but what are evidently proved and made good by diligent observation, and luciferous experiments; that such may be recorded in a general history of natural things, that so every age and generation, proceeding in the same way, and upon the same principles, may dayly go on with the work, to the building up of a well-grounded

and lasting Fabrick, which indeed is the only true way for the instaura-
tion and advancement of learning and knowledge.[3]

Reference is very clearly made to Bacon's natural history, and it is
interesting to note that its compilation is made the goal of scientific
education.

Chemistry, physics, geography, astronomy (Copernican, not Ptole-
maic), botany, anatomy, including vivisection and dissection, and all
kinds of scientific instruments were advanced as proper academic subjects. Puritan scientists who had been appointed to various positions at
Oxford, and who were influential in the development of the scientific
movement, drew up a design for the establishing of a school for the
study of magnetism, mechanics, and optics in the university. A proposition published at the end of the Puritan era, entitled *A Modell for a
Colledge Reformation,* proposes nothing less than that Christ Church,
which was or soon became the most conservative college in Oxford,
should be thoroughly overhauled, the dean and canons ousted, and the
funds thus released used for training the fellows to be exact experimental
scientists in geography, magnetism, mechanics, optics, chemistry, anatomy, and medicine. Special provision was made for a professorship
both of Cartesianism and of the Greek atomic philosophy as revived
by Gassendi. This proposal differs from other treatises in that it demands that a definite institution be taken over and that its very real
funds be diverted from their futile (in Puritan eyes) employment to
the support of instruction in experimental science. We are not surprised
to find near the end of the century Christ Church lined up solidly with
those who were attacking the Royal Society.

But even greater emphasis was placed upon utilitarian or applied
science than upon pure. Only practical mathematics was to be taught,
for as one worthy says mathematics exists only to enable men to build
houses and to assist mechanical operations. Another says that physics
is to be studied not so much to secure knowledge of nature as to use
this knowledge 'for the general good and benefit of mankind.' Medicine,
agriculture, horticulture, surveying, and kindred subjects are given a
prominent place in the curriculum. Mechanical knowledge is emphasized. In fact one reformer insists that every mechanical art, no matter
how humble, should have its professor or lecturer. All these treatises
reveal a spirit quite familiar to our academic world to-day, a spirit
which insists upon the practical and useful in education, which emphasizes scientific rather than humanistic subjects, and which would load

the curricula of our colleges of liberal arts with professional and vocational courses. The modern reader, perusing them for the first time, finds them strangely familiar.

What social sciences were taught at the universities fared better than humanistic studies. History was to remain. In political science, however, Aristotle was no longer to be studied, but in his place Machiavelli and, to quote one writer, 'our own Countreyman master *Hobbs* [who] hath pieces of more exquisiteness, and profundity in that subject than ever the Grecian wit was able to reach unto.'[4] These are indeed queer birds to be recommended by the 'godly men,' as they liked to be called. But Hobbes the Atheist had joyfully joined forces with the Puritans in the assault on the universities, and they loved him for it. It is worthy of notice that the most serious attempt ever made in the past to drive humanistic studies from the curriculum to provide space for scientific and technological subjects was made in hearty co-operation with a complete apostle of totalitarianism and with the encouragement of an undisguised dictator.

When the scientific movement emerged from this era, it bore on its face such an indubitable expression of scientific utilitarianism and Puritan Philistinism that authentic scientists themselves became duly alarmed. It is rather amusing to witness the alacrity with which the Royal Society, through its historian Thomas Sprat, sought to assure the world that its members had not the least desire or intention to introduce any changes into the universities.

> Men are not ingag'd in these *studies*, [he says] till the Course of *Education* be fully compleated; the *Art of Experiments*, is not thrust into the hands of Boyes, or set up to be perform'd by Beginners in the School; but in an Assembly of Men of Ripe years; who while they begin a *new Method* of Knowledge, which shall consist of *Works,* and is therefore most proper for Men: they still leave to Learners and Children, the old talkative *Arts* which best fit the younger Age. From hence it must follow, that all the various manners of *Education,* will remain undisturb'd; because the practises of them, and the labors of this, are not appointed to meet in the same *Age,* or *Persons.*[5]

Joseph Glanvill, a most ardent propagandist of the new science, strenuously denies that he entertains any designs against the schools, and he insists that the development of experimental science will leave them untouched. But one may with little difficulty read between the lines of what Sprat and Glanvill say, and perceive a great dissatisfaction with university education, stifled because of an outraged public opinion. It is quite possible that the Puritan treatises on education had something to do with the delay in the introduction of scientific courses into the curriculum of English universities.

It is not difficult to imagine the resentment over the proposed educational innovations which burned in the hearts of the conservatives, nor to realize the odium that became attached to experimental science because of its association with them. The age was much closer than we are to the great contributions which antiquity had made to the beginnings of modern civilization. With spirits nourished by classical literature and philosophy the conservatives of the period were greatly disturbed by the effort to judge humanistic studies by materialistic and utilitarian standards. Where they made their serious mistake was in trying to maintain the natural philosophy of the past, which the new scientists were tearing into shreds, in not perceiving that the world of nature was the peculiar province of the scientists, and in not realizing that the latter were pursuing the right path to its truth. They were quite correct in repelling the attack on humanistic studies and the exaggerated emphasis upon materialistic values which were characteristic of the Puritans and which continued into the Restoration. The learned Meric Casaubon, prebendary of Canterbury, was severely critical of the materialistic standards by which science would measure utility. If, he says, usefulness were found only in what affords the necessities of life, brewers and bakers, smiths and veterinarians would have to be looked upon as equal or superior to those who have been considered the great lights of learning. Henry Stubbe, a well-known doctor of the day, who waged unrelenting warfare against the Royal Society, scornfully contrasts such vocational subjects as the making of cider, the planting of orchards, the grinding of optic glasses to the logic and moral philosophy taught in the universities. 'What *contempt*,' he exclaims, 'is there raised upon the . . . *Ethics* of *Aristotle,* and the *Stoiques*? And these Moral instructions that have produced . . . the *Pompeys* and *Ciceroes*, are now slighted in comparison of day-laboring,' and he continues to attack the substitution of the study of mechanical trades, such as the making of wine and the art of dyeing, for the philosophy taught in the schools.[6] Other critics, like Thomas Hall, maintain the same attitude. The resentment against the Royal Society because of the previous attacks of scientific Puritans upon the universities was strong. Peter Gunning, bishop of Chichester, preached regularly against the scientists, and objected to the publication of a volume of verses, simply because it contained a poem in praise of the Society. Though the Society, warned by the strong reaction against the Puritans, honestly disclaimed any intention of meddling with the schools, the values which the members continued to hold were exactly those which would militate against liberal education. The fight was really one between humanism and naturalistic materialism.

But humanistic critics of experimental science began to discover another danger in the emphasis placed upon sense-observation and in the absorbing study of external nature. They began to fear that the world of man would be sunk in the world of nature, that man would seek in nature the laws that govern his being, and would forget the distinction which Emerson was later to make between the law of the thing and the law of man. They had reason to fear. In the history of the Royal Society, which though written by Sprat was an official pronouncement of the whole organization, some remarkable claims are made; such, for instance, as the statement that 'by long studying of the *Spirits* of the *Blood*, of the *Nourishment,* of the parts, of the Diseases, of . . . humane bodies . . . there [may] without question be very neer ghesses made, even at the more *exalted* and *immediate* Actions of the *Soul*'; and again, spiritual truth 'cannot seem incredible [to man] when he perceives the numberless particles that move in every man's *Blood*.'[7] In another passage Sprat asserts, in a manner prophetic of Wordsworth, that the pleasant images of nature will purify thoughts and make men morally better than moral precepts will. Statements like these filled religious souls with fear and resentment. Henry Stubbe, an embittered foe of the experimental philosophers, answered that as long as man sought proof of spiritual truth in the material world he would certainly go astray. Meric Casaubon, the most intelligent critic of experimental science, insists upon the difference between the moral and material worlds. ridiculing the belief that science can moralize man, and laughing at Gassendi's claim that he learned to control his passions by observing how all the blood of a louse when angered ran into its tail. Can a louse, he asks, do what philosophers and the Bible cannot? Casaubon clearly perceived the danger of placing morality upon a naturalistic basis, by which, he says, reason is prostituted to nature instead of ruling nature, and as an example he cites the justification of sexual freedom on biological grounds. This clash between naturalistic science and humanistic philosophy does much to explain the angry reaction to the attempts of the Puritans to abolish humanistic studies. The critics of science believed that religion, morality, education, and art were so closely associated with the past that a contempt for antiquity, generated by an overweening faith in, and by an exaggerated emphasis upon, the superiority of modern science over all other learning, would tend towards the destruction of the Church, the corruption of education, and the brutalization of man. They viewed with great concern the perils, as regards man's moral and spiritual interests, of a naturalistic philosophy based upon the new science, and they supported the cause of a humanistic culture against the aggressive demands of a utilitarian and mechanistic science.

The greatest danger to science, however, and the cause of the most strenuous opposition in religious quarters came from across the Channel, where Descartes had developed his mechanistic scheme of things. This mechanical philosophy, as it was called, laid out a pattern for explaining all natural phenomena on a basis of matter, motion, and mathematics, thus at one blow sweeping aside all the specious theories of traditional philosophies. Descartes saw in nature one vast machine filled with innumerable smaller ones. Animals were mere automata, and so were the bodies of men. Light, life, and beauty left nature. But he was pious and sincerely believed in God and men's spirit. He did not try to mechanize the rational soul of man, but postulated for its base a thinking substance, different from the substance of matter; in other words, an immaterial substance. In England the experimental scientists were carrying out Bacon's injunction to observe and experiment, but being human they could not altogether observe his caution against using reason in seeking explanations of the data secured by their scientific activities. More and more they discovered that the mechanical philosophy furnished clearer and more convincing explanations of these data than any which they had inherited or devised. The frequent expressions of this discovery brought it about that the scientific movement became closely associated with Descartes's philosophy, an association which at first promised to be a great asset but which later caused the Baconians many a headache.

All might have gone well had it not been for a certain gentleman whom we have already noticed as a companion of the Puritan brethren. Descartes had saved man's soul and made God's support necessary for the running of the machine. Thomas Hobbes, whose hard-headed philosophy was as rigid as cast iron and as hard as adamant, heartily subscribed to matter, motion, and mathematics, but his dogmatic, unfeeling, and materialistic soul, a soul he would have denied, took from man that spiritual comfort which Descartes's dualism had furnished him in compensation for what the French philosopher had done to nature. By ignoring Descartes's assertion that God's support was necessary to the functioning of the machine, and by means of his famous dictum that there is no such thing as an immaterial substance, Hobbes took God from his heavens and the soul from man. So man's mind as well as his body becomes mechanistic, and mental as well as physical phenomena are explained by the formula of matter and motion. Inasmuch as Hobbes's philosophy was only an extension of the Cartesian, the latter became suspect. In many minds Hobbes had made Descartes's philosophy atheistic. So here is the situation. On one side the mechanical philosophy was associated with experimental science, and on the other with atheism, so that the Baconians suddenly discovered that they possessed a strange and decidedly unwanted bedfellow.

The alacrity with which they tried to get rid of this bedfellow, to distinguish, at one time between experimental science and Cartesianism, and at another between this science and Hobbes, is at this distance amusing. Two considerations moved them to this action. One was their own genuine alarm at discovering their association with a philosophy now abhorrent to them. We must remember that the scientific movement, as distinguished from scientific discovery, was partly fostered by the clergy. The membership of the Royal Society contained the two archbishops, numerous bishops, and many of lower rank. To discover suddenly that the philosophy which had proved so serviceable to the experimenters had turned atheistic in Hobbes's hands was a rude awakening. The other consideration was a well-justified fear that the charge of atheism would be brought against the Baconians themselves. And it was, though not as vigorously as it would have been had not so many been clergymen. The scientists were on the defensive. Their first step was to keep Hobbes out of the Royal Society, even though he was genuinely interested in science and tried to edge into the organization. This they did with ease. Their next was to discredit him as a scientist. This also they did with ease, Wallis wiping up the ground with him in mathematics and Boyle in physics. Their third step was to refute his dictum that there was no such thing as an immaterial substance. Here they were stumped. In fact they were forced to adopt means which have puzzled some historians of science and caused some scientists to lift their eyebrows. They literally went witch-hunting and ghost-hunting. Richard Baxter, the nonconformist, and Henry More, the Cambridge Platonist, both good friends of experimental science, try their hands at showing the authenticity of witches and ghosts in order to prove the existence of immaterial substances and thus refute Hobbes. But it was Joseph Glanvill, ardent propagandist of the new philosophy, who, egged on by Robert Boyle, was most concerned to free science from the imputation of atheism by gathering all the data he could to support belief in ghosts and witches. No member of the American Society for Psychical Research ever collected occult data with more assiduity than Glanvill sought out witch- and ghost-stories, which he published in 1668 in a book the sub-title of which is 'A full and plain Evidence Concerning Witches and Apparitions.' The great Robert Boyle expressed an emphatic belief in the usefulness of Glanvill's investigation, only cautioning him to use well-authenticated stories. It is quite possible that the desire to refute Hobbes strengthened and prolonged belief in witches. It is indeed strange to find science seeking refuge in ghosts.

There was, however, a more important, and certainly a more rational, way out of the dilemma in which the Baconians found themselves, a dilemma which, as I have said, arose from the fact that the philosophy which they found most useful in explaining experiments had in the eyes of many turned out to be atheistic. The experimentalists could draw, and insist upon, a clear line of distinction between the mechanical philosophy, which was a theory, and the experimental, which rested on sense-observation only. This they did. As we have already seen, Bacon insisted upon the need of extensive and prolonged observation and experiment in order to secure data for his comprehensive natural history, and he had solemnly warned against the danger of employing reason to formulate theories before all the evidence was in. Descartes, on the other hand, had emphasized reason and somewhat discounted the evidence of the senses. The scientists seize upon the difference. They assert that the experimental philosophy demands only that men patiently gather data, the explanation of which may be found elsewhere than in Descartes's philosophy. On the other hand Cartesianism was but a theory or hypothesis, rendered insecure because erected on too slim a factual foundation. They frequently point out Descartes's deficiency in that he did not experiment sufficiently, and where possible they take pleasure in pointing out his mistakes due to his failure to experiment. Boyle also remarks that the Cartesian hypothesis only furnishes delight to reasoning, speculative men, whereas Baconianism deals with nature and confers material benefits upon man. The scientists reduce the matter to a struggle between Bacon and Descartes, with God on Bacon's side. The experimenter who uses his eyes to observe nature may see the goodness and wisdom of God reflected in it; the speculator, unrestrained by sense-observation, is likely to reason himself out of the privilege. Henry More, who had tried to make a synthesis of Cartesianism, Platonism, and Christianity, discovered an alloy in his metal, and hastily shifted his allegiance from the mechanical to the experimental philosophy. He says, 'But the philosophy which they [i.e. experimental philosophers] aim at, is a more *perfect philosophy*, as yet to be raised out of faithful and skilful *Experiments* in Nature, which is so far from tending to *Atheism*, that I am confident, it will utterly rout it and the *Mechanical Philosophy.*'[8] It was perfectly natural that when Sprat, under the supervision of the Royal Society, wrote his history of the Society, he should mention Descartes only once or twice, and that in no very complimentary way.

Sprat realized how dangerous to science was the imputation of atheism to the mechanical philosophy. In fact, when he comes to discuss the relationship of science and religion, he remarks on the 'slippery place' in which he stood. In a manner peculiar to him he met the charge of atheism by exaggerating to an incredible degree the religious nature of experiments and experimenters. Miracles he calls God's 'Divine Experiments,' the purpose of which, like that of human experiments, was to convince men through their senses. The Apostles would have made good scientists for they were men of honesty, trades, and business. Furthermore, Christ, like the experimenter, commanded his disciples to believe his works rather than his words. Sprat equates the qualities of a humble Christian with those of a true experimenter: he must judge himself aright, doubt his own thoughts, and be conscious of his ignorance. Certainly, he says, the sceptical, scrupulous, diligent observer of nature is nearer to the modest, meek, severe Christian than the proud speculative man. Moreover, he claims, science and Christianity join in a common humanitarian purpose, for Christ by feeding the hungry, healing the lame, and curing the blind showed that 'it is the most honourable Labour to study the benefit of Mankind; to help their infirmities; to supply their wants, to ease their burdens . . . all which may be called *Philosophical Works* performed by an *Almighty Hand.*'[9] Sprat seems to be on the point of inviting God to become an honorary fellow of the Royal Society. Needless to say, religious souls were shocked by his blasphemous enthusiasm, and another demerit was registered against science.

Not only did Restoration science have to struggle against anti-Puritan sentiment and the atheistic reputation of the mechanical philosophy; in an even more fundamental way it ran counter to the age. We have already noticed the distrust of reason which Bacon imposed upon his followers. Sir Francis had noted the misuse of reason conspicuous in the schoolmen and he was familiar with large philosophical systems which men had raised on very flimsy factual foundations. So he had acquired on the one hand an exaggerated idea of the amount of data requisite for true scientific thinking, and on the other a depreciation of reason, which he thought lured men to the airy regions of speculation. Furthermore, he found it especially necessary to warn men against the too ready use of reason if his natural history, the very foundation of his whole *Magna Instauratio,* was to be completed. His followers, who were almost fanatically committed to the history, continued the anti-rational spirit. The age, however, partly under the influence of ancient philosophy, partly under the influence of Descartes, and partly in reaction against Puritan religious fanaticism, was insisting that reason should be basic in religion, philosophy, morality, and æsthetics. So the anti-rationalistic spirit of science ran directly against one of the main values of the times, perhaps the most important. The opposition to science because of its attitude toward reason was so deep-seated and fundamental that it does not find frequent direct expression but plays an almost unconscious part in criticism of science expressed in other ways. It is true some of the scientists themselves were uneasy over the matter. Timothy Clerke, a very intelligent member of the Royal Society, in a manner contrary to the optimism of his fellow members says, 'I rather fear our tumbling into the greatest barbarity and most profound ignorance; the way to solid knowledge by cultivating of our reasons, and inuring them to compare, compute, and estimate well, begins now to be wholly despised.' [10] The hostile reaction to this aspect of the scientific movement, however, is seldom revealed in direct condemnation. It lies at the base of the scorn and satire which literary writers like Shadwell, Swift, Arbuthnot, and Pope later directed against the scientists. It is partly responsible for the fact that in spite of the enthusiasm and strenuous activity which characterized science in the early Restoration the experimental philosophy did not capture the imagination of the rising generation. It is true that Newton, a tireless experimenter and a distruster of theories, astonished his age, but his principal work represented a triumph for Descartes and the mechanical philosophy more than for experimental science. Though the observers and experimenters moved along the highest level of the early Restoration they gradually sank to a less important plane and pursued a relatively obscure path, satirized and abused by literary men, until the middle of the next century.

This undervaluing of reason led to yet another condition injurious to the reputation of science. Both the theory of nature's decay and the immense amount of work necessary for the compilation of his natural history compelled Bacon to express a very unflattering estimate of the intellectual qualifications required of scientists. He asserted that the method of observing and experimenting demanded of its operators nothing but the most mediocre mental powers. This idea he passed on to his followers. Though Boyle demurred somewhat, as well he might, to Bacon's estimate of the brains necessary for an experimenter, he, together with other scientists, supported it in another way. Not once but a number of times he declared that he could learn more about nature from humble ignorant people and simple artisans, who were in direct contact with nature, than from the aristocrats of learning. In view of the modest requirements of an experimenter and in view of the tribute paid the most humble by distinguished scientists, was there anyone who could not aspire to be a scientist? When the bandwagon of experimental science began rolling in the Restoration, with men mighty in Church, state, and literature occupying prominent seats, and with trumpets proclaiming the glory of Bacon, observation, and experiment, it was soon surrounded by a mob of tatterdemalions eagerly reaching dirty hands to secure a position on it. The removal of the bars of learning and intellectual competence let loose a crowd of astrologers, empirics, magicians, alchemists, rosicrucians, and a host of others who defy name and classification, all eager to pursue a path that seemed to lead to money, respectability, and fame. Their ways were unlovely and their writings mere jargon, but they could at least despise the ancients, praise the name of Bacon, and shout Experiment! Experiment! Authentic scientists were somewhat confused and inconsistent in their attitude toward them, at one time reaching out helping hands, at another trying to dissociate themselves entirely from them. It is not hard to guess what the intelligent, non-scientific observer of the times thought of a science accompanied by this rabble. The result was that the bad company which the scientific movement kept, in spite of spasmodic efforts to get rid of them, lowered its dignity, which had with difficulty been rescued from the Puritans, and injured its credit with the intelligent public. This fact becomes all the more apparent when we remember that the critics of science had inherited a fastidious aversion to manual contact with material things, a characteristic of aristocratic learning, and did not view those beyond the social pale with any democratic sympathy. There were other reasons for the satiric attack on the experimental philosophy, but the presence of these Ishmaels in the Baconian cohorts increased the contempt with which science was viewed.

The extent to which opposition to experimental science discussed here appears in the anti-scientific literature of the Neo-Classical period can only be suggested now. The atheistic associations of the scientific movement would have produced much more satiric opposition, had so many supporters of the movement not been religious men and had great scientists like Boyle and Newton not remained on the side of the angels. Another reason is discovered in the fact that the charge of atheism was in general diverted from the scientists to the free-thinkers, who had been greatly influenced by science. The anti-rationalistic spirit and the emphasis upon sense-observation characteristic of Baconism played a fundamental part in the satire directed against it. For the chief sin which the satirists find in the experimentalists was the glaring faults of judgement which failed to distinguish between the worth of things and which proposed silly and impossible projects. The importance ascribed to small and insignificant matters by the scientific emphasis upon non-rational observation violated the hierarchy of values upon which neo-classical writers insisted. The naturalistic tendency of the new science and the utilitarian and vocational ideas of education which this science fostered were repugnant to the humanism of Pope's age. And last, the association of science with those low in the social scale and with the much abused Puritans or Dissenters did not recommend it to the undemocratic souls of the neo-classicists. Thus religious, intellectual, and social values influenced the attitude of literature. There were other elements in the scientific movement which inspired satire. The hostility of the new philosophy to the ancients was hardly agreeable to writers who admired them, and the general progressive spirit of Baconianism was antipathetic to the conservatism of the neo-classicists. But those suggested above seem to be the most important.

NOTES

1. See a letter by John Wallis dated 17 July 1669 in Robert Boyle's *Works*, ed. Birch, v. 514.

2. See Richard F. Jones, *Ancients and Moderns*, chap. v. A few passages from this volume are incorporated in the present article.

3. *Academiarum Examen* (1654), p. 105.

4. John Webster, *op. cit.*, p. 88.

5. *History of the Royal Society* (1667), pp. 323–4.

6. Henry Stubbe, *Legends no Histories* (1670), preface.

7. Op cit., pp. 83, 348.

8. See Joseph Glanvill, *A Prefatory Answer to Mr. Henry Stubbe* (1671), p. 155.

9. *History of the Royal Society*, p. 352.

10. *Some Papers Writ in the Year 1664* (1670), p. 2.

HERBERT DAVIS

The Conciseness of Swift

LORD ORRERY was, I think, the first to draw attention to one of the most obvious marks of Swift's style: 'If we consider his prose works, we shall find a certain masterly conciseness in their style, that has never been equalled by any other writer.' In reply to a critic who had said that to judge from the rest of his argument he must really have meant to say correctness, not conciseness, he wrote in one of the interleaved copies of his *Remarks*, now in the Harvard library:

> I am afraid that in this Instance I am vulnerable. *Correctness* would be a better word, in this place, although the conciseness of Swift's Style is very remarkable. . . . I may boldly answer, that *Swift* is in many places as easy and delicate as *Addison*, as grave and majestic as *Tillotson*, but neither *Tillotson* nor *Addison* are in any part of their works as concise as *Swift*.

If, as I suppose, no one would dispute this, it might be useful to extend this comparison further in order to discover whether there is anyone among Swift's friends or contemporaries who is as concise as he is. Certainly not Arbuthnot or Gay, or even Pope, when he writes in prose, though Swift himself remarks upon the conciseness of Pope's verse, and envies him for it:

> When he can in one Couplet fix
> More sense than I can do in six.

Certainly not Bolingbroke or Pulteney, though he complains that they drove him out of date by the vigour of their political writings. Certainly

---

From *Essays on the Eighteenth Century Presented to David Nichol Smith* (Clarendon Press, 1945), 15–32. Reprinted by permission of the author.

not any of his circle of Irish friends, though they tried to imitate him and sometimes succeeded in passing off their imitations as his work. Is it possible then that this quality is so remarkable in all his work that it may be recognized and used as evidence of his hand?

In attempting to separate Swift's authentic work from the large mass of doubtful material that has at one time or another been attributed to him, it is dangerous to make any conjectures which depend on internal evidence of style alone. But when we have reason to suspect an attribution, because it was never acknowledged by Swift or reprinted in any edition in his lifetime, or because doubt has been expressed by his friends or earliest editors, it may be well to examine such a work carefully and try to decide whether he could have written it or not. We may possibly find something that would be enough to turn the scale.

I doubt whether it would ever be safe to assume that we could isolate a certain quality of biting humour or of irony, and say, this must be Swift's. For we know that many papers were printed by the booksellers as his on such grounds, and contemptuously rejected by him. And I doubt also whether we can find any particular mannerisms or tricks of phrase in his work so individual that they would give him away. His style is never mannered, and it is well to remember that even Stella and his friends in Dublin were never quite sure about his contributions to the *Tatler* and the *Examiner*, or even his separate political tracts written in London during the Queen's reign. Swift delighted to mislead them; but then, and much more emphatically later on, he seemed to expect that his friends ought to be able to recognize clearly that there were certain things which he could not have written, certain limits which they should know he could never be guilty of crossing. And likewise he would expect his editors and critics to-day to be sure that even in his most careless moments or in his lightest and most trivial mood he could never have written such sloppy, slovenly stuff as some of the papers still included among his works, or those paragraphs in *Gulliver's Travels* which were inserted in the earliest editions 'contrary to the Author's manner and style and intention.'

Others among his friends and enemies could write political satires with biting power; others could use the weapons of raillery and irony with success; others could be humorous and sceptical in their formal sermons or their essays and letters; and others could use plain simple language, and avoid technical jargon and learned terms. But in all these different forms of writing, and even in his most hurried as well as in his most deliberate work, I shall try to show that Swift is a master of conciseness, unequalled and unmistakable by reason of that quality alone, which gives a flavour as of salt to all his work, and preserves it from certain levels of dullness, banality, or mere impoverishment of style liable to appear in the writings of all his contemporaries.

I use the term 'conciseness' not quite as Ben Jonson used it to describe the style 'which expresseth not enough, but leaves somewhat to be understood,' though that is perhaps the reason why we feel in Swift a strength and force lacking in other plain writers. He leaves somewhat to be understood. But I use the term rather as Dryden used it, when he spoke of 'the conciseness of Demosthenes,' quoting the remark of Speroni, the Italian wit, that Tully wished to achieve the copiousness of Homer, and Virgil the conciseness of Demosthenes. It will be remembered that Swift compares the art of Demosthenes and Cicero in his *Letter to a Young Clergyman,* recommending the former, with whom most divines were less conversant, as the more excellent orator. And he draws attention to the chief purpose of their oratory, 'to drive some one particular Point, according as the Oratory on either Side prevailed.' Swift's experience as a political journalist had formed his style and made it rigorously functional, because he had learned in that school similarly to be concerned 'to drive some one particular point' for the immediate purpose of supporting or opposing some definite course of action. He never deviated from this particular purpose, never allowed himself to hesitate, to make qualifications or concessions.

After *A Tale of a Tub* was put behind him, he rarely permitted himself to indulge his humour or his literary skill in parody or raillery or any of the tricks of his trade for his amusement only. His irresponsible play was almost entirely limited to verse and the various bagatelles in which the little group of Dublin friends engaged for sport. In his satires and sermons and political tracts he was careful never to spoil the immediate effect he wanted by any display of 'learning or oratory or politeness.' He speaks from his own experience when he says so confidently in 1720:

> When a Man's Thoughts are clear, the properest Words will generally offer themselves first; and his own Judgment will direct him in what Order to place them, so as they may be best understood.

Then he adds a sentence which is a complete revelation of himself, an artist and a master of his craft, recognizing the quality of perfect work, but valuing it only as it performs a useful function:

> In short, that Simplicity, without which no human Performance can arrive to any great Perfection, is no where more eminently useful than in this.

Though Addison with his ease and delicacy also attains a perfection of simplicity, his writing can be differentiated from Swift's, because he is never quite so concise, never quite so rigorously and exclusively concerned with making his point. This may be clearly seen if we compare a passage from one of Addison's Saturday papers, written for the *Tatler*, 17 December 1709, with Swift's use of the same theme in the *Intelligencer*, No. 9. Addison writes in a mood almost of reminiscence, as he tries to convey to us the opportunities for pleasure and profit through a proper commerce with men and books:

> I must confess, there is nothing that more pleases me, in all that I read in Books, or see among Mankind, than such Passages as represent humane Nature in its proper Dignity. As Man is a Creature made up of different Extremes, he has something in him very great and very mean: A skilful Artist may draw an excellent Picture of him in either of these Views. The finest Authors of Antiquity have taken him on the more advantagious Side. They cultivate the natural Grandeur of the Soul, raise in her a generous Ambition, feed her with Hopes of Immortality and Perfection, and do all they can to widen the Partition between the Virtuous and the Vicious, by making the Difference betwixt them as great as between Gods and Brutes. In short, it is impossible to read a Page in *Plato, Tully,* and a Thousand other ancient Moralists, without being a greater and a better Man for it.

Swift makes of it a weapon to attack the wealthy and the noble for neglecting their sons' education.

> The Books read at *Schools* and *Colleges,* are full of Incitements to Virtue and Discouragements from Vice, drawn from the wisest Reasons, the strongest Motives, and the most influencing Examples. Thus, young Minds are filled early with an Inclination to Good, and an Abhorrence of Evil, both which encrease in them, according to the Advances they make in Literature. . . .
>
> The present Scope I would aim at is to prove, that some Proportion of human Knowledge appears requisite to those, who, by their Birth or Fortune, are called to the making of Laws, and in a subordinate Way to the Execution of them; and that such Knowledge is not to be obtained without a Miracle under the frequent, corrupt and sottish Methods, of educating those, who are born to Wealth or Titles. . . .

Swift is rarely content to make an observation, much less to speculate or indulge in 'an amusement of agreeable words,' which he always suspects are intended to put false colours upon things and make the worse reason appear to be the better. He writes either to prove or to disprove; to urge some action, or oppose it.

We may follow Orrery a step farther and examine his comparison between the style of Swift and Tillotson. They both mistrusted theological speculation and regarded it as a snare rather than an aid to religion. Tillotson gravely rebukes the 'speculative Christian' who finds the knowledge of religion a good ornament of conversation:

> and because he doth not intend to practise it, he passeth over those things which are plain and easie to be understood, and applies himself chiefly to the Consideration of those things which are more abstruse, and will afford matter of Controversie and subtle Dispute, as the Doctrine of the *Trinity, Predestination, Freewill* and the like.

Swift, however, spurns the whole thing with an almost brutal gesture, using the harshest figure of compulsion by process of law:

> I defy the greatest Divine to produce any Law either of God or Man which obliges me to comprehend the meaning of *Omniscience, Omnipresence, Ubiquity, Attribute, Beatifick Vision,* &c.

But the most excellent example of Swift's conciseness, in the larger sense of its effect not upon the phrase or the sentence but upon the construction and shape of the whole piece, is his sermon 'On Doing Good,' which I shall compare with Tillotson's sermon on the same subject and the same text, preached at Christ Church on Easter Tuesday, 14 April 1691. The text—'As we have therefore opportunity, let us do good unto all men'—is rather an obvious one for a 'spital sermon'; and Tillotson uses his sermon to introduce a direct appeal for the chief hospitals in the city. It is clearly a sermon with a specific purpose. Nevertheless, it is arranged according to a conventional pattern in which the subject of Doing Good is discussed under five heads—the nature of the Duty, the extent of it, the measure of it, unwearied perseverance in it, and encouragement to it. Each of those is further divided into several sections until the main theme has been drawn out into all its various ramifications, leading up to a final solution to persuade his hearers to the practice of it. It remains a sermon for general edification, with the particular charitable appeal added.

Swift's sermon on the text is, as he termed it himself, a pamphlet against Wood's halfpence. He admits in the course of his sermon that it may perhaps be thought by some that this way of discussing is not so proper from the pulpit. Nevertheless he preaches only good sound ethical doctrine—the importance of the public good, which is a perfectly reasonable interpretation of the text, 'let us do good unto all men.'

> Beside this love we owe to every man in his particular capacity under the title of our neighbour, there is yet a duty of a more large, extensive nature, incumbent on us; which is, our love to our neighbour in his public capacity, as he is a member of that great body, the commonwealth, under the same government with ourselves; and this is usually called love of the public. . . .
>
> Therefore, I shall think my time not ill spent, if I can persuade most or all of you who hear me, to shew the love you have for your country, by endeavouring, in your several stations, to do all the public good you are able.

The whole of the sermon is then pointed with great directness at Wood's project. It is short, clear, concise in its whole argument, and no one could at any moment have been mistaken about Swift's intention and the immediate effect he hoped it would have upon his audience. He tells them plainly that it was the consideration of their great danger which led him to discourse on this subject and to exhort them to prefer the public interest before that of one destructive impostor, and a few of his adherents. He admits further that his sermon was intended also to stir up others of the clergy to exhort their congregations to show their love for their country on this important occasion. And in a final superb gesture, with the impunity of the Dean who knows no higher authority, ecclesiastical or lay, within the walls of his own cathedral, he permits himself a momentary glance over the head of the mechanic Wood and his miserable project, challenging and defying the power of his real enemy, the Whig government, with the briefest flash of irony—'And this, I am sure, cannot be called meddling in affairs of state.' Nothing is quite so concise as the conciseness of irony; the meaning is tight-closed, until the reader stays to pick it up and open it. We are left with the question: When should a Dean, when should anyone, meddle with affairs of state? His irony embraces the answer of Demosthenes: 'When all our national interests are imperilled; when the issue lies between the people and their adversaries. Then such is the part of a chivalrous and patriotic citizen.'

There is the same method and the same irony in the sermon, a diatribe against faction and party spirit, which was preached on 29 November 1717, with the title, 'On Brotherly Love.' It is almost a parody of the conventional sermon in which the subject is carefully divided into three heads: first, the causes of this lack of brotherly love; second, the effects of it; and third, persuasions to continue in it. But the real theme is stated in a preliminary sentence which sums up the whole course of the ecclesiastical history of the Christian Church:

> The last Legacy of *Christ* was Peace and mutual Love; but then he foretold that he came to send a Sword upon the Earth: The primitive Christians accepted the Legacy, and their Successors, down to the present Age, have been largely fulfilling his Prophecy.

When that theme is fully exhausted, Swift again reminds us of his text only to confess that he had treated it in a manner much more suited to the present times than to the nature of the subject in general; but again he cannot resist the temptation to make use of an ironical excuse for his conduct by quoting the epistle to the Thessalonians: 'Touching brotherly love ye need not that I write unto you, for ye yourselves are taught of God to love one another.' Considering the noisy disputes of the times and the whole course of Church history alike, he is of the opinion that God alone can teach men to love one another!

The more closely we analyse the few sermons that remain, the more difficult it is to understand why it has been customary to dismiss them casually with a reference to some phrase of Swift in which he disparages his own powers as a preacher. They are the work of a man who refused even in the pulpit to waste words, who despised unction and distrusted the eloquent appeal to the passions, but who performed the duties of his office with sincerity, using even in his sermons the full force of all his gifts, his intelligence, his humour, his mastery of language, and his hatred of hypocrisy and injustice.

Burke knew better, and his praise is unmeasured when he says that Swift's 'sermon upon Doing Good . . . contains perhaps the best motives to patriotism that were ever delivered within so small a compass.' But the sermons were not all political pamphlets; and I am not sure that the utmost perfection of form—in unity and simplicity and conciseness—is not rather to be found in the sermon on the Trinity, and the fullest play of his art to be seen when he preached against sleeping in church, 'with the design, if possible, to disturb some part in this audience of half an hour's sleep, for the convenience and exercise whereof this place, at this season of the day, is very much celebrated.'

Though as far as I know no manuscript exists of any of these sermons except the manuscript of the sermon on Brotherly Love which is in Trinity College, Dublin, and though none of them were printed until after Swift's death, I submit that those I have referred to are not less certainly recognizable as his handiwork than they would be if we could read them in his own autograph. Can we also, on the other hand, now safely attempt to analyse another sermon, to which the following note was attached when it was first printed?

> The Manuscript Title Page of the following Sermon being lost, and no Memorandums written upon it, as there were upon the others, when and where it was preached, made the Editor doubtful whether he should print it as the DEAN's, or not. But its being found amongst the same Papers; and the Hand, although written somewhat better, bearing a great Similitude to the DEAN's, made him willing to lay it before the Publick, that they might judge whether the Stile and Manner also do not render it still more probable to be his.

Orrery seems to put it aside as obviously not Swift's work, and the only claim to be made for it is that Sheridan, when he reprinted it in his edition, states that the manuscript was in the hand of Stella.

But I am here concerned to examine it on the evidence of the style, the quality of the writing and the plan of it, as an experiment on a doubtful piece to see whether it is possible to find negative proof on which we might risk the statement that Swift could not have written it.

The framework is the conventional one that Swift often uses—first an introduction, explaining the text, then a division of the subject into three main heads, each considered separately again in a series of paragraphs with a final exhortation and prayer, the common form of hundreds of volumes of sermons.

Before examining the statement of the particular topic to be treated, it is well to remember the precision and vigour which Swift uses at this point in other sermons, e.g.

> It is upon this Subject of Brotherly Love, that I intend to discourse at present, and the Method I shall observe shall be as follows:

or,

> This Day being set apart to acknowledge our Belief in the Eternal TRINITY, I thought it might be proper to employ my present Discourse entirely upon that Subject; and, I hope, to handle it in such a Manner, that the most ignorant among you, may return home better informed of your Duty in this great Point, than probably you are at present.

In these he uses a directness, and force, and plainness to make sure that even the sleepiest of his hearers might know at the beginning exactly what instruction he intends to give them. There is no such conciseness in the overweighted wordiness of this sentence:

> Therefore, to bring down the Words of my Text to our present Occasion, I shall endeavour, in a further Prosecution of them, to evince the great Necessity of a nice and curious Inspection into the several Recesses of the Heart, that being the surest and the shortest Method that a wicked Man can take to reform himself:

or in the formless meandering of the rest of the paragraph, with its worn imagery:

> For let us but stop the Fountain, and the Streams will spend and waste themselves away in a very little Time; but if we go about, like Children, to raise a Bank, and to stop the Current, not taking Notice all the while of the Spring which continually feedeth it, when the next Flood of a Temptation riseth and breaketh in upon it, then we shall find that we have begun at the wrong End of our Duty, and that we are very little more the better for it, than if we had sat still, and made no Advances at all.

No wonder that the next sentence is introduced by the phrase 'But, in order to a clearer explanation of the point,' a phrase which Swift would never have allowed himself to pen without immediately recognizing the need to rewrite the previous statement. There are innumerable passages of this sort throughout, which lack all force and clarity, and there is not one single sentence that I can find which bears the certain marks of Swift's shaping.

If we are to take any account of the possibility that the sermon was preserved and attributed to Swift because it was in the handwriting of Stella, there is the obvious explanation that Stella might well have been generous enough to copy out a sermon of his own for the Rev. Thomas Sheridan, who may have needed the help of his friends to ensure that he had something written out in time for him to perform his duties in the pulpit. But in the absence of any manuscript signed by Swift himself or any definite statement that he wrote it, I submit that the internal evidence of style alone is enough to justify the statement that Swift was incapable of writing so badly as this.

It is true that in the eighteenth century some of Swift's critics objected that his style was not always impeccably correct and disapproved of his trifling; and in the nineteenth century the style of some of his political journalism was even described as 'sometimes loose and slovenly'; but his critics have not always been careful to set aside papers which were wrongly attributed to him, in spite of his care to make clear to his friends the real authorship of the John Bull papers, the point at which he was no longer responsible for the *Examiner,* and the exact division of labour between Sheridan and himself in the *Intelligencer* papers, which were reprinted in London in 1730 as by the author of *A Tale of a Tub.*

I should not wish to claim that Swift is at his best in the *Intelligencer,* but his characteristic quality is nevertheless clearly recognizable here, especially if we compare No. 15, which is a reprint of his *Short View of the State of Ireland* with Nos. 6 and 17, in which Sheridan writes with considerable vigour on the same topic. They both alike resented the blindness of those who refused to see the misery and poverty of Ireland and spoke of it as a rich country. Sheridan speaks of his 'Indignation against those vile Betrayers and Insulters of it, who insinuate themselves into Favour, by saying, it is a rich Nation; and [his] *sincere Passion* for the Natives, who are sunk to the lowest Degree of Misery and Poverty.' It might be almost enough to note how different this is in its tone from the words of Swift:

> I have been using all Endeavours to subdue my Indignation, to which indeed I am not provoked by any personal Interest, being not the Owner of one Spot of Ground in the whole *Island* . . .

but I am concerned rather to show again the 'conciseness' of Swift in his enumeration of the deficiencies of the people of Ireland and the powerful directness of his reply, compared with the detailed evidence which Sheridan reports from the actual sights and occurrences that had stirred him to rage and compassion on his last journey through the country.

The picture Sheridan gives is a complete one: first, the evidences of trade:

> I met nine Cars loaden with old musty, shriveled Hides; one Car-Load of Butter; four Jockeys driving eight Horses, all out of Case; one Cow and Calf driven by a Man and his Wife; six tattered Families flitting to be shipped off to the *West-Indies*; a Colony of a hundred and fifty Beggars. . . .

second, the appearance of travellers on the road:

> Travellers enough, but seven in ten wanting Shirts and Cravats; nine in ten going bare Foot, and carrying their Brogues and Stockings in

their Hands; one Woman in twenty having a Pillion, the rest riding bare
Back'd: Above two hundred Horse-Men, with four Pair of Boots amongst
them all; Seventeen Saddles of Leather (the rest being made of Straw)
and most of their Garrons only shod before. . . .

third, the condition of the houses on the farms and in the towns:

his whole Furniture consisted of two Blocks for Stools, a Bench on each
Side the Fire-Place made of Turf, six Trenchers, one Bowl, a Pot, six
Horn Spoons, three Noggins, three Blankets, one of which served the
Man and Maid Servant; the other the Master of the Family, his Wife
and five Children; a small Churn, a wooden Candlestick, a broken Stick
for a Pair of Tongs.

When he considers the ruined churches of Drogheda he is led to
contrast the spirit of Ireland with the spirit of the Athenians who resolved to leave their ruined temples as monuments to posterity for a
witness against the barbarians, and when he views the desolation
around Dundalk he is led to quote the philosophical reflections of
Cicero on the ruins of Greece. And in his second paper he elaborates an
ironical proof of the prosperity of Ireland by reference to wealthy
absentee landlords, its attractiveness to the robbers who come from
England, and to the idle beggars at home, and the great numbers of its
inhabitants who are able to take the long voyage to America. Sheridan's
papers are entirely concerned with his own observations and somewhat
literary-philosophical reflections. Their tendency is unmistakable, but
their aim is not wholly clear. He has only conveyed to us his feelings, a
mixture of rage and compassion which leave us helpless in face of the
situation.

There is no doubt about the purpose of Swift's *Short View of the State
of Ireland.* He wishes to prove the stupidity and dishonesty of all those
who cannot see that in spite of great natural advantages Ireland has
been utterly ruined by the way in which it has been governed 'against
every law of Nature and Reason,' 'a condition I must not call by its true
uncontroverted Name.' Like Sheridan he describes ironically the riches
of the country, but he sharpens his irony by associating this fair picture
with the visiting commissioners from England.

Let [them] ride round the Kingdom, and observe the Face of Nature,
or the Faces of the Natives; the Improvement of the Land; . . . the com-
modious Farmers-Houses and Barns; . . . the comfortable Dyet, and
Dress, and Dwellings of the People; . . . the Roads crowded with Carriers
laden with rich Manufactures; . . .

> With what Envy and Admiration would these Gentlemen return from so delightful a Progress? What glorious Reports would they make when they went back to *England*?

And when he turns with too heavy a heart from this irony to the actual situation, and sums up shortly and bitterly the general desolation, the English standards of the English visitor are used again the other way round to redouble the attack.

> . . . the Families of Farmers who pay great Rents, living in Filth and Nastiness upon *Butter-milk* and *Potatoes*, without a Shoe or Stocking to their Feet, or a House so convenient as an *English* Hogsty to receive them: These indeed may be comfortable Sights to an *English* Spectator, who comes for a short Time, only *to learn* the *Language*, and returns back to his own Countrey, whither he finds all our Wealth transmitted.

And once more the visitors from England are drawn unfavourably into the argument:

> I think it a little unhospitable, and others may call it a subtil Piece of Malice, that, because there may be a Dozen Families in this Town able to entertain their *English* Friends in a generous Manner at their Tables, their Guests, upon their Return to *England*, shall report that we wallow in Riches and Luxury.

Sheridan speaks of his indignation against the betrayers and insulters of his country and his sincere passion for the natives; but Swift's compassion and indignation are fused together into one deadly purpose, which turns every sentence into a blow against the tyranny which had enslaved the people of Ireland.

Either of necessity or choice Swift published nearly all his work anonymously, and he was perfectly ready to allow Pope to look after the publication of the volumes of *Miscellanies* in 1727–32, containing—without any separate ascription—their work and some of Arbuthnot's. But when he finally decided to allow Faulkner to prepare a collected edition of his works to be printed in Dublin, though in the early volumes his name still did not appear on the title-page, he showed some desire to have nothing included in the volumes which he supervised that was not entirely his own. It seems evident that the text was set up from the volumes of the *Miscellanies* printed in London, as it contains corrections made by Swift in a copy from his own library, now in the possession of Lord Rothschild.

It is rather curious, therefore, that *A Letter of Advice to a Young Poet*, which had been published in Dublin in 1721 and reprinted in London over Swift's name, was omitted both in the *Miscellanies* and also in the *Collected Works*. Neither was it included even later in any of the volumes added to Faulkner's edition. Mr. John Hayward was, I believe, the first editor to call attention to this in his Nonesuch edition of Swift's *Selected Writings*; but even he does not express any doubt as to the authenticity of the *Letter*. Although it is a witty piece of writing and seems better than we could expect from an imitation, I can find no satisfactory reason to explain why Swift did not reprint it, if it was his work. I must regard it therefore as doubtful. If then, with this doubt in our minds, we examine it carefully and compare it with *A Letter to a Young Clergyman* and *A Letter to a Very Young Lady* we notice that it lacks this very quality of directness and conciseness which we are considering. It is full of literary references, witty sallies, and humorous tricks; and it ends with a proposal for the encouragement of poetry in Dublin so loose and slovenly in style that I cannot think Swift in any way responsible for these final pages. I will give only this sample:

> I would now offer some poor Thoughts of mine for the Encouragement of *Poetry* in this Kingdom, if I could hope they would be agreeable. I have had many an aking Heart for the ill plight of that noble Profession here, and it has been my late and early Study how to bring it into better Circumstances. And surely, considering what *Monstrous* Wits in the Poetick way, do almost daily start up and surprize us in this Town; what *prodigious* Genius's we have here (of which I cou'd give Instances without number;) and withal of what great benefit it might be to our Trade to encourage that Science here, . . . I say, these things consider'd, I am humbly of Opinion, it wou'd be worth the Care of our Governours to cherish Gentlemen of the *Quill*, and give them all proper Encouragements here. And since I am upon the Subject, I shall speak my Mind very *freely*, and if I added *sawcily*, it is no more than my Birthright as a *Briton*.

We know now from Swift's letters to Charles Ford that he took particular interest in Faulkner's third volume, which was to contain *Gulliver's Travels*. He admits that he had been annoyed by the changes introduced in the original edition, owing to the fears of the printer, not so much because of the things omitted as because of certain passages which were added in a style so slovenly that he was unwilling to have them remain in a volume which would be known as his work. Here then are samples of writing which Swift himself felt should be recognizable as something he could never have done. Here are passages which have been printed in some later editions of *Gulliver,* which the critics ought to have suspected from internal evidence of style alone. He had written, for instance, with little attempt to disguise the real object of his attack:

> I told him, that in the Kingdom of *Tribnia,* by the Natives called *Langden,* where I had long sojourned, the Bulk of the People consisted wholly of Discoverers, Witnesses, Informers, Accusers, Prosecutors, Evidences, Swearers; etc.

This is pointed and definite and unhesitating. He continues to charge the politicians in that kingdom with arranging plots to answer their private advantage and describes the methods of dealing with those who are to be accused. In the first edition, to remove the sting, it is all made hypothetical and carefully packed in soft layers of verbiage:

> I told him, that should I happen to live in a Kingdom where Plots and Conspiracies were either in vogue from the turbulency of the meaner People, or could be turned to the use and service of the higher Rank of them, I first would take care to cherish and encourage the breed of Discoverers, Witnesses, etc.

Once given the clue it is certainly not difficult to detect the padding:

> Men thus qualified and thus empowered might make a most excellent use and advantage of Plots. . . .
> This might be done by first agreeing and settling among themselves. . . .
> They should be allowed to put what Interpretation they pleased upon them, giving them a Sense not only which has no relation at all to them, but even what is quite contrary to their true Intent and real Meaning; thus for Instance, they may, if they so fancy, interpret a *Sieve* etc.

For Swift rarely follows that loose fashion of coupling his verbs and nouns like this—qualified and empowered, use and advantage, agreeing and settling—and is incapable of such clumsiness as 'not only which has no . . . but even what.'

But the chief changes were made in the Fourth Book, to cushion the blows which Swift had dealt against the profession of the Law and against a First or Chief Minister of State. I do not think we could find anywhere a better proof of the conciseness of Swift than in the fifth and sixth chapters of the Fourth Book of *Gulliver,* if we read what he wrote as printed in Faulkner's edition:

I said there was a Society of Men among us, bred up from their Youth in the Art of proving by Words multiplied for the Purpose, that *White* is *Black,* and *Black* is *White,* according as they are paid. To this Society all the rest of the People are Slaves.

That is surely Brobdingnagian in style—clear, masculine, and smooth; without multiplying unnecessary words or using various expressions. The attack is direct and unqualified, and therefore dangerous. Again Swift was justified in expecting his critics to recognize that the substituted passage which appears in the early London editions could not have come from his pen, for it is cautious and qualified, and therefore out of key with the context; and its meaning is completely clouded by the multiplication of unnecessary words.

I said that those who made profession of this Science were exceedingly multiplied, being almost equal to the Caterpillars in Number; that they were of diverse Degrees, Distinctions, and Denominations. The Numerousness of those that dedicated themselves to this Profession were such that the fair and justifiable Advantage and Income of the Profession was not sufficient for the decent and handsome Maintenance of Multitudes of those who followed it. Hence it came to pass that it was found needful to supply that by Artifice and Cunning, which could not be procured by just and honest Methods: The better to bring which about, very many Men among us were bred up from their Youth in the Art of proving by Words multiplied for the Purpose that *White* is *Black,* and *Black* is *White,* according as they are paid. The Greatness of these Mens Assurance and the Boldness of their Pretensions gained upon the Opinion of the Vulgar, whom in a Manner they made Slaves of, and got into their Hands much the largest Share of the Practice of their Profession.

The attack in the sixth chapter on the First or Chief Minister of State was not tampered with, but instead the danger was removed by introducing it with an extraordinary piece of patchwork intended to prevent the reader from a malicious interpretation at the expense of any recent British statesman. Again the style is so entirely unlike Swift and the change in tone so sudden that a careful reader could not fail to be suspicious of some tampering with the text. Had Swift been concerned to avoid any possible reference to Harley and Queen Anne, he would not have trusted to such a preposterous sentence of clumsy compliment; nor would he have ruined the whole effect of his satire by assuring his master that he was referring only to former times in Britain and to other courts in Europe now:

where Princes grew indolent and careless of their own Affairs through a constant Love and Pursuit of Pleasure, they made use of such an Administrator, as I had mentioned, under the Title of *first* or *chief Minister of State*, the Description of which, as far as it may be collected not only from their Actions, but from the Letters, Memoirs, and Writings published by themselves, the Truth of which has not yet been disputed, may be allowed to be as follows: . . .

So long as this kind of writing was reprinted over and over again as part of the Swift canon, and included in the text of his greatest and best-known work, and so long as other papers which we now know were certainly not his and a great many very doubtful pieces, like the sermon I have examined, have been included in every fresh edition of his collected works, it is difficult to set precise limits to possible variations of quality in his work, and to be sure that there is a point where we can boldly say: Thus far he might go, but no farther, from the essentials of good prose, which he himself set down so clearly.

Whether he wrote as Drapier, Bickerstaff, or Gulliver, or as the Dean of St. Patrick's, there were, I believe, certain standards which we may always apply, certain qualities which we can always recognize; for they are the marks of the mind and of the art of Jonathan Swift. And the particular quality of his prose that we have been considering as something both distinctive and remarkable—its conciseness—is also an essential mark of his mind and his art. That explains his greatness and his intensity; it explains also what were the things he could not do. In order to be plain and simple it is necessary to clear the mind of speculation and compromise, and to avoid in art the distortions of height and depth and the deception of colour.

He held that all knowledge is intended for use, not for idle curiosity or the pleasure of speculation. In matters of belief there must be boundaries between the spheres of faith and reason, and limits set to prevent disorder from the revolutionary forces of scepticism and critical inquiry. In matters of ethics he was content with a simple form of dualism, which defines the borders of right and wrong and when applied to political and social matters divides everything into a system of parties, Whigs and Tories, Ancients and Moderns, conformists and nonconformists, the forces of enlightenment and the forces of dullness—and finally a world of friends and enemies. In matters of political and ecclesiastical history he makes astonishing simplifications which provide a series of political parallels endlessly recurring, and of constant validity for all mankind. It is evidently a pattern simplified for common use which sometimes surprises us almost into a belief that it must be true, when it enables him to pack into a concise statement such a telling political generalization as this:

> in the course of many Ages they have been troubled with the same Disease, to which the whole Race of Mankind is subject; the Nobility often contending for Power, the People for Liberty, and the King for absolute Dominion.

Like most of his contemporaries he approved of the activities of the scientists in so far as their work could be of practical use in agriculture and manufactures and navigation and medicine. But he feared the quackery and conceit of these investigators and logically was driven to make his attack on all kinds of technical jargon, as the very symbol of that kind of speculation which was in danger of separating its activities from all connexion with the common needs of man, and becoming, as law and theology and medicine had already done, a separate guild whose activities had long been of questionable value to the public, whom they had each in their own way made their ignorant slaves.

And finally, the art of the writer is likewise for use, not for his own pleasure, nor for the pleasure of his readers. It is functional. Therefore the method will vary whether it is for edification in sermons, for moral or political instruction in essays and pamphlets, or whether it is intended to sting and vex the world into a greater concern for political justice or the decencies and proprieties of social life. But it will always be short, clear, and concise, and directed to the immediate purpose. And there is a further requirement: if it is to be effective, it must never be dull. The task of the satirist is attack, and the weapons in his hands must be sharp and keen. His strokes must be brilliant and rapid. He must overcome his antagonist by cunning and surprise. He must lure him on by raillery and irony, and confound him by the brilliant flashing of wit. But above all he must preserve all his strength and force, avoiding unnecessary flourishes. His vision must be clear and his glance unwavering until the bout is over and his opponent is overcome. There is no place here for heroic boasting or laughter, for the wildness of anger and rage, for primitive outbursts of hatred and lust. He cannot cry to the gods to help him or rouse the spirits from the vasty deep. He cannot lift his eyes to the hills for help or wait for the right configuration of the stars to give him confidence. He has nothing but his own skill and his own knowledge of the weakness of his adversaries. His art is confined within very human boundaries, within the limits of his own age and social order and of the common idiom of his time.

But if he succeeds in attaining that 'Simplicity without which no human Performance can arrive to any great Perfection,' he may not only be eminently useful to his own age but also by reason of that perfect simplicity may continue to be eminently useful at other times and in other places, wherever men may still be concerned to probe into the causes and cure of those same diseases which are common to the whole race of mankind. Although it is often said that *Gulliver's Travels* is such a good story that for more than two hundred years it has delighted children and ceased to hurt their parents, the truth is that, if we may judge by the comments of some of his critics who have been rash enough to read it all, Swift is, in fact, still successful in what he set himself to do: he is still able to vex the conscience of his readers. And there are not many who have written in English who are envied so much as he is to-day for that quality in him which is most distinctive and remarkable—that conciseness which gave such concentrated force and perfect clarity to his style.

LOUIS A. LANDA

A *Modest Proposal* and Populousness

AMONG Swift's Irish tracts is one entitled *Maxims Controlled* [i.e., confuted] *in Ireland,* written probably about the time of *A Modest Proposal* (1729), though published later. In this lesser known tract Swift examined 'certain maxims of state, founded upon long observation and experience, drawn from the constant practice of the wisest nations, and from the very principles of government.'[1] His purpose was to demonstrate that however much these maxims applied to other countries they had no application to Ireland. Among the maxims examined and confuted is one that was cherished by the mercantilist economic writers of the last half of the seventeenth and the first half of the eighteenth centuries: that people are the riches of a nation. The passage in which this maxim is presented would seem to be the germ of *A Modest Proposal:*

> It is another undisputed maxim in government, 'That people are the riches of a nation'; which is so universally granted, that it will be hardly pardonable to bring it in doubt. And I will grant it to be so far true, even in this island, that if we had the African custom, or privilege, of selling our useless bodies for slaves to foreigners, it would be the most useful branch of our trade, by ridding us of a most unsupportable burthen, and bringing us money in the stead. But, in our present situation, at least five children in six who are born, lie a dead weight upon us, for want of employment. And a very skilful computer assured me, that above one half of the souls in this kingdom supported themselves by begging and thievery; whereof two thirds would be able to get their bread in any other country upon earth. Trade is the only incitement to labour; where that fails the poor native must either beg, steal, or starve, or be forced

From *Modern Philology*, November 1942, pp. 161–170. Reprinted by permission of the publisher and author.

to quit his country. This hath made me often wish, for some years past, that instead of discouraging our people from seeking foreign soil, the public would rather pay for transporting all our unnecessary mortals. . . . .[2]

The parallelism in ideas between this passage and *A Modest Proposal* is striking. In each there is the complaint that the people, for want of employment, must turn to begging and thievery, that a portion of the population is a useless burden, and that under certain conditions these useless people could become a source of wealth to the nation. The ironic solution for Ireland's economic difficulties in each instance is the selling-off of human bodies, as slaves in the one case and as food in the other. In effect, Swift is maintaining that the maxim—people are the riches of a nation—applies to Ireland only if Ireland is permitted slavery or cannibalism. In both the *Maxims Controlled in Ireland* and *A Modest Proposal* populousness is overtly and impliedly made a vicious economic condition for Ireland. The methods are, of course, different in the two, with *A Modest Proposal* gaining its effects through broad and sustained irony; but for fear that the reader may miss his telling point, that people are not the riches of Ireland whatever they may be in other countries, Swift inserts at the close of *A Modest Proposal* a more direct statement of his purpose:

I can think of no one objection, that will possibly be raised against this proposal, unless it should be urged that the number of people will be thereby much lessened in the kingdom. This I freely own, and was indeed one principal design in offering it to the world. I desire the reader will observe, that I calculate my remedy *for this one individual Kingdom of Ireland, and for no other that ever was, is, or, I think, ever can be upon earth.*[3]

The satirical point of *A Modest Proposal* would have been sharpened for Swift's contemporaries to the extent to which they believed the maxim it refuted. How much more damaging to England that her drastic policies had forced Ireland outside the pale in which universally valid economic laws could operate!

An examination of economic tracts in the second half of the seventeenth century reveals constant iteration of the principle that people are the riches of a nation. Sir William Petty, whose views on Ireland were widely quoted in Swift's day, wrote that 'Fewness of people is real poverty; and a Nation wherein are Eight Millions of People, are more than twice as rich as the same scope of Land wherein are but Four.'[4] People, wrote William Petyt, the supposed author of *Britannia Languens*

(1680), are 'in truth the chiefest, most fundamental, and precious commodity.'[5] Sir Josiah Child, great merchant and expounder of mercantilist ideas, maintained that 'most Nations in the Civilized Parts of the World, are more or less Rich or Poor proportionably to the Paucity or Plenty of their People, and not to the Sterility or Fruitfulness of their Lands.'[6] These statements are frequently repeated in the early eighteenth century. In *New Essays on Trade* (1702), Sir Francis Brewster wrote: 'Nothing makes Kingdoms and Commonwealths, Mighty, Opulent and Rich, but multitudes of People; 'tis Crowds bring in Industry.'[7] From Defoe came a similar expression: '. . . . the glory, the strength, the riches, the trade, and all that is valuable in a nation as to its figure in the world, depends upon the number of its people, be they never so mean and poor. . . .'[8] These are typical expressions and could be multiplied. In their context and with their supporting arguments, these expressions, it is true, are not tantamount to an unqualified assertion that people are the riches of a nation. People are conceived of as a source of riches; their labor is potential wealth but it must be utilized. As one writer expressed it, the people are *'capital material . . . raw* and indigested..'[9]

Yet often the maxim was stated without qualification or without any attempt to equate the number of people and the employment available to them, although there was likely to be an assumption that employment could be provided.[10] The mercantilist wanted a large or dense population in order to keep wages low[11] and manufactures cheap, a condition by which a country gained an advantage in export trade, the great desideratum of the mercantilist. As William Petyt wrote: 'The *odds in Populacy* must also produce the like odds in Manufacture; plenty of people must also cause *cheapnesse of wages:* which will cause cheapnesse of the Manufacture; in a scarcity of people wages must be dearer, which must cause the dearnesse of the Manufacture. . . .'[12] Mandeville was thinking in the same terms when he declared that 'in a free Nation where Slaves are not allow'd of, the surest Wealth consists in a Multitude of laborious Poor.'[13] Though the insistence on populousness received support from serious economic writers by serious arguments, the maxim was as likely as not to be set down in nontechnical and popular writings without consideration of the implications and assumptions involved, as it was, for example, in the *Weekly Journal, or Saturday's Post,* April 11, 1724, and in the Irish weekly, the *Tribune,* No. 17 (1729).

Against the uncritical enunciation of the maxim there were sporadic protests. In an *Essay upon the Probable Methods of Making a People*

Gainer in the Ballance of Trade (1699), Charles Davenant declared: 'Their's is a wrong Opinion who think all Mouths profit a Country that consume its Product; And it may more truthfully be affirmed, That he who does not some way serve the Commonwealth, either by being employed, or by employing Others, is not only a useless, but a hurtful member to it.'[14] A similar protest came from Laurence Braddon in 1723:

> But tho' Populousness be designed as the greatest Blessing to a Nation, yet, in fact, it proves a Blessing only to that Kingdom and State, where due care is taken ... that none, who are willing to work, shall be forced to be Idle for want of Employment. . . . And where none who are able are permitted to live idle, by begging, or other more Vicious Practices. . . .[15]

Swift, too, made a protest of the same nature. In *The History of the Four Last Years of the Queen,* which he was writing in the trying days near the end of Anne's reign, he complained that 'The maxim, "That people are the riches of a nation," hath been crudely understood by many writers and reasoners upon that subject.' At the moment his animus was directed against the Palatines, whose numbers immigrating into England had increased the population by just so many dissenters; yet he was also establishing a general point: that populousness per se is not a blessing; that a person who does not function productively in economic or political society makes the nation poorer, not richer; and that such a person is comparable, to use Swift's own figure, to a wen, which, although it makes a man fatter, is 'unsightly and troublesome, at best, and intercepts that nourishment, which would otherwise diffuse itself through the whole body.'[16]

Viewed against this background, *A Modest Proposal* is seen to be another protest, in Swift's unique manner, against the unqualified maxim that people are the riches of a nation. The tract was written for a public in whose consciousness the maxim was firmly implanted, in the expectation that the ironic impact would thus be greater. The terrible irony in the bare maxim, divested of its supporting arguments, was even more apparent at this time than usual because of the famine conditions which prevailed in Ireland after three successive failures in harvests; and Swift takes occasion in two other tracts, one written in 1728 and one in 1729, to insist that 'the uncontrolled maxim, "That people are the riches of a Nation," is no maxim here under our circumstances.'[17] Here, at least, was one country where populousness was not a virtue. Swift seemed to be aware—the evidence was before his eyes—of the contradiction in the mercantilist attitude that the wealth of a country was based on the poverty of the majority of its subjects. However, we must guard against endowing Swift with unusual knowledge of or insight into economic matters,[18] or even seeing him as moving against the trend of mercantilist thought. His purpose was not primarily to expose an economic fallacy; it was purely propagandistic: to put the onus on England of vitiating the working of natural economic law in Ireland by denying Irishmen 'the same natural rights common to the rest of mankind.'

It would seem, on merely logical grounds, that Swift should have favored a reduction of the population to achieve a higher level of subsistence, that he should have defended, for example, the emigration of the Irish people to the American colonies; and he did pretend to see in emigration a partial solution. In *Maxims Controlled in Ireland* he wrote that he has often wished 'for some years past, that instead of discouraging our people from seeking foreign soil, the public would rather pay for transporting all our unnecessary mortals, whether Papists or Protestants, to America.'[19] He repeats the view in the *Intelligencer,* No. 19: 'It must needs be a very comfortable circumstance, in the present juncture, that some thousand families are gone, or going, or preparing to go, from hence, and settle themselves in America.'[20] But these statements, viewed in their context, are seen to be ironic, their function being to emphasize the dire position of a country which must resort to emigration. In the light of contemporary economic theory, with its insistence on an increasing population, emigration could not be viewed with complacency; it was not acceptable as a solution. There was much concern that England's population was declining or was not increasing at a sufficiently rapid rate; and many mercantilists advocated encouragements to marriage, to achieve a higher birth rate,[21] and laws to facilitate immigration.[22] There were complaints that emigration to the colonies has been detrimental to the nation. 'The peopling of the American Plantations subject to the Crown of England,' wrote Roger Coke, 'hath diminished the strength of England.'[23] It is not, Slingsby Bethel maintained, in 'the interest of State, to suffer such multitudes of people to pass out of his Majesties Kingdoms into other Princes Dominions, or the Western Plantations, thereby to disfurnish our selves of people; the sad consequences and effects whereof, are too visible in the misfortunes of *Spain.*'[24] The author of *Britannia Languens* argued in the same vein: '. . . our *Plantation-Trade* hath robbed and prevented us of some Millions of our People, amongst which very many being, or might have been Manufacturers, the Nation hath also lost more Millions of Pounds in the loss of their Manufactures.'[25] Those Irishmen, Swift among them,[26] who had observed the losses to Ireland resulting from the emigration of workers in the Irish woolen industry to France, Spain, Germany, and the Low Countries—an exodus caused by the restrictive acts passed by the English Parliament at the close of the seventeenth century—would have read such complaints understandingly.

Many mercantilists found, however, that they could reconcile emigration to colonies with the desire for an increasing population and the fear of loss of numbers. It could not be denied that by reducing the number of laborers in the nation emigration tended to raise the costs of labor and manufactures and thus to put the country in a less favorable position for advantageous foreign trade; yet it could be and was argued that colonies compensated for the disadvantages created by providing raw materials to be manufactured in the mother-country and a market for the finished products. Emigration to colonies whose trade was carefully controlled by navigation acts was justifiable, therefore, if such colonies created employment at home and swelled the exports to a value greater than that lost by the numbers who emigrated. Thus Sir Josiah Child wrote: 'That all Colonies and foreign Plantations do endamage their Mother-Kingdom, whereof the Trades (of such Plantations) are not confined to their said Mother-Kingdom, by good Laws and severe Execution of those Laws.'[27] He continued:

> *Plantations* being at first furnished, and afterwards successively supplied with People from their Mother-Kingdoms, and People being Riches, that loss of People to the Mother-Kingdoms, be it more or less, is certainly a damage, except the employment of those People abroad, do cause the employment of so many more at home in their Mother-Kingdoms. . . .[28]

The argument is more fully expressed by John Cary:

> . . . it having been a great question among many thoughtful Men whether our Foreign Plantations have been an advantage to this Nation, the reasons they give against them are, that they have drained us of Multitudes of our People who might have been serviceable at home and advanced Improvements in Husbandry and Manufacture; That the Kingdom of *England* is worse Peopled by so much as they are increased; and that Inhabitants being the Wealth of a Nation, by how much they are lessened, by so much we are poorer than when we first began to settle our Foreign Colonies; Though I allow the last Proposition to be true, that People are or may be made the Wealth of a Nation . . . . Its my Opinion that our Plantations are an Advantage . . . every one more or less, as

they take off our Product and Manufactures, supply us with Commodities which may be either wrought up here, or Exported again, or prevent fetching things of the same Nature from other Princes for our home Consumption, imploy our Poor, and encourage our Navigation. . . .[29]

Such justifications, as Swift was aware, had no application to Ireland, which was itself treated as a colony, with its trade strictly controlled by the Navigation Acts in the interests of England. An emigrant from England, Holland, or France might be looked upon as a unit of economic value who would eventually return his value to the mother-country; but one could hardly apply the same economic logic to the Irish emigrant, whose country was peculiarly removed from the operations of economic law, 'I have often taken notice,' Swift wrote, 'both in print and in discourse, that there is no topic so fallacious . . . as to argue how we ought to act in Ireland, from the example of England, Holland, France, or any other country, whose inhabitants are allowed the common rights and liberties of humankind.'[30] Public-spirited Irishmen were concerned at the numbers who were departing. Even Lord Primate Boulter, whose first thought was for the welfare of England rather than for Ireland, was disturbed in 1728, when famine was widespread, at the size of the emigration. In a letter written to the Duke of Newcastle, then Secretary of State, Boulter brought the problem before the English Cabinet for possible parliamentary action:

I am very sorry I am obliged to give your Grace so melancholy an account of the state of this kingdom. . . . For we have had three bad harvests together there [in the north], which has made oatmeal, which is their great subsistence, much dearer than ordinary. . . . We have had for several years some agents from the colonies in *America*, and several masters of ships that have gone about the country, and deluded the people with stories of great plenty and estates to be had for going for in those parts of the world: and they have been better able to seduce people, by reason of the necessities of the poor so late. . . . But whatever occasions their going, it is certain that above 4,200 men, women, and children have been shipped off from hence for the *West Indies* within three years, and of these above 3,100 this last summer. . . . The whole north is in a ferment at present, and people every day engaging one another to go next year to the *West Indies*. The humour has spread like a contagious distemper, and the people will hardly hear any body that tries to cure them of their madness.[31]

Swift, too, was genuinely perturbed. In 1728 and 1729 he refers several times to the subject of emigrating Irishmen, particularly to those who are leaving for America, which for several reasons he thinks no better than Ireland. Like Boulter, he believed that they had been given false representations and that they were doomed to disappointment; yet he is not at a loss to understand their motives for going, since 'men in the extremest degree of misery, and want, will naturally fly to the first appearance of relief, let it be ever so vain, or visionary.'[32] It was at this time that Swift wrote *A Modest Proposal* and its lesser known companion piece, *An Answer to the Craftsman*. This last tract was occasioned by the license given to France to recruit Irishmen for military service in the French army; and it too is a bitter and ironic commentary, among other matters, on the subject of Ireland's depopulation by England. As he had done in *A Modest Proposal*, Swift makes in this tract an ironical computation of the monetary profit to Ireland from the reduction and destruction of its people. And he adds this recommendation: '. . . for fear of increasing the natives in this island, that an annual draught, according to the number born every year, be exported to whatever prince will bear the carriage, or transplanted to the English dominions on the American continent, as a screen between his Majesty's English subjects and the savage Indians.'[33]

What Swift wanted for Ireland was not fewer people but more opportunities—opportunities that would present themselves if England adopted a less restrictive policy, if the Irish absentees were regulated, and if the Irish people could be made to see wherein their welfare lay. He maintained, as did many contemporary Irishmen,[34] that Ireland possessed the potentialities of a rich country and could, under proper conditions, easily support its population. Ireland, he wrote, 'is the poorest of all civilized countries in Europe, with every natural advantage to make it one of the richest.'

NOTES

1. *The Prose Works of Jonathan Swift, D.D.*, ed. Temple Scott (London, 1897–1908), VII. 65. This edition will hereafter be referred to as *Works*.
2. *Ibid.*, p. 70.
3. *Ibid.*, pp. 214–15.
4. *A Treatise of Taxes and Contributions*, in *The Economic Writings of Sir William Petty*, ed. Charles H. Hull (Cambridge, 1899), I, 34.
5. Reprinted in *A Select Collection of Early English Tracts on Commerce*, ed. J. R. McCulloch (London, 1856), p. 458.
6. *A New Discourse of Trade* (London, 1698), p. 179.
7. P. 51.

8. *Giving Alms No Charity* (1704); reprinted in *A Collection of Pamphlets Concerning the Poor*, ed. Thomas Gilbert (London, 1787), p. 71.

9. William Petyt, *Britannia Languens*, in *A Select Collection* . . . . ed. McCulloch, p. 458.

10. See the discussion on this point in Eli F. Heckscher, *Mercantilism*, trans. Mendel Shapiro (London, 1935), II, 159 ff. Heckscher writes: 'It is natural to wonder how the notion that there could never be too great a population could ever be reconciled with the anxiety concerning the insufficiency of employment. In actual fact, this contradiction was never resolved.'

11. See Jacob Viner, *Studies in the Theory of International Trade* (New York and London, 1937), pp. 56–57, where it is pointed out that commentators on mercantilism have neglected to take sufficiently into account dissent—on economic and humanitarian grounds—from the dominant doctrine that low wages are desirable. Viner's first two chapters, with their clear exposition of seventeenth- and eighteenth-century economic theory and their rich documentation from writers in the period, are of great value to the student of the period.

12. *Britannia Languens*, in *A Select Collection* . . . , p. 349.

13. *The Fable of the Bees*, ed. F. B. Kaye (Oxford, 1924), I, 287.

14. P. 51.

15. *To Pay Old Debts Without New Taxes* (London, 1723), p. xi.

16. *Works*, X, 114–15.

17. *Ibid.*, VII, 114, 139.

18. There is no evidence that Swift did any extended or systematic reading in economic theory. His library contained the following: Josiah Child, *Discourse on Trade* (1693); Charles Davenant, *Picture of a Modern Whig: with Other Tracts* (1701); John Browne, *Essays on the Trade and Coin of Ireland* (1729); John Locke, *Tracts Relating to Money, Interest and Trade* (1696); William Petty, *Essays in Political Arithmetick* (1699); Samuel Madden, *Reflections and Resolutions for the Gentlemen of Ireland* (1738). I have listed these in the order in which they appear in the Sales Catalogue reprinted by Harold Williams in *Dean Swift's Library* (Cambridge, 1932), Nos. 276, 288, 300, 412, 435, 444. To these may be added the economic tracts of Sir William Temple.

19. Works, VII, 70.

20. *Ibid.*, IX, 328.

21. In *A Modest Proposal* Swift lists among the ironical advantages of his proposal that it 'would be a great inducement to marriage, which all wise nations have either encouraged by rewards, or enforced by laws and penalties' (*Works*, VII, 214). Charles Davenant complained that the duties imposed on marriages and birth were detrimental: 'a very grievous Burthen upon the poorer Sort, whose Numbers compose the Strength and Wealth of any Nation.' He adds: 'In order to have Hands to carry on Labour and Manufactures, which must make us Gainers in the Ballance of Trade, we ought not to deterr but rather invite Men to marry . . .' (*An Essay Upon the Probable Methods of Making a People Gainers in the Ballance of Trade* [London, 1699], p. 33). Contrast Swift's statement in *A Proposal for Giving Badges to the Beggars of Dublin* (1737): 'As this is the only Christian country where people contrary to the old maxim, are the poverty and not the riches of the nation, so, the blessing of increase and multiply is by us converted into a

curse: and, as marriage hath been ever countenanced in all free countries, so we should be less miserable if it were discouraged in ours, as far as can be consistent with Christianity (*Works*, VII, 330).

22. In *The History of the Four Last Years of the Queen*, Swift makes an interesting application of the maxim, that people are the riches of a nation, to the problem of immigration (*Works*, IX, 114–15). On the immigration and naturalization of foreigners see Slingsby Bethel, *An Account of the French Usurpation Upon the Trade of England* (London, 1679), p. 15; Charles Davenant, *Discourses on the Public Revenues and Trade of England* (London, 1698), II, 199; William Wood, *A Survey of Trade* (London, 1718), pp. 299 ff.

23. *A Treatise Wherein is Demonstrated that the Church and State of England are in Equal Danger with the Trade of It* (London, 1671), p. 26.

24. *An Account of the French Usurpation upon the Trade of England* (London, 1679), p. 16.

25. P. 370.

26. Any reader of the Irish tracts will recall examples of Swift's laments about the Irish woolen industry.

27. P. 194.

28. *Ibid.*, p. 195.

29. *An Essay on the State of England, in Relation to its Trade, Its Poor, and Its Taxes* (Bristol, 1695), pp. 65–66.

30. *Works*, VII, 196; see also VII, 66, 123, 339.

31 *Letters Written by His Excellency Hugh Boulter . . . to Several Ministers of State in England* (Dublin, 1770). I, 209–10.

32 *Works*, IX, 330; see also VII, 120, 123.

33. *Ibid.*, VII, 222. Compare this passage with what Swift has to say in the *Intelligencer*, No. 19, on the conditions which confront the Irish emigrant to America: 'The English established in those colonies, are in great want of men to inhabit that tract of ground, which lies between them, and the wild Indians who are not reduced under their dominion. We read of some barbarous people, whom the Romans placed in their armies, for no other service, than to blunt their enemies' swords, and afterward to fill up trenches with their dead bodies. And thus our people who transport themselves, are settled in those interjacent tracts, as a screen against the insults of the savages, and may have as much land, as they can clear from the woods, at a very reasonable rate, if they can afford to pay about a hundred years' purchase by their labor' (*Works*, IX, 329–30).

34. Cf. John Browne, *An Essay on Trade in General, and on That of Ireland in Particular* (Dublin, 1728), pp. 38–39; George Berkeley, *The Querist* (1735), Nos. 123–24, 132–34, 272–73; *Some Thoughts on the Tillage of Ireland* (Dublin, 1738), pp. 52 f.

SAMUEL HOLT MONK

———

The Pride of Lemuel Gulliver*

GULLIVER'S TRAVELS is a complex book. It is, of course, a satire on four
aspects of man: the physical, the political, the intellectual, and the
moral. The last three are inseparable, and when Swift writes of one he
always has in view the others. It is also a brilliant parody of travel
literature; and it is at once science fiction and a witty parody of science
fiction. It expresses savage indignation at the follies, vices, and stupidi-
ties of men, and everywhere implicit in the book as a whole is an
awareness of man's tragic insufficiency. But at the same time it is a great
comic masterpiece, a fact that solemn and too-sensitive readers often
miss.

A friend once wrote me of having shocked an associate by remarking
that he had laughed often on rereading *Gulliver's Travels*. 'What should
I have done?' he asked me. 'Blown out my brains?' I am sure that Swift
would have approved my friend's laughter. To conclude that *Gulliver's
Travels* expresses despair or that its import is nihilistic is radically to
misread the book. All of Swift's satire was written in anger, contempt,
or disgust, but it was written to promote self-knowledge in the faith that
self-knowledge will lead to right action. Nothing would have bewildered

---

* Students of Swift will recognize my very great indebtedness to the work
of other critics and scholars. It would be pedantic to acknowledge borrowings
so numerous and so self-evident. I hope that it is sufficient here to acknowledge this general indebtedness and to express my gratitude to those who, over
a period of twenty-five years, have helped me to better understand Jonathan
Swift.

From *The Sewanee Review*, Winter 1955, pp. 48–71. Reprinted by permission
of the publisher and author.

him more than to learn that he had led a reader to the desperate remedy of blowing out his brains. But the book is so often called morbid, so frequently have readers concluded that it is the work of an incipient madman, that I think it worth while to emphasize the gayety and comedy of the voyages as an indication of their author's essential intellectual and spiritual health. True, seventeen years after finishing *Gulliver's Travels,* Swift was officially declared *non compos mentis.* But his masterpiece was written at the height of his powers, and the comic animation of the book as a whole rules out the suspicion of morbidity and mental illness.

We laugh and were meant to laugh at the toy kingdom of the Lilliputians; at the acrobatic skill of the politicians and courtiers; at the absurd jealousy of the diminutive minister who suspects an adulterous relationship between his wife and the giant Gulliver. We laugh at the plight of Gulliver in Brobdingnag: one of the lords of creation, frightened by a puppy, rendered ludicrous by the tricks of a mischievous monkey, in awe of a dwarf; embarrassed by the lascivious antics of the maids of honor; and at last content to be tended like a baby by his girl-nurse. We laugh at the abstractness of the philosophers of Laputa, at the mad experimenters of Balnibarbi. And I am sure that we are right in at least smiling at the preposterous horses, the Houyhnhnms, so limited and so positive in their knowledge and opinions, so skilled in such improbable tasks as threading needles or carrying trays, so complacent in their assurance that they are 'the Perfection of Nature.' Much of the delight that we take in *Gulliver's Travels* is due to this gay, comic, fanciful inventiveness. Swift might well say in the words of Hamlet: 'Lay not that flattering unction to your soul/That not your trespass but my madness speaks.' Swift did not wish us to blow out our brains; he did wish us to laugh. But beyond the mirth and liveliness are gravity, anger, anxiety, frustration—and he meant us to experience them fully.

For there is an abyss below this fantastic world—the dizzying abyss of corrupt human nature. Swift is the great master of shock. With perfect control of tone and pace, with perfect timing, he startles us into an awareness of this abyss and its implications. We are forced to gaze into the stupid, evil, brutal heart of humanity, and when we do, the laughter that Swift has evoked is abruptly silenced. The surface of the book is comic, but at its center is tragedy, transformed through style and tone into icy irony. Soft minds have found Swift's irony unnerving and depressing and, in self-protection, have dismissed him as a repellent misanthrope. Stronger minds that prefer unpalatable truths to euphoric illusions have found this irony bracing and healthful.

Before I discuss the book itself it is necessary to speak of certain ideas and tendencies that were current in Swift's world. *Gulliver's Travels* was written at the height of that phase of European civilization which we know as the Enlightenment, and the Enlightenment was the first clearly defined manifestation of modernity—the modernity of which our age may be the catastrophic conclusion. Swift wrote always in opposition to the Enlightenment and as an enemy of 'modernism.' He detected with uncanny prescience the implications of such characteristic ideas as the following: (1) Rationalism, especially Cartesianism, with its radical tendency to abstract truth into purely intellectual concepts, and its bold rejection of the experience and wisdom of the past. Swift doubted the capacity of human reason to attain metaphysical and theological truth. A safer guide in this life seemed to him to be what he called 'common forms,' the *consensus gentium,* the time-approved wisdom of the race. (2) Experimental and theoretical science, fathered by Bacon and Galileo, vindicated by Newton, and propagandized and nourished by the Royal Society. The science of Swift's day was predominantly concerned with physics and astronomy. Swift, I think, could not imaginatively relate to the moral—*i.e.,* the totally human—life of man the efforts of an astronomer to plot the trajectory of a comet or of a physicist to comprehend a universe that is 'really' no more than abstract mass, extension, and motion. Moreover science gave sanction to the idea of progress, deluding men with the promise of an ever-expanding and improving future, which to Swift seemed necessarily chimerical, man being limited as he is. And finally science unwittingly fostered the secularization of society and of human values, promising men mastery of nature and the abolition of all mysteries, and, by implication at least, of religion. Swift was a religious man. (3) The new conception of man, which was the result of both rationalism and science. It taught the essential goodness of human nature in a sentimental and optimistic tone of voice that irritated Swift and compelled him to reply with all his powers in *Gulliver's Travels.* (4) The new moneyed wealth of England, based upon trade and speculation and bolstering up the national importance of the middle class. Swift regarded this wealth and its owners as irresponsible and dangerous to the state. Divorced from land and the responsibilities implied in the ownership of land, it seemed to him abstract and at the same time frighteningly ambitious; and he had to look only to London and the Court to be assured that this new, vulgar, wealthy class was corrupting both the individual and the social and political institutions of England. (5) The increasing power of centralized government—in Swift's day a few ministers, the

Crown, and the court. To Swift, such power seemed necessarily evil since it was divorced from concrete human needs.

Why was Swift inimical to these tendencies—all of which are familiar aspects of our world today? Very simply, I think, because he was a Christian and a humanist. As a Christian he believed that man's fallen nature could never transcend its own limitations and so fulfil the hopes of that optimistic age; as a humanist he was concerned for the preservation of those moral and spiritual qualities which distinguish men from beasts and for the health and continuity of fruitful tradition in church, state, and the sphere of the mind. As both Christian and humanist, he knew that men must be better than they are and that, though our institutions can never be perfect, they need not be corrupt. The 'savage indignation' which motivates all of Swift's satires arises from his anger at the difference between what men are and what they might be if they only would rise to the full height of their humanity. If he indulged no Utopian hopes, he also never gave way to cheap cynicism.

Two famous letters, written in the fall of 1725, the year before *Gulliver's Travels* was published, tell us much about Swift's state of mind at this time. In the first, to Pope, he writes:

> . . . when you think of the world, give it one lash the more at my Request. I have ever hated all Nations, Professions, and Communities; and all my love is towards Individuals; for Instance, I hate the Tribe of Lawyers, Physicians . . . Soldiers, English, Scotch, French, and the rest. But principally I hate and detest that animal called Man, although I heartily love John, Peter, Thomas, and so forth. This is the system upon which I have governed myself many Years . . . and so I shall go on until I have done with them. I have got Materials toward a Treatise, proving the falsity of that Definition, *Animal rationale* and to show that it should be only *rationis capax*. Upon this great foundation of Misanthropy (although not in Timon's Manner) the whole building of my travels is erected; and I will never have Peace of Mind until all honest Men are of my Opinion. . . .

This letter makes three important points.

(1) Swift's life and letters support his assertion that he could and did love individuals. His hatred was directed against abstract man, against men existing and acting within semi-human or dehumanized racial or professional groups. Apparently he felt that when men submerge their individual judgments and moral beings in such groups, they necessarily further corrupt their already corrupted natures. When for example an individual thinks or acts or feels not as a free moral agent responsible to

God, but as a politician, a lawyer, a bishop, he abrogates to some degree his humanity. He becomes the instrument of a force that is larger than himself, but not so large as the moral law: and in so doing he becomes at least potentially evil. We hear a great deal today of group dynamics, group psychology, and mass communication. Swift would oppose these forces on the ground that they abridge the freedom which is necessary to the completely moral and responsible life.

(2) Swift dissociates his 'misanthropy' from that of Plutarch's Timon of Athens, the hero of Shakespeare's play, who withdrew in bitter disillusionment merely to rail in solitude against mankind. Swift knew how sterile such an attitude is. His own satire is seldom merely invective. It is not paradoxical to say that it arises from philanthropy, not misanthropy, from idealism as to what man might be, not from despair at what he is.

(3) Swift rejects the definition of man as *animal rationale* in favor of the definition *animal capax rationis*. I think that he has Descartes in mind here, Descartes, who apparently had forgotten that God made man a little lower than the angels (pure intelligences) and consequently capable of only enough reason to order his world here and to find his way, with God's grace, to the next. The second letter, to Pope and Bolingbroke, amplifies this point.

> I tell you after all I do not hate Mankind, it is *vous autres* who hate them, because you would have them reasonable Animals, and are angry at being disappointed: I have always rejected that Definition, and made another of my own. I am no more angry with——than I was with the Kite that last Week flew away with one of my Chickens; and yet I was pleased when one of my servants shot him two days after.

Swift argues that the man really in danger of becoming a misanthrope is he who holds an unrealistic view of the potentialities of human nature and who expects that men can somehow transcend their limitations and become, shall we say, angels. In the phrase *vous autres,* Swift includes all the secular, scientific, deistic, optimistic—in a world, liberal—thinkers of the Enlightenment; and he turns in anger from them. The philanthropist will not be angry when he has to recognize the corruptions and limitations of human nature; he will settle for a creature who is *capable* of reason and will do the best he can with him. The word *capable* is a positive concept, not a negative one. It imposes a sort of moral imperative on man to exploit his capability to its fullest. As Swift makes plain in *Gulliver's Travels*, this task is large enough to occupy the whole attention of man. It is fallacious and stupid to attribute to our race qualities that it can never possess. To do so is pride, the besetting sin of men and angels, the sin that disrupts the natural and supernatural order of God's creation. The theme of pride looms large in all four voyages.

Seven years after the publication of *Gulliver's Travels*, Pope published his well-known comment on the tragic duality of man:

> Placed on this isthmus of a middle state,
> A being darkly wise, and rudely great:
> With too much knowledge for the Sceptic side,
> With too much weakness for the Stoic's pride,
> He hangs between; in doubt to act, or rest;
> In doubt to deem himself a God, or Beast;
> In doubt his Mind or Body to prefer;
> Born but to die, and reas'ning but to err;
> Alike in ignorance, his reason such,
> Whether he thinks too little, or too much:
> Chaos of Thought and Passion, all confused:
> Still by himself abused, or disabused;
> Created half to rise, and half to fall;
> Great lord of all things, yet a prey to all;
> Sole judge of Truth, in endless Error hurl'd:
> The glory, jest, and riddle of the world!

The idea that man occupies an anomalous, a middle, state in creation was a familiar one in Swift's day. The whole of living creation was conceived to be carefully ordered and subtly graded in one vast 'chain of being,' descending from God, through an almost infinite number of pure intelligences, to man, and thence through the lower animals to microscopic forms of life, which finally end in nothing. Man occupies the most uncomfortable position in this chain, since to a limited degree he shares the intelligence of higher creatures, and to an unlimited degree the sensuality of animals. He is the middle link because he is the transitional point between the purely intelligent and the purely sensual. With Pope, with Addison, and a number of other writers this image, for reasons which we shall not inquire into, became one of the chief supports of the optimism of the Enlightenment—optimism concerning God, nature, and man. To Pascal, in his moving 72nd *Pensée*, it had suggested tragic thoughts about the disproportion of man. Swift used it as an instrument of comedy, of irony, and of satire. In three of the four voyages, it plays an important role.

So much for background. Let us turn to the book. The first character to demand our attention is Gulliver himself. He is the narrator, the principal actor. We see through his eyes, feel his feelings, share his thoughts. We are in his company from first to last, and it is important that we come to know him as quickly as possible. What is he like and what is his role in the book? He is first of all a bit of a bore, for his mind is irritatingly circumstantial and unimaginative: observe the numerous insignificant biographical details which he gives us in the first pages of the book. Gradually, however, we come to like him and to enjoy his company. In all respects he is an average good man. He has had some university education both at Cambridge and at Leyden, where he studied medicine. He is observant (and we eventually come to be grateful for his gift of close observation and circumstantial reporting, once he has something worth observing and reporting), reasonably intelligent, thoroughly capable in an emergency, and both brave and hopeful. If he lacks imagination and inventiveness, so much the better; for we can be sure that what he tells us, no matter how strange, is true. He is simple, direct, uncomplicated. At the outset he is full of naive good will, and, though he grows less naive and more critical as a result of his voyaging among remote nations, he retains his benevolence throughout the first three voyages. It is a pity that so fine an example of the bluff, good-natured, honest Englishman should at last grow sick and morbid and should be driven mad—but that, I am afraid, is what befalls him.

All of this Gulliver is; but let us notice carefully what he is NOT. He is NOT Jonathan Swift. The meaning of the book is wholly distorted if we identify the Gulliver of the last voyage with his creator, and lay Gulliver's misanthropy at Swift's door. He is a fully rendered, objective, dramatic character, no more to be identified with Swift than Shylock is to be identified with Shakespeare. This character acts and is acted upon; he changes, he grows in the course of his adventures. Like King Lear, he begins in simplicity, grows into sophistication, and ends in madness. Unlike King Lear he is never cured.

The four voyages 'into several remote nations of the world,' are so arranged as to attain a climactic intensification of tone as we travel through increasing darkness into the black heart of humanity. But the forward movement is interrupted by the third voyage, a macabre scherzo on science, politics, economics as they are practiced by madmen—Swift's term for those who misuse and abuse human reason. Observe that the tone of each voyage is established by the nature of the event that brings about the adventure: in the first voyage (the most benign and the gayest) accident, or at worst, the carelessness of the lookout, accounts for the shipwreck; in the second, much more savage in tone,

Gulliver is left alone in a strange land, through the cowardice of his shipmates; in the third, he is captured and later abandoned by pirates (evil in action); in the fourth, his crew of cutthroats mutinies, seizes the ship, and leaves him to starve on a near-by island. Gulliver thus describes this crew to his Houyhnhnm master:

> I said they were Fellows of desperate Fortunes, forced to fly from the Places of their Birth, on Account of their Poverty and their Crimes. Some were undone by Lawsuits; others spent all they had in Drinking, Whoring, and gaming; others fled for Treason; many for Murder, Theft, Poisoning, Robbery, Perjury, Forgery, Coining false Money; for committing Rapes and Sodomy; for flying from their Colours, or deserting to the Enemy; and most of them had broken Prison. . . .

The good ship *Adventure* was a little world which housed the whole of unregenerate human nature.

It is best to consider the first two voyages together and to notice how effectively Swift uses the idea of the great chain of being. Pascal, writing of man's disproportion, had asked: 'For in fact, what is man in nature? A nothing in comparison with the Infinite, an All in comparison with the Nothing, a mean between nothing and everything.' Swift transposes this theme into another key, and makes it the major instrument of his satire. In the first two voyages, Gulliver is made aware of his disproportion; placed on this isthmus of a middle state, in the voyage to Lilliput he looks down the chain of being and knows himself an awkward, if kindly, giant in that delicate kingdom; in the voyage to Brobdingnag he looks up the chain and discovers a race of 'superior beings,' among whom his pride shrivels through the humiliating knowledge of his own physical insignificance. The emphasis here is upon size, the physical; but it is none the less notable that Lilliputia calls into operation Gulliver's engaging kindliness and gentleness, and that Brobdingnag brings out his moral and physical courage. Though comically and tragically disproportioned, man has moral virtues which he can and does exercise.

But Swift's satire is a two-edged sword. What of the inhabitants of these strange lands? They too are disproportioned. From the start the Lilliputians win our interest and liking: these pigmies ingeniously capture the Hercules whom chance has cast on their shore; they humanely solve the problem of feeding him; their pretty land and their fascinating little city take our fancy. But in the end what do they prove to be? prideful, envious, rapacious, treacherous, cruel, vengeful, jealous, and hypocritical. Their primitive social and political systems have been corrupted; they are governed by an Emperor who is ambitious totally to destroy the neighboring kingdom, and by courtiers and ministers who are chosen not for their fitness for office, but for their skill in walking the tightrope, leaping over sticks or creeping under them. 'Climbing,' Swift once remarked, 'is performed in the same Posture with Creeping.' These little people, like Gulliver himself, are an instance of the disproportion of man. Their vices, their appetites, their ambitions, their passions are not commensurate with their tiny stature. They appear to Gulliver as he and his kind must appear to the higher orders of beings—as venomous and contemptibly petty.

In Brobdingnag we meet creatures ten times the size of Europeans, and we share Gulliver's anxiety lest their moral natures be as brutish as their bodies. But the reverse is true; and through a violent and effective shift of symbol, tone, and point of view, Gulliver, who seemed lovable and humane among the Lilliputians, appears an ignominious and morally insensitive being in contrast to the enlightened and benevolent Brobdingnagians. Since Gulliver represents us, his shame, insufficiency, and ludicrousness are ours.

When the peasants discover him, they feel both curiosity and repulsion: the farmer picks him up 'with the Caution of one who endeavours to lay hold on a small dangerous Animal in such a Manner that it shall not be able either to scratch or to bite him, . . .' Gulliver fears that his captor may dash him to the ground, 'as we usually do any little hateful Animal which we have a Mind to destroy.' The change in tone and intent is obvious.

Gulliver is submitted to one humiliation after another, but he is still capable of a fatuous blindness to the defects of European society, and when the King questions him about England he describes with uncritical enthusiasm its class system, its constitution, its laws, its military glory, and its history. In the questions which the king asks and which Gulliver meets with only an embarrassed silence, the voice of morality is heard condemning the institutions of the modern world. And the verdict of a moral being on European man is given in words as icy as controlled contempt can make them: 'But, by what I have gathered from your own Relation, and the Answers I have with much Pains wringed and extorted from you; I cannot but conclude the Bulk of your Natives to be the most pernicious Race of little odious Vermin that Nature ever suffered to crawl upon the Surface of the Earth.'

Such a conclusion is inevitable, for the King is high-minded, benevolent, and, in Swift's sense of the word, rational: i.e., he and his people think practically, not theoretically; concretely, not metaphysically; simply, not intricately. Brobdingnag is a Swiftian Utopia of common good sense and morality; and Gulliver, conditioned by the corrupt society from which he comes, appears naive, blind, and insensitive to moral values. His account of the history of England in the seventeenth century evokes the King's crushing retort:

> . . . it was only an Heap of Conspiracies, Rebellions, Murders, Massacres, Revolutions, Banishments; the very worst Effects that Avarice, Faction, Hypocracy, Perfidiousness, Cruelty, Rage, Madness, Hatred, Envy, Lust, Malice and Ambition could produce.

Notice the carefully arranged disorder of that list, the calculated avoidance of climax. This is a favorite device of Swift: the irrational, the appetitive, the evil nature of man *is* disorder.

The King is horrified when Gulliver offers him a way to complete dominion over his subjects by teaching him to make gunpowder. And Gulliver, speaking as a European, feels contemptuous surprise. 'A strange Effect of *narrow Principles* and *short Views*!' The King is baffled by the concept of political *science*—how can the *art* of government be reduced to a science?

> He confined the knowledge of governing within very *narrow Bounds;* to common Sense and Reason, to Justice and Lenity, to the Speedy Determination of Civil and criminal Causes; with some other obvious Topicks which are not worth considering. And he gave it for his Opinion; that whoever could make two Ears of Corn, or two Blades of Grass to grow upon a Spot of Ground where only one grew before would deserve better of Mankind, and do more essential Service to his Country, than the whole Race of Politicians put together.

The learning of the Brobdingnagians is simple and practical, 'consisting only in Morality, History, Poetry, and Mathematicks.' Observe that Swift omits metaphysics, theoretical science, and theology from the category of useful knowledge.

Swift's attack on pride in the first two voyages is made more powerful because of his brilliant use of the chain of being. In so far as we recognize ourselves in the Lilliputians or in Gulliver in Brobdingnag, we become aware of our pettiness—of the disproportion of our race and of the shocking difference between what we profess and what we are. But Swift uses the good giants to strike an unexpected blow at human vanity and to introduce a motif which he employed with deadly effect in the last voyage. That motif is disgust, of which, as T. S. Eliot has remarked, he is the great master. Philosophers of the century were never tired of admiring the beautiful perfection of the human body, its intricateness, its perfect articulation, its happy appropriateness to the particular place that men occupy in the scheme of things. But how does this glorious body appear to lesser creatures—say to an insect? Swift forces us to answer by making us share Gulliver's disgust at the cancerous breasts and lousy bodies of the beggars; at the blotched color, the huge pores, the coarse hairs, and the nauseous odors of the maids of honor. Such is the skin, presumably, that the Brobdingnagians love to touch. Our beauty is only apparent; our disproportion is real.

The third voyage has always been considered the least successful; that may well be, but it is none the less interesting. Structurally it is loosely episodic, lacking unity of action and tone. Into it Swift seems to have put all the material that he could not work into the other three voyages. It is a fantasia on two themes which Swift treats under a single metaphor: the metaphor is science, the themes are politics and the abuse of reason. In short, the voyage is a digression on madness, on the divorce of man and good sense in the modern world.

At this point, I fear, it is necessary to defend Swift, since he will seem merely stupid and prejudiced to a generation that enjoys the blessings of television, the common cold, and the hydrogen bomb. Moreover, to liberals he will appear an unenlightened political reactionary. I have said earlier that in my opinion Swift distrusted science because it seemed irrelevant to the moral life of man. Though no scientist, he was not an ignoramus. He had read contemporary science—Descartes, Newton, and the yearly *Transactions of the Royal Society*. The Flying Island is conceived on sound scientific principles; some of the mad experiments of the scientists of Balnibarbi are grotesque distortions of ideas actually advanced by members of the Royal Society. The philosophers of the Flying Island are lost in the abstractions of mathematics, music, and astronomy to the great neglect of all practical reality, including their wives. The very tailors measure Gulliver for clothes by abstruse mathematical processes and contrive a suit which fits him not at all. Swift lived before the age of applied science, but I do not think that he would be surprised to learn that modern citizens of his Flying Island contrived the most significant event of the twentieth century—Hiroshima.

It is also necessary to apologize for Swift's political views. He was a Tory, a conservative—opprobrious terms today. In economics he was an agrarian; in politics a royalist; in religion a high churchman. He disapproved the founding of the National Bank; could make no sense of a national debt, a gadget invented in his time; he distrusted the new moneyed wealth, the ancestor of modern capitalism, which increased the political power and importance of the merchant class, and he found his distrust justified in 1720 by the disastrous collapse of South Sea stocks. Innovation and experimentation in politics he detested and fought. He would have hated the improvisations of the New Deal; he would have deplored the vast powers of our Federal Government; he would have loathed the whole program of the Labor Party in Britain. And were he alive, he would fight the abstract state of this century with every weapon within reach.

Too many liberals are unaware of the fact that a man may be a non-liberal without being illiberal; that he may distrust the abstract power of government, the theoretical formulae of economists, politicians, and social scientists and the like without ceasing to be actively and effectively concerned for human welfare. Swift was a Tory who fought valiantly and at times successfully for the oppressed. Living in Ireland, contemptuous of the Irish, detesting their Catholicism, he none the less became their champion against the oppression and exploitation of his adopted country by the English Court and Parliament. He is one of the heroes of modern Ireland because he first gave effective expression to Irish nationalism. He earned the right to the last sentence of the epitaph which he composed for his own tombstone: *Abi Viator/ et imitare, si poteris/ Strenuum pro virili/Libertatis Vindicatorem.*

The Flying Island is not only a trope for science; it is also a mordant image of the concentration of political power in the hands of a clique remote from human needs, motivated by pure theory, and given to experiment and improvisation. Laputa (perhaps, as has been suggested, Spanish *La Puta*, 'the whore') is a symbol of such government: it is controlled by madmen who govern scientifically, not morally; it is a *flying* island, and hence out of touch with subject territories, which it exploits and tyrannizes over by means of what we call today air power; it can withhold sun and rain as a punitive device, or can harass through bombing raids, or even tyrannously crush all opposition by settling its great weight upon the land below. One contrasts this form of government with that of the wise and good King of Brobdingnag.

When Gulliver visits the subject land of Balnibarbi, which is of course England, he sees the result of statism.

The People in the Streets walked fast, looked wild, their Eyes fixed, and were generally in Rags. We passed through one of the Town Gates, and went about three Miles into the Country, where I saw many Labourers working with several Sorts of Tools in the Ground, but was not able to conjecture what they were about; neither did I observe any Expectation either of Corn or Grass, although the Soil appeared to be excellent.

This is what comes of experimentation in government and of financial speculation. It strongly suggests the memories that some of us have of the great depression. A modern Tory used it effectively as the basis of an attack on the post-war Labor Government.

But there are other ills consequent to the abstract state. Too great a concentration of power leads to tyranny; tyranny breeds fear; fear breeds the obnoxious race of spies and informers. The abstract state becomes the police state.

I told him that in the Kingdom of *Tribnia* [Britain], by the Natives called *Langden* [England], where I had sojourned some time in my Travels, the Bulk of the People consist in a manner wholly of Discoverers, Witnesses, Informers, Accusers, Prosecutors, Evidences, Swearers; together with their several subservient and subaltern Instruments; all under Deputies. The Plots in that Kingdom are usually the Workmanship of those Persons who desire to raise their own Character of profound Politicians; to restore new Vigour to a crazy Administration; to stifle or divert general Discontents; to fill their Pockets with Forfeitures; and raise or sink the Opinion of publick Credit, as either shall best answer their private Advantage. It is first agreed and settled among them, what suspected Persons shall be accused of a Plot: then, effectual Care is taken to secure all their Letters and Papers, . nd put the Criminals in Chains. These Papers are delivered to a Set of Artists, very dexterous in finding out the mysterious Meanings of Words, Syllables, and Letters. For Instance, they can decypher a Close-stool to signify a Privy-Council; a Flock of Geese, a Senate; a lame Dog, an Invader; a Codshead, a [King]; the Plague, a Standing Army; a Buzzard, a Prime Minister; the Gout, a High Priest; a Gibbet, a Secretary of State; a Chamber pot, a Committee of Grandees; a Sieve, a Court Lady; a Broom, a Revolution; a Mouse-trap, an Employment; a bottomless Pit, The Treasury; a Sink, the C[our]t; a Cap and Bells, a Favourite; a broken Reed, a Court of Justice; an empty Tun, a General; a running Sore, the Administration.

One cannot read that passage without thinking of certain testimony given of late years in Washington.

Such are the fruits of madness—of that pride which impels us to trust our reason beyond its proper scope and which suggests that we can build a heavenly city on earth on principles divorced from humanity and morality.

The climactic fourth voyage is the great section of *Gulliver's Travels*. It has provoked violent attacks on Swift and his book, entirely, I think, because it has been misunderstood. It has offended the unreflective and pious Christian, the sentimentalist, and the optimist. Thackeray, lecturing to the ladies in London in 1851, the year in which the Great Exhibition seemed to give the lie to every opinion that Swift held, may serve as an example, by no means unique, of the capacity of this voyage to shock. He advised his ladies not to read the last voyage, and to hoot the Dean. And the meaning that he found in it was 'that man is utterly wicked, desperate, and imbecile, and his passions are monstrous, and his boasted power mean, that he is and deserves to be the shame of brutes, and ignorance is better than his vaunted reason.' 'It is Yahoo language,' he continues, 'a monster gibbering shrieks and gnashing imprecations against mankind . . . filthy in word, filthy in thought, furious, raging, obscene.'

The legend of Swift as a savage, mad, embittered misanthrope largely rests upon this wrong-headed, sensational reading of the last voyage. In my opinion the work is that of a Christian-humanist and a moralist who no more blasphemes against the dignity of human nature than do St. Paul and some of the angrier prophets of the Old Testament. Swift has been misunderstood for several reasons.

1. The sheer intensity and violent rhetoric of the voyage are overwhelming and may well numb the critical sense of certain readers.

2. Gulliver in the frenzy of his mad misanthropy has been too facilely identified with Swift. Gulliver speaks for Gulliver and not for his creator in the final pages of the book, and careful reading should reveal the plain fact that he becomes the victim of Swift's irony as he grows to hate the human race. The final pages of the book are grimly comic.

3. The primary symbols of the voyage have been totally misunderstood. The Houyhnhnms have been regarded as Swift's ideal for man, and the Yahoos have been identified as his representation of what men are. Neither of these opinions, I believe is correct.

Let us begin with the Houyhnhnms and the Yahoos. In the first two voyages Gulliver is shown uncomfortably situated on the isthmus of a middle state between the very large and the very small. In this voyage he also stands on an isthmus, but now it is between the purely rational and the purely sensual—between Houyhnhnm and Yahoo. Neither of these symbols can stand for man, since Gulliver himself is the symbol of humanity. Unfortunately for poor Gulliver, he shares somehow in the nature of both extremes. Swift simply isolates the two elements that combine in the duality of man, the middle link, in order to allow Gulliver to contemplate each in its essence.

Does Swift recommend that Gulliver should strive to become a Houyhnhnm? We discover that in every sense Houyhnhnmland is a rationalistic Utopia. The Houyhnhnms are the embodiment of pure reason. They know neither love nor grief nor lust nor ambition. They cannot lie; indeed they have no word for lying and are hard put to it to understand the meaning of *opinion*. Their society is an aristocracy, resting upon the slave labor of the Yahoos and the work of an especially-bred servant class. With icy, stoical calm they face the processes of life—marriage, childbirth, accident, death. Their society is a planned society that has achieved the mild anarchy that many Utopian dreamers have aspired to. They practice eugenics, and since they know no lust, they control the size of their population; children are educated by the state; their agrarian economy is supervised by a democratic council; government is entirely conducted by periodic assemblies. The Houyhnhnms feel natural human affection for each other, but they love every one equally. It is all very admirable, but it is remote from the possibilities of human life.

Does Swift intend us to accept this as his ideal way of life? He who loved and hated and fought and bled internally through *saeva indignatio*? I think not. The Houyhnhnms resemble Cartesians and are clearly stoics. 'Neither is *Reason* among them a Point problematical as with us,' reports Gulliver, 'where Men can argue with Plausibility on both Sides of a Question; but strikes you with immediate Conviction; . . .' This is the Houyhnhnm version of Descartes' rational intuition of clear and distinct ideas. Now Swift was anti-Cartesian from his first published satire, for the simple reason that he held that Descartes was self-deluded and that man's reason was incapable of the feats that Descartes attributed to it. The Houyhnhnms are stoics, and Swift recorded his view of stoicism in *Thoughts on Various Subjects*: 'The Stoical Scheme of supplying our Wants, by lopping off our Desires, is like cutting off our Feet when we want Shoes.' It is Gulliver, not Swift, who is dazzled by the Houyhnhnms and who aspires to rise above the human condition and to become pure intelligence as these horses and the angels are.

The most powerful single symbol in all Swift is the Yahoos. They do not represent Swift's view of man, but rather of the bestial element in man—the unenlightened, unregenerate, irrational element in human nature. Hence the Houyhnhnms classify Gulliver with them; hence the female Yahoo wishes to couple with him; hence despite his instinctive recoiling from them, Gulliver has to admit with shame and horror that he is more like them than he is like the Houyhnhnms. This I think is clear. Because of his neglect or misuse of human reason, European man has sunk nearer to the Yahoo pole of his nature than he has risen toward the Houyhnhnm pole. The seeds of human society and of human depravity, as they exist in Europe, are clearly discerned in the society and conduct of the Yahoos. Gulliver looks into the obscene abyss of human nature unlighted by the frail light of reason and of morality, and the sight drives him mad.

Repelled by what he sees, he, not Swift, identifies the Yahoos with man; and he, not Swift, turns misanthrope. Since he will not be a Yahoo, he seeks to become, as nearly as possible, a Houyhnhnm. But he can do so only by denying his place in and responsibility to humanity, by aspiring above the middle link, which is man, to the next higher link, that of the purely rational. The wise Houyhnhnm, to whom he gives his terrifying account of European man and society, concludes that 'the corruption of reason' is worse than brutality itself, and that man is more dangerous than the Yahoo. This is profoundly true. But its effect on Gulliver is to awaken loathing of all that is human.

Lear, gazing on the naked, shivering Edgar, disguised as a Tom o' Bedlam, cries: 'Thou art the thing itself; unaccommodated man is no more but such a poor, bare, forked animal as thou art.' And in that intense moment, he goes mad. Something of the same thing befalls Gulliver. He thinks he has seen the thing itself. Though the Houyhnhnms never acknowledge that he is more than an unusually gifted Yahoo, he aspires to their rationality, stoicism, and simple wisdom; and persuaded that he has attained them, he feeds his growing misanthropy on pride, which alienates him not only from his remote kinsmen, the Yahoos, but eventually from his brothers, the human race. Looking back with nostalgia on his lost happiness in Houyhnhnmland, he recalls:

I enjoyed perfect Health of Body, and Tranquility of Mind; I did not feel the Treachery or Inconstancy of a Friend, nor the Injuries of a secret or open Enemy. I had no Occasion of bribing, flattering, or pimping, to procure the Favour of any great Man, or of his Minion. I wanted no Fence against Fraud or Oppression: Here was neither physician to destroy my Body, nor Lawyer to ruin my Fortune: No Informer to Watch my Words and Actions, or forge Accusations against me for Hire: Here were no Gibers, Censurers, Backbiters, Pickpockets, Highwaymen, Housebreakers, Attorneys, Bawds, Buffoons, Gamesters, Politicians, Wits, Spleneticks, tedious Talkers, Controvertists, Ravishers, Murderers, Robbers, Virtuoso's; no Leaders or Followers of Party and Faction; no

Encouragers to Vice, by Seducement or Examples: no Dungeon, Axes, Gibbets, Whippingposts, or Pillories; No cheating Shopkeepers or Mechanicks; No Pride, Vanity or Affection: No Fops, Bullies, Drunkards, strolling Whores, or Poxes: No ranting, lewd, expensive Wives: No stupid, proud Pedants: No importunate, over-bearing, quarrelsome, noisy, roaring, empty, conceited, swearing Companions: No Scoundrels raised from the Dust upon the Merit of their Vices; or Nobility thrown into it on account of their Virtues: No Lords, Fiddlers, Judges or Dancing-masters.

From the moment that the banished Gulliver despairingly sets sail from Houyhnhnmland, his pride, his misanthropy, his madness are apparent. Deluded by his worship of pure reason, he commits the error of the Houyhnhnms in equating human beings with the Yahoos. Captured by a Portuguese crew and forced to return from sullen solitude to humanity, he trembles between fear and hatred. The captain of the ship, Don Pedro de Mendez, like Gulliver himself, shares the nature of the Houyhnhnm and the Yahoo; and like the Gulliver of the first voyage he is tolerant, sympathetic, kindly, patient, and charitable; but Gulliver can no longer recognize these traits in a human being. With the myopic vision of the Houyhnhnms, he perceives only the Yahoo and is repelled by Don Pedro's clothes, food, and odor. Gradually, however, he is nursed back to partial health, and is forced to admit in the very accent of his admired horses, that his benefactor has a 'very good *human* Understanding.' But the Gulliver who writes this book is still under the control of his *idée fixe,* and when we last see him he prefers the smell and conversation of his two horses to the company of his wife and children. This is misanthropy in Timon's manner, not Swift's. In the brilliant and intricately ironic coda with which the book ends, Swift directs his savage, comic gaze straight at Gulliver and his insane pretensions.

My Reconcilement to the *Yahoo*-kind in general might not be so difficult, if they would be content with those Vices and Follies only which Nature hath entitled them to. I am not in the least provoked at the Sight of a Lawyer, a Pickpocket, a Colonel, a Fool, a Lord, a Gamester, a Politician, a Whoremunger, a Physician, an Evidence, a Suborner, an Attorney, a Traytor, or the like: This is all according to the due Course of Things: But when I behold a Lump of Deformity, and Diseases both of Body and Mind, smitten with *Pride,* it immediately breaks all the Measures of my Patience; neither shall I ever be able to comprehend how such an Animal and such a Vice could tally together.

The grim joke is that Gulliver himself is the supreme instance of a creature smitten with pride. His education has somehow failed. He has voyaged into several remote nations of the world, but the journeys were not long, because of course he has never moved outside the bounds of human nature. The countries he visited, like the Kingdom of Heaven, are all within us. The ultimate danger of these travels was precisely the one that destroyed Gulliver's humanity—the danger that in his explorations he would discover something that he was not strong enough to face. This befell him, and he took refuge in a sick and morbid pride that alienated him from his species and taught him the gratitude of the Pharisee—'Lord, I thank Thee that I am not as other men.'

Swift himself, in his personal conduct, displayed an arrogant pride. But he was never guilty of the angelic, dehumanizing pride of Gulliver, who writes in a letter to his Cousin Sympson:

> I must freely confess, that since my last Return, some corruptions of my *Yahoo* Nature have revived in me by Conversing with a few of your Species, and particularly those of my own Family, by an unavoidable Necessity; else I should never have attempted so absurd a Project as that of reforming the *Yahoo* Race in this Kingdom; but, I have now done with all such visionary Schemes for ever.

Jonathan Swift was stronger and healthier than Lemuel Gulliver. He hated the stupidity and the sinfulness and the folly of mankind. He could not accept the optimistic view of human nature that the philosophers of the Enlightenment proposed. And so he could exclaim to his contemporaries: 'O wicked and perverse generation!' But, until he entered upon the darkness of his last years, he did not abandon his fellow man as hopeless or cease to announce, however indirectly, the dignity and worth of human kind.

JAMES SUTHERLAND

John Gay

THE serious temper of the present age, the contemporary tendency to
think of literature as a discipline rather than a delight, and to value
the literature of the past in proportion as it is relevant to our present
distresses and has power to 'interpret life for us, to console us, to sustain
us,' all this creates a rather astringent atmosphere which is unfriendly
to the reputation of such a writer as John Gay. If Gay is not actually a
forgotten poet, he is not very actively remembered to-day except as the
friend of Swift and Pope; he remains, like so many literary and other
monuments in England, not so much because he has an important
function to perform as because he is already there. He is not doing any
harm, and no one is particularly interested in removing him. His surest
hold upon immortality is the *Beggar's Opera,* and any dividends that
may come to him from a revival of that charming piece he must share
with the modern producer, the costumier, the adaptor of the music, and
the contemporary impersonators of Polly Peachum and Macheath. Certainly, if he is still among the English poets, he hardly owes that position
to the literary critics. He has suffered, in fact, from that most damaging
kind of criticism that gives with one hand and takes away with the
other: everyone rather likes Gay, and no one is prepared to make any
serious claims for him as a poet. 'It would be idle to pretend . . .', the
critics say in unison, 'it would be foolish to suggest . . .'; and Gay,
waiting anxiously in the wings for the verdict of posterity, hears only a
little tepid applause falling like coppers into a charity-box.

The critical attitude to Gay (as to most other eighteenth-century
poets) is probably still influenced, if no longer determined, by the
judgment of Dr. Johnson. In his account of the poet he decided that

---

From *Pope and His Contemporaries: Essays Presented to George Sherburn*
(Clarendon Press, 1949), 201–14. Reprinted by permission of the author.

Gay could not be rated high; he was, as Johnson had once heard a female critic remark, 'of a lower order.' That is bad enough for a start, but worse is to follow. Johnson proceeds to consider Gay's works one by one, and by nicely balancing the blame with the praise he casts up his poetical account and finds him not much more than solvent. The *Rural Sports* are 'never contemptible, nor ever excellent'; *Trivia* may be allowed 'all that it claims'; the minor poems are 'neither much esteemed, nor totally despised.'[1] In the end Johnson leaves his readers with the impression that if they skip Gay altogether they will not be missing much. Two years later Joseph Warton dismisses him in much the same style: 'He wrote with neatness and terseness, *aequali quadam mediocritate*, but certainly without any elevation.'[2]

It must be added that Gay's own friends rarely asserted his claims as a poet. They thought of him, and when he was dead they remembered him, as a man—gentle, good-natured, indolent, lovable in the extreme, shiftless, impracticable, innocent, volatile, a sort of Augustan Peter Pan riding in the coaches of his noble friends, dining at their tables, shooting their pheasants, but quite incapable of attending to his worldly affairs. They all loved him, and they all looked after him; he was a sort of joint responsibility, and he repaid them by his wit and geniality and by his unselfish interest in their own concerns. Swift in particular tried to instil into Gay some of his own sense of husbandry and responsibility. He urged his friend to take more exercise, and to plan some big work that would take several years to write; he should think of laying up something for his old age. And Gay really tried—as an undergraduate will try to please his tutor. 'I remember your prescription,' he tells Swift, 'and I do ride upon the Downs, and at present I have no asthma.' Or again: 'I find myself dispirited for want of having some pursuit. . . . If you would advise the Duchess to confine me four hours a day to my own room, while I am in the country, I will write; for I cannot confine myself as I ought.'[3] No wonder Swift complained on one occasion to Pope:

> I suppose Mr. Gay will return from the Bath with twenty pounds more flesh, and two hundred less in money. Providence never designed him to be above two-and-twenty, by his thoughtlessness and cullibility. He has as little foresight of age, sickness, poverty, or loss of admirers, as a girl at fifteen.[4]

Spiritually, indeed, Gay did remain about two-and-twenty all his life, and in the rather too-adult eighteenth century that is one of his most endearing qualities. When he died in 1731 and was buried in Westminster Abbey (as if, Arbuthnot remarked to Swift, he had been a peer of the realm), his friends in their various ways all felt that they had lost a part of themselves. None of them, perhaps, expressed so completely what Gay had meant to those who knew him best as the Duchess of Queensberry, with whom the last years of his life had been spent in such debonair and unaffected friendship. Writing almost three years after his death, she mentions the successful purchase of some property which 'for this four or five years last past we had set our hearts on.' And yet, she reflects:

> I have not felt delighted, only mighty well satisfied: is not this astonishing? I often want poor Mr. Gay, and on this occasion extremely. Nothing evaporates sooner than joy untold, or even told, unless to one so entirely in your interest as he was, who bore at least an equal share in every satisfaction or dissatisfaction which attended us.[5]

To live on so in the memory of one's friends is indeed something. To those friends, so various in temperament and character, he was a sort of extension of their own personalities; he entered into their schemes, he gave them his time and his affection, he was never too busy or too preoccupied with his own affairs to break off and attend to theirs. He was therefore the perfect companion, equally welcome at the tea-table or in the coffeehouse or over a bottle of claret, the right man for a walking tour (if he had ever been willing to walk), the amiable and adaptable guest, the delightful correspondent. It was so that they all tended to think of him and to value him, and only secondarily as the author of the *Shepherd's Week*, or *Trivia*, or even the *Beggar's Opera*. This affectionate and faintly protective attitude of his friends has descended to those who never knew him. Not, it is true, to Johnson, for whom Gay's unassertive and accommodating nature had little appeal. But few later critics have written of him without betraying a slightly patronizing affection, and without referring (even Johnson does this once) to 'poor Gay.' No one ever thinks of saying 'poor Swift,' and only, perhaps, Miss Sitwell of saying 'poor Pope.'

What men *are* lives after them, and often gets between us and what they wrote. The world's verdict on an author is based, more often than we are apt to believe, on the impression made by his personality, and not solely on what he wrote. It is notorious that Matthew Arnold, who warned us against this very error, went on to commit it himself in his estimates of Byron, of Shelley, of Keats; and with reputations less secure than those, some weakness or ineffectiveness of character may lead to the partial or total neglect of a reputable author.[6] Of Gay it may perhaps be said that while his attractive and unassertive character has to some slight extent helped to keep his memory alive, it has tended at the same time to blur his achievement as a poet. The habit among critics of patronizing Gay, of not taking him quite seriously *as a man*, has spread to his poetry. When Johnson wrote of him that he had not in any degree 'the *mens divinior*, the dignity of genius,'[7] we may perhaps suspect that the judgement is partly due to the impression made by Gay the man, who had not, in Johnson's opinion, 'the character of a hero.'[8] It is true enough ('it would be idle to pretend') that Gay is the wrong man to go to if you are looking for the *mens divinior* in its most pronounced degree. But how much of it would you find in Horace, in Herrick, in Cowper, in Lamartine? Does the *'mens divinior*, the dignity of genius' turn out to be something, like Arnold's 'grand style,' that helps us to a qualitative rather than a quantitative distinction?

The only way to do Gay justice is to accept his poetry on its own terms. If we look to him for 'a criticism of life,' or expect to find in his poetry a substitute for religion, we shall look for what he is hardly ever concerned to give. His poetry bears about as much relation to contemporary eighteenth-century life as a Victorian sampler bears to the flowers and trees and cottages that it reproduces in bright needlework. Gay did not run away from life; he accepted it as his point of departure. In the medium of poetry he did what had long been familiar in the medium of pottery—he produced *objets d'art*, delicate, formalized, artificial, glazed and polished by his poetic diction, and removed from actuality by a process of refining and idealizing that was his own peculiar secret. What Gay had in a high degree, and what he has rarely been given sufficient credit for, was a delicate and sophisticated craftsmanship. The thing perfectly said, the tone perfectly caught and maintained: are these so common that we can take them for granted?

If we want the actual movement and stench and uproar of the London streets (as in certain moods we may) we can go to, say, Ned Ward; if we want to get the feeling—coarse, vulgar, palpitating—of a London crowd on holiday in the eighteenth century, we may find what we are looking for in the contemporary newspapers:

> The Holidays coming on, the Alewives of Islington, Kentish Town, and several other adjacent Villages, are in great Expectation of a considerable Trade from the Citizens, as Harlots are from their Apprentices. If the Weather proves favourable, whole Shoals of the former, with all

their Living Utensils, viz. Their Wives and Children, will be flocking thither, to the utter Destruction of Stuff'd Beef, Gammon of Bacon, Cheese-cakes, Bottle-Ale, and Cyder, which will be devour'd like Custard on a Lord-Mayor's Day, or Flummery by a Club of Welsh Attorneys. . . . The Fields will swarm with Butchers Wives, and Oyster-Women, known by wadling Gates, and Gold Chains; with a Medley of other frail Matrons and Damsels diverting themselves with their snotty Offspring, whilst their Spouses and Sweethearts are sweating at Nine-pins, some at Cricket, others at Stool-Ball, besides an amorous couple in every corner; so that the poor Town will be left as empty as a long Vacation, or a Pawnbroker's Conscience; only Stock-Jobbers will stick close to Business, to find the Way to the Devil, at Jonathan's. Much Noise and Guttling in the Morning; much Tippling all Day; and much Reeling and Kissing at Night.[9]

How remote from Gay is this guzzling, sweating, jostling crowd! He knows, of course, how the citizens eat and drink and amuse themselves, and how they smell; but before they are fit for his verse they must be devitalized, deodorized, and gently formalized. They must, in fact, be transformed into Chelsea shepherds and shepherdesses:

> When the sweet-breathing Spring unfolds the buds,
> Love flys the dusty town for shady woods.
> Then Totenham fields with roving beauty swarm,
> And Hampstead Balls the city virgin warm;
> Then Chelsea's meads o'erhear perfidious vows,
> And the prest grass defrauds the grazing cows. [10]

The two last lines are pure Gay; they have his own special note of delicate absurdity and sophisticated mockery. But the whole passage is characteristic of his habit of refining the raw materials of life. In *Rural Sports* he explains to the angler in georgic fashion how to clean the worms he is going to use as bait:

> Cleanse them from filth, to give a tempting gloss,
> Cherish the sully'd reptile race with moss;
> Amid the verdant bed they twine, they toil,
> And from their bodies wipe their native soil.[11]

Gay submits contemporary life to this same self-cleaning process until it shines with a delicate and not quite earthly lustre. The actual, the real, are of interest to this poet mainly because they enable him, as in the *Shepherd's Week* and *Trivia*, to obtain a kind of contrapuntal effect with the artificiality of his glossy diction and the orderliness of his balanced rhythm. The gently deliberate contrast comes out in *Trivia*:

> When all the Mall in leafy ruin lies,
> And damsels first renew their oyster cries . . .[12]

or in the *Shepherd's Week*:

> Lost in the musick of the whirling flail,
> To gaze on thee I left the smoaking pail . . .[13]

or, again in *Trivia*:

> When on his box the nodding coachman snores,
> And dreams of fancy'd fares . . .[14]

or finally, in a winter scene in the steets of London:

> On silent wheel the passing coaches roll;
> Oft' look behind, and ward the threatning pole.
> In harden'd orbs the school-boy moulds the snow,
> To mark the coachman with a dext'rous throw.
> Why do ye, boys, the kennel's surface spread,
> To tempt with faithless pass the matron's tread?
> How can ye laugh to see the damsel spurn,
> Sink in your frauds, and her green stockings mourn?
> At *White's* the harness'd chairman idly stands,
> And swings around his waste his tingling hands:
> The sempstress speeds to *'Change* with red-tipt nose;
> The Belgian stove beneath her footstool glows;
> In half-whipt muslin needles useless lie,
> And shuttle-cocks across the counter fly.
> These sports warm harmless; why then will ye prove,
> Deluded maids, the dang'rous flames of love?[15]

In the picture of the frozen Thames that follows, Nature has come half-way to meet the poet by herself appearing in an artificial dress; it is just this natural artificiality that Gay seeks habitually to create. On this occasion Nature has saved him the trouble by effecting the delicate transformation herself. To get the precise effect of Gay's habitual softening of the actual it is sometimes necessary to substitute the England of the twentieth century for the London of Queen Anne—to replace the waterman, the hackney coachman, the sempstress by the taxidriver, the bus-conductor, the typist. How is the typist, for instance, to become a piece of Chelsea china? By the same delicate process of formalizing her, emptying her of all seriousness, and glazing her with poetic diction. There she sits at her machine (Gay would have done it better, but we may at least make the attempt)

> And dreams of Damon still with melting eye,
> While rattling stops beneath her digits fly.

Life was indeed a jest to Gay. Cheerful, sociable, kind-hearted, he nevertheless remained slightly aloof from human concerns. Confronted by life he had the detachment of the artist, just as at a death-bed his friend Arbuthnot had the detachment of the physician. His special kind of perception was for the ironical, the delicately absurd, the piquant contrast between the growing artificialities of town life and the natural man or the natural background. When Spring comes to the Town,

> The ladies gayly dress'd the *Mall* adorn
> With various dyes, and paint the sunny morn;
> The wanton fawns with frisking pleasure range,
> And chirping sparrows greet the welcome change.[16]

The ladies, the fawns, the sparrows: it is characteristic of Gay to bring them together in this way, the sophisticated and the natural. When a rainstorm threatens,

> The bookseller, whose shop's an open square,
> Foresees the tempest, and with early care
> Of learning strips the rails. . . .[17]

Again the delicate contrast: the books in the street, the rain on the books. An umbrella is perhaps the perfect symbol for the world of Gay's peculiar, half-mocking vision; an umbrella that 'guards from chilly show'rs the walking maid,' faintly absurd in itself, an apparatus devised by civilized man and yet spread out in the face of a hostile nature.

This contrast between the natural and the artificial runs through all Gay's work. Sometimes it is emphasized, as when he notes how

> On doors the sallow milk-maid chalks her gains;
> Ah! how unlike the milkmaid of the plains! [18]

Sometimes it is only implied, as when he goes on to remark upon the ass's milk which was prescribed by physicians for 'the love-sick maid' and 'dwindling beau' (even here the contrast is implicit), and which was brought to the invalid not in milk-pails but in the still-unmilked ass herself:

> Before proud gates attending asses bray,
> Or arrogate with solemn pace the way. . . .[19]

It was, we may be sure, the odd solemnity of those patient animals picking their way over the London cobblestones that caught and held Gay's attention. With Gay we have at last reached a genuinely urban civilization (a state of affairs so frequently and so superfluously deplored by critics of a romantic turn), and we can recognize in him the town-dweller's delighted interest in such manifestations of natural life as come his way—the cat caught in a tree and rescued by the fire brigade, the pigeons in Trafalgar Square (citizens of a smaller growth), the well-groomed greys at a royal wedding.

Aware of this contrast between the natural and the artificial, Gay is constantly modifying the one by the other: the natural becomes artificial, and the artificial natural. But Gay's tendency is always, if not actually to idealize, to soften and harmonize. He presents his world not under fluorescent lighting but in the kindlier glow of candlelight. In *Trivia* (where the joke begins with the sedentary Gay writing a poem on walking at all) the disorderly human material of the London streets is quietly folded away in his orderly couplets, patted gently into place, and scented with lavender. His method of dealing with the poor and the humble was made possible by the wide gap between the educated and the uneducated in the early eighteenth century, but again Gay has his own special perception of their touching and amusing simplicity. His own peculiar note of kindly sophistication comes out in the charming ballad, 'Sweet William's Farewell to Black-ey'd Susan.' When William, high on the ship's mast, 'rock'd with the billow to and fro,' heard the voice of his sweetheart,

> He sigh'd and cast his eyes below:
> The cord slides swiftly through his glowing hands
> And (quick as lightning) on the deck he stands.

It is a drawing-room piece, another perfect example of Gay's Chelsea china. So is the equally sophisticated ' 'Twas when the seas were roaring,' and so are most of the earlier Fables, and many of the songs scattered through the *Beggar's Opera* (e.g. 'Before the barn door crowing,' 'Were I laid on Greenland's coast').

In the *Fables*, once so popular and now hardly read at all, Gay is, as usual, taking his art seriously and wearing his morality lightly. Written for the edification of the young Prince William, Duke of Cumberland, they have sometimes the most unexpected application. 'The Tame Stag' (No. XIII) recounts pleasantly the progress of a young stag which has been captured by a country clown and kept in captivity. Timid at first, he soon begins to feel at home in his new surroundings, 'munches the linen on the lines,' expects to be fed by the servants ('examines every fist for meat'), and ends at last by attacking his captors. The moral of all this?

> Such is the country maiden's fright,
> When first a red-coat is in sight,
> Behind the door she hides her face,
> Next time at distance eyes the lace,
> She now can all his terrors stand,
> Nor from his squeeze withdraws her hand;
> She plays familiar in his arms,
> And ev'ry soldier hath his charms;
> From tent to tent she spreads her flame:
> For custom conquers fear and shame.

So far as Gay's moral purpose is concerned, it could not have been much less if he had been illustrating the behaviour of stags by that of country wenches. What concerns him here, as always, is the polished and precise statement, the nice conduct of a critical intelligence, and the urbane cultivation of a literary 'kind.'

If Gay was not an earnest moralist, neither was he a determined satirist. We may suspect that his satirical tone was acquired mainly from living among satirists in a satirical age. We can see him occasionally in his letters working himself up to a fashionable indignation with the age in which he lives, but there is no conviction in his protests. When in verse he attempts the mode of Juvenal, he is 'a little o'erparted'; his indignation is no more than what he thinks the occasion requires, not what he really feels or has ever had much occasion to feel. Of this kind are some lines on the Parisian dames:

> This next the spoils of fifty lovers wears,
> Rich Dandin's brilliant favours grace her ears;
> The necklace Florio's gen'rous flame bestow'd,

Clitander's sparkling gems her finger load;
But now, her charms grown cheap by constant use,
She sins for scarfs, clock'd stockings, knots, and shoes.
This next, with sober gait and serious leer,
Wearies her knees with morn and ev'ning prayer;
She scorns th'ignoble love of feeble pages,
But with three Abbots in one night engages. . . .[20]

Gay knew about as much of such things as a precocious schoolboy; he
is right out of his element here. He was happy enough bringing down
the Duke of Queensberry's partridges; he had no experience of hunting
the more dangerous creatures of the woods or of eighteenth-century
society. There is one poem, however, 'The Birth of the Squire,' in which
his satire takes on a deeper tone. It begins quietly enough:

Hark! the bells ring; along the distant grounds
The driving gales convey the swelling sounds;
Th'attentive swain, forgetful of his work,
With gaping wonder, leans upon his fork.
What sudden news alarms the waking morn?
To the glad Squire a hopeful heir is born.

The poet goes on to describe the duteous offerings of the tenants on this
joyful occasion and the beer-swilling that accompanies it, the young
Squire's early introduction to the glories of the hunting field, his furtive
amours with the milkmaid in dairy, barn, and hayloft, his broken collar-
bone at the five-bar gate, his translation to Westminster 'to snore away
debates in Parliament,' his pompous activities as a Justice of the Peace
whose chief concern is the enforcement of the game laws, until finally
we reach the last scene of all:

Methinks I see him in his hall appear,
Where the long table floats in clammy beer,
'Midst mugs and glasses shatter'd o'er the floor,
Dead-drunk his servile crew supinely snore;
Triumphant, o'er the prostrate brutes he stands,
The mighty bumper trembles in his hands;
Boldly he drinks, and like his glorious Sires,
In copious gulps of potent ale expires.

We might have expected this Hogarthian poem to figure prominently
in the anthologies, if anthologies were not so often compiled with an eye
to the young and the timid. In 'The Birth of the Squire' Gay had behind

him a long satirical tradition; he was the man of wit and taste mocking at the booby squire, as Farquhar had mocked at Squire Sullen, and Congreve at Sir Wilful Witwoud, and Ravenscroft at Sir Simon Soft-head, and Crowne at Sir Mannerly Shallow—and so back to their an-cestors in Caroline and Jacobean comedy. But Gay's tone is, for him, oddly uncompromising; it comes near to disgust. We may perhaps suspect that he had some particularly unfavourable specimen of the squirearchy in mind, some arrogant lout remembered from his boyhood years in Devon.

With Gay the tone is all important. Criticism is apt not to talk at all about those matters which it finds difficult to discuss on easily intel-ligible terms. The poet's rhythm (as distinct from his metre) is one of those topics that most critics pass by rather uneasily: on such matters criticism has not yet got much farther than using words like 'magical' and 'hypnotic.' Similar difficulties are felt in discussing the poet's tone, his attitude to his readers. 'Tone' is something of which any sensitive reader of Pope or Gay or Johnson is subconsciously aware (it is an element in the poetical experience that is peculiarly relevant to eight-eenth-century poetry) but which, for lack of a critical vocabulary or any accepted means of measuring it, is usually passed over in silence.[21] Gay's tone varies, of course, from poem to poem; but he is almost every-where in polite touch with his reader, walking slightly ahead of him to point out this object or that, dwelling with his habitual mock-seriousness on some homely detail; adding a touch of humorous exaggeration or picturesque embellishment to some familiar appearance. In 'A Journey to Exeter,' for instance, where he is addressing himself to the Earl of Burlington, he has nothing very remarkable to tell, but the poem is a minor triumph of the politely familiar mode. And once again Gay manages to transform the ordinary into that something more delicate and remote that is his most characteristic achievement. He contrives even to throw this 'unbought grace' of style over the very meals he ate on his journey. At Stockbridge—

> O'er our parch'd tongue the rich metheglin glides,
> And the red dainty trout our knife divides. . . .

and, at Bridport:

> On unadulterate wine we here regale,
> And strip the lobster of his scarlet mail.[22]

On both occasions the gross act of feeding has taken on something of the precision and formality of an anatomical dissection: the heroic couplet alone would have seen to that. Yet quite apart from the balanced metre, with its tendency, as Wordsworth noted, to 'divest language, in a certain degree, of its reality, and thus to throw a sort of half-consciousness of unsubstantial existence over the whole composition,' the effect is also due to Gay's cool detachment, that delicate withdrawal from the object contemplated which was, with him, the essential preliminary to seeing it.

Gay raises in an acute form the problem of the right critical attitude to minor poets. In the eighteenth century they were accepted without question. Johnson had no illusions about the importance of many of the poets whose lives he wrote, but (with one or two possible exceptions) he obviously thought that they were worth writing about, and that their poetry (judiciously selected) was worth reading. The modern attitude is apt to be far less tolerant. The sort of fluctuation in taste which is represented by 'Who now reads Cowley?' is natural and almost inevitable. But in the increasingly astringent atmosphere of twentieth-century criticism the question is as likely to be: 'Who now would dream of reading Cowley?'—or Cotton, or Matthew Prior, or Beddoes? This new tendency, not merely to neglect the minor poet but to insist that he is not worth reading, may derive from Matthew Arnold, a potent critic, but a very busy man, who (as Saintsbury put it with a nice meiosis) had no special bent towards literary history. Certainly, if a man's time is limited, he would do well to restrict his reading to the greatest writers. No doubt, too, the intelligent critic, particularly if he moves in academic circles, may be forgiven if he reacts sharply against the modern tendency to encourage the young scholar to spend several years in exacavating the life and literary remains of some irredeemably minor poet. But this will hardly explain or excuse the uncompromising attitude of some modern critics to writers of long-established reputation whose work is not of the very first order of importance. Among the literary achievements of the twentieth century may be reckoned a much closer and more detailed investigation of the work of art than was normally attempted in earlier periods; but as the criticism of poetry becomes more and more intensive the law of the conservation of energy seems to come into play, and it is found that fewer and fewer poets are worth reading at all. This exclusiveness, which is associated, not entirely to its credit, with a school of criticism at Cambridge,[23] seems to arise from a disproportionate emphasis on values: the critic who is preoccupied with the question of values is in danger of discounting any writer who has not got an impressive balance at the bank. With such a critic the best becomes too great an enemy to the good; but to neglect or denigrate the good because it is not the best is to leave the best in an unnatural and misleading isolation, and to make poor use of the great resources of English poetry. 'Shine, Poet! in thy place, and be content.' The attitude of Wordsworth to the minor poet is generous and reasonable:

> The stars pre-eminent in magnitude,
> And they that from the zenith dart their beams . . .
> Are yet of no diviner origin,
> No purer essence than the one that burns
> Like an untended watch-fire on the ridge
> Of some dark mountain; or than those which seem
> Humbly to hang, like twinkling winter lamps,
> Among the branches of the leafless trees.
> All are the undying offspring of one Sire:
> Then, to the measure of the light vouchsafed,
> Shine, Poet! in thy place, and be content.

Shine, Critic, too, in thy place, and be content. And one part of the critic's function, when he is not just pontificating, or effecting the dislodgement of Milton, or Shelley, or whoever else owing to some change in the intellectual climate may have gone temporarily out of fashion, is to act, more humbly and usefully, as a sort of caretaker for literary reputations. In this capacity he can at least open the front door for visitors, see that the rooms are kept dusted and ventilated, and, if need be, comment on the exhibits if any visitors arrive. Such employment is not spectacular, but it is honourable; it expresses the relative importance of the critic and the creative writer, and it keeps the critic in the place that heaven has assigned for him.

NOTES

1. Samuel Johnson, *Lives of the English Poets*, ed. G. B. Hill (1905), ii. 282–4.

2. Joseph Warton, *An Essay on the Writings and Genius of Pope* (1782), ii. 314.

3. *The Correspondence of Jonathan Swift, D.D.*, ed. F. E. Ball (1913), iv. 134, 173, 272, 286, 294.

4. Ibid. 39.

5. *Letters to and from Henrietta, Countess of Suffolk . . .* (1824), ii. 109.

6. Who would guess from the histories of literature that the *Duke of Lerma* is almost the finest English tragedy written in the second half of the seventeenth century? But the author, Sir Robert Howard, appears to have been a pompous ass, and was generally recognized and satirized as such by his contemporaries. The character of the man prejudiced the reputation of his tragedy, and though his character is now as little known as his play the harm had been done.

7. *Lives*, ed. cit. ii. 282.

8. Ibid. 272.

9. *The Weekly Journal; Or, British Gazetteer*, 4 June 1720. If this is not by Ned Ward it is by one of his imitators.

10. *An Epistle to the Right Honourable William Pulteney, Esq.*, 101 ff.

11. Op. cit. i. 167 ff.

12. Op. cit. i. 27 f.

13. Op. cit. 'Tuesday,' 57 f.

14. Op. cit. i. 153 f.

15. *Trivia*, ii. 327 ff.

16. Ibid. i. 145 ff.

17. *Trivia*, i. 161 ff.

18. Ibid. ii. 11 f.

19. Ibid. 13 f.

20. *An Epistle to the Right Honourable William Pulteney, Esq.*, 167 ff.

21. But not by Mr. I. A. Richards, who has some admirable remarks on Gray's attitude to the reader of the *Elegy*, and who concludes: Indeed, many of the secrets of "style" could, I believe, be shown to be matters of tone, of the perfect recognition of the writer's relation to the reader in view of what is being said and their joint feelings about it' (*Practical Criticism* (London, 1929), pp. 206–7). One might have expected Mr. Richards's preoccupation with theory to interfere with his response to the individual work of art; but he has remained the perfect reader, and his ability to draw from a poem all that is there, and no more, gives authority to his criticism, and should procure a willing suspension of disbelief for his theory.

22. Op. cit. 49–50, 99–100. 'Unadulterate' is a good example of Gay's keeping in touch with his reader, and appealing to his past experience. At the time (1715) when Gay wrote this poem, complaints about the adulteration of wine by vintners were frequent. (See, for example, *Brooke and Hellier: a Satyr*, 1712.) Gay's reference to the adulteration of wines would arouse the same ready response as a reference to whalemeat or snoek in war-time England.

23 Cambridge, Eng., not Mass.

C. S. LEWIS

Addison

'I HAVE always,' said Addison, 'preferred cheerfulness to mirth. The latter I consider as an act, the former as an habit of the mind';[1] or again, 'Though I am always serious, I do not know what it is to be melancholy.'[2] These sentences pretty well give us the measure, if not of the man, yet of the work; just as the limpidity of their style, conveying a distinction of almost scholastic precision in such manner that even a 'tea-table' could not fail to understand it, gives us the measure of his talent. They serve also to mark the most profound difference between the Whig essayist and his two great Tory contemporaries.

Swift and Pope were by no means always serious and they knew very well what it was to be melancholy. One would have found more mirth in their conversation than in Addison's: not only epigram and repartee, but frolic and extravaganza—even buffoonery. It is true that they regarded satire as a 'sacred weapon,' but we must not so concentrate on that idea as to forget the sheer *vis comica* which brightens so much of their work. Swift's 'favourite maxim was *vive la bagatelle*.'[3] *Gulliver* and the *Dunciad* and the whole myth of Scriblerus have missed their point if they do not sometimes make us 'laugh and shake in Rabelais' easy chair.' Even their love of filth is, in my opinion, much better understood by schoolboys than by psychoanalysts: if there is something sinister in it, there is also an element of high-spirited rowdiness. Addison has a sense of humour; the Tories have, in addition, a sense of fun. But they have no 'habit' of cheerfulness. Rage, exasperation, and something like despair are never far away. It is to this that they owe their sublimity —for Pope, no less than Swift, can be sublime. We suspect that the picture he paints of himself is historically false—

From *Essays on the Eighteenth Century Presented to David Nichol Smith* (Clarendon Press, 1945), 1–14. Reprinted by permission of the author.

Yes, I am proud; I must be proud to see
Men not afraid of God, afraid of me.

But it is a sublime poetical image. The picture of surly, contemptuous
virtue had often been attempted before—in Chapman's Bussy and
Clermont, in Dryden's Almanzor, in Wycherley's Manly, even in the
Christ of *Paradise Regained*; but I would give Pope the palm, for in
Milton the discrepancy between the known historical character of his
Hero and the 'Senecal man' he has painted is more shocking than that
between the real and the imagined Pope. There is nothing of so high a
reach in Addison. The grandeur of 'cynical asperity' is a flower that
grows only in a tropical climate, and in passing to Addison's world we
pass to a world where such things are impossible. Surly virtue is not
cheerful nor equable: in the long run it is not, perhaps, perfectly
consistent with good sense.

This contrast between Addison and the Tories comes out with special
clarity in their treatment of enemies. For the Tories, every enemy—
whether it be the Duchess of Marlborough or only a Shakespearian
editor found guilty of some real English scholarship—becomes a grotesque. All who have, in whatever fashion, incurred their ill will are
knaves, scarecrows, whores, bugs, toads, bedlamites, yahoos; Addison
himself a smooth Mephistopheles. It is good fun, but it is certainly not
good sense; we laugh, and disbelieve. Now mark Addison's procedure.
The strength of the Tory party is the smaller country gentry with their
Jacobite leanings and their opposition to the moneyed interest. All the
material for savage satire is there. Addison might have anticipated
Squire Western (as he did later in the *Freeholder*) and painted merely
the block-headed, fox-hunting sot, the tyrant of his family and his village. Instead, with the help of Steele, he invents Sir Roger de Coverley.
The measure of his success is that we can now think of Sir Roger for a
long time without remembering his Toryism; when we do remember
it, it is only as a lovable whimsy.

In all our journey from London to his house, we did not so much as
bait at a Whig inn. This often betrayed us into hard beds and bad cheer;
for we were not so inquisitive about the inn as the innkeeper; and provided our landlord's principles were sound, did not take any notice of
the staleness of his provisions.

As a natural consequence, Mr. Spectator soon 'dreaded entering into
an house of any one that Sir Roger had applauded for an honest man.'[4]

It is so beautifully done that we do not notice it. The enemy, far from being vilified, is being turned into a dear old man. The thought that he could ever be dangerous has been erased from our minds; but so also the thought that anything he said could ever be taken seriously. We all love Sir Roger; but of course we do not really attend to him as we do—well, to Sir Andrew Freeport. All through the century which Addison ushered in, England was going to attend more and more seriously to the Freeports, and the de Coverleys were to be more and more effectually silenced. The figure of the dear old squire dominates—possibly, on some views, corrupts—the national imagination to the present day. This is indeed to 'make a man die sweetly.' That element in English society which stood against all that Addison's party was bringing in is henceforth seen through a mist of smiling tenderness—as an archaism, a lovely absurdity. What we might have been urged to attack as a fortress we are tricked into admiring as a ruin.

When I say 'tricked' I am not implying that Steele and Addison calculated the whole effect of their creation just as I have set it down. The actual upshot of their work is obvious; their conscious intentions are another matter. I am inclined to think that Addison really loved Sir Roger—with that 'superior love' which, in England, the victorious party so easily accords to the remnants of a vanishing order. Addison is not a simple man; he is, in the older sense of the word, 'sly.' I do not believe for one moment that he was the fiendlike Atticus; but one sees how inevitably he must have appeared so to the losers. He is so cool, so infuriatingly sensible, and yet he effects more than they. A satiric portrait by Pope or Swift is like a thunderclap; the Addisonian method is more like the slow operations of ordinary nature, loosening stones, blunting outlines, modifying a whole landscape with 'silent overgrowings' so that the change can never quite be reversed again. Whatever his intentions, his reasonableness and amiability (both cheerful 'habits' of the mind) are stronger in the end than the Tory spleen. To rail is the sad privilege of the loser.

I have used the word 'amiability.' Should we go further and say 'charity'? I feel that this Christian word, with its doctrinal implications, would be a little out of place when we are speaking of Addison's essays. About the man, as distinct from the work, I will not speculate. Let us hope that he practised this theological virtue. The story that he summoned Lord Warwick to his deathbed *to see how a Christian can die* is ambiguous; it can be taken either as evidence of his Christianity or as a very brimstone proof of the reverse. I give no vote: my concern is with books. And the essays do not invite criticism in terms of any very definite theology. They are everywhere 'pious.' Rational Piety, together with Polite Letters and Simplicity, is one of the hallmarks of the age which Addison was partly interpreting but partly also bringing into existence. And Rational Piety is by its very nature not very doctrinal. This is one of the many ways in which Addison is historically momentous. He ushers in that period—it is just now drawing to a close—in which it is possible to talk of 'piety' or (later) 'religion' almost in the abstract; in which the contrast is no longer between Christian and Pagan, the elect and the world, orthodox and heretic, but between 'religious' and 'irreligious.' The transition cannot be quite defined: absence of doctrine would have to become itself doctrinal for that to be possible. It is a change of atmosphere, which every reader of sensibility will feel if he passes suddenly from the literature of any earlier period to that of the eighteenth century. Hard rocks of Calvinism show up amidst the seemingly innocuous surface of an *Arcadia* or a *Faerie Queene*; Shakespearian comedy reckons on an audience who will at once see the point of jokes about the controversy on Works and Faith. Here also, no doubt, it is difficult to bring Addison to a point. Perhaps the most illuminating passage is the essay on 'Sir Roger at Church,' and specially the quotation from Pythagoras prefixed to it—'Honour first the immortal gods according to the established mode.'[5] That is the very note of Rational Piety. A sensible man goes with his society, according to local and ancestral usage. And he does so with complete sincerity. Clean clothes and the sound of bells on Sunday morning do really throw him into a mood of sober benevolence, not 'clouded by enthusiasm' but inviting his thoughts to approach the mystery of things.

In this matter of Rational Piety one must not draw too sharp a contrast between Addison and the Tories. They are infected with it themselves, and Swift quotes with equal approval the Pagan maxim about worshipping 'according to the laws of the country.'[6] But I think there is *some* contrast. The Tories are a little nearer than Addison to the old period with its uncompromising creeds. Pope's Romanism is not nearly so superficial as some have supposed, and the 'Pantheism' of the *Essay on Man* owes a good deal of its notoriety to critics who would make a very poor shape at defining pantheism. He made an edifying end, and he perhaps understands the conflict in Eloise's mind—it is not simply a conflict of virtue and vice—better than Addison would have done. Swift is harder to classify. There is, to be sure, no doubt of his churchmanship, only of his Christianity, and this, of itself, is significant. If Swift were (as I do not think he is) primarily a Church of England man, only secondly a Christian, and not 'pious' or 'religious' at all, we might say that in Addison's writings the proportions are reversed. And some things would lend colour to such an interpretation of Swift. In the *Sentiments* his religion seems to be purely political. 'I leave it among the divines to dilate upon the danger of schism, as a spiritual evil, but I would consider it only as a temporal one.'[7] Separation from the established worship, 'though to a new one that is more pure and perfect,' is dangerous. More disquieting still are the tormented aphorisms of *Thoughts on Religion*. To change fundamental opinions is ordinarily wicked 'whether those opinions be true or false,' and 'The want of belief is a defect that ought to be concealed when it cannot be overcome.'[8] Some parts of *Gulliver* seem inconsistent with any religion—except perhaps Buddhism. The *Further Thoughts on Religion* open with the assertion that the Mosaic account of creation is 'most agreeable of all other to probability' and immediately cite—the making of Eve out of Adam's rib![9] Is it possible that this should not be irony? And yet there is much to set on the other side. His priestly duties were discharged with a fidelity rare in that age. The ferocity of the later *Gulliver* all works up to that devastating attack on Pride which is more specifically Christian than any other piece of ethical writing in the century, if we except William Law. The prayers offered at Stella's deathbed have a scholastic firmness in their implied moral theology. ('Keep her from both the sad extremes of presumption and despair.' 'Forgive the sorrow and weakness of those among us who sink under the grief and terror of losing so dear and useful a friend.') The sermon 'On the Trinity,' taken at its face value, preaches a submission of the reason to dogma which ought to satisfy the sternest supernaturalist. And I think it should be taken at its face value. If we ever think otherwise, I believe the explanation to lie in that peculiar ungraciousness which Swift exercised upwards as well as downwards. He gave alms 'without tenderness or civility,' so that 'those who were fed by him could hardly love him.'[10] As below, so above. He practises obedience without humility or meekness, takes his medicine with a wry face. But the alms, however given, were hard cash, and I think his acceptance of Christian doctrine is equally real, though offered (as it were) under protest, as if he were resentful of Heaven for putting him in such a ridiculous position. There is a tension and discomfort about all this, but that very tension suggests depths that Addison never knew. It is from those depths that Swift is writing when he says there can be no question in England of any but a nominal Christianity—'the other having been for some time wholly laid aside by general consent as utterly inconsistent with our present schemes of wealth and power.'[11]

This is a far cry from Mr. Spectator's pleasing reflections on the Royal Exchange.

> As I am a great lover of mankind, my heart naturally overflows with pleasure at the sight of a happy and prosperous multitude, insomuch that at many public solemnities I cannot forbear expressing my joy with tears that have stolen down my cheeks. For this reason I am wonderfully delighted to see such a body of men thriving in their own private fortunes, and at the same time promoting the public stock; or, in other words, raising estates for their own families, by bringing into their country whatever is wanting, and carrying out of it whatever is superfluous.[12]

Compared with this, Swift's remark is like a scorching wind from the hermitages of the Thebaid.

Addison is never blasphemous or irreverent; Swift can be both. That, I think, helps to confirm the kind of distinction I am drawing between them. Swift still belongs, at any rate in part, to the older world. He would have understood Rochester in both Rochester's phases better than he could understand Addison. Rochester unconverted was a Bad Man of the old, thoroughgoing kind,

> he drunk, he fought, he whored,
> He did despite unto the Lord.

Rochester converted was a deathbed penitent. One cannot imagine Mr. Spectator or Sir Andrew emulating him in either achievement.

The mention of Rochester suggests yet another gulf between Addison and the preceding age. We may be sure that Rochester's manners lacked that 'simplicity' which the Whig essayists recommended. It is, of course, a commonplace that they addressed themselves to the reform of manners; but I sometimes wonder whether the very degree of their success does not conceal from us the greatness of the undertaking. I sometimes catch myself taking it for granted that the marks of good breeding were in all ages the same as they are to-day—that swagger was always vulgar, that a low voice, an unpretentious manner, a show (however superficial) of self-effacement, were always demanded. But it is almost certainly false. We catch a glimpse of the truth in Johnson's remark: 'Lord Southwell was the highest bred man without insolence that I ever was in company with. . . . Lord Orrery was not dignified; Lord Chesterfield was, but he was insolent.'[13] Insolence, for us, is a characteristic of the 'beggar on horseback,' a mark of ill breeding; we have little idea of the genuine 'high' manners that bordered on it. We catch another glimpse in Polonius's advice, 'Costly thy habit as thy purse can buy,' and again in Hotspur's humorous indignation at the 'sarcenet' insipidity of his wife's oaths. We perceive from many scenes of Elizabethan comedy and from the stir among the servants at Gawain's arrival in the *Green Knight* that the old courtesy was not a 'pass school' (as it is with us where a man either knows the right thing to do or not) but an 'honours school' where competing extravagances of decorum and compliment could go to any height. I am inclined to think that if we saw it now we should mistake that high breeding for no breeding at all. The walk of the courtier would seem to us a Janissary's strut, his readiness to find quarrel in a straw would seem a yokel touchiness, his clothes an intolerable ostentation. Even to this day, when we meet foreigners (only think of some *young* Frenchmen) who have not been subjected to the Addisonian 'reform,' we have to 'make allowances' for them. I do not suggest that Addison and Steele, simply by writing essays, abolished the old flamboyancy. Doubtless they gave expression to a tendency which would have existed even without them. But to express is partly to mould. That sober code of manners under which we still live to-day, in so far as we have any code at all, and which foreigners call hypocrisy, is in some important degree a legacy from the *Tatler* and the *Spectator*. It is certainly not to be explained as a mere imposition of the code of the citizens upon the gentry. No one denies that a *rapprochement* between the 'cit' and the courtier was an essential part of the Addisonian synthesis. Sir Andrew Freeport mixes with those whose grandfather would have regarded his grandfather simply as a 'cuckoldand.' But the shop and the counting-house are not of themselves schools of modest and obliging deportment: least of all when they are prosperous. There was real novelty in the new manners.

These new manners were a little restrictive; in adopting them we lost, along with some cruelties and absurdities, a good deal of 'the unbought grace of life.' But in other respects Addison is a liberator. His famous defence of 'Chevy Chase' is sometimes taken to show a 'romantic' side in him, but that, I think, is not the best way of considering it. The word 'romantic' is always ambiguous. The paper on 'Chevy Chase' is to be taken in its context. It follows a discussion on False Wit. False Wit is taken up by poets who lack the 'strength of genius' which gives 'majestic simplicity to Nature' and who are therefore forced 'to hunt after foreign ornaments.' These writers are to poetry what the Goths were to architecture. Ovid is the type of such 'Gothic' poets, and 'the taste of most of our English poets, as well as readers, is extremely

Gothic.'[14] One mark of true poetry is that it 'pleases all kinds of palates,' whereas the Gothic manner pleases 'only such as have formed to themselves a wrong artificial taste upon little fanciful authors.'[15] It is, therefore, to be expected that common songs or ballads which are 'the delight of the common people' should be 'paintings of Nature.' It is after this preamble that Addison proceeds to examine 'Chevy Chase'—according to the rules of Le Bossu—and pronounces in its favour.

No more classical piece of criticism exists. In it Addison touches hands with Scaliger on the one side and Matthew Arnold on the other. What complicates it is, of course, his peculiar use of the word 'Gothic.' Addison must have known perfectly well that the ballad is just the sort of thing to which his contemporaries would spontaneously have applied that word, and that Ovid and Cowley are not. Very well, then; he will prove that it is the ballad which really follows Nature and that the true Goths are the authors whom the Town in fact prefers. In other words he is calling the neo-classical bluff. It is as if he said, 'You all profess to like a great subject, a good moral, unity of action, and truth to Nature. Well, here they all are in the ballad which you despise; and yonder, in the Cowley which you really enjoy, they are not.' One cannot be certain here, as one could not be certain about the invention of Sir Roger, whether Addison is being 'sly' or really innocent. One sees again what is behind the image of Atticus. The man who writes thus will certainly appear 'sly' to his opponents. But is he consciously setting a trap, or is he merely following the truth as he sees it in all simplicity? Perhaps it does not much matter, for the trap is inherent in the facts, and works whether Addison meant to set it or no; in the sense that if the *nominal* standards of Augustan criticism are ever taken seriously they must work out in favour of the ballads (and much medieval literature) and against most of the poetry the Augustans themselves produced. In other words, if we insist on calling an appreciation of ballads 'romantic,' then we must say that Addison becomes a romantic precisely because he is a *real* classic, and that every real classic must infallibly do the same. It is inconceivable that Aristotle and Horace, had they known them, should not have put the *Chanson de Roland* above the *Davideis*. Antiquity and the Middle Ages are not divided from each other by any such chasm as divides both from the Renaissance.

But it is better not to use the word 'romantic' in this context at all. What Addison really shows by his appreciation of the Ballad is his openmindedness, his readiness to recognize excellence wherever he finds it, whether in those periods which Renaissance Humanism had elected to call 'classical' or in those far longer extents of time which it ignored. The obscurantism of the Humanists is still not fully recognized. Learning to them meant the knowledge and imitation of a few rather arbitrarily selected Latin authors and some even fewer Greek authors. They despised metaphysics and natural science; and they despised all the past outside the favoured periods. They were dominated by a narrowly ethical purpose. 'Referenda ad mores omnia,' said Vives;[16] and he thought it fortunate that the Attic dialect contained nearly all the Greek worth reading—'reliquis utuntur auctores carminum quos non tanti est intelligi.'[17] Their philistine attitude to metaphysics is prettily carried off in modern histories by phrases about 'brushing away scholastic cobwebs,' but the Humanist attack is really on metaphysics itself. In Erasmus, in Rabelais, in the *Utopia* one recognizes the very accent of the angry *belle-lettrist* railing, as he rails in all ages, at 'jargon' and 'strawsplitting.' On this side Pope and Swift are true inheritors of the Humanist tradition. It is easy, of course, to say that Laputa is an attack not on science but on the aberrations of science. I am not convinced. The learning of the Brobdingnagians and the Horses is ruthlessly limited. Nothing that cannot plead the clearest immediate utility—nothing that cannot make two blades of grass grow where one grew before—wins any approval from Swift. Bentley is not forgiven for knowing more Greek than Temple, nor Theobald for knowing more English than Pope. Most of the history of Europe is a mere wilderness, not worth visiting, in which 'the monks finished what the Goths begun.'[18] The terror expressed at the end of the *Dunciad* is not wholly terror at the approach of ignorance: it is also terror lest the compact little fortress of Humanism should be destroyed, and new knowledge is one of the enemies. Whatever is not immediately intelligible to a man versed in the Latin and French classics appears to them to be charlatanism or barbarity. The number of things they do not want to hear about is enormous.

But Addison wants to hear about everything. He is quite as good a classical scholar as the Tories but he does not live in the Humanist prison. He notes with satisfaction 'that curiosity is one of the strongest and most lasting appetites implanted in us, and that admiration is one of our most pleasing passions.'[19] He delights to introduce his readers to the new philosophy of Mr. Locke and to explain by it, with aid from Malebranche, 'a famous passage in the Alcoran.'[20] He remembers with pleasure how 'Mr. Boyle, speaking of a certain mineral, tells us that a man may consume his whole life in the study of it, without arriving at the knowledge of all its qualities.'[21] He gazes on the sea ('the heaving of this prodigious bulk of waters') with 'a very pleasing astonishment.'[22] Astronomy, revealing the immensities of space, entertains him with sublime meditations,[23] and his reading, he tells us, 'has very much lain among books of natural history.'[24] Mysteries attract him. He loves to lose himself in an *o altitudo* whether on the marvels of animal instinct[25] or on those of the powers enjoyed by the soul in dreams—on which he quotes Browne himself.[26] He lives habitually in a world of horizons and possibilities which Pope touched, I think, only in the *Essay on Man,* and Swift hardly touches at all. It is a cool, quiet world after that of the Tories—say, a water-colour world, but there is more room in it. On those things which it illuminates at all, the wit of Swift and Pope casts a sharper and (in a sense) more beautiful light; but what huge regions of reality appear to them, as Addison says that life itself appears to ignorance and folly, a 'prospect of naked hills and plains which produce nothing either profitable or ornamental'!²⁷

This open-mindedness is not particularly 'romantic,' though without it we should have had no Wartons, no Ritson, no Percy, and perhaps no Scott; for the medievalism of the eighteenth century, whatever else it may be, is a mighty defeat of sheer ignorance. But Addison is much more closely connected with the Romantic Movement in quite a different way. He stands at the very turning-point in the history of a certain mode of feeling.

I think that perhaps the best piece of criticism Raleigh ever wrote is in the fourth chapter of his *Wordsworth,* where he sets Claudio's shuddering speech ('To be imprisoned in the viewless winds') beside Wordsworth's longing to retain a body 'endued with all the nice regards of flesh and blood' and yet surrender it to the elements 'as if it were a spirit.' He points out, quite justly, that what is Hell to Claudio is almost Heaven to Wordsworth. Between the two passages a profound change in human sentiment has taken place. Briefly put—for the story has often been told before—it is the change from an age when men frankly hated and feared all those things in Nature which are neither sensuously pleasing, useful, safe, symmetrical, or gaily coloured, to an age when men love and actually seek out mountains, waste places, dark forests, cataracts, and storm-beaten coasts. What was once the ugly has become a department (even the major department) of the beautiful. The first conflict between the old and the new taste received striking expression when Addison was already nine years old, in Thomas Burnet's *Telluris Theoria Sacra.* Burnet cannot quite conceal a certain joy in the awfulness of the Alps, but his very argument depends on the conception that they are deformities—*longaeva illa, tristia et squalentia corpora.*[28] Not that they are the only offence. In the face of this Earth as a whole we find *multa superflua, multa inelegantia*: such beauty (*ornamentum*) as it possesses comes chiefly *cultu et habitatione hominum.*[29]

The position of Addison in this story is very interesting. He divides the sources of imaginative pleasure into three classes—the Great, the Uncommon, and the Beautiful. As specimens of the Great he mentions 'an open champaign country, a vast uncultivated desert, huge heaps of mountains, high rocks and precipices, or a wide expanse of waters'—all of which produce 'a delightful stillness and amazement in the soul.'[30] To a later writer many of these things would have seemed beautiful; to an earlier one they would have seemed simply unpleasant. Addison does not find beauty in them, but he includes them among the sources of pleasure. His category of the Great, clearly distinguished from the Beautiful, exists precisely to make room for them. A similar distinction was, of course, the basis of Burke's treatise on *The Sublime and Beautiful,* and dominated the aesthetic thought of the century. Whether it was not much more sensible than the modern practice of bundling Alps and roses together into the single category of Beauty, I do not here inquire. The interesting thing is that Addison stands exactly at the turn of the tide.

Equally important for the historian of taste is *Spectator,* No. 160, where he contrasts the original 'genius' (which tends to be 'nobly wild and extravagant') and the *Bel Esprit* 'refined by conversation, reflection, and the reading of the most polite authors.' The taste for 'noble extravagance' is not itself a novelty, for audacities in art and graces that overleap the rules are praised by Dryden, Boileau, and Pope. What is interesting is Addison's belief that even the greatest genius is 'broken' by the rules and in becoming learned 'falls unavoidably into imitation.' This pessimistic view of culture as something naturally opposed to genius received, no doubt, its extreme expression in Macaulay's essay on Milton; but I think it had also a great deal to do with that crop of forgeries which the eighteenth century produced. If sublime genius lies all in the past, before civilization began, we naturally look for it in the past. We long to recover the work of those sublime prehistoric bards and druids who *must* have existed. But their work is not to be found; and the surviving medieval literature conspicuously lacks the sublimity and mysteriousness we desire. In the end one begins *inventing* what the 'bards,' 'druids,' and 'minstrels' ought to have written. Ossian, Rowley, and *Otranto* are wish-fulfilments. It is always to be remembered that Macpherson had written original epics about prehistoric Scotland before he invented Ossian. By a tragic chance he and Chatterton discovered that their work was marketable, and so make-believe turned into fraud.

But there was a sincere impulse behind it: they were seeking in the past that great romantic poetry which really lay in the future, and from intense imagination of what it must be like if only they could find it they slipped into making it themselves.

So far I have been trying to obey Arnold's precept—to get myself out of the way and let humanity decide. I have not attempted to assess the value of Addison's work, having wished rather to bring out its immense potency. He appears to be (as far as any individual can be) the source of a quite astonishing number of mental habits which were still prevalent when men now living were born. Almost everything which my own generation ignorantly called Victorian seems to have been expressed by Addison. It is all there in the *Spectator*—the vague religious sensibility, the insistence on what came later to be called Good Form, the playful condescension towards women, the untroubled belief in the beneficence of commerce, the comfortable sense of security which, far from excluding, perhaps renders possible the romantic relish for wildness and solitude. If he is not at present the most hated of our writers, that can only be because he is so little read. Everything the moderns detest, all that they call *smugness, complacency,* and *bourgeois ideology,* is brought together in his work and given its most perfect expression.

And certainly, if it were at all times true that the Good is the enemy of the Best, it would be hard to defend Addison. His Rational Piety, his smiling indulgence to 'the fair sex,' his small idealisms about trade, certainly fall short of actual Christianity, and plain justice to women, and true political wisdom. They may even be obstacles to them; palliatives and anodynes that prolong the disease. In some moods I cannot help seeing Addison as one who, at every point, 'sings charms to ills that ask the knife.' I believe he could defend himself. He is not attempting to write sermons or philosophy, only essays; and he certainly could not foresee what the search for markets would finally make of international trade. These hostile criticisms, made on the basis of our modern experience when all issues have become sharper, cannot really be maintained. All we can justly say is that his essays are rather small beer; there is no iron in them as in Johnson; they do not stir the depths.

And yet, if I were to live in a man's house for a whole twelve-month, I think I should be more curious about the quality of his small beer than about that of his wine; more curious about his bread and butter and beef than about either. Writers like Addison who stand on the common ground of daily life and deal only with middle things are unduly depreciated to-day. Pascal says somewhere that the cardinal error of Stoicism was to suppose that we can do always what we do sometimes. No one lives always on the stretch. Hence one of the most pertinent questions to be asked about any man is what he falls back on. The important thing about Malory's world, for example, is that when you fall back from the quest of the Grail you fall back into the middle world of Arthur's court: not plumb down into the level of King Mark. The important thing about many fierce idealists in our own day is that when the political meeting or the literary movement can be endured no longer they fall plumb down to the cinema and the dance band. I fully admit that when Pope and Swift are on the heights they have a strength and splendour which makes everything in Addison look pale; but what an abyss of hatred and bigotry and even silliness receives them when they slip from the heights! The Addisonian world is not one to live in at all times, but it is a good one to fall back into when the day's work is over and a man's feet on the fender and his pipe in his mouth. Good sense is no substitute for Reason; but as a rest from Reason it has distinct advantages over Jargon. I do not think Addison's popularity is likely to return; but something to fill the same place in life will always be needed— some tranquil middle ground of quiet sentiments and pleasing melan- cholies and gentle humour to come in between our restless idealisms and our equally restless dissipations. Do we not after all detect in the charge of *smugness* and *complacency* the note of envy? Addison is, above all else, comfortable. He is not on that account to be condemned. He is an admirable cure for the fidgets.

NOTES

1. *Spectator*, 381.
2. Ibid. 26.
3. Johnson, *Life of Swift*.
4. *Spectator*, 126.
5. *Spectator*, 112.
6. *Sentiments of a Church of England Man*.
7. *Sentiments of a Church of England Man*.
8. Ibid.
9. *Further Thoughts on Religion*.
10. Johnson, *Life of Swift*.
11. *Argument against Abolishing Christianity*.
12. *Spectator*, 69.
13. Boswell, 23 March 1783.
14. *Spectator*, 62.
15. Ibid. 70.
16. *De Tradendis Disciplinis*, iv.

17. Ibid. iii.
18. *Essay on Criticism*, l. 692.
19. *Spectator*, 237.
20. Ibid. 98.
21. Ibid. 94.
22. Ibid. 489.
23. Ibid. 565.
24. Ibid. 120.
25. Ibid.
26. *Spectator*, 487.
27. Ibid. 94.
28. *Telluris Theoria Sacra*, 1. ix.
29. *Telluris Theoria Sacra*, 1. x.
30. *Spectator*, 412.

IAN WATT

―――

Robinson Crusoe as a Myth

We do not usually think of *Robinson Crusoe* as a novel. Defoe's first full-length work of fiction seems to fall more naturally into place with *Faust, Don Juan* and *Don Quixote,* the great myths of our civilization. What these myths are about it is fairly easy to say. Their basic plots, their enduring images, all exhibit a single-minded pursuit by the protagonist of one of the characteristic aspirations of Western man. Each of their heroes embodies an *arete* and a *hubris,* an exceptional prowess and a vitiating excess, in spheres of action that are peculiarly important in our culture. Don Quixote, the impetuous generosity and the limiting blindness of chivalric idealism; Don Juan, pursuing and at the same time tormented by the idea of boundless experience of women; Faustus, the great knower, his curiosity always unsatisfied, and therefore damned.

Crusoe does not at first seem a likely companion for these other culture-heroes. They lose the world for an idea; he for gain. Their aspirations are conscious, and defiant, so that when retribution comes it is half expected and already understood; whereas Robinson Crusoe disclaims either heroism or pride; he stolidly insists that he is no more than he seems, that you would do it too in the circumstances.

Yet of his apotheosis there can be no doubt. By the end of the nineteenth century, there had appeared at least 700 editions, translations and imitations, not to mention a popular eighteenth-century pantomime, and an opera by Offenbach.[1] There are other more picturesque examples of his fame. In 1848, an enterprising French industrialist started a restaurant up a tree, a particularly fine chestnut in a wood near Paris: he called it 'Robinson,' and now restaurateurs vie for the title in a village

―――

From *Essays in Criticism: a Quarterly Journal of Literary Criticism,* April 1951, pp. 95–119. Reprinted by permission of the publisher and author.

of that name.[2] In France, again, 'un robinson' has become a popular term for a large umbrella.

Nor, as Virginia Woolf has pointed out,[3] is he usually thought of as a hero of fiction. Instead, partly because of Defoe's verisimilitude and partly for deeper reasons, his author's name has been forgotten, while he himself has acquired a kind of semi-historical status, like the traditional heroes of myth. When his story appeared it is reported to have been 'universally received and credited as a genuine history';[4] and we today can surely apply to it Malinowski's description of primitive myths: 'It is not of the nature of fiction, such as we read today in a novel, but it is a living reality, believed to have once happened in primeval times, and continuing ever since to influence the world and human destinies.'[5]

Almost universally known, almost universally thought of as at least half real, he cannot be refused the status of myth. But the myth of what?

It is at first difficult to answer, especially if we take into account the later portions of the Crusoe trilogy. For Defoe at once cashed in on the success of the *Strange and Surprising Adventures of Robinson Crusoe* with two other books, the *Farther Adventures* and the *Serious Reflections*. They complicate the answer because, though the character is the same, he is no longer on the island. But, perhaps, there is no need to consider them in detail. Myth always tends in transmission to be whittled down to a single, significant situation. Hardly anyone knows the later books of the trilogy; the stark facts of the hero's island existence occupy almost all our attention, and the rest is largely forgotten, or plays a very secondary role. Even the other portions of the first volume of the trilogy, comprising the early adventures and the eventual return to civilization, though better known, are hardly part of the myth, which retains only the island episode. But even if we ask what is the essential social meaning of that one episode, that solitude, many answers suggest themselves.

Defoe himself gives two main explanations for Crusoe's solitude. At times Crusoe feels he is being punished for irreligion;[6] at others for his filial disobedience in leaving home—in the *Farther Adventures* he even accuses himself of having 'killed his father.'[7] But Crusoe as a man isolated from God, or as a modern Oedipus, is not our subject here. For the myth as it has taken shape in our minds is surely not primarily about religious or psychological alienation, nor even about solitude as such. Crusoe lives in the imagination mainly as a triumph of human achievement and enterprise, and as a favourite example of the elementary processes of political economy. So, in our attempt to understand the causes for Crusoe's apotheosis, we will look first at the relationship of his story to some of the enduring traits of our social and economic history.

It is easy to see that *Robinson Crusoe* is related to three essential themes of modern civilization—which we can briefly designate as 'Back to Nature,' 'The Dignity of Labour' and 'Economic Man.' Robinson Crusoe seems to have become a kind of culture-hero representing all three of these related but not wholly congruent ideas. It is true that if we examine what Defoe actually wrote, and may be thought to have intended, it appears that *Robinson Crusoe* hardly supports some of the symbolic uses to which the pressure of the needs of our society has made it serve. But this, of course, is in keeping with the status of *Robinson Crusoe* as a myth, for we learn as much from the varied shapes that a myth takes in men's minds, as from the form in which it first arose. It is not an author, but a society, that metamorphoses a story into a myth, by retaining only what its unconscious needs dictate, and forgetting everything else.

The term 'Back to Nature' covers the many and varied forms of primitivism, of revulsion from the contemporary complexities of civilization into a simpler and more 'natural' order. The movement necessarily features two forms of regress: technological and topographical; a simpler economic structure and its associated rural setting. Both are involved in *Robinson Crusoe*, and it is interesting to see that Rousseau, the great prophet of both these trends, was the first to see in it something which far transcended the status of a mere adventure story. The book played an important role in his imaginative experience, and he frequently referred to it. The most famous reference occurs in *Émile*.[8] There, after announcing that in principle 'he hates books' and that he is determined to correct the predominantly bookish tendency of traditional methods of education, Rousseau solemnly proclaims an exception. One book exists which teaches all that books can teach. It is 'the first that my Émile will read; it will for a long time be the whole contents of his library; and it will always hold an honoured place there . . . What then is this marvellous book? Is it Aristotle? Is it Pliny? Is it Buffon? No, it is *Robinson Crusoe.*'

The hero, alone on his island, deprived of all assistance from his fellows, and nevertheless able to look after himself, is obviously a figure that will enthral readers of all ages. The book's consequent entertainment value renders palatable its moral and philosophical merits which are Rousseau's main concern. We cannot here give a full account of them, but two are particularly relevant. One is based on the descriptions of Crusoe's labours: they will fire Émile's imagination with the practical, natural, and manual education to which he is destined. Bacon, Comenius and Locke had urged this change of emphasis, but Rousseau takes it very much further; Defoe's story, a box of tools, and the philosopher of Geneva, these will suffice Émile: anything more would be superfluous, nay vicious.

But the pattern which Émile must imitate is not only that of the simple life of toil. Crusoe also stands for another of Rousseau's favourite ideas—radical individualism. To attain this way of life, Rousseau believes that 'the surest way to raise oneself above prejudices and to order one's judgment on the real relationship between things, is to put oneself in the place of an isolated man, and to judge of everything as that man would judge of them, according to their actual usefulness.'[9] Hence, again, the pre-eminent utility of *Robinson Crusoe* as a basic text: for the hero's life is its demonstration.

The book as Defoe wrote it (strictly speaking, the *Life and Strange Surprising Adventures* as Saint Hyacinthe and Van Effen transposed it into the more formal French literary tradition)[10] is not perfect. So Rousseau proposes a version freed of all 'fatras';[11] one which was in fact that of the myth. The story was to begin with the shipwreck and to end with the rescue: Émile's book would be less instructive if it ended in the way it actually does—with a return to civilization.

Defoe, of course, would have been surprised at this canonization of his story. His surprise would have been increased by Rousseau's other references where Crusoe becomes a sort of John the Baptist, who in his solitude made straight the ways of the final incarnation of the extravagancies of romantic individualism. For Crusoe is after all a 'solitaire malgré lui,' as Paul Nourrison points out in his *Jean-Jacques Rousseau et Robinson Crusoë*.[12] He is an involuntary and unappreciative prisoner of the beauties of nature. Rousseau was a botanist but Crusoe is a seed merchant: and the moral of his activities is quite different from that which Rousseau extracts. Indeed, if we, perhaps unwisely, attempt to draw any general conclusions from Crusoe's life on the island, it must surely be that out of humanity's repertoire of conceivable designs for living, rational economic benaviour alone is entitled to ontological status. Crusoe 'returns to nature' only according to Defoe's characteristic definition of that accommodating word: in his newspaper the *Review*, Defoe had written that 'Nothing follows the course of Nature more than Trade. There Causes and Consequences follow as directly as day and night.'[13] So in the island the nature of the universe is most importantly manifested in the rationality of the processes of economic life.

There are the 'real relationships between things' which Crusoe discovers, relationships whose value and interest come from the way they help man to secure the maximum utility from his environment.

Defoe's 'nature' appeals not for adoration but for exploitation: the island solitude is an exceptional occasion not for undisturbed self-communion, but for strenuous efforts at self-help. Inspired with this belief, Crusoe observes nature, not with the eyes of a pantheist primitive, but with the calculating gaze of colonial capitalism; wherever he looks he sees acres that cry out for improvement, and as he settles down to the task he glows, not with noble savagery, but purposive possession.

The interest of Rousseau and Defoe in a 'state of nature' has only one motive in common: it and it alone will allow them to realize without interference their own thwarted vocations. The island offers exemplary opportunities for total *laisser-faire*: or perhaps we should say, for 'Laisse-moi faire'—to put the doctrine in psychological terms, terms which help to explain its appeal to Rousseau.

But the vocations are different, and indeed contradictory. The primitive setting of the island which is Rousseau's goal is only a starting point for Crusoe. He finds himself on a desert island, but he has no intention of letting it remain as such. Rousseau wanted to flee the complication and corruptions of the town, to take refuge in a solitary pastoral retreat: Defoe's solution of the dilemma is much more deeply representative of our culture. If the pace gets too fast at home—go overseas. Not to pastoral retreats but to colonies. There the imagination is fired by a splendid prospect which shows the true and necessary conclusion of the ancient conflict between urban and rural ways of life. That conflict can only be resolved in one way—by the urbanization of the countryside. The new culture-hero's task is done only when he has taken possession of his colony and stocked it with an adequate labour force; presumably Rousseau did not read *The Farther Adventures of Robinson Crusoe* where his favourite hero rejoices that 'never was there such a little city in a wood.'[14] But this is the ultimate message of Defoe's story. The most desolate island cannot retain its natural order; wherever the white man brings his rational technology there can only be man-made order, and the jungle itself must succumb to the irresistible teleology of capitalism.

That is the direction which Defoe gives his story. It is fundamentally anti-primitivist. If many readers have interpreted it as a 'back to nature' story, they have done so to satisfy their own needs, and contrary to

Defoe's general development of his theme. The implications of *Robinson Crusoe* are equally equivocal as regards the 'Dignity of Labour': but the immediate justification for seeing in it a panegyric of work is a good deal stronger.

Rousseau saw Defoe's story as an object lesson in the educational virtues of manual labour; and Crusoe does indeed draw the correct moral from this activity:

> By stating and squaring everything by reason, and by making the most rational judgment of things, every man may be in time master of every mechanic art. I had never handled a tool in my life, and yet in time, by labour, application and contrivance, I found at last that I wanted nothing but I could have made it, especially if I had had tools.[15]

The pleasures of this discovery to Crusoe and his readers are largely the result of the Division of Labour. The terms is Adam Smith's, but he was to a large extent anticipated by Defoe's contemporary, Bernard Mandeville.[16] The process to which the term refers, and which, of course, began very early in human history, was at that time as far advanced in England as anywhere. This advanced development of the division of labour is an important condition of the creation and immediate success of *Robinson Crusoe,* just as the later accelerated development of the process is a condition of the subsequent triumph of the myth. For the main processes by which man secures food, clothing, and shelter are only likely to become interesting when they have become alien to his common, everyday experience. To enjoy the description of the elementary productive processes reveals a sophisticated taste. Obviously, primitive peoples can never forget for a day what Crusoe announces with the tones of one making a discovery: 'It might be truly said that now I began to work for my bread. 'Tis a little wonderful, and what I believe few people have thought much upon, viz., the strange multitude of little things necessary in the providing, producing, curing, dressing, making and finishing this one article of bread.'[17] The account continues for seven pages, and each detail is new or at least unfamiliar, and reminds us of the vast ignorance that separated production and consumption in the London of Defoe's day, an ignorance that has inevitably increased since then, and that surely explains much of the fascination we find in reading the detailed descriptions of Crusoe's island labours.

Rousseau was very much aware of these factors. In his political and economic writings the development of the arts and sciences past the stage of patriarchal simplicity, and the consequent growth of the division of labour, urbanization, and the political state, are the villains.[18] One deplorable result is to separate manual from mental labour. For Rousseau's purposes, therefore, *Robinson Crusoe* was a valuable corrective to the unnatural intellectualism which society inflicts upon the middle class.

Progressive education and the arts and crafts movement owe a good deal to Rousseau's pages on *Robinson Crusoe* in *Émile*. Educationalists try to rectify many of the results of the division of labour and of urbanization, by including in the curriculum many of the practical and manual activities which Crusoe pursued on the island, and which Rousseau recommended for his pupil. In the adult sphere, many reformers have attempted to bridge the gap between the allegedly inventive, satisfying and humanizing processes of primitive methods of production, and the dehumanizing effects of most economic activities under capitalism. The Arts and Crafts movement, for example, and the cult of the rough edge, are two of the most obvious attempts to remedy the social and esthetic effects of the division of labour in industrial capitalism with an artificial primitivism in technique and way of life. The same attempted diagnosis and remedy—in which one can often detect a residue of moral and religious overtones—can be traced in many of the modern forms of leisure activity. It seems typical of our civilization to try to palliate the distortions of specialization by re-introducing the basic economic processes in the guise of recreations. In school, and in later life, it is suggested, by such pursuits as gardening, home-weaving, woodwork, the keeping of pets, we can all partake of Crusoe's character-forming satisfactions.

There are other aspects of the glorification of labour which are relevant to the function of *Robinson Crusoe* as a myth. Many political reformers since Rousseau have been occupied with the idea of rectifying the effects of the division of labour in the whole of the economic and political system. Both on the right and the left they have tried to realize in practice, by new social arrangements, the ideal of the dignity of labour.

For Marx, man and man's universe are the products of work, and his political system was designed with the idea that human labour under changed conditions could undo the contemporary estrangement of most men from their labour, and recreate a society where all economic activities would increase each individual's moral stature. William Morris and the Guild Socialists in advocating a return to a simpler communal economy suggested a different road: but they were trying to achieve the same moral end, and accepted, in the main, Marx's analysis of the real conditions of human labour in the society of their day. And on the right, Samuel Smiles, for example, was also trying to persuade us that hard work even in the present state of society is the key to all: that 'labor omnia vincit.'[19] Much of Carlyle's political theory and moral teaching derives from his idea that the great lesson is 'Know what thou canst work at.' All these and many others—educationalists, moralists, social and political reformers, publicists, economic theorists—seem to base themselves upon a dogma which finds its supreme narrative realization on Crusoe's island.

The reader's ignorance of the basic processes of production is not the only source of the appeal of Crusoe's island labours. He is also affected by the obscure ethical and religious overtones which pervade Defoe's intense concentration upon each stage of Crusoe's exertions. Eventually, they fasten upon our imaginative life a picture of the human lot as heroic only when productive, and of man as capable of redemption only through untiring labour. As we read we share in an inspiring and yet wholly credible demonstration of the vitality and interest of all the basic economic pursuits. If we draw a moral, it can only be that for all the ailments of man and his society, Defoe confidently prescribes the therapy of work.

The extent both of Defoe's concern with labour, and that of the whole ideology of our culture, is certainly unprecedented. Older cultural traditions would probably have seen *Robinson Crusoe* as a glorification of the purely contingent (if not wholly deplorable) aspects of human experience. Certainly most of their myths, the Golden Fleece, Midas, and the Rheingold are concerned, not with the process by which people ordinarily manage to subsist, but with the sudden magical seizure of wealth: they are inspired by the prospect of never having to work again.

Defoe's interest in labour is part of the ideology of a new and vast historical process. The dignity of labour is ultimately the creed of the religion of capitalism. In this religion Marx figures as the arch-schismatic who—like all heretics—became so by taking one part of the creed too seriously and trying to apply it universally and inconveniently.

It is impossible to deal summarily with this creed. But some attention to that part of it which is directly related to the creation of *Robinson Crusoe* seems necessary.

It is no accident that the idea of the dignity of labour sounds typical of the Victorian Age, for it was then that the new ideology was most publicly and variously established. But actually, of course, the Gospel of Work was by no means new even in 1719. In Greece, Cynics and Stoics had opposed the denigration of manual labour which is a necessary part of a slave-owning society's scale of values. In the Christian tradition labour had never been a dishonourable estate. In the sixteenth century, Protestantism, in harmony with the obscure needs of social and economic change, revived and expanded an old belief until it loomed much larger in the total picture of the human lot. The Biblical view that labour was a curse for Adam's disobedience was displaced by the idea that hard work—untiring stewardship of the gifts of God— was a paramount ethical obligation.

The extent of this shift of values can be measured by comparing Defoe's attitude to work with that of Sir Thomas More. In More's *Utopia* hours of work are limited to six, and all surpluses of production are redistributed in the form of extra holidays.[20] Defoe, in *The Complete Tradesman,* proposes very long hours, and insists that leisure activities, even an inordinate craving for sermons, must be kept in check.[21] The same tendency can be observed in the practice of Robinson Crusoe, to whom More's ideal would have seemed moral laxness. For Crusoe hard work seems to be a condition of life itself, and we notice that the arrival of Friday is a signal, not for increased leisure, but for expanded production.

One of the reasons for the canonization of *Robinson Crusoe* is certainly its consonance with the modern view that labour is both the most valuable form of human activity in itself, and at the same time the only reliable way of developing one's spiritual biceps. Defoe's version of this attitude is at times overtly religious in tone. Crusoe's successful improvisations, his perfectly controlled economy, foreshadow his ultimate standing in the divine design. Defoe has taken the idea from his own dissenting milieu, and from its conduct books, whose message has been made familiar to us today in the writings of Weber, Troeltsch and Tawney, and given it a fascinating narrative form.

The combination of this aspect of the ideology of Ascetic Protestantism, or Puritanism, with a kind of return to nature, is particularly happy. Defoe thereby embodies in the same story two historically associated aspirations of the bourgeois class with whom he and his hero have been long and justly identified. In his epic of individual enterprise he bequeathed them both a programme of further economic action, and a figure on whom to project a quasi-religious mystique which retained from the ebbing fervours of Calvinism its essential social and economic teaching. The programme of action is Empire: and it includes, as we have seen, temporary submission to primitivism, or at least to the lure of the wide open places. The mystique is one which distracts attention from the enormous and rapidly growing differences between the kinds of work and their economic rewards, by lumping them together under the one word 'labour,' and erecting a creed which bestows the same high 'dignity' on *all* forms of activity which are subsumed under that one word.

That the mystique of the Dignity of Labour helped to ensure the later success of *Robinson Crusoe* as a myth seems certain. It needed a gospel. But much of what Defoe actually wrote had to be overlooked. This may seem surprising, since Defoe, the complacent apologist of nascent industrial capitalism, certainly approved of the new ideology. But as a writer his eye was so keenly on the object, and second thoughts so rarely checked the flow of his pen, that he reported, not his wishes, but the plausible image of the moment, what he knew people would actually do. So it is that he tells us much which, if analysed, questions not only the simple message of the myth, but even some of his own cherished beliefs. And as these details do not protrude, we must consider them a little more closely.

On the desert island Robinson Crusoe turns his forsaken estate into a triumph. This is a flagrant unreality. Other castaways in the past, including Defoe's main model, Alexander Selkirk, were reduced to an extremely primitive condition, and in the space of a few years.[22] Harassed by fear, dogged by ecological degradation, they sank more and more to the level of animals: in some authentic cases they forgot the use of speech, went mad or died of inanition. One book which Defoe had almost certainly read, *The Voyages and Travels of J. Albert de Mandelso,* tells of two such cases: of a Frenchman who, after two years of solitude on Mauritius, tore his clothing to pieces in a fit of madness brought on by a diet of raw tortoise;[23] and of a Dutch seaman on St. Helena who disinterred the body of a buried comrade and set out to sea in the coffin.[24]

Defoe's readers, perhaps, from their own ordinary experiences of solitude, may suspect as much, even if in a less dramatic form. But as they read *Robinson Crusoe* they forget that isolation can be painful or boring, that it tends in their own lives towards apathetic animality and mental derangement. Instead, they rejoice to find that isolation can be the beginning of a new realization of the potentialities of the individual. Their inertias are cheered by a vicarious participation in Crusoe's twenty-three years of lonely and triumphant struggle. They imagine themselves to be sharing each representative step in his conquest of the environment, and perform with him a heartening recapitulation of humanity's success story.

To all who feel isolated or who get tired of their job—and who at times does not?—the story has a deep appeal and sends our critical faculties asleep. Inspired by the theme, and blinded, perhaps, by our wishes and dreams, we forget the subtle ways by which a consolatory unreality has been made to appear real.

The psychological unreality has its complement in the material one. The normal economic picture—that known to most of Defoe's readers—has been tampered with, unobtrusively but decisively. Defoe's hero—unlike most of us—has been endowed with the basic necessities for the successful exercise of free enterprise. He is not actually a primitive or a proletarian or even a professional man, but a capitalist. He owns, freehold, an estate which is rich, though unimproved. It is not a desert island in the geographical sense; it is merely barren of owners or competitors, and, above all, the very event which brings him there, the shipwreck, which is supposed to be a retributive disaster, is in fact a miraculous present of the means of production, a present rendered particularly felicitous by the death of all the other passengers. Crusoe complains that he is 'reduced to a state of nature'; in fact he secures from the wreck 'the biggest magazine of all kinds . . . that ever was laid out . . . for one man.'[25]

The possession of this original stock, which Defoe's imitators usually retain, usually on a more lavish and less utilitarian scale, is the major practical unreality overlooked by many of his admirers of the classic idyll of individual enterprise. Yet it alone is enough to controvert the myth's wishful affirmation of a flagrant economic naivety—the idea that anyone has ever attained comfort and security entirely by his own efforts.

The myth demanded that the storm be presented as a tragic peripety, although it is really the *deus ex machina* which makes its message plausible. Some such legerdemain was necessary before solitary labour could even appear to be not an alternative to a death sentence, but a solution to the perplexities of economic and social reality.

The dignity of labour is salvaged, then, under the most apparently adverse conditions, mainly because Crusoe has been lucky with capital stock. One wonders whether his 'instinct of workmanship' would have been of any avail if he had really begun from scratch. Certainly Johann Heinrich Campe, the head master of the *Philanthropium* at Dessau, felt that there was a logical objection here which should be countered. He acted on Rousseau's suggestion that only the island episode was improving, and produced a *Nouveau Robinson* for the young which superseded Defoe's original version both in France and Germany. In it, the stock of tools was omitted.[26]

This version imposes a severe strain on the credulity of its readers; at least on that of anyone who does not live in a *Philanthropium*. But even if we grant the possibility of an isolated man reaching a high technological level unaided, there remain other more drastic difficulties in interpreting *Robinson Crusoe* as a myth of autarkic individual enterprise—difficulties based on the fact that the island is, after all, an island, and that whatever happens there is exceptional and does not seem to happen anywhere else.

On the island there is—with one exception to which we shall return— only real wealth. The perplexities of money and the price mechanism do not exist. There is there, as perhaps nowhere else, a direct relation between production and consumption. That is one obvious reason why we should not argue from it to our society; another follows from the fact that Crusoe did not want to go to the island, and once there, doesn't want to stay. The fact that he is forced to be a model of industry does not mean that he likes work. Actually, in the total setting of the trilogy, it becomes quite clear that Crusoe regards his little profits on the island only as a consolation prize. What he wanted (and later obtained) were unearned increments from the labour of others. In Brazil, he had soon tired even of the tasks of a sugar plantation owner, and it was his quest of the more spectacular rewards of the slave trade which took him to the island.[27] To use Max Weber's distinction, he preferred the speculative rewards of 'adventurer's capitalism' to the uneventful, though regular, increments which are typical of the modern economic order.[28] And after Crusoe leaves the island, he again succumbs to the lure of foreign trade, which at that time gave the highest and quickest returns on capital.[29] It is only on his island that Crusoe shows the regulated diligence combined with accurate planning and stocktaking which is so important in modern economic organization. Defoe knew this theoretically; he dealt with such matters in his economic manuals. But he himself had not been able to carry out his economic ideals into practice. They were to be realized only on Crusoe's 'island of despair' which is actually a utopia, though of a new and peculiar kind.

Most utopias have been based upon the ideal of a more harmonious relationship among men. Those of Plato and More are wholly social in inspiration. They, and many later utopias, are also characterized by a certain static quality, and by the fact that people seem to do much less work and get much more for it than in the real world. But this new utopia is the answer, not to the easy and expansive yearnings of the heart for individual happiness and social harmony, nor even to Crusoe's acquisitive instincts; it is the answer only to a very rigorous conception of what kind of life Defoe feels is good for other people.

Crusoe, in fact, has been stranded in the utopia of the Protestant Ethic. There temptation, whether economic or moral, is wholly absent. Crusoe's energies cannot be deflected, either by the picnic promises of pastoral utopias, or by the relaxing and uneconomic piety of the hermits and mystics who are the heroes of an earlier form of Christianity, heroes whose faith is measured by their certainty that 'God will provide.' On Crusoe's island, unremitting toil is obligatory; there, and only there, it is instinct both with moral value and calculable personal reward.

If we look further afield for economic motivation in Defoe, if we leave the island, we find a very different picture. The other adventures of Robinson Crusoe, and the lives of Defoe's other heroes and heroines do not point in the direction of the dignity of labour. Defoe knew very well that the normal social conditions of his time caused very different adjustments to the environment. Moll Flanders, Roxana, and Colonel Jacque satisfy their needs in ways which no one would propose for imitation. Indeed their exploits demonstrate quite another type of political economy, and point the moral that—to those outside Crusoe's island, and without his heaven-bestowed capital—'La propriéte, c'est le vol.'[30]

Defoe, then, is a realist about the individual and his economic environment. He has no illusions about the dignity of the labours of most people in the England of his day. He expressed their lot in a moving passage which William Morris used as epigraph to his lecture on 'The Art of the People'; 'And the men of labour spend their strength in daily struggling for bread to maintain the vital strength they labour with: so living in a daily circulation of sorrow, living but to work, and working but to live, as if daily bread were the only end of a wearisome life, and a wearisome life the only occasion of daily bread.'

If we wish to trace in Defoe any universal and overriding idea it is certainly not that of the dignity of labour as a social fact or even as a moral dogma. The key to the basic motivation of his characters and the hypothesis that best explains their history both apply to Crusoe. For he is only a special case of economic man. Just as the doctrine of the dignity of labour can be understood as the optimistic and deluding myth which hides the realities involved in the division of labour, so the fortitude of Defoe's isolated man withdraws from general attention the true lineaments of that lonely and unlovely archetype of our civilization, *homo economicus*, who is also mirrored in *Robinson Crusoe*.

Homo economicus is, of course, a fiction. There has long been a conflict about the utility of the abstraction. Briefly, the classical political economists found in the idea of Robinson Crusoe, the solitary individual on a desert island, a splendid example for their system-building. On the other hand, their critics who, like Marx, were concerned to prove that economics can be a guide to reality only when it is a historical and a social science, have denied the relevance of Robinson Crusoe to any realistic economic thinking.

Marx began his polemic against classical political economy by insisting on the social nature of production. He, therefore, attacked the starting points of Adam Smith and Ricardo—the isolated hunters and fishers, who were, he said, 'Robinsonades,' and belonged to 'the insipid illusions of the Eighteenth Century.'[31] Later, in *Capital*, he appropriated Crusoe to support his own theory of value. For Crusoe, 'in spite of the variety of his work . . . knows that his labour whatever its form, is but the activity of one and the same Robinson, and consequently, that it consists of nothing but different modes of human labour . . . All the relations between Robinson and the objects that form this wealth of his own creation, are here so simple and clear as to be intelligible without exertion.'[32] But it is only on the island that the value of any object is directly proportional to the quantity of labour expended upon it. In Western capitalism the rewards of labour and the price of commodities are subject to market considerations which are capricious and unjust, especially to labour.[33] The use of Crusoe as an example therefore distracts attention from the dark realities of the economic system as it is.

Marx does not make the useful polemic point which Crusoe's fortunate acquisition of capital might have afforded him. Nor does he mention the extent to which his personality embodies the moral evils which he ascribed to capitalism. This is no doubt because he is using Crusoe only as an example of one particular theme, and not for any general purpose. For actually Crusoe exemplifies another aspect of Marx's thought; the process of alienation by which capitalism tends to convert man's relationships with his fellows, and even to his own personality, into commodities to be manipulated.

This view of economic man is not, of course, limited to Marx. Max Weber's idea that the Protestant Ethic involves a thorough systematization of behavior according to rational norms of personal profit is very similar,[34] and so is Tawney's picture of the acquisitive society composed of individuals pursuing their individual interests without any recognition of social or moral solidarity.[35] But these theoretical formulations had long before been anticipated by literary realization. For, as an ironic commentary upon the myth, the book of *Robinson Crusoe* depicts in its casual reports of the hero's behaviour and of his occasional parenthetic reflections, the shameless and pervasive impact of the cash nexus upon the character and personal relationships of the archetypal economic man. Defoe has supplied the antidote to the myth of his unwitting creation—not only in the incidental unrealities of the plot mentioned above, but also in the sombre touches which are an overt part of his picture of the personality of the protagonist.

Crusoe treats his personal relationships in terms of their commodity value. The Moorish boy, Xury, for example, helps him to escape from slavery, and on another occasion offers to prove his devotion by sacrificing his own life. Crusoe very properly resolves 'to love him ever after,'[36] and promises 'to make him a great man.' But when chance leads them to the Portuguese trader, and its Captain offers Crusoe sixty pieces of eight—twice Judas's figure—he cannot resist the bargain and sells Xury into slavery. He has momentary scruples at the betrayal, it is true, but they are soon economically satisfied by securing from the Captain a promise 'to set him free in ten years if he turn Christian.'[37] Remorse later supervenes, but only when the tasks of his island existence renew his need for a slave.[38]

Slaves, of course, were his original objective in the voyage which brought him to the island. And eventually Providence and his own exertions provide him with Man Friday, who answers his prayers by 'swearing to be my slave for ever.'[39] The unsolicited promise is prophetic, and the development of the relationship is instructive. Crusoe does not ask Friday his name, he gives him one; and there is throughout a remarkable lack of interest in Friday as a person, as someone worth trying to understand or converse with. Even in language—the medium whereby human beings may achieve something more than animal relationships with each other—Crusoe is a strict utilitarian. 'I likewise taught him to say yes and no,'[40] he tells us, though, as Defoe's contemporary critic Gildon not unjustly remarked,[41] Friday still speaks pidgin English at the end of their long association.

Yet Crusoe regards the relationship as ideal. In the period alone with Friday he was 'perfectly and completely happy, if any such thing as complete happiness can be found in a sublunary state.'[42] A functional silence, apparently, adds to the charms of the idyll, broken only by an occasional 'No, Friday' or an abject 'Yes, Master.' Man's social nature is wholly satisfied by the righteous bestowal, or grateful receipt, of benevolent but not undemanding patronage.[43]

Only one doubt ruffles Crusoe's proprietary equanimity. He becomes obsessed with the fear that Friday may be harbouring an ungrateful wish to return to his father and his tribe. But the fear proves groundless and they leave the island together. Crusoe later avoids any possible qualms about keeping Friday in servitude by the deferred altruism of a resolution 'to do something considerable for him, if he outlived me.'[44] Fortunately, no such sacrifice is called for, as Friday dies at sea, faithful to the end, and rewarded only by a brief word of obituary compassion.

Crusoe's attitude to women is also marked by an extreme inhibition of what we now consider to be normal human feelings. There are, of course, none on the island, and their absence is not deplored. When Crusoe does notice the lack of 'society,' he prays for company, but it is for that of a male slave. With Friday, he is fully satisfied by an idyll without benefit of woman. It is an interesting break from the traditional expectations aroused by desert islands, from the *Odyssey* to the *New Yorker*.

Defoe's view of the individual was too completely dominated by the rational pursuit of material self-interest to allow any scope either for natural instinct or for higher emotional needs. Even when Crusoe returns to civilization, sex is strictly subordinated to business. Only after his financial position has been fully secured by a further voyage does he marry, 'and that not either to my disadvantage or dissatisfaction.'[45]

Some of Crusoe's colonists have the same attitude. He tells how they draw lots for five women, and strongly approves of the outcome: 'He that drew to choose first . . . took her that was reckoned the homeliest and eldest of the five, which made mirth enough among the rest . . . but the fellow considered better than any of them, that it was application and business that they were to expect assistance in as much as anything else; and she proved the best wife of all the parcel.'[46]

The conflict is put very much in Weber's terms.[47] Sex is seen as a dangerously irrational factor in life which interferes with the pursuit of rational self-interest: and economic and moral worth in the male does not guarantee him a profitable matrimonial investment. On his colony 'as it often happens in the world (what the wise ends of God's Providence are in such a disposition of things I cannot say), the two honest fellows had the two worst wives; and the three reprobates, that were scarce worth hanging, . . . had three clever, diligent, careful and ingenious wives.'[48] It is therefore no accident that love plays a very minor part in Crusoe's own life, and is eliminated from the scene of his greatest triumphs.

One could illustrate the ideology of *homo economicus* at much greater length from *Robinson Crusoe*. Everything is measured from the rational, a-social, and anti-traditional standards of individual self-interest, and some of the results are not pleasant. But these results are surely lamentable, but necessary, corollaries of the social process which the story reflects; and the common tendency to overlook them in the hero must be attributed to the obscure forces that guard the idols of our society and shape its myths.

Malinowski has said that 'myth is . . . an indispensable ingredient of all culture.'[49] It would indeed appear to be so, but I have no wish to be numbered among those who would prove our common humanity by putting us back on a level with the Trobriand islanders. The aim of this essay is rather to do something they don't do; that is, scrutinize one small item of our cultural repertoire in the hope of clarifying its role in the past and present of our society.

Much has had to be omitted. The appeal of the adventure in itself, for example, and the theological aspect of the story, which modifies the picture considerably. Some of the social and economic matters have been treated somewhat cavalierly. The case of Robinson Crusoe as *homo economicus* has been somewhat oversimplified. For Defoe does suggest on at least one occasion (the famous episode when Crusoe comes across a hoard of gold on the island and, after declaiming on its uselessness, 'upon second thoughts' takes it away)[50] the irrationality of the goals which shape the character of economic man and which affect his actions more powerfully than his own understanding of his real needs. And, of course, in a wintry sort of way, Crusoe has his pleasures. He does not, as Selkirk had done, dance with the goats, but he does at least occasionally supplement occupational by recreational therapy. Still, it seems true to say that the reality of Defoe's masterpiece, its ultimate referent, is economic man. So that if we seek a general meaning for his solitude it must be the social atomization which *homo economicus* brings in his train. That, surely, is the main historical basis of this metaphor of human solitude which has haunted the western consciousness. And the need to obscure the regrettable social and psychological corollaries of the rise of economic individualism must explain much of the very general disinclination to see the darker side of Defoe's hero.

174

It is certainly curious to observe how all but universal has been the reluctance to challenge Crusoe as a model for imitation and inspiration. In some cases there may be other explanations for this. The myth of national character, for example. Some foreign commentators have had ulterior motives in presenting Robinson Crusoe as the typical Englishman. Marx calls him a 'true-born Briton';[51] and Dibelius echoes the impeachment of a nation of shopkeepers with more obvious venom.[52] For France, de Vogüé, in his study of what he calls 'Le livre anglais,' though more polite, is equally disparaging by implication.[53] What is curious is to find that most English writers, too, have tended to accept Crusoe as the typical Englishman, apparently undeterred by any of his anti-social idiosyncrasies.

There have been occasional dissentients. Dickens, for example, was revolted by Crusoe's attitude to the death of Friday, and to women generally; and he wrote in a letter that Defoe must have been a 'precious dry and disagreeable article himself.'[54] Ruskin—another critic of the mentality of industrial capitalism—uses the phrase 'a very small, perky, contented, conceited, Cock-Robinson-Crusoe, sort of life.'[55] Yet on the whole, Crusoe has been accepted as the typical Englishman by his fellow-countrymen, although, as it happens, Defoe made his father 'a foreigner of Bremen.'

In some ways, of course, the character of Robinson Crusoe is a national one. Courage, practical intelligence, not making a fuss, these are not the least of the virtues, and their combination in Crusoe does seem to be according to an English pattern. But these virtues cannot be regarded as exemplary and sufficient. Dickens wrote of *Robinson Crusoe* that it is 'the only instance of a universally popular book that could make no one laugh and no one cry.'[56] This suggests the major flaw. Defoe's epic of the stiff upper lip does not propose a wholly satisfactory ideal. For Crusoe's merits are combined with a stolid and inhibited self-sufficiency which is disastrous both for the individual and for society. That is Crusoe's *hubris*—a defect not unlike Rousseau's 'hypertrophie du moi.'

There is, even on Crusoe's own showing, very little content or peace in this way of life. Pascal said that the misery of man can be traced from a single fact, his inability to stay still in his own room. Crusoe can never stay still. His brisk and businesslike exterior cannot wholly conceal the deadening compulsion of an alienation which is assuaged only by ceaseless economic activity. He is modern economic man putting a poker face on the fate that Pascal found intolerable. 'Nothing else offering, and finding that really stirring about and trading, the profit being so great, and, as I may say, certain, had more pleasure in it, and more satisfaction to the mind, than sitting still, which, to me especially, was the unhappiest part of life. . . .'[57] So, in the *Farther Adventures*, he sets out on yet another lucrative Odyssey.

His author, deeply implicated in the character that Walter de la Mare has called Defoe's 'Elective Affinity,'[58] appears to approve. But he certainly does not see his work in an optimistic vein: 'Nothing else offering . . .' suggests why. Defoe wrestles with the meanings of his creation in the essay 'On Solitude' which begins the *Serious Reflections*. The essay is inconclusive, and there are several different strands of thought in it. But the bitterness of isolation as the primordial fact repeatedly moves Defoe to a great fervour of communication. One of the passages seems a particularly moving commentary on the isolation which the pursuit of individual self-interest creates in the human spirit.

What are the sorrows of other men to us, and what their joy? Sometimes we may be touched indeed by the power of sympathy, and a secret turn of the affections; but all the solid reflection is directed to ourselves. Our meditations are all solitude in perfection; our passions are all exercised in retirement; we love, we hate, we covet, we enjoy, all in privacy and solitude. All that we communicate of those things to any other is but for their assistance in the pursuit of our desires; the end is at home; the enjoyment, the contemplation, is all solitude and retirement; it is for ourselves we enjoy, and for ourselves we suffer.[59]

The loneliness of economic man was a tragic fact. Many Stoic or Christian thinkers might have said 'We love, we hate . . . all in privacy and solitude.' But 'we covet, we enjoy' is characteristic of a later ideology. To the solitude of the soul which so many have expressed, Defoe adds 'all we communicate of those things to any other is but for their assistance in the pursuit of our desires.' A rationally-conceived self-interest makes a mockery of speech, and suggests silence.

So, although *Robinson Crusoe* is a mutation of a very ancient theme, its specific cause and nature are wholly modern. And now that it is possible to see fairly clearly the realities of which Crusoe is the menacing symbol, we must surely question his desirability as an ideal prototype. What has happened in the last 200 years has shown that where Defoe's new culture-hero is admitted into the pantheon of myth, he soon crowds out or subjugates the other figures, whether comic or tragic, round whom have gathered those more generous aspirations that occasionally mitigate the bitterness of history.

NOTES

1. For a survey of the work done on this subject, with very full references, see PHILIP BABCOCK GOVE, *The Imaginary Voyage in Prose Fiction* . . . (New York, 1941). The study of *Robinsonaden* is particularly connected with the name of Hermann Ullrich, author of *Robinson und Robinsonaden* (Weimar, 1898), and *Defoes Robinson Crusoe, Geschichte eines Weltbuches* (Leipzig, 1924). H. C. Hutchins has studied the early editions of *Robinson Crusoe* in his *Robinson Crusoe and Its Printing* (New York, 1925), and William-Edward Mann is responsible for a useful study of *Robinson Crusoë en France* (Paris, 1916).

2. RENÉ POTTIER, *Histoire d'un Village* (Paris, 1941), pp. 171–4.

3. DEFOE, *The Common Reader*, First Series (London, 1925).

4. Cit. MAX GÜNTHER, *Entstehungsgeschichte von Defoes Robinson Crusoe* (Griefswald, 1909), p. 29.

5. *Myth in Primitive Psychology* (London, 1926), pp. 18–9.

6. *The Life and Strange Surprising Adventures of Robinson Crusoe*, ed. George A. Aitken (London, 1902), pp. 41–3, 95–100 and *passim*.

7. *The Farther Adventures of Robinson Crusoe*, ed. G. A. Aitken (London, 1902), pp. 149–50. Also, *Life*, p. 216.

8. *Émile, ou De L'Éducation*, ed. F. and P. Richard (Paris, 1939), pp. 210–4.

9. Ibid., p. 211.

10. See GOVE, *The Imaginary Voyage*, p. 36; MANN, *Robinson Crusoë en France*, pp. 51–5 and 102; W. J. B. PIENAAR, *English Influences in Dutch Literature and Justus Van Effen as Intermediary* (Cambridge, 1929), pp. 248–9.

11. *Émile*, p. 211.

12. Paris, 1931, p. 30. This hostile and somewhat exaggerated polemic discusses Rousseau's other references to *Robinson Crusoe*.

13. *Review*, II, 26; cit., WALTER WILSON, *Memoirs of the Life and Times of Daniel Defoe* (London, 1830), II, 319.

14. p. 118.

15. *Life*, p. 74.

16. *The Fable of the Bees*, ed. F. B. Kaye (Oxford, 1924), I, cxxxiv–cxxxv, II, 142n.

17. *Life*, p. 130.

18. See ARTHUR LOVEJOY, 'The Supposed Primitivism of Rousseau's *Discourse on Inequality*', *Essays in the History of Ideas* (Baltimore, 1948).

19. Smiles gives this epigraph to his delightfully entitled *Life and Labour or Characteristics of Men of Industry, Culture and Genius*, attributing it to Virgil. Virgil actually wrote, of the coming of the Age of Iron:

labor omnia vicit
improbus et duris urgens in rebus egestas. (*Georgics*, I, 145–6)

The time-hallowed misquotation is an interesting example of the forces which have made *Robinson Crusoe* into a myth. That labour does and always will conquer all is a modern view which cannot be derived from Virgil. There seems no reason to consider *vicit* as a gnomic perfect: Conington remarks that 'the poet is narrating, not uttering a sentiment,' although he approves of the general characterization of the *Georgics* as a 'glorification of labor.' (*P. Vergili Maronis Opera* . . . (London, 1881), I, 151–5). F. Plessis and P. Lejay comment acidly: 'Le poëte n'éxalte pas le travail pour lui-même, ce qui est une affectation toute moderne, une idée d'Encyclopédiste, mais pour ses résultats.' (*Œuvres* (Paris, 1945), p. 29). L. P. Wilkinson, in a recent article, writes, 'The text of Virgil's Gospel of Work was not *laborare et orare,* as some have suggested, but *laborare et vivere.*' ('The Intention of Virgil's *Georgics,' Greece and Rome,* XVIII (1950), 24.) Virgil's interpretation of the end of the Golden Age, bears obvious resemblances to the Christian, and especially Protestant, welcome to the loss of Eden; as Adam says in *Paradise Lost,* 'Idleness had been worse.' See also A. LOVEJOY and G. BOAS, *Primitivism and Related Ideas in Antiquity* (Baltimore, 1935), p. 370.

20. *Ideal Commonwealths,* ed. H. Morley (London, 1899), pp. 97, 101.

21. *The Complete English Tradesman* (Oxford, 1841), I, 32–4. See also, A. E. LEVETT, 'Daniel Defoe,' *Social and Political Ideas of Some English Thinkers of the Augustan Age,* ed. F. J. C. Hearnshaw (London, 1928), p. 180.

22. A. W. SECORD, *Studies in the Narrative Method of Defoe* (Illinois, 1924), p. 26.

23. Ibid., p. 28.

24. Ibid.

25. *Life,* p. 60.

26. See MANN, *Robinson Crusoë en France,* pp. 85–101. It was this version which H. H. Gossen used in deriving economic laws from *Crusoe* (W. STARK, *The Ideal Foundations of Economic Thought* (London, 1948), p. 159): and was probably that of FRÉDÉRIC BASTIAT, *Harmonies Économiques* (Bruxelles, 1850), pp. 99f, 214f.

27. *Life,* pp. 40–2. See also, *Farther Adventures,* p. 66, where Defoe shows his awareness of the dangers of this type of enterprise by attributing it to idle ne'er-do-wells.

28. WEBER, *The Protestant Ethic and the Spirit of Capitalism,* trans. T. Parsons (London, 1930), pp. 21, 74–8 and *The Theory of Economic and Social Organization,* trans. T. Parsons and A. M. Henderson (New York, 1947), pp. 50–2, 279ff.

29. A. L. MERSON, 'The Revolution and the British Empire,' *The Modern Quarterly,* IV (1949), 152.

30. J. Sutherland points out that on the island, although stealing is impossible the satisfactory emotions of successful theft are suggested by the looting of the wreck. *Defoe* (London, 1937), p. 232.

31. *A Contribution to the Critique of Political Economy* (1st ed., 1859: New York, 1904), pp. 265–6.

32. Chap. I, section iv.

33. Defoe had experienced this for himself. His bookseller, Taylor, owned the whole share of all three parts of *Robinson Crusoe* and is said to have made his fortune by it. (HUTCHINS, *Robinson Crusoe and Its Printing,* p. 185.)

Defoe worked indefatigably for most of his seventy years of life, and though he was at times rich, he died alone, hiding from a creditor. (SUTHERLAND, *Defoe*, pp. 269–74.)

34. WEBER, *Theory of Economic and Social Organization*, pp. 191–249 *et passim*.

35. R. H. TAWNEY, *The Acquisitive Society* (London, 1921), p. 32.

36. *Life*, p. 27.

37. Ibid., p. 36.

38. Ibid., p. 164.

39. Ibid., p. 226.

40. Ibid., p. 229.

41. *Robinson Crusoe Examin'd and Criticis'd;* . . . ed. P. Dottin (London and Paris, 1923), pp. 70, 78, 118.

42. *Life*, pp. 245–6.

43. The Crusoe-Friday relationship is representative in many other ways. Not least in showing how the quest for the white man's burden tends to end in the discovery of the perfect porter and personal servant.

44. *Farther Adventures*, p. 133.

45. *Life*, p. 341.

46. *Farther Adventures*, p. 77.

47. MAX WEBER, *Essays in Sociology*, trans. H. H. Gerth and C. Wright Mills (New York, 1946), p. 350.

48. *Farther Adventures*, p. 78.

49. *Myth in Primitive Psychology*, p. 125.

50. *Life*, p. 62.

51. *Capital*, chap. I, section vi.

52. *Englische Romankunst* (Berlin, 1910), I, 36.

53. *Revue des Deux Mondes*, October 1st, 1895. As is Jean Giraudoux in *Suzanne et le Pacifique* (Paris, 1921), pp. 228–33.

54. JOHN FORSTER, *Life of Charles Dickens*, rev. J. W. T. Ley (London, 1928), p. 611.

55. PETER QUENNELL, *John Ruskin* (London, 1949), p. 15.

56. Loc. cit.

57. p. 214.

58. *Desert Islands and Robinson Crusoe* (London, 1930), p. 7.

59. *Serious Reflections of Robinson Crusoe*, ed. G. A. Aitken (London, 1902), pp. 2–3.

D. NICHOL SMITH

———

Thomson and Burns

EVERYONE of us who is concerned with the teaching of English literature
is aware that whereas there is general agreement about Elizabethan
poetry and the poetry of the seventeenth century, there are at least two
'schools of thought' about the poetry of the eighteenth. To one school
the century is mainly of interest as being the seed-time of the poetry
which blossomed in the days of Wordsworth and Coleridge. Even those
who do not profess adherence to this school can remember the occasions
when as the spirits failed and the eyes grew dim and two or three
questions had yet to be set before the examination paper was complete,
the temptation to jot down something about the first signs of the
'Romantic Revival' proved irresistible. All of us, at least the older of us,
have at some stage been taught to picture the marches and the counter-
marches which, about the middle of the century, began to disturb the
Peace of the Augustans, and the final triumphal onslaught of *Lyrical
Ballads*. The good verse, we were asked to believe, belonged to the
future, and the poor verse or the indifferent verse was in its proper place.
Good poets, like Gray, were said to be born out of their time. Somehow
Nature had made a slip and dropped a poet in an age of prose.

Others prefer the modest alternative that when a poet seems to have
got into the wrong place what is wrong is our idea of the place. Like
every other century the eighteenth was an age of transition, but we need
not therefore assume that its poets were engaged in one long campaign.
The good poets of the eighteenth century spoke frankly about each
other, as poets usually do; and though their aims might be divergent,
they were always as ready as poets have ever been to acknowledge
merit when they found it.

———

From *Some Observations on Eighteenth Century Poetry* [The Alexander Lectures, University of Toronto, 1937] (University of Toronto Press, 1937), 56–
80. Reprinted by permission of the publisher and author.

So far I have chosen to speak mainly of Pope and Johnson.[1] I now turn to two other representative poets of the century—James Thomson and Robert Burns.

Both of them were Scots, and neither could have written as he did had he not been a Scot. Each has been hailed, rightly or wrongly, as introducing a new element into our poetry. The work of every good poet must be in some sense novel. No man, as Johnson said, was ever great by imitation; and whether or not this is invariably true, it is certainly true of the artist. But neither Thomson nor Burns ever imagined himself to be a rebel.

Nor must we imagine that Pope, or Johnson, believed the empire of Wit to be limited and defined. They may have charted the portions of it with which they were familiar, but they knew that it was always expanding. Pope had maintained in the *Essay on Criticism* that anything is permissible provided it succeeds, but that the poet was less likely to succeed if he neglected what could be learned from his great predecessors. Should

> Some lucky licence answer to the full
> The intent proposed, that licence is a rule.

Thomson's *Winter* was a new kind of poem, but it fulfilled its purpose, and Pope welcomed it. He came to know Thomson and in the next edition of *Winter* Thomson inserted a glowing tribute to his friendship:

> Or from the muses' hill will *Pope* descend,
> To raise the sacred hour, to make it smile,
> And with the social spirit warm the heart:
> For tho' not sweeter his own *Homer* sings,
> Yet is his life the more endearing song.

Similarly Pope urged the publication of Akenside's *The Pleasures of Imagination,* a poem so novel that the publisher to whom it was submitted did not know what to make of it. 'I have heard Dodsley, by whom it was published, relate,' says Johnson, 'that when the copy was offered him the price demanded for it, which was an hundred and twenty pounds, being such as he was not inclined to give precipitately, he carried the work to Pope, who, having looked into it, advised him not to make a niggardly offer; for "this was no every-day writer." '

Pope's very excellence, as I have already had occasion to say, was an incentive to younger poets to seek new fields; and they had Pope's encouragement when they proved their competence. This side of Pope's relations with his contemporaries has not yet received the attention which it deserves. The best of all the poets whom he encouraged was Thomson.

With the Union of England and Scotland came the long and endless procession of Scots intent on finding their livelihood in London or elsewhere in the richer south, and among the early stragglers was James Thomson. He left Scotland at the age of twenty-five with 'a poem in his pocket.' It was his *Winter*. Within a few years it was to be one of the four parts of *The Seasons*. He had spent all his youth on the Scottish Border, where his father was a parish minister, or in Edinburgh, where he had himself studied for the ministry at the University.

The traveller who enters Scotland by the Cheviots finds a change in the prospect as he reaches the Border at Carter Bar. He has been passing through miles and miles of the moorland of Northumberland, but on a sudden he looks down, over a hilly foreground, to a richly wooded and cultivated country, with Jedburgh in the near distance, and further off Hawick and Kelso. This was Thomson's country. His early home lay between the rich district to the north and the rough hill country of the Cheviots to the south. The scenery which inspired *The Seasons* was the daily scenery of his youth, viewed through 'a kind of glory.' He may refer to many countries, but what he has experienced as a lad is behind what he tells us. When he writes of frost in winter, and frozen rills, and the death of the shepherd, he is thinking of the Cheviots. The fishing he describes was in the tributaries of the Tweed. His agricultural pictures are suggested by farming in the Merse, one of the richest agricultural districts of Scotland. When he speaks of the joys of bathing in summer, he is recollecting through the beautifying mists of memory the warm seasons by the burns of the Jed Water in the parish of Southdean. That *The Seasons* is in origin a poem from the Scottish Border is disguised by the absence of local references and the purposely general description of the great movements of Nature. Sooner than speak of the Border, Thomson will draw imaginary pictures of the Sahara, or Lapland, or the fate of Siberian exiles. Such passages were introduced when his poem became more ambitious, while he was living in the gentler climate of the south of England. But even in them we discover the recollected emotion as, amid the distractions of the great city, he cherishes the memory of his early home.

Nothing in *The Seasons* has given English readers more trouble than the diction. What Pope thought of it is not on record; evidently it did not obscure the merits of the poem for him. But Johnson could not praise it: 'His diction is in the highest degree florid and luxuriant. . . .

It is too exuberant, and sometimes may be charged with filling the ear more than the mind.' Wordsworth is less judicial, and says bluntly that 'he writes a vicious style.' And I think that all English purists regard it as a vicious style, produced in the main by a forced imitation of Milton. But the English reader is here at a disadvantage. Thomson was a Scot, and to the educated Scot—who has always excelled in compiling dictionaries of the English language, but has not quite the Englishman's sense of the usage of the words which he is so proficient in collecting and defining—the language of *The Seasons* does not offer so great difficulties.

When Thomson was at the University of Edinburgh studying for the ministry, he was reprimanded by the Professor of Divinity for being too poetically splendid in an exercise on the 119th Psalm. He was told that 'if he thought of being useful in the ministry he must keep a stricter rein upon his imagination, and express himself in language intelligible to an ordinary congregation.' A wholesome censure no doubt, and a common censure in Scotland. The Scottish student has always been prone to rhetoric, and his tastes have been judiciously encouraged. The best English treatises on rhetoric were produced by Scottish professors in the eighteenth century. The English chair at Edinburgh is still called the chair of 'Rhetoric and English Literature'; it used to be called the chair of 'Rhetoric and Belles Lettres.' To the present day the Scottish student dearly loves a well-rounded resounding sentence. Not so the English undergraduate. If I may cite my own experience I have never known him rhetorical. His danger is of quite another kind. He may strain after epigram. He likes a sparkling style. If when you are rhetorical you run the risk 'of filling the ear more than the mind,' when you cultivate the epigram there is the risk that your cleverness may miss fire. Both faults are linked to virtues: rhetoric encourages attention to the rhythm of the sentence, and the epigram may conduce to the simple style in which words are not wasted. I believe it is still the experience of a large number of Scots who have followed Thomson and set up their rest in England that they become aware of the need of simplifying their style—of using shorter words now and again, and perhaps fewer words. And again if I may cite my experience, when I return to Scotland and read the leading articles in the newspapers, I get the impression that the vocabulary is slightly heavier than I have become used to in the journalism of the South.

We are apt to forget the large place occupied by Latin in vernacular Scots. Latin was at one time as familiar to the educated Scot as his mother-tongue, and was his means of communication with foreigners.

The Scot abroad made his way with Latin. The Scottish authors who were known abroad wrote in Latin. Scots Law, which is founded on Roman Law, has a larger Latin element than English Law. Latin words were bound to creep into the vernacular. More than that, Latin words have come into English from Scottish usage. An instance is 'narrate,' which is thus defined by Johnson in his *Dictionary*—'to relate, to tell; a word only used in Scotland.' Richardson in his *Clarissa* has 'when I have least to narrate, to speak in the Scottish phrase, I am most diverting.' Here we have the explanation why the Scottish historians and philosophers of the eighteenth century write in a style which seems to the English reader to be over-Latinized in vocabulary, and, as our schoolmasters know, is eminently suitable for conversion into Latin prose. I have heard a speaker in one of the debating societies of Edinburgh use these words when he wished to express agreement with what had just been said—'I homologate the sentiments of the previous speaker.' In Scotland the housewife does not make tea, she infuses it.

On a style naturally rhetorical, and Latinized, Thomson superimposed a Miltonic element. He found in Milton a language after his heart. 'Chimeras huge,' 'in endless mazes, intricate, perplexed,'—such words and phrases as these made their way into *The Seasons* much more easily than we are apt to suppose. *The Seasons* is sometimes spoken of as if it were a long exercise in aureate diction; but it is too vital a poem for its language to be a continuous artifice. The style came easily to Thomson; it was natural to him. We can understand why Wordsworth called it vicious, for it is not a style which could have been cultivated by any good English poet. But I should be surprised if, even to-day, it is perplexing to the home-bred Scot. For myself, who may now have to be excluded from that category, I confess that I am attracted by it. Thomson always seems to me to succeed in conveying the impression which he means to convey.

Johnson detected a change of style in the revisions of *The Seasons*. 'I know not whether they have not lost part of what Temple calls their *race*; a word which, applied to wines, in its primitive sense, means the flavour of the soil.' His observation of the change is only less interesting than his admission of his regret. Thomson's way of writing, like that of other Scots who have left Scotland, was probably modified unconsciously. But after more than twenty years' residence by the banks of the Thames he preserved the Scottish vernacular in his talk. In the brief life written by Robert Shiels, one of Johnson's Scottish assistants on the *Dictionary*, the story is told of a visit paid by an old Edinburgh friend who refused to give his name:

Mr. Thomson came forward to receive him, and looking steadfastly at him (for they had not seen one another for many years) said, 'Troth Sir, I cannot say I ken your countenance well—Let me therefore crave your name.' Which the gentleman no sooner mentioned but the tears gushed from Mr. Thomson's eyes. He could only reply, good God! are you the son of my dear friend, my old benefactor; and then rushing to his arms, he tenderly embraced him; rejoicing at so unexpected a meeting.

This is a vivid picture of a sudden access of emotion on remembering happy days, and Thomson's feelings were always easily moved. We should not be far wrong if we called him the first of the Scottish sentimentalists in English literature. It is sentiment which gives *The Castle of Indolence* its peculiar grace—sentiment which never gets out of control, which is never false or aggressive. Remembrance of Scotland inspires the most famous lines of that poem:

> As when a Shepherd of the *Hebrid-Isles*,
> Plac'd far amid the melancholy Main.

Thomson had seen no more of the Hebrides than of the Sahara or Lapland, but the Hebrides are in Scotland. The emotional element to be found in all his nature pictures in *The Seasons* is their most characteristic quality.

He begins his *Winter* by describing the delight which as a boy he took in wandering over the hilly country near his home in frost and snow:

> Pleas'd, have I, in my cheerful Morn of Life,
> When, nurs'd by careless *Solitude,* I liv'd,
> And sung of Nature with unceasing Joy,
> Pleas'd, have I wander'd thro' your rough Domains;
> Trod the pure, virgin, Snows, my self as pure:
> Heard the Winds roar, and the big Torrent burst:
> Or seen the deep, fermenting, Tempest brew'd,
> In the red, evening, Sky.—Thus pass'd the Time,
> Till, thro' the opening Chambers of the South,
> Look'd out the joyous *Spring,* look'd out, and smil'd.[2]

He knows the

> sensations sweet
> Felt in the blood, and felt along the heart,

that are given by the 'beauteous forms' of Nature; but that other gift 'of aspect more sublime' which Wordsworth speaks of in *Tintern Abbey* Thomson does not reveal. He remains the observer and lover of nature. Her secrets have to be won from her; she is not an *active* teacher; we have to draw our own lessons from what she provides. 'I know no subject more elevating, more amusing,' he says, 'more ready to awake the poetical enthusiasm, the philosophical reflection, and the moral sentiment, than the works of Nature.' He will

> solitary court
> Th' inspiring Breeze; and meditate the Book
> Of Nature, ever open, aiming thence,
> Warm from the Heart, to learn the moral Song.

He meditates the book of Nature. His interests are partly intellectual, partly moral, and we shall agree that what he says comes 'warm from the heart.'

The emotional bearings of Nature on man are his true theme. The fault of Pope's early poems, his *Pastorals* and his *Windsor Forest,* was that they were too purely descriptive. They are accurate in detail, for Pope had lived in the country all his life till he wrote them—and for that matter the Twickenham at which he afterwards lived was still the country by our standards. But they were written 'while pure description held the place of sense.' They do not give us the clue to his own mood. That was the great lesson which Thomson taught the nature poets of the eighteenth century. Johnson has put it in a memorable sentence: 'The reader of *The Seasons* wonders that he never saw before what Thomson shews him, and that he never yet has felt what Thomson impresses.' But of all Thomson's critics I think that Hazlitt is still the best. Like other Englishmen he did not appreciate Thomson's language, but it could not hide from him the poet.

> Thomson [he says] is the best of our descriptive poets, for he gives most of the poetry of natural description. Others have been quite equal to him, or have surpassed him, as Cowper for instance, in the picturesque part of his art, in marking the peculiar features and curious details of objects;—no one has yet come up to him in giving the sum total of their effects, their varying influences on the mind. . . . Nature in his descriptions is seen growing around us, fresh and lusty as in itself. . . . In a word, he describes not to the eye alone, but to the other senses, and to the whole man. He puts his heart into his subject, writes as he feels, and humanises whatever he touches.

High praise, and the more remarkable as it was written when Hazlitt was familiar with the poetry of Wordsworth. But Wordsworth is not primarily a descriptive poet. He has an unsurpassed power of suggesting a scene in a few words, but he soon takes us far beyond it. The art of Thomson remains purposely pictorial; and this is true of the best nature poetry of the century.

Treating Nature pictorially, he presents it as a background to human activity, the scene on which man has his being. It was more than a background to Wordsworth. But I would suggest that it is not more than a background to most of us, and that even among Wordsworth's most ardent admirers there are few who can bring themselves to think of it habitually, or for any length of time, as he did.

The Seasons won immediate popularity. No one attacked it, no one considered its novelty to be rebellious. It went into many editions, each one of which Thomson carefully revised and augmented; the final edition of the four parts is some fifteen hundred lines longer than the first. Its popularity continued till well into the nineteenth century. I have known a house—it was in Scotland—where a well-bound copy lay on the drawing-room table.

The language of Burns, unlike that of Thomson, does not seem to have detracted from his appreciation by English readers. They may have difficulty in understanding it, but they never mistake it for 'vicious' English. They accept its strange idiom, and, in company with a large number of Scottish enthusiasts, make the best of it.

In one sense Burns was less original than Thomson. He did not have a new subject, or a new manner. He began by imitation, and to the end of his life his ambition was to excel within the tradition. His originality consists of doing better than his Scottish predecessors what they had done. He is content with what he finds, knowing what he can make of it. What generations of Scots had been saying, or trying to say, finds in him its rememberable expression.

We are not to think that Burns's mastery of the craft of words came to him without long practice, nor to forget the old proverb that Heaven helps them who help themselves. In a brave moment he had affected to despise book-learning and had proclaimed the sufficiency of his untutored gifts:

> Gie me ae spark o' Nature's fire,
> That's a' the learning I desire.

187

He had been given this spark of Nature's fire, but no one knew better than he did that he had to learn how to make use of it. 'Excellence in the profession,' he says in a letter written after he had come to his fame, 'is the fruit of industry, labour, attention, and pains'; and there he is talking seriously. From the days when he first had the ambition to write poems of his own he had studied the poems of others.

In a long autobiographical letter he included a full account of his early reading:

> My knowledge of ancient story was gathered from Salmon's and Guthrie's geographical grammars; my knowledge of modern manners, and of literature and criticism, I got from the Spectator.—These, with Pope's works, some plays of Shakespear, Tull and Dickson on Agriculture, The Pantheon, Locke's Essay on the human understanding, Stackhouse's history of the bible, Justice's British Gardiner's directory, Boyle's lectures, Allan Ramsay's works, Taylor's scripture doctrine of original sin, a select Collection of English songs, and Hervey's meditations had been the extent of my reading.

In this remarkable list only Allan Ramsay's works are in the Scottish vernacular; and Burns goes on to show that they were of much less importance to him than the 'select Collection of English songs.'

> The Collection of Songs was my vade mecum.—I pored over them, driving my cart or walking to labor, song by song, verse by verse; carefully noting the true tender or sublime from affectation and fustian.— I am convinced I owe much to this for my critic-craft such as it is.

This Collection has not been convincingly identified; but we have to note that it contained English songs, not Scottish.

> My reading [he continues] was enlarged with the very important addition of Thomson's and Shenstone's works. . . . I had met with a collection of letters by the Wits of Queen Ann's reign, and I pored over them most devoutly. . . . The addition of two more Authors to my library gave me great pleasure; Sterne and McKenzie. Tristram Shandy and the Man of Feeling were my bosom favorites.

Still later he read stray volumes of Richardson's *Pamela* and Smollett's *Count Fathom*.

Burns gave himself an English training. From this account it appears that his reading was mainly in the English literature of his own century, though he also read Shakespeare and Milton. What he thus learned about the art of writing he was to turn to account in his Scottish poems. The crisis in his career came at the age of twenty-three, when he read the poems of Robert Fergusson, and was moved to follow their example. Fergusson, a lawyer's clerk in Edinburgh, had drawn pictures of the life of the capital in the vernacular as it was there spoken, and in traditional Scottish measures. What Fergusson had done for Edinburgh, Burns was to do for his Ayrshire. A few years later, at the age of twenty-seven, he brought out the famous Kilmarnock edition.

A comparison of this edition with Fergusson's *Scots Poems* shows almost at a glance how closely it is imitative. Burns has not an easier command of the language, nor has he a more caustic wit, but he excels in his greater range of mood and in his fuller sense of the joy of life. Fergusson had recently died insane; and much of the attraction of the Kilmarnock volume lies in the impression which it gives us of sheer health. But Fergusson had revealed to Burns the possibilities of their native tongue, and Burns never forgot his debt to

> my elder brother in misfortune,
> By far my elder brother in the Muse.

With the publication of the Kilmarnock volume the unknown Ayrshire farmer, who held the plough and himself worked his land, leapt to fame with a bound. And no wonder. It was a remarkable volume that opened with *The Twa Dogs* and contained *The Holy Fair*, the *Address to the Deil, Halloween, The Cotter's Saturday Night*, the poems *To a Mouse* and *To a Mountain-Daisy*, besides some of his very best epistles to his friends—a kind of epistle in which he has no rival. But the volume did not contain one song that is generally known. Burns made his name by poems which were descriptive of Scottish life and gave opportunities for a mingled display of wit, and satire, and sentiment; and there was nothing novel in them beyond their excellence.

Most of us read Burns in collected editions, or in selections, but we had better try to see the Kilmarnock edition as it appeared should we want to understand the effect which it produced. If none of the twenty-four original copies which are known to survive should be available, we can always handle to our heart's content a facsimile or reprint. We may be struck by the absence of songs, but nothing will strike us more than the number of well-known pieces or familiar passages which crowd upon each other as we turn its pages.

The new edition of his poems which was brought out the next year at Edinburgh—whither his fame had taken him away from his Ayrshire farm—contains new pieces of the same kind, *Death and Dr. Hornbook, The Brigs of Ayr,* and *Address to the Unco Guid,* and only a few songs, the best known of which are *John Barleycorn* and *Green Grow the Rashes.* It did not contain *The Jolly Beggars* and other songs which had been written in Ayrshire and might have been included. In the choice of his poems Burns was still influenced by the example of Fergusson, and only his intimate friends would think of him as a song-writer.

While he was in Edinburgh he became acquainted with the music engraver who was producing *The Scots Musical Museum.* This engraver, James Johnson by name, could attend to the music, but he asked for help with the words; and from this time to the end of his life Burns's main occupation as a poet was the refurbishing of old songs, and the writing of new songs to old airs. Some of the songs which he had already written he was now to publish; and he was not to confine himself to songs—he was still to write, for example, *Tam o' Shanter.* But henceforward he was to be, pre-eminently, a song-writer. He was to be the great song-writer of Scotland, and one of the greatest song-writers of the world.

Altogether he wrote or rewrote between three hundred and four hundred songs. The great example of his rewriting is *Auld Lang Syne.* In a primitive form it is as old as the seventeenth century, and it had been twice doctored editorially, first in James Watson's *Choice Collection of Scots Poems* in 1711, and again by Allan Ramsay for his *Tea-Table Miscellany* in 1724. Had the poem survived only in the version of Watson or Ramsay, it would itself have been 'forgot and never brought to mind.' Instead it is the parting song of good fellowship not only in Scotland, but in England, and, I understand, wherever English is spoken. (How many know the meaning of all the words, how many Scots can repeat it correctly, need not be enquired.) In the difficult art of preserving the floating fragments of national song, Burns, for all I know, may have his equal in some other country, but I cannot believe that he has ever been surpassed. No praise can be too high for his mastery in giving new life to the remnants of an old tradition. We may wonder what would have become of Scottish song without Burns.

He is no less within the tradition in his own Scottish songs. There, too, he had no thought of reform; he had no attack to make on convention; his function was to carry on. He took lessons from the English poets, but only when he is conscious of his Scottish inheritance does he write with ease and conviction. 'I think my ideas are more barren in English than in Scotish,' he said. And again, 'Are you not quite vexed to think that these men of genius, for such they certainly were, who composed our fine Scotish lyrics, should be unknown? It has given me many a heart-ach.' In that spirit he became their successor.

Burns generally wrote his songs to a tune. 'To sough [*i.e.*, hum] the tune over and over,' he says, 'is the readiest way to catch the inspiration and raise the Bard into that glorious enthusiasm so strongly characteristic of our old Scotch poetry.' He has described his method even minutely:

> Untill I am compleat master of a tune, in my own singing, (such as it is) I never can compose for it.—My way is: I consider the poetic Sentiment, correspondent to my idea of the musical expression; then chuse my theme; begin one Stanza; when that is composed, which is generally the most difficult part of the business, I walk out, sit down now and then, look out for objects in Nature around me that are in unison or harmony with the cogitations of my fancy and workings of my bosom; humming every now and then the air with the verses I have framed: when I feel my Muse beginning to jade, I retire to the solitary fireside of my study, and there commit my effusions to paper; swinging, at intervals, on the hind-legs of my elbow-chair, by way of calling forth my own critical strictures, as my pen goes on.—Seriously, this, at home, is almost invariably my way.—What damn'd Egotism!

He made no claims for himself as a musician.

> You know [he writes] that my pretensions to musical taste, are merely a few of Nature's instincts, untaught and untutored by Art.—For this reason, many musical compositions, particularly where much of the merit lies in Counterpoint, however they may transport and ravish the ears of you, Connoisseurs, affect my simple lug no otherwise than merely as melodious Din.—On the other hand, by way of amends, I am delighted with many little melodies, which the learned Musician despises as silly and insipid.

And he goes on to tell how he composed *Scots Wha Hae* to an old air.

These airs were the old Scottish airs, traditional airs; and by composing to them Burns preserved the tradition in his original compositions—he reproduced it in his own medium, the medium of words. What was this tradition but the genius of the people expressing itself from generation to generation in the way in which it could express itself best? In the poetry of Burns it found clear and unwavering voice. The traditional element in his work has contributed to make him the national poet of Scotland, more incontestably than any poet is the national poet of England.

It may be doubted if England, with all her unmatched wealth of poetry, has a national poet. Even Shakespeare is too great, too individual, too much by himself, to be accepted as speaking for his fellow-men. Not so Burns. He is never beyond their capacity. He does not speak to them so much as for them; and he could have had no higher ambition. There was much in Scottish life at his time against which, in common with many others, he rebelled, but there was nothing to be overthrown in Scottish poetry. He kept to the old subjects, the old measures, and the old manner, and was original in the mastery with which he used them.

If in view of Burns's world-wide reputation I should seem to you to have laid too great stress on the national qualities of his verse, I would plead that my intention has been to give due prominence to his historical position, and thus to view him clearly in his relation to the great revival of poetry that came in England with the nineteenth century. Burns perfected the Scottish tradition in poetry at a time when English poetry was passing through one of its poorer periods, when, as Blake lamented, the sounds were forced, the notes were few. In the pages of Burns Scottish poetry was brought to the notice of English readers. They mistook him for a reformer, they looked upon him as a herald of a new age, because they found in him the lost charm of spontaneous song. But a long history lies behind his work, and much discipline had gone to its making. No wonder that they hailed him as a great original genius, as indeed he was. But Burns was a true child of the Scottish eighteenth century.

Let us not forget, however, that England has her own songs in the eighteenth century. She did not excel then in love songs, but she gave us songs that we all know, and though we may not think of them as outstanding works of poetical art, we should be sorry to be without them. The great lyrical utterances come from the heart of man in solitude, when he is driven in upon himself and must speak. Are not love songs usually inspired by regrets at one's solitude? As I have already remarked, the century may strike us as being a little too grown-up to indulge in pining for what is not. But it was an eminently social century, and it gave us songs that are sung in unison, songs with a chorus, songs for jovial companies or for crowds. It gave us *God Save the King*, which dates from about 1745 but did not become the national anthem till many years later. It gave us *Rule Britannia* about the same time, in 1740. It gave us *Heart of Oak* and *The British Grenadiers*. It gave us *A Hunting We Will Go*, and *The Roast Beef of Old England*, and *Tom Bowling*. These are social songs—songs for men in the company of their fellows.

And it gave us most of our best hymns. This is the century of Isaac Watts, the Wesleys, and Cowper.

NOTES

1. In preceding lectures of the Toronto series.
2. As in the first edition. The edition of 1730 has 'the lucid chambers.'

MARJORIE HOPE NICOLSON

Aesthetic Implications of Newton's *Opticks*

MIND, MIND ALONE, BEAR WITNESS, EARTH AND HEAV'N!
THE LIVING FOUNTAIN IN ITSELF CONTAINS
OF BEAUTEOUS AND SUBLIME.[1]

THE extent to which Newtonian theories of color and light in the *Opticks* affected the theory or technique of painters is a question which lies beyond the scope of this study. Certainly Newton himself showed a good deal of interest in problems of mixing colors, in differences between artificial colors and those of the spectrum, particularly in differences between 'whites' produced artificially and the 'white' of light. As in their descriptive writing the poets showed themselves studying colors in nature in an attempt to describe them more accurately, so they became more self-conscious about color and light as used by painters, and often expressed their tributes in Newtonian terms.[2] Thus Christopher Pitt wrote to Sir James Thornhill:

> Th' exalted strokes so delicately shine,
> And so conspire to push the bold design;
> That in each sprightly feature we may find
> The great idea of the master's mind,
> As the strong colours faithfully unite,
> Mellow to shade, and ripen into light.[3]

Savage's tribute 'To Mr. John Dyer, a Painter,' included these lines:

> Such vivid tinctures sure through aether glow,
> Stain summer clouds, or gild the watery bow: . . .
> Still stream your colours rich with Clio's rays! . . .
> Clear, and more clear, your golden genius shines.[4]

From *Newton Demands the Muse: Newton's 'Opticks' and the Eighteenth Century Poets* (Princeton University Press, 1946), Chapter V, pp. 107–31. Reprinted, with excisions, by permission of the publisher and author.

194

James Cawthorn, like various other poets, used the relationship between color and light to point a moral:

> Passions, like colours, have their strength and ease,
> Those too insipid, and too gaudy these: . . .
> Wouldst thou then reach what Rembrandt's genius knew,
> And live the model that his pencil drew,
> Form all thy life with all his warmth divine,
> Great as his plan, and faultless as his line;
> Let all thy passions, like his colours, play,
> Strong without harshness, without glaring gay.[5]

Various of the poets were groping toward what might be called an aesthetic of color and light, but Thomson and Akenside here, as elsewhere, went beyond their contemporaries.

In the Preface to the second edition of 'Winter,' after discussing the relation between poetry and 'the most charming power of imagination,' Thomson said:

> I know no subject more elevating, more amusing; more ready to awake the poetical enthusiasm, the philosophical reflection, and the moral sentiment, than the works of Nature. Where can we meet with such variety, such beauty, such magnificence? All that enlarges and transports the soul! What more inspiring than a calm, wide survey of them? In every dress nature is greatly charming—whether she puts on the crimson robes of the morning, the strong effulgence of noon, the sober suit of the evening, or the deep sables of blackness and tempest! How gay looks the Spring! how glorious the Summer! how pleasing the Autumn! and how venerable the Winter! [6]

In his phrases, 'such variety, such beauty, such magnificence,' Thomson was probably paraphrasing Addison's familiar distinction in *Pleasures of the Imagination*, 'the great, the new, the beautiful,' as did various other poets who developed the Addisonian categories in their poetry. So, too, Addison's ideas may have been in Thomson's mind when, in his tribute to Newton, he stressed the fact that Newton's wisdom had called forth 'from a few causes such a scheme of things, Effects so *various, beautiful,* and *great.*' In *Pleasures of the Imagination*, Addison had associated color with 'the beautiful.'[7] Yet he seems to have felt little association of *light* with the *sublime.*[8]

Thomson's distinction between 'color' as 'beautiful,' and 'light' as 'sublime' is shown more fully in his practice than in his theory; yet it is implied in phrases in the Preface already quoted: 'How gay looks the Spring! how glorious the Summer!' It is even more clear in the 'Hymn on the Seasons,' first published in 1730, included in all succeeding versions in the author's lifetime:

> These, as they change, Almighty Father! these
> Are but the varied God. The rolling year
> Is full of thee. Forth in the pleasing Spring
> Thy *beauty* walks, thy *tenderness* and *love*.
> *Wide flush the fields*; the softening air is balm;
> Echo the mountains round; the forest smiles;
> And every sense, and every heart, is joy.
> Then comes thy *glory* in the Summer-months,
> *With light and heat refulgent*. Then thy sun
> Shoots full perfection through the swelling year:
> And oft thy voice *in dreadful thunder* speaks. . . .[9]

'Spring' is filled with color; 'Summer' with light. It is in 'Spring' that we are most conscious that 'moist, bright, and green, the landscape laughs around.' 'Spring' is the season in which garden-colors are most vivid.[10]

In this season the poet shows us the colors of the rainbow, of 'broken clouds, gay-shifting to his beam,'[11] of flowers in an English garden,[12] colors everywhere in nature, when 'undisguis'd by mimic art, she spreads Unbounded beauty to the roving eye.' Thomson's 'roving eye' in spring was constantly on the watch for color: 'where the raptured eye Hurries from joy to joy,'[13] he saw 'the country, far-diffused around One boundless blush.'[14] As he found himself incapable of describing the spring flowers 'with hues on hues expression cannot paint,'[15] so he indicated the general poverty of poetic vocabulary when it attempted to describe color.[16] 'Spring' is mild, lovely, charming, delightful; it has in it little terror; upon it the poet lavished all the soft—even lush—adjectives of poets at all times. Spring is the creation of Deity, yet in a sense very familiar in the eighteenth century, the creation less of the awful, radiant, effulgent God who reigns in 'darkness visible,' than of the Second Person of the Trinity, the kind, humane, tender aspect which God shows His followers in His Son.[17]

In 'Summer' we find ourselves in a different world. Here the poet is concerned not only with light, but with excess of light. Even in the moderate climate of England, when the 'sun looks in boundless majesty abroad,' there enters into *The Seasons* the pleasure-pain theory, of which

Burke was to make so much; as 'vertical, the sun Darts on the head direct his forceful rays':

> In vain the sight dejected to the ground
> Stoops for relief; thence *hot ascending steams*
> And *keen reflection pain*.[18]

As the poet retires to the 'sweetness of the shade,' 'bold fancy' sends him on a 'daring flight' to the torrid zone, where the excesses of heat and light are constant, where the sun 'looks *gaily fierce* o'er all the dazzling air.'[19] Here he feels the excess of light, in which sublimity—combined of majesty and terror—is found:

> The parent sun himself
> Seems o'er this world of slaves to tyrannize,
> And, with oppressive ray the *roseate bloom*
> *Of beauty blasting*, gives the gloomy hue
> And feature gross.[20]

In these regions the poet finds none of the tender, kind, placid, charming emotions which he had discovered in 'Spring':

> Love dwells not there,
> The *soft regards*, the *tenderness* of life,
> The heart-shed tear, the *ineffable delight*
> Of sweet humanity. . . .
> The very brute creation there
> *This rage partakes*, and *burns with horrid fire*.[21]

This is a region of 'the rage intense Of brazen-vaulted skies,' of thunderstorms, of the lurid blaze of volcanoes, of earthquakes; here Nature suffers in excess. This is also a region of perpetual light, more severe, more extreme than even the light of midsummer in the British Isles. There is majesty in the light of these regions—but there is also danger. Even when we return with Thomson to the British Isles, we are conscious still of the excesses of nature, of summer thunderstorms with flashing lightning, of light too strong for man to bear. 'Beauty' appears in 'Summer' only at those times of day when the full force of light is abated: the early morning; calm following a summer storm; evening when 'the Sun has lost his rage,' and, heat and light assuaged, the time comes for the poet to walk abroad among the delightful hills of England. Upon one occasion in 'Summer,' Thomson compares the 'beauty' of familiar and quiet light with the former 'sublimity,' when after a summer storm, 'from the face of Heaven the shattered clouds Tumultuous rove,' and Nature 'shines out afresh,' while in the rainbow appears the yellow 'glittering robe of joy'; here alone he says: ' 'Tis beauty all.' [22] Except for such occasional moments, 'Summer' is a season of majesty and terror, so far as light is concerned; and, for the most part, color is conspicuous by its absence.

Occasionally—but only momentarily—in 'Autumn' and 'Winter' we feel the sublimity of light. Light is 'infinite splendor! wide-investing all' [23]; 'Earth's universal face . . . Is one wild dazzling waste' [24]; 'The full ethereal round . . . Shines out intensely keen, and all one cope Of starry glitter' [25]; the earth in winter is a 'glittering waste' of 'unbounded wilds,' when 'snows swell on snows amazing to the sky.' [26] Thomson's important distinction between the 'beautiful' and 'sublime,' so far as light and color were concerned, occurred in 'Spring' and 'Summer.' That the distinction was self-conscious and not merely fortuitous, and that it had been made even more clear to Thomson by the Newtonian discoveries, certain chronological facts would seem to indicate. Thomson was working upon 'Summer' in 1726 or early 1727; before he published it, he interrupted his labors in order to write the memorial verses to Newton, which involved a careful study of the theories of the *Opticks*. Unlike the majority of his poetical predecessors (with the exception of Blackmore), Thomson really understood the implications of the *Opticks* in 1727. At the same time, Thomson was in close touch through correspondence with his Scottish friend, David Mallett, who was writing his *Excursion* as a complement to the earlier 'Seasons.' [27] 'Sublimity,' Thomson wrote to Mallett, 'must be the character of your piece,' and he suggested to his friend subjects and themes which might well be added to *The Excursion*. Mallett and Thomson interchanged their manuscripts, and as in 'Summer,' published in 1727 after the death of Newton, Thomson drew from Mallett, so Mallett in *The Excursion* drew from Thomson. 'Sublimity' was the 'character' of both their pieces. Indeed, Mallett's practice in his poem affords an interesting commentary upon Thomson's self-conscious development of the 'sublime' in 'Summer.' Mallett, too, went back to Addison's categories in *Pleasures of the Imagination*:

> Thus roaming with adventurous wing the globe
> From scene to scene excursive, I behold
> In all her workings, *beauteous, great, or new,*
> Fair Nature, and in all with wonder trace
> The sovereign Maker.[28]

Mallett divided his attention equally between the terrestrial world and the cosmic universe, devoting one book to each; in that division Thomson's distinction between the beauty of color and the sublimity of light was implicit. While there is Color in *The Excursion*, it is confined to the first book; there is—on an even more prodigal scale than in 'Summer'—the sublimity of light, which, in the first book dealing with the terrestrial world, appears chiefly in connection with storms, volcanoes, and other dire manifestations of nature, and in the second book in connection with ethereal light, as the poet's imagination journeys to the stars, the planets, and the sun.

One other element in Thomson's 'aesthetic' of light must be considered before we pass on to the further development of such an aesthetic in Akenside and Burke. If light may be sublime, so, too, may darkness and obscurity, consisting in the absence of light. The eighteenth century 'school of night' felt sublimity not less but sometimes more than did the descriptive poets of day—as Young's *Night Thoughts* amply proves, for Young was a poet not of the beautiful, but of the sublime. In 'the midnight depth' Thomson experienced 'horror' as in the blaze of tropical sun:

> Deep-roused, I feel
> A sacred terror, a severe delight
> Creep through my mortal frame.[29]

As night blotted out day in 'Autumn' the poet was aware of an emotional response to the 'sublime' as the vast, the grand, the magnificent. He himself suggested the contrast between the 'infinite splendour' of the light of day, and the magnificence and vastness of night, in which beauty is lost:

> Now black and deep the night begins to fall,
> A shade immense! Sunk in the quenching gloom,
> Magnificent and vast, are heaven and earth.
> Order confounded lies, *all beauty void*. . . [30]

The effect of darkness to various eighteenth century poets was often analogous to the effect of excessive light. Locke to the contrary notwithstanding, it, too, was a sense-impression: 'So Darkness strikes the sense no less than Light,'[31] said Pope, expressing a truism of the period. Locke, in his *Essay*, had discussed both darkness and the effect of excessive light[32] and, moreover, had quoted a letter from Newton, in which the great scientist had commented upon his own experience in observing light which caused temporary blindness and almost cost him his sight.[33]

> Excessive beauty, like a flash of light,
> Seems more to weaken, than to please the sight,

wrote Walter Harte in his 'Essay on Painting.'[34] Aaron Hill made the same point more verbosely in speaking about the comparative effect of color and light upon man's sense:

> [God] veil'd each path
> To heaven's blue lawns, with clouds, that shift each hour,
> Form, texture, hue—to suit their painted glow
> To man's undazzled gaze—attemp'ring lights
> That teach the sun's too fervid beam to break
> In colouring rays, and touch the sight, *more safe*.[35]

It was Akenside rather than Thomson who brought into a semiphilosophical system the theories of the 'sublime' and 'beautiful' in relation to light and color. Thomson was primarily a descriptive poet; interested in and responsive to philosophical theories though he was, he remained a poet of nature rather than of the mind of man. Akenside prided himself upon being a 'philosophical' poet, an eclectic who drew from many systems of philosophy, and welded those systems into still another which he felt his own. He was abstract rather than concrete, as Thomson was concrete rather than abstract. In *The Pleasures of Imagination,* first published in 1744, he attempted to bring Addison's earlier categories up-to-date for the mid-eighteenth century:

> Know then, whate'er of nature's pregnant stores,
> Whate'er of mimic art's reflected forms
> With love and admiration thus inflame
> The pow'rs of fancy, her delighted sons
> To three illustrious orders have referr'd:
> Three sister-graces, whom the painter's hand,
> The poet's tongue confesses: the *sublime*,
> The *wonderful*, the *fair*.[36]

In one of his most familiar passages, Akenside classified the different types of imagination in accordance with their chief response to the 'sublime' and 'beautiful':

> Diff'rent minds
> Incline to different objects: one pursues
> The vast alone, the wonderful, the wild;
> Another sighs for harmony, and grace,
> And gentlest beauty.[37]

In his early version of *The Pleasures of Imagination*, Akenside equated color with beauty. While, in his invocation to Beauty, the poet hailed her as 'Brightest progeny of heav'n,' it is clear that response to beauty was a simpler matter than response to sublimity. The idea of 'order' was fundamental to Akenside.[38] It is not Reason, but the lesser faculty, 'indulgent Fancy' (a term which Akenside, unlike Addison, frequently distinguished from 'Imagination'), which delights in color; she finds pleasure less, as Reason, in 'majestic Truth' than in

> Fiction . . . upon her vagrant wings
> Wafting ten thousand colours thro' the air,
> And, by the glances of her magic eye,
> Combining each in endless, fairy forms,
> Her wild creation.[39]

In a long passage (a combination of Addison, Shaftesbury, and various Neoplatonic predecessors) in which Akenside attempted 'to trace the rising lustre' of Nature's charms 'thro' various being's fair proportion'd scale,' from their 'first twilight' to 'meridian splendour,' the beauty of simple color found the lowest place in the 'scale':

> Of degree
> The least and lowliest, in th'effusive warmth
> Of colours mingling with a random blaze,
> Doth beauty dwell. Then higher in the line
> And variation of determin'd shape,
> Where truth's eternal measures mark the bound
> Of circle, cube, or sphere. The third ascent
> Unites this varied symmetry of parts
> With colour's bland allurement. . . .
> But more lovely still
> Is nature's charm, where to the full consent
> Of complicated members, to the bloom
> Of colour, and the vital change of growth,
> Life's holy flame and piercing sense are giv'n,
> And active motion speaks the temper'd soul.[40]

The untutored peasant, watching the sunset, might be as responsive to the simple beauty of color as the man of learning who understands the nature of things:

> Ask the swain
> Who journeys homeward from a summer day's
> Long labour, why, forgetful of his toils,
> And due repose, he loiters to behold
> The sunshine gleaming as thro' amber clouds,
> O'er all the western sky; full soon, I ween,
> His rude expression and untutor'd airs,
> Beyond the pow'r of language, will unfold
> The form of beauty smiling at his heart.[41]

In the various 'excursions,' in which Akenside's imagination ranged over the world and through the cosmic universe seeking the sources of the 'sublime, the wonderful, the fair,' and in the many 'visions,' we find the constant association of color with beauty. In his invocation to Beauty, he said:

> How shall I trace thy features? where select
> The roseate hues to emulate thy bloom? [42]

Flying with 'laughing Autumn to th' Atlantic isles,' he saw that

> where'er his fingers touch the fruitful grove,
> The branches shoot with gold; where'er his step
> Marks the glad soil, the tender clusters glow
> With purple ripeness, and invest each hill
> As with the blushes of an evening sky.[43]

So far, however, Akenside has suggested little more than the conventional and orthodox association of color with beauty. In at least one instance he departed from mere convention, attempting to determine how color may ascend from the 'beautiful' to the 'sublime.' While color is ordinarily charming, delightful, beautiful, yet, carried to excess, involved with vastness or extraordinary emotion—particularly with the sublimity of light—it may momentarily become sublime:

> when to raise the meditated scene,
> The flame of passion, thro' the struggling soul
> Deep-kindled, shows across that sudden blaze
> The object of its rapture, vast of size,
> With fiercer colours and a night of shade.[44]

In this passage we approach Akenside's theory of the sublimity of light. To be sure, there are moments in *The Pleasures of Imagination*, when Akenside merely followed the Scriptural, Pythagorean and Miltonic fashion of referring 'sublime' light to the 'Author of Sublimity.'[45]

While beauty and color, in their simpler manifestations, might be associated with Fiction and appeal to 'indulgent Fancy,' 'majestic Truth' dwelt in sublime light:

> shall I mention, where coelestial truth
> Her awful light discloses, to effuse
> A more majestic pomp on beauty's frame?[46]

For true sublimity, light must be either excessive, sudden, painful to the observer, associated with vastness, or in marked contrast to darkness. One of Akenside's 'visions' of sublimity occurred 'in the windings of an ancient wood' at evening on an autumn day, when 'the shade More horrid nodded o'er me,' and 'dark As midnight storms'

> the scene of human things
> Appear'd before me; desarts, burning sands,
> Where the parch'd adder dies; the frozen north
> And desolation blasting all the west
> With rapine and with murder . . .[47]

Across this fearful scene, combining, in characteristic eighteenth century style both 'horrid' dark and 'horror,' came sudden light:

> A flashing torrent of coelestial day
> Burst thro' the shadowy void. With slow descent
> A purple cloud came floating thro' the sky,
> And pois'd at length within the circling trees,
> Hung obvious to my view; till opening wide
> Its lucid orb, a more than human form
> Emerging lean'd majestic o'er my head,
> And instant thunder shook the conscious grove.[48]

In another 'vision,' the beauty and the sublimity of light are contrasted, as two ethereal visitants appeared to the poet. One was the essence of beauty, involving both color and light:

> Eternal youth
> O'er all her form its glowing honours breath'd;
> And smiles eternal, from her candid eyes,

Flow'd like the dewy lustre of the morn
Effusive trembling on the placid waves.
The spring of heav'n had shed its blushing spoils
To bind her sable tresses: full diffus'd
Her yellow mantle floated in the breeze.[49]

The other visitant was symbolic not of the beautiful, but of the sublime:

More sublime
The heav'nly partner mov'd. The prime of age
Composed her steps. The presence of a god
High on the circle of her brow inthron'd,
From each majestic motion darted awe, . . .
A matron's robe,
White as the sunshine streams thro' vernal clouds,
Her stately form invested.[50]

As 'the immortal pair forsook th' enamell'd green,' and rising above the atmosphere ascended into ether, Akenside brought together his various theories of the sublimity of light:

Rays of limpid light
Gleam'd round their path; coelestial sounds were heard,
And thro' the fragrant air aethereal dews
Distill'd around them; till at once the clouds
Disparting wide in midway sky, withdrew
Their airy veil, and left a bright expanse
Of empyrean flame, where spent and drown'd,
Afflicted vision plung'd in vain to scan
What object it involv'd. My feeble eyes
Indur'd not.[51]

In *The Pleasures of Imagination* Akenside, the eclectic, taking his point of departure from Addison, had gathered together theories of the 'sublime' and 'beautiful,' which had been emerging in the first half of the eighteenth century. He prided himself upon being a 'philosophical' poet; while he was no true philosopher, he went far in his attempt at not only a systematization of the theories of his time, but a versified illustration of them. To what extent *The Pleasures of Imagination* served as the specific point of departure for the philosophical work in which these tendencies of the time were finally reduced to order and method remains a matter of surmise. Yet in seeking the ancestry of Burke's *Philosophical Enquiry into the Origin of Our Ideas of the Sublime and Beautiful*, it is well to remember that eighteenth century philosophers read poetry and popular essays, as essayists and poets read philosophy. Burke's essay was not published until 1756 or 1757,[52] but there is little reason to doubt the statement that its original draft was written about 1748, when Burke was not more than nineteen, and was read before the club he had founded at Trinity College, Dublin. Addison's *Pleasures of the Imagination* had been 'classic' for many years; Thomson's *Seasons,* in various editions, particularly in the revision of 1744, was immensely popular, and Akenside's *Pleasures of Imagination* was rapidly becoming one of the most widely read poems of the period.[53] Similarities between Burke's *Enquiry* and Addison's essays clearly exist and have always been recognized. Not only did Burke pick up many of Addison's points in the *Pleasures,* agreeing and disagreeing, but in later editions, he, too, prefaced his discussion of the imagination, as had Addison, with a disquisition upon 'Taste,' in which he took exception to the earlier essayist's theory that Taste was a 'faculty' of the soul. Whatever Burke's actual debt to Thomson and Akenside, he showed in his treatment of color and light many similarities with the theories of the latter and the practice of the former.

In his treatment of color in relationship to beauty, Burke said little that was not entirely conventional. He listed as 'qualities of beauty, as they are merely sensible qualities,' smallness, smoothness, gradual variation, delicacy, and color, and discussed in some detail the kinds of color which make for beauty.[54] Later in considering the effect of the qualities of beauty he had already discussed, he returned to his statement that 'the colours of beautiful bodies must not be dusky or muddy, but clean and fair,' explaining 'the agreeable effects' upon principles of optics.[55] Ordinarily, color belongs to the realm of beauty, but it may produce an effect of sublimity if it is strong and violent on the one hand or sad and melancholy on the other:

Among colours, such as are soft and cheerful (except, perhaps, a strong red which is cheerful) are unfit to produce grand images. An immense mountain, covered with a shining green turf, is nothing, in this respect, to one dark and gloomy; the cloudy sky is more grand than the blue, and night more sublime and solemn than day. Therefore in historical painting, a gay or gaudy drapery can never have a happy effect: and in buildings, when the highest degree of the sublime is intended, the materials and ornaments ought neither to be white, nor green, nor yellow, nor blue, nor of a pale red, nor violet, nor spotted, but of sad and fuscous colours, as black, or brown, or deep purple, and the like.[56]

Burke's sections upon light are more interesting and significant than those on color. 'Mere light' is too common and ordinary to be associated aesthetically with either beauty or sublimity, though we have seen that the clarity of light might contribute to beauty:

> With regard to light, to make it a cause capable of producing the sublime, it must be attended with some circumstances besides its bare faculty of showing other objects. Mere light is too common a thing to make a strong impression on the mind; and without a strong impression nothing can be sublime. But such a light as that of the sun, immediately exerted on the eye, as it overpowers the sense, is a very great idea. Light of an inferior strength to this, if it moves with great celerity, has the same power; for lightning is certainly productive of grandeur, which it owes chiefly to the extreme velocity of its motion. A quick transition from light to darkness, or from darkness to light, has yet a greater effect. But darkness is more productive of sublime ideas than light. . . . Thus are two ideas, as opposite as can be imagined, reconciled in the extremes of both; and both, in spite of their opposite nature, brought to concur in producing the sublime.[57]

Among the qualities of the sublime, Burke listed astonishment, terror, obscurity, power, vastness, and magnificence. The sublimity of light partakes in some degree of each of them: light may astonish by its suddenness, overwhelm by its vastness and power, evoke an aesthetic response by its magnificence, or rouse the passions either by its terror in excess or by its 'privation.' Burke showed himself of the post-Newtonian generation in the many passages in which he paused to analyze the effects of the sublime in connection with the processes of sight, as for example in his discussion 'Why visual objects of great dimension are sublime.'[58]

'All *general* privations are great,' Burke declared, 'because they are all terrible: *Vacuity, Darkness, Solitude,* and *Silence*.'[59] While light may involve sublimity because of either magnificence or 'horror,' the 'privation' of light is even more a cause of terror. Darkness, Burke said, is more productive of sublime ideas than light; light, too excessive for human sight, inevitably becomes darkness. The sublimity of darkness might, on the one hand, rise from pain, as in excessive light; on the other hand, it might arise from terror. Here, in his attempt to develop his own most characteristic thesis, Burke departed from Locke:

> It is Mr. Locke's opinion, that darkness is not naturally an idea of terror; and that, though an excessive light is painful to the sense, that the greatest excess of darkness is in no way troublesome. . . . The authority of this

great man is doubtless as great as that of any man can be, and it seems to stand in the way of our general principle. We have considered darkness as a cause of the sublime; and we have all along considered the sublime as depending on some modification of pain or terror; so that, if darkness be in no way painful or terrible . . . it can be no source of the sublime.[60]

The long, carefully reasoned sections which follow are most interesting in showing the extent to which the generation which followed Locke and Newton found it necessary to enter into close analysis of the physiological processes of sight in order to explain its psychological effects. Here Burke added still another character to the procession of the blind: a boy born blind who gained sight at the age of thirteen or fourteen, and who, immediately upon seeing a black object, displayed great uneasiness—a circumstance which served to aid Burke in his insistence that the fear of darkness is not merely the result of childhood association, engendered by nurses' tales of ghosts and goblins. Burke analyzed in detail various theories of the physiological effects of darkness, entering into a lengthy discussion of its effects upon the human eye, insisting that there are such effects, and that 'any one will find, if he opens his eyes, and makes an effort to see in a dark place, that a very perceptible pain ensues.' The passage—with the accompanying discussion of the difference between 'darkness' and 'blackness'—serves as an excellent summary of various attitudes toward darkness, in contrast with light, which we have seen in some of the poets, and with which we are well acquainted in other 'melancholy,' 'midnight,' and 'graveyard' writers. While Burke discussed the association of darkness with superstition and legend, which may be peculiar to an individual and the result of early experience, he was convinced that the terror of darkness is not an individual but a universal instinct. This was in part because of its potential danger:

. . . for, in utter darkness, it is impossible to know in what degree of safety we stand; we are ignorant of the objects that surround us; we may every moment strike against some dangerous obstruction; we may fall down a precipice the first step we take; and, if an enemy approach, we know not in what quarter to defend ourselves; in such a case strength is no sure protection; wisdom can only act by guess; the boldest are staggered; and he who would pray for nothing else towards his defence, is forced to pray for light.[61]

Even apart from danger, darkness remained to Burke an object of uneasiness. Blackness, which 'is but a partial darkness' has in it—as to Burke's blind boy—something painful to the sight, even though custom may reconcile us to it, so that the terror abates with familiarity. Yet 'black will always have something melancholy in it, because the sensory will always find the change to it, from other colours, too violent; or, if it occupy the whole compass of the sight, it will then be darkness; and what was said of darkness, will be applicable here.'[62] Characteristic product of the 'Age of Reason' as he was, Burke's objectivity and dispassionateness, his analytical mind, his literal style, striving for exactness rather than for beauty, were far removed from mysticism or mystery. But in his prolonged discussion of darkness, and in his insistence that the terror of darkness is not peculiar to an individual but is 'an association of a more general nature, an association which takes in all mankind,' we feel a momentary stirring of some instinct deep-planted in humanity, a universal terror of the human race. The unreasoning fear of the child 'afraid of the dark,' the superstitious dread of the savage, was in kind if not degree the response of even the 'philosophic mind' in the Age of Enlightenment, attempting to dispel by the cool light of reason the terrors of darkness which oppressed man. Light might be sublime, because magnificent, painful, or dangerous; darkness, even more than the other 'general privations' was still more sublime, because still more terrible. One kind of sublimity was experienced and expressed by the great poet 'blinded by excess of light' who closed his eyes in endless night; another was that of Akenside's vision, beginning with the magnificence of light, ending with its pain, when 'afflicted vision plung'd in vain to scan What object it involv'd. My feeble eyes endured not.' Thomson felt both the grandeur and terror of the deprivation of light; at one moment he experienced 'a sacred terror, a severe delight,' at another he felt the 'privation' of night, with its obliteration of all that man calls beautiful:

> Order confounded lies, all beauty void,
> Distinction lost, and gay variety
> One universal blot. . . .[63]

And yet it was not Burke nor Akenside nor Thomson who gave the finest expression to the deep-seated eighteenth century response to that great 'privation.' It was Pope, who at the end of *The Dunciad* expressed in truly 'sublime' style both the majesty and the terror of universal darkness:

In vain, in vain—the all-composing Hour
Resistless falls: the Muse obeys the Pow'r.
She comes! she comes! the sable Throne behold
Of Night primaeval and of Chaos old.
Before her, Fancy's gilded clouds decay,
And all its varying Rain-bows die away.
Wit shoots in vain its momentary fires,
The meteor drops, and in a flash expires. . . .
Thus at her felt approach and secret might,
Art after Art goes out, and all is Night.
See skulking Truth to her old cavern fled,
Mountains of Casuistry heaped o'er her head!
Philosophy, that lean'd on Heav'n before,
Shrinks to her second cause, and is no more.
Physic of Metaphysic begs defence,
And Metaphysic calls for aid on Sense!
See Mystery to Mathematics fly!
In vain! they gaze, turn giddy, rave, and die. . . .
Lo! thy dread Empire, CHAOS! is restor'd;
Light dies before thy uncreating word;
Thy hand, great Anarch! lets the curtain fall,
And universal Darkness buries All.

The rest should be silence; as Pope said the last word on the sublimity of darkness, so, for many poets of his time, he said the last word on 'Physic' and 'Metaphysic.'

NOTES

1. Mark Akenside, *The Pleasures of Imagination*, I. 481–483.

2. In reading through the various collections which I used in preparing this study, I noticed in passing a good deal of this sort of thing, but noted only a few instances of it, since it seemed at the time less significant for my purposes than other treatments of the Newtonian theories.

3. 'To Sir James Thornhill'; Chalmers, XII, 376. The poem was written in 1718.

4. *Works*, edited Johnson, Vol. 45, pp. 128–129.

5. James Cawthorn, 'The Regulation of the Passions'; Chalmers, XIV. 242–243.

6. *Complete Poetical Works, ed. cit.*, pp. 240–241. The Preface continued to be printed with successive editions of the poem until 1730.

7. *Spectator* 412.

8. The use of the word 'sublime' here is, I realize, inexact, since Addison

himself carefully refrained from using it in connection with the effects of external objects upon the imagination. In my forthcoming book I have considered in detail the general background of the 'sublime' and 'beautiful' in this period; in this section, I am using the words as they have been used since Burke.

9. 'A Hymn on the Seasons,' in *Complete Poetical Works, ed. cit.*, p. 245. The italics in these passages are mine.

10. 'Spring,' ll. 95–98.

11. Ibid., l. 191.

12. Ibid., ll. 516 ff.

13. Ibid., ll. 111–112.

14. Ibid., ll. 109–110.

15. Ibid., l. 554.

16. Ibid., ll. 467–476.

17. Ibid., ll. 861-862. This distinction is common among the poets; the 'awful' God creates whirlwinds, volcanoes, tempests, earthquakes; the 'smiling' God is responsible for the loveliness, charm, delicacy of external nature.

18. 'Summer,' ll. 437-439. The italics in these passages are, of course, mine.

19. Ibid., ll. 637-638.

20. Ibid., ll. 884-888.

21. Ibid., ll. 890-897.

22. Ibid., l. 1233.

23. 'Autumn,' l. 1210.

24. 'Winter,' ll. 238-239.

25. Ibid., ll. 738-741.

26. Ibid., l. 905.

27. Cf. Peter Cunningham, 'James Thomson and David Mallett,' *Miscellanies of the Philobiblon Society*, IV, 1857–1858; McKillop, *Background of Thomson's Seasons*, pp. 70, 129; Samuel Monk, *The Sublime*, New York, 1935, pp. 89-90.

28. *The Excursion*; Chalmers, XIV. 21.

29. 'Summer,' ll. 540–541.

30. 'Autumn,' ll. 1138–1144.

31. Locke denied that it was a sense-impression; see pp. 206–7.

32. *Essay Concerning Human Understanding*, II, vii, 4.

33. Newton's letter to Locke is mentioned in the *Essay*, I. 237; and quoted in a note, I. 237–238.

34. 'Essay on Painting'; Chalmers, XVI. 322.

35. 'Free Thoughts upon Faith,' in *Works of the Late Aaron Hill*, London, 1753, IV. 240.

36. *Pleasures of Imagination*, I. 139–146. The italics in this case are Akenside's.

37. *Ibid.*, III. 546–550.

38. Cf. Alfred O. Aldridge, 'The Eclecticism of Mark Akenside's "The Pleasures of Imagination,"' *Journal of the History of Ideas*, V. 292–314.

39. *Pleasures of Imagination*, I. 14–18.

40. *Ibid.*, I. 442–480.

41. *Ibid.*, III. 526–534.

42. *Ibid.*, I. 281–287.

43. *Ibid.*, I. 290–294.

44. *Ibid.*, II. 136–140.

45. *Ibid.*, III. 485–489.

46. *Ibid.*, II. 97–99.

47. *Ibid.*, II. 205–212.

48. *Ibid.*, II. 221–230.

49. *Ibid.*, II. 409–416.

50. *Ibid.*, II. 420–433.

51. *Ibid.*, II. 435–444.

52. The date commonly given for the *Enquiry* is 1756, but there is good reason for dating it 1757; see F. A. Pottle, *Notes and Queries*, CXLVIII (1925), p. 80; Helen Drew, *Modern Language Notes*, I (1935), pp. 29–31.

53. I am not, of course, suggesting that the various critical and philosophical works treating the sublime and beautiful were not influential; discussion of them may be found conveniently brought together in Samuel Monk, *The Sublime*, particularly in Chapters III and IV. It merely seems to me that Akenside's poem might well have served as a point of departure for the young student at Trinity College.

54. *A Philosophical Enquiry into the Origin of Our Ideas of the Sublime and Beautiful*, Philadelphia, 1806, Part III, Section XVII.

55. *Ibid.*, Part IV, Section XXVI.

56. *Ibid.*, Part II, Section XVII.

57. *Ibid.*, Part II, Section XV. The omitted passage is a tribute to the sublimity of Milton's handling of light and darkness, in connection with Deity.

58. *Ibid.*, Part IV, Section IX.

59. *Ibid.*, Part II, Section VII.

60. *Ibid.*, Part IV, Section XIV.

61. *Ibid.*

62. *Ibid.*, Part IV, Section XVIII.

63. 'Autumn,' ll. 1141-1143.

GEOFFREY TILLOTSON

Eighteenth-Century Poetic Diction

IT is true of most of those who are likely to read this article that they approach eighteenth-century poetry by way of nineteenth-century poetry. They have been brought up to expect poetry to be written in a certain way, its words to be chosen in accordance with certain principles. They know what Wordsworth said about Pope before they read Pope. And this means that when they read Pope and other eighteenth-century poets, they apply the wrong criteria: criteria which are wrong because irrelevant.

These wrong criteria are often applied to the poetic diction of eighteenth-century poetry. In using the terms 'eighteenth-century' and 'nineteenth-century' I do not intend to imply that they carry any well-defined meanings for the historian or critic of the poetic diction. Blake, who uses almost none of the diction, is an eighteenth-century poet. On the other hand, poets born later are not necessarily immune from the waning infection. The passionate attack on the diction made by Wordsworth and Coleridge, whom we think of as nineteenth-century poets, is all the more passionate because the eighteenth century is in their blood and will not be expelled. Byron, of course, glories in the ancestral germs. Keats and, to a smaller extent, Shelley use the diction more than is generally seen, and even Tennyson does not cut himself off from it, though he seems to discover it again for himself rather than to use it from habit. Browning appears to be the first poet of the nineteenth century who is not indebted to the diction.

From *Essays and Studies by Members of the English Ass'n, 1939*, XXV (1940), 59–80; reprinted in *Essays in Criticism and Research* (Cambridge University Press, 1942), 63–85. Reprinted with revisions by permission of The English Ass'n, The Cambridge University Press, and the author.

The generalizations made below will apply in various degrees to the poets of the two centuries and also to poets of the seventeenth and the sixteenth, since the methods of forming the diction, and even part of the diction itself, are already found in Spenser, in Sylvester's translation of Du Bartas, and in most succeeding poets except, broadly speaking, the metaphysicals.

It is generally true that the vocabulary of nineteenth-century poetry is restricted only in so far as the vocabulary of any poetry is restricted, i.e. only in so far as the subject-matter is restricted. Poems in the nineteenth century tend to be written on what were then considered 'poetical' subjects. The reservation is a serious one when we consider the poetry of other centuries, including our own since 1920; but, barring it, there is no limitation of vocabulary. There still remains, therefore, a great deal of the dictionary out of which the nineteenth-century poet can choose his words. The nineteenth-century poet may be said to provide each poem (whatever the subject, whatever the form) with new diction. He writes almost as if he were the first and the only poet in the world:

> As if he were Earth's first-born birth,
> And none had lived before him.[1]

The nineteenth-century poet discovers a new poetic territory and maps it out by himself.

Writing poetry was different in the eighteenth century. Then the kinds of poetry were still seen as distinct. And these different kinds entailed the use of different kinds of vocabulary, of diction. In the eighteenth century, writing poems was a communal art in the sense that the poet was not free to write as he chose. Much had to be learnt before he could write correctly, without offending the rules and distinctions acknowledged by poets and readers. A poet did not have to create the taste by which he was enjoyed to the same extent as a nineteenth-century poet was conscious of having to. The kinds were ready waiting for him, and, if the rules for the kinds in which he elected to write were properly complied with, the products were recognizable as poems of those kinds. It goes without saying that for the products to be good poems the 'material' to which the rules were applied had to be good. The kinds included epic, tragedy in verse, pindaric, elegy, heroic and familiar epistle, pastoral, georgic, occasional verse, translation and

213

imitation. Pope chooses to tackle all these kinds in turn. He sees them as distinct. He tells Spence, for instance, how he takes a poem and corrects it:

> After writing a poem, one should correct it all over, with one single view at a time. Thus for language; if an elegy; 'these lines are very good, but are they not of too heroical a strain?' and so *vice versa*. It appears very plainly, from comparing parallel passages touched both in the Iliad and Odyssey, that Homer did this; and it is yet plainer that Virgil did so, from the distinct styles he uses in his three sorts of poems. It always answers in him; and so constant an effect could not be the effect of chance.[2]

This observation is modified later:

> Though Virgil, in his pastorals, has sometimes six or eight lines together that are epic: I have been so scrupulous as scarce ever to admit above two together, even in the Messiah.[3]

Sometimes Pope keeps the kinds distinct: when he introduces different kinds into the same poem, he knows what he is doing and marks off the component parts by the use of different kinds of diction (diction includes larger matters such as personification, apostrophe, exclamation). These rules and principles may seem curious pedantry after the practice of nineteenth-century poets. But they were based on first-hand scrutiny of good poetry in the past (witness the above quotations from Spence) and so were as unpedantic in the hands of a poet as, say, the study of Spenser was unpedantic in the hands of Keats: or in the hands of Dryden or Pope, for that matter.

For Pope, then, poetic diction would cover all the words used in all the kinds (which meant virtually all the words in the dictionary, except those which nobody knew the meaning of without intense specialization in technical fields). When Pope speaks of words in *An Essay on Criticism* his criterion of their correct use is appropriateness. He makes no reference to poetic diction.

He does use the term, however, in the 'Preface' to his translation of the *Iliad*, but not in Wordsworth's sense.[4] He uses it to mark the difference between the vocabulary of poetry and prose, and his instances are figures and compound epithets:

> If we descend from hence [i.e. from remarking Homer's descriptions, images and similes] to the *Expression*, we see the bright Imagination of

Homer shining out in the most enliven'd Forms of it. We acknowledge him the Father of Poetical Diction, the first who taught that *Language of the Gods* to Men. His Expression is like the colouring of some great Masters, which discovers itself to be laid on boldly, and executed with Rapidity. It is indeed the strongest and most glowing imaginable, and touch'd with the greatest Spirit. *Aristotle* had reason to say, He was the only Poet who had found out *Living Words;* there are in him more daring Figures and Metaphors than in any good Author whatever. An Arrow is *impatient* to be on the Wing, a Weapon *thirsts* to drink the Blood of an Enemy, and the like. Yet his Expression is never too big for the Sense, but justly great in proportion to it: 'Tis the Sentiment that swells and fills out the Diction, which rises with it, and forms itself about it. For in the same degree that a *Thought* is warmer, an *Expression* will be brighter; and as That is more strong, This will become more perspicuous: Like Glass in the Furnace which grows to a greater Magnitude, and refines to a greater Clearness, only as the *Breath* within is more powerful, and the *Heat* more intense.[5]

What follows in the next paragraph must be read in the light of this:

To throw his Language more out of Prose, *Homer* seems to have affected the *Compound-Epithets*. This was a sort of Composition peculiarly proper to Poetry, not only as it heighten'd the *Diction*, but as it assisted and fill'd the *Numbers* with greater Sound and Pomp, and likewise conduced in some measure to thicken the *Images*.[6]

This statement concerning the diction of poetry has a general validity. It would be subscribed to by almost all poets and critics: one exception would be Malherbe. 'In the same degree that a *Thought* is warmer, an *Expression* will be brighter. . .' Even Wordsworth, despite statements implying the contrary, is found allowing Pope's general position. He seems indeed to be repeating Pope's words—it was to be expected that he should pay attention to Pope's 'Preface' before attacking the diction which he considered to have sprung from the translation that 'Preface' introduced. Wordsworth writes:

The earliest poets of all nations generally wrote from passion excited by real events . . . feeling powerfully as they did, their language was daring and figurative.[7]

Pope's use of the term poetical diction has nothing to do with the narrower sense in which it was used by Wordsworth and others in relation to the poetry of the eighteenth century.

Poetic diction, in Wordsworth's sense, can only be said to exist in certain kinds of eighteenth-century poetry. As Wordsworth and Coleridge saw, there is little or no poetic diction in the satires, familiar epistles, and occasional verse. (In the elegy and the heroic epistle the poetic diction is of a kind that has passed almost unnoticed by the critics: this diction includes such words as *sad, beauteous, trembling, pensive.*) In the satires and familiar epistles the vocabulary is as free in principle as that used in any nineteenth-century poem—*The Ring and the Book,* for example. The vocabulary of all nineteenth-century poetry cowers into a corner when the *Dunciad* walks abroad, seeking whom it may devour. And this applies even to those parts of it where the subject is a favourite one of nineteenth-century poetry, where the material is external nature. In the same way that the primary human emotions tended to mean for Matthew Arnold only the noble primary human emotions, external nature tended to mean for the nineteenth-century poets only what was 'beautiful' and noble in it. But Pope knew no such distinction. In the *Dunciad* there are the isles of fragrance, the lily-silver'd vales, but also other things:

> So watchful Bruin forms, with plastic care,
> Each growing lump, and brings it to a Bear.[8]

Or

> Next, o'er his Books his eyes began to roll,
> In pleasing memory of all he stole,
> How here he sipp'd, how there he plunder'd snug,
> And suck'd all o'er, like an industrious Bug.[9]

The nineteenth-century poets were squeamish about external nature. So that even on their chosen ground the eighteenth-century poets can beat them in variety of appreciation. There is obviously no poetic diction in the *Dunciad*: except of course where Pope is deliberately mimicking the epic manner. When writing satire the eighteenth-century poet chose his words as freely as any poet. And the same is true when he was writing several of the other kinds.

But when writing epic, pastoral, and georgic the eighteenth-century poet was not so free.[10] No eighteenth-century poet of much distinction writes an epic (Pope started to write one). But Milton wrote one, and Dryden translated one and part of another: here the term eighteenth-century extends itself backward spiritually as for certain nineteenth-century poets it extends itself forward. Pope followed Dryden's example.

There is no need, however, to examine the epic diction here because the nineteenth-century attackers, though they single out Pope's *Homer* as the source of the diction, select for examination that passage which could have stood equally in a pastoral or georgic. Coleridge, it seems, was the first to examine the 'popular lines' from Book VIII of the *Iliad*—

As when the moon, refulgent lamp of night. . . .[11]

Southey followed in the *Quarterly Review* (October 1814), and Wordsworth, a year later, in his 'Essay, Supplementary to the Preface' of the first collective edition of his poems in 1815.

It was in the pastoral and georgic, then, and in pastoral and georgic material intruding into other kinds, that the diction of the eighteenth-century poets came to be most despised. This fate was inevitable since it was by jealously extending the descriptive element in these two kinds that the nineteenth-century poets found the form for much of their own best writing. The champion of eighteenth-century diction must take his stand on pastoral and georgic, insisting, of course, that the eighteenth-century poets, unlike those of the nineteenth century, did not do their best work in those kinds. The best poetry of the eighteenth century is generally that of man (any man of a liberal education, of a certain reach of mind) and his fellow-men. The best poetry of the nineteenth century is generally that of man (an individual man of unusual distinction) and external nature: that is, the poet himself in a world of dawns and sunsets, streams and trees, mountains and sea. This difference of favourite subject-matter is at the root of all the differences between the poetry of the two centuries. In discussing poetic diction, therefore, we are comparing the best poetry of the nineteenth century with the less-than-best poetry of the eighteenth.

Nineteenth-century poets have a strong sense of the individual quality of each moment of experience. Late in their day, the 'Epilogue' to Pater's *Renaissance* enunciated this part of their creed with exquisite finality. The nineteenth-century poets are humble—one is forced to the conclusion—because they see the external world as more startlingly beautiful than anything they have of their own, than anything they themselves can make. When they experience any natural phenomenon, they offer as white a mind as possible to receive it. They tremblingly hold up the mirror to nature. Their business as poets is to prove to their readers that they have been worthy of a unique experience. And so they write of skies, for instance, in the following ways:

217

> . . . the western sky,
> And its peculiar tint of yellow green.[12]

> Deep in the orange light of widening morn.[13]

> . . . a bed of daffodil sky.[14]

> The orange and pale violet evening-sky.[15]

Coleridge, in the first of these quotations, feels it necessary to excuse his perception of a green sky by allowing that it was 'peculiar.' Later poets (green skies are frequent throughout the nineteenth century, and even survive as late as Empson) make no apology.

The eighteenth-century poets were not so humble. They saw external nature not as culminating in its own most exquisite moments, but as culminating in man. Thomson, for instance, who looked at external nature as long and as lovingly as any nineteenth-century poet except Wordsworth, considered that

> . . . Man superior walks
> Amid the glad creation.[16]

Thomson forgets this superiority at times and so do many eighteenth-century poets, but this is their attitude in the main. The glad creation provides them with many instances of individual beauty, but they differ from the nineteenth-century poets in being impressed only up to a point. They seldom present a white mind to experience. They present a mind already coloured with all their past experience of all kinds: experience of other past instances of the beauty of external nature (they tend to generalize a description), experience of man, and experience of books (man's record of his experiences). Whereas the nineteenth-century poet is interested in the freshness of his response to experience, the eighteenth-century poet is interested in that response at a later stage: when the new has been welcomed by the old, when it has been accommodated to the existing harmony. It is this presence of a stage intermediary between the fresh response and the written poem that accounts for much of the difference between an eighteenth-century nature-poem and a nineteenth-century one. In every eighteenth-century pastoral and georgic there is something expected, predictable. And it is this element which requires and receives its poetic diction. The poetic diction represents the existing mind, the new words represent the freshness of the response. The poet's value is measured by the quality of the new, and also by the quality of the new art with which he manipulates the old. Shelley, Newman and Bergson held that fresh experience is itself poetry. The mere fact that there is seen to be an orange and pale violet evening sky is poetry. The art in that phrase is negligible, the fact is everything. But an eighteenth-century nature-poem depends for half its existence on its paper and ink, on its words as words. When you read Arnold's line it is the thing, not the words, that you are given. Arnold—for all his mind—does not exist except as a finger pointing to a unique sky. We praise him for his discovery.

It is another matter when we read the following lines from Pope's juvenile pastoral, 'Spring':

> Soon as the flocks shook off the nightly dews,
> Two swains, whom Love kept wakeful, and the Muse,
> Pour'd o'er the whitening vale their fleecy care. . . .[17]

Here in the first and third lines (we must neglect the second because the human element in 'Thyrsis' is unrepresented in the line selected) we find a combination of new and old. Actually there is such a combination in Arnold's line: Shelley, as my quotations show, had already seen an orange sky. But the combination in Arnold's line is accidental. His line is not, so to speak, built on Shelley's,[18] and he does not expect us to remember Shelley's 'orange.' He expects us to think both 'orange' and 'pale violet' original and striking. Pope knows of course that the reader will recognize 'fleecy care' as a common phrase in pastorals. And whereas 'fleecy care' is old, a quotation from the poetic diction, there is new and old simultaneously in the preceding phrase: 'Pour'd o'er the whitening vale.' Here *vale* (for *valley*) is old, a quotation from Spenser. *Whitening* is old, but also new. It goes back to Virgil where it is used of the light of dawn (*ut primum albescere lucem Vidit*).[19] Pope wishes us to recognize that whitening is a process noted by Virgil and therefore of interest to later poets. But he applies the process to something more surprising than the morning sky. He applies it to the colour of a pasture into which sheep, perhaps newly shorn, are given entry. They appreciably alter the general colour of a field. That this latter sense is intended is shown by the use of Pope's verb by later eighteenth-century poets: Shenstone in his 'Pastoral Ballad' writes:

> . . . my hills are white-over with sheep;

and Cowper:

> . . . The sheep-fold here
> Pours out its fleecy tenants o'er the glebe.
> At first, progressive as a stream. they seek
> The middle field; but, scatter'd by degrees,
> Each to his choice, soon whiten all the land.[20]

and even one poet in the nineteenth century:

> Now rings the woodland loud and long,
> The flocks are whiter down the vale.[21]

Then again, take *pour'd*. It is unpoetically, startlingly new. Pope seems to have been the first and only poet to observe the effect of sheep bursting out of a fold: they seem to be poured out, like porridge from a pan. Then in the first line there is the unpredictable verb, *shook off*.

In summary, then, we can say that Pope has observed something new, as Arnold has. His discoveries are as valuable, and surely as spectacular, as those of Arnold. But the record of the discovery is all that there is in Arnold, whereas in Pope the discovery represents only a part of the whole. Pope is using his whole mind.

One of the major elements included in the whole mind evident in eighteenth-century pastorals and georgics—what is 'old' in it—may be compendiously stated as Virgil's *Georgics*. It is the *Georgics* more than anything else that prepare the mind of the eighteenth-century poet for writing his nature-poem, which are responsible for the element of the old. Virgil helped the eighteenth-century nature-poet in something like the same way that the Bible helped Bunyan. And the value of eighteenth-century nature-poetry suffered in the nineteenth-century, when the reverence for Virgil faded, in the same way that the value of *The Pilgrim's Progress* suffers whenever there is a decline in Bible reading. Not that the nineteenth century did not honour Virgil. Keats as a boy translated the *Aeneid* into prose. Tennyson saluted Virgil's centenary with a sumptuous ode. In Max Beerbohm's cartoon, the nineteenth-century 'Statesman . . . [makes] without wish for emolument a . . . version of the Georgics, in English hexameters.' But that version is confessedly 'flat but faithful.' And we find Hazlitt recording in his 'First Acquaintance with Poets' that on one occasion 'Coleridge spoke of Virgil's "Georgics," but not well. I do not think he had much feeling for the classical or elegant.' Keats as a boy translates the *Aeneid* into prose. But Dryden as an old man translates not only the *Aeneid* but the *Pastorals* and *Georgics,* and not into prose but into splendid verse. The eighteenth century feels Virgil as a divine presence. Hazlitt's 'classical or elegant,' even when allowance is made for contemporary usage, were words too cold to describe their reverence for 'the best of the Ancients.'[22] He is Pope's favourite poet, and one of the four busts in his garden is Virgil's. Gray habitually reads him under the beeches at Burnham.[23] Shenstone has his Virgil's Grove at the Leasowes. They arrange part of their very lives about him. Thomson in the first edition of *Winter* cries:

> Maro, the best of poets, and of men!

In the second:

> Maro! the glory of the poet's art!

Later editions read:

> Behold who yonder comes! in sober state,
> Fair, mild, and strong as is a vernal sun:
> 'Tis Phoebus' self, or else the Mantuan swain![24]

The same thing is even true of prose writers: Gilbert White's

mind is haunted by the classics. He sounds a Latin phrase now and then as if to tune his English. The echo that was so famous a feature of Selborne seems of its own accord to boom out 'Tityre, tu patulae recubans. . . .' It was with Virgil in his mind that Gilbert White described the women making rush candles at Selborne.[25]

And it is the *Georgics* that for Dryden, and so for most eighteenth-century poets, are 'the divinest part' of Virgil.[26]

Virgil helps the eighteenth-century nature-poets in a dozen ways. He helps them technically. They try to get his 'strength,' 'sweetness,'[27] and smoothness of tone, to write lines the music of which is as solid, as exquisite, as his. In his translation of Virgil Dryden seems at times to be trying to suggest something of the Latin versification by letting the stress of the lines fall on syllables with long vowels.[28] Virgil also helps them to concentrate their meaning into fewer words, to combine words in new ways. He shows them how subtly meaning may be embodied in appropriate sound (a lesson they usually find too difficult). He furnishes them with many actual words: *liquid, involve, purple,*[29] *irriguous, refulgent, conscious, gelid, crown* (verb), *invade, painted* (used adjectively). *Care* comes straight from the *Georgics: cura* is Virgil's constant word for the job of the shepherd and farmer. *Fleecy care* itself, in an age of poets who liked adjectives ending in -y and invented them by the hundred,[30] springs readily from the juxtaposition: 'superat pars altera *curae, Lanigeros* agitare greges.'[31] The phrase *sylvan scene* comes from another juxtaposition, this time in the *Aeneid:* 'silvis scaena coruscis.'[32] Dryden spoke for many of these poets when he praised 'the *dictio Virgiliana,*' adding 'in that I have always endeavoured to copy him.'[33]

And while Virgil improved the eighteenth-century sense of metre, the diction which he contributed to forming was found useful in a more readily practical way. Many of the nouns in the diction are monosyllables: '*race, tribe, train, gale, vale, swain, tide,* and so on. They also have long vowels or diphthongs. And so for poets who held that rime should have just those qualifications,[34] here was a body of words suitable for the rime position in which they usually placed them.[35] It has also been pointed out that the trochaic adjectives belonging to the diction, when linked to nouns of one or two syllables, formed convenient units for getting that balance in a line which was considered musically valuable.[36]

By virtue of the words and phrases borrowed or adapted from Virgil, the nature-poems of the eighteenth century have a quality which is usually denied them, the quality of 'atmosphere.' The diction is coloured with Virgilian connotation. Critics have been too apt to dismiss the words merely as derived from Latin, as if their previous life lay only in the double-columned pages of the dictionary. But it is because these words leapt to the eye whenever the poet opened his Virgil that they appear whenever he writes nature-poems for himself. Too much attention has been paid to that dictum of Crabbe on some of Pope: 'actuality of relation, . . . nudity of description, and poetry without an atmosphere.'[37] The dictum only applies to eighteenth-century nature-poems when the reader fails to supply the Virgilian connotation. As the reverence for Virgil faded, the capacity to supply the connotation faded with it. In the eighteenth century the meanings of the favourite Virgilian words are not defined in the dictionaries. They are beyond definition in the same way that Keats's words are, though often for other reasons. They are indefinable because the dictionary cannot assess the Italian light they derive from the *Georgics.* Take for example, *gelid.* Johnson defines it as 'extremely cold,' and this is sometimes its meaning: Professor Sherard Vines, for instance, comments as follows on the use of the word in Thomson's *Winter*:

> 'The horizontal sun
> Broad o'er the south, hangs at his utmost noon
> And ineffectual strikes the gelid cliff,

tells us in words what Claude would have told us on canvas; he would have seen, not as Ruskin, the tertiary cliff with inclined strata, or glacial curvatures, particular after particular, but in all its essential and generalised dignity, the gelid cliff.'[38]

Gelid sometimes has this zero temperature in the *Georgics*: it is applied, for instance, to *antrum*. But it is a warmer word on other occasions, when, for instance, it describes valleys that Virgil longs to idle in.[39] And it has this warmer connotation when Goldsmith writes in *The Traveller*:

> While sea-born gales their gelid wings expand
> To winnow fragrance round the smiling land.

(*Smiling*, a common word in eighteenth-century pastoral, may be considered the equivalent of *laetus*, which Virgil constantly applied to crops.) When Joseph Warton translated *gelidi fontes* (among *mollia prata*)[40] he was right to render it as 'cooling fountains.'

Virgil suits these poets for another reason. The *Georgics* are an exaltation of human control over the stubbornness and fertility of the earth and of the beast. The men of the eighteenth century, like those of any other century, admired this control, but sought more intelligently to refine and enlarge the amount of it which had already been secured: witness their landscape gardening, the improvements in agriculture and in the breeding of stock. But the control which is most worthy of celebration by poets is that of a stubbornness and fertility which almost have their own way, which need a ceaseless vigilance. Virgil, therefore, had also celebrated the severe act of labour which is the means to the control. He had experienced the realities of the land on his own farm. And, further, he had laboured like any peasant on the furrows of his poem: the *Georgics*, we are told, cost him seven years to perfect. But it must be confessed that in the georgics of the eighteenth century there is not always much evidence of a struggle. The control which

they assume is dry-browed and sometimes almost automatic. A stubbornness which is shown so thoroughly tamed risks the suspicion that
it was never stubborn enough. The poets of the eighteenth-century
georgics are too much like the absentee gentleman farmer who comes
down from town and does his controlling with a straight back and a
walking-stick. What Virgil won with pain, they take with a bow. Moreover, it is often the same bow: because, whereas you know that minor
nineteenth-century poetry will be bad, you know that minor eighteenth-
century poetry will be bad in a certain way. And it is partly because of
their more facile harvest that the eighteenth-century poets take certain
lines in the *Georgics* too seriously. Writing for Augustus and Maecenas,
and being himself a poet naturally prone to grandeur rather than to
simplicity, Virgil did not always feel that he could write straight ahead
as if he were writing merely for farmers. At least he feels the need for
an apology before doing so:

> Nec sum animi dubius, verbis ea vincere magnum
> Quam sit, et angustis hunc addere rebus honorem. [41]

But after this apology his words say frankly what he means. It is not
because of any abstention that Virgil's poem remains poetical: he uses
the words he obviously needs. It is what may compendiously be called
the versification that sheds the glory on the poem. By virtue of the
richness of the sound, Virgil, in Addison's words, 'breaks the Clods and
tosses the Dung about with an Air of Gracefulness.' [42] Some of this glory
is present in Dryden's translation, and perhaps it is not without significance that we find Beattie censuring him for 'being less figurative than
the original [and] in one place exceedingly filthy, and in another
shockingly obscene.' [43] The georgic writers of the eighteenth century
may not have been writing for the great of Rome, but no more than
Virgil were they writing simply for farmers. They had in mind readers
of poetry who had also, actually or potentially, the interests of gentlemen farmers, farmers in a comfortable mood of contemplation. They
also, therefore, had their problems of vocabulary, and, of course, they
often take the easy path of solving them by glossing. But it must be
remembered that their problems were real ones, and that they had at
least two strong reasons for being squeamish about using 'low' words in
'serious' poems. Even if they saw that Virgil was often using realistic
words, they were conscious that the words were more 'sounding' (to
use Dryden's epithet) than their English equivalents. Beside Virgil's
Latin, the Saxon and 'low' element in English seemed like human life

itself, 'nasty, brutish, and short.' In his life of John Philips, George Sewell put his finger on

> the great Difficulty of making our *English* Names of Plants, Soils, Animals and Instruments, shine in Verse: There are hardly any of those, which, in the *Latin* Tongue, are not in themselves beautiful and expressive; and very few in our own which do not rather debase than exalt the Style.[44]

And it was not only the words 'in themselves' which were the trouble. During the latter half of the seventeenth century and the earlier eighteenth century, burlesque was busy blackening the Saxon elements in the English language. These words were being rotted by gross ridicule. None of the 'serious' kinds of poetry were exempted from brutal parody, and to use any of the enemy's words would be to instigate the laugh you dreaded.[45] It is not too much to say that in the eighteenth century part of the English vocabulary was rendered temporarily unusable in 'serious' poetry.[46] Dr. Johnson discussing the passage from *Macbeth* (a passage he greatly admires) which includes the words *dun, knife,* and *blanket,* finds that he 'can scarce check [his] risibility,' and one of the reasons for this lies in his sensitiveness to the occasions when these words or their like have occurred in amusing or offensive contexts which he himself cannot forget:

> if, in the most solemn discourse, a phrase happens to occur which has been successfully employed in some ludicrous narrative, the gravest auditor finds it difficult to refrain from laughter. . . .[47]

So that for the 'serious' eighteenth-century poet, a periphrasis was often a means for skirting the company of such parodists as (to name only the greatest) Cotton, Butler, Gay, and Swift.[48] It is inevitable that when there is no other reason for a periphrasis than this strictly temporary one, the periphrasis itself will seem ludicrous to a later, cleaner age. But this does not alter the fact that the periphrasis did once seem preferable. Pope, anticipating ourselves, laughed at the periphrasts.[49] The remedy, he saw, was sometimes worse than the disease. But the disease was a real one.

Some of the poets use the diction as stilts to escape the mud. But not the good poets. It is true to say that the good poets of the eighteenth century use language, including the poetic diction, with a scrupulousness far in advance, say, of Shelley's use of language. Examine, for instance, this excerpt from a snow scene in Thomson's *Winter*:

> . . . The foodless wilds
> Pour forth their brown inhabitants. The hare,
> Though timorous of heart, and hard beset
> By death in various forms, dark snares, and dogs,
> And more unpitying men, the garden seeks,
> Urg'd on by fearless want. The bleating kind
> Eye the bleak heaven, and next the glistening earth,
> With looks of dumb despair; then, sad-dispersed,
> Dig for the withered herb through the heaps of snow.[50]

Here the diction is parcel of the meaning. 'Brown inhabitants' is a neat way of grouping creatures which inhabit the scene described and whose browness is the most evident thing about them in the snow. 'Bleating kind' is anything but an unthinking substitute for 'sheep.' Thomson is saying: we think of sheep as creatures who bleat, but they are silent enough in the snow; it is the dumb eye and not the voice that tells us of their despair.

There is at least one more reason why the diction is called for. It helps to express some part of the contemporary interest in the theological and scientific significance of natural phenomena.[51] If external nature was not much regarded for its own sake, it was often regarded for the sake of a straightforward theology and an everyday science. The creatures were a continual proof of the wisdom and variety of the mind of the Creator, and a continual invitation for man to marvel and understand. The eighteenth-century theologian and scientist (they were frequently the same man) often see themselves in the position of the writer of Psalms viii and civ, which appear as follows in the version of George Sandys:

> . . . O what is Man, or his frail Race,
> That thou shouldst such a Shadow grace!
> Next to thy Angels most renown'd;
> With Majesty and Glory crown'd:
> The King of all thy Creatures made;
> That all beneath his feet hath laid:
> All that on Dales or Mountains feed,
> That shady Woods or Deserts breed;
> What in the Airy Region glide,
> Or through the rowling Ocean slide. . . .

And

> ... Great God! how manifold, how infinite
> Are all thy Works! with what a clear fore-sight
> Didst thou create and multiply their birth!
> Thy riches fill the far extended Earth.
> The ample Sea; in whose unfathom'd Deep
> Innumerable sorts of Creatures creep:
> Bright scaled Fishes in her Entrails glide,
> And high-built Ships upon her bosome ride.´. . . [52]

Like the Psalmist, they are conscious of the separate wonders of the different elements:

> Whate'er of life all-quick'ning æther keeps,
> Or breathes thro' air, or shoots beneath the deeps,
> Or pours profuse on earth . . .
> Not man alone, but all that roam the wood,
> Or wing the sky, or roll along the flood. . . .[53]

And above all they are interested in the adaptation of life to environment. To draw only on one instance. The Rev. William Derham in 1713 published his Boyle lectures with the title *Physico-Theology: or, a Demonstration of the Being and Attributes of God, from his Works of Creation.* The book went into many editions. One chapter concerns the *Clothing of Animals* 'in which we have plain Tokens of the Creator's Art, manifested in these two Particulars; the *Suitableness of Animals Cloathing to their Place and Occasions,* and the *Garniture and Beauty thereof.*' [54] The poetic diction is obviously a means of differentiating the creatures in this way: *the scaly breed, the feather'd race,* and so on. It is not surprising to find it cropping up in brief descriptions of the genesis of the world: see, for instance, Sylvester's *Du Bartas,*[55] John Hanson's 'Time is a turnecoate':

> The winged-people of the various Skie,
> The scalie Troupe which in the Surges lie;[56]

Davenant's *Gondibert:* [57] Dryden's *State of Innocence,* where the newly created Eve, seeking to distinguish what she is, sees

> from each Tree
> The feather'd Kind peep down, to look on me;[58]

and Blackmore's *Creation*.[59] The notion of the great Scale of Being, which Professor Lovejoy has so thoroughly interpreted for us,[60] provided for an infinite scale of creatures, ranging from angels, whom Dryden calls 'Th'Etherial people'[61] to

> . . . the green myriads in the peopled grass.[62]

All these 'people' were variously adapted to their place in the sublime chain. Life manifested itself on every link, and the grouped bearers of that life (*people, inhabitants, race, train, troop, drove, breed*) are clothed in appropriate bodies. Derham, for example, uses terms such as *vegetable race, winged tribes, watery inhabitants*.[63] The diction, then, is not simply 'poetic' diction: it is also 'physicotheological' nomenclature. All this tells against Owen Barfield's suggestion in his brilliant book on *Poetic Diction*:

> No one would have dreamed of employing the stale Miltonics [Barfield followed Sir Walter Raleigh in deriving the poetic diction from Milton], which lay at the bottom of so much eighteenth-century 'poetic diction', in *prose*, however imaginative.[64]

The evidence, however, runs the other way, and we msut allow for this in estimating the degree to which the poetic diction was poetic to contemporary eyes. Among Derham's terms for dividing the creation into groups of creatures is the term 'heavenly bodies.' This term alone has survived into the scientific usage of our own century. We should not suspect any poet who dared to use this term of attempting decoration. And with this as evidence we may believe that those terms of the poetic diction which were also the terms of the moralists and scientists had an intellectual toughness about them as well as a neatness and fashionable grace. It is possible to argue that the poets ceased to use the diction only when the scientists did.

Enough has been said of the poetic diction of the eighteenth century to indicate that when it comes to be examined as thoroughly as it never yet has been, much of eighteenth-century poetry will be seen more clearly. The reasons why eighteenth-century poets use the diction share in the central reasons why they write poetry at all.

NOTES

1. Wordsworth, 'Expostulation and Reply.' II. 11f. (adapted).

2. J. Spence, *Ancedotes, Observations, and Characters, of Books and Men,* ed. S.W. Singer, 1820, pp. 23f.

3. *Ibid.,* p. 312.

4. Dennis apparently invents the term (see F. W. Bateson, *Poetry and Language,* 1934, p. 71n.): Dryden had used the phrase *dictio Virgiliana* (see above, p. 222, and ten years before, in 1685, had half anglicized it: 'diction, or (to speak English) . . . expressions' (*Essays,* ed. Ker, 1900, I, 266).

5. Pope, *The Iliad of Homer,* I (1715: folio ed.), D 2ᵛ.

6. *Ibid.,* E. Iʳ.

7. 'Appendix' (on poetic diction) added in 1802 to the 'Preface' (1800) to the *Lyrical Ballads* (Oxford Poets ed., 1916, p. 942).

8. I, 101f. Cf. Dryden's inventive translation (11.559 ff.) of Ovid's *Metamorphoses,* XV, 379 ff.

9. I, 127 ff.

10. I denote by the terms *pastoral* and *georgic* not only poems like Pope's *Pastorals,* Thomson's *Seasons,* Grainger's *Sugar-cane* but local poems like *Windsor Forest,* and Goldsmith's *Traveller.*

11. *Biographia Literaria,* ed. J. Shawcross, 1907. I, 26f. For Southey see the *Review of English Studies,* V (1929), pp. 441f. The passage, which struck eighteenth-century readers the more forcibly perhaps because of the interest in night-pieces shown by Rymer in the preface to his translation of Rapin, had been praised in the eighteenth century by James Ralph in the preface to his *Night* (1728) and by William Melmoth, who preferred Pope's version to Homer's (*Letters on Several Subjects by the late Sir Thomas Fitzosborne,* 1748, p. 44). Ralph, it may be noted, anticipates Southey in finding certain inconsistencies in the passage which he puts down to the tyranny of rime. Arnold cites the passage for dispraise in *On the Story of Celtic Literature,* 1867, p. 164.

12. Coleridge, 'Dejection: An Ode,' ll. 28 f.

13. Shelley, *Prometheus Unbound,* II, i, 18.

14. Tennyson, *Maud,* I, XXII, ii, 4.

15. Arnold, 'Thyrsis,' XVI, 9.

16 *Spring,* ll. 170 f.

17. ll. 17 ff.

18. Keats, and to some extent Shelley, seem to build on the poetic diction of the eighteenth century. Following an age which, for example, delighted in *soft, blooming, sylvan, trembling, purple, blush,* Keats writes with a recognizable variation: 'While barred clouds bloom the soft-dying day' ('To Autumn'), 'Sylvan historian' ('Grecian Urn'), 'trembled blossoms' ('Psyche'), 'a thought . . . in his pained heart Made purple riot' ('Eve of St Agnes'), 'scutcheon blush'd with blood' (ibid.). There are many more instances. In the same way Coleridge's lines in the 'Ancient Mariner': 'As idle as a painted ship Upon a painted ocean' dealt a contemporary shock by using *painted* literally.

19. *Aeneid*, IV, 586 f.

20. *The Task*, i. 290 ff.

21. Tennyson, *In Memoriam*, CXV, 6.

22. J. Oldmixon, *Amores Britannici*, 1703, A 7^r.

23. Letter to Walpole, Aug. 1736.

24. Oxford Poets ed., 1906, p.205.

25. Virginia Woolf, 'White's Selborne' (*New Statesman and Nation*, 30 Sept. 1939, p.460).

26. *Essays*, ed. Ker, I, 16: cf. I, 259.

27. Two qualities Dryden insists on as essential in poetry.

28. Dryden also sometimes appears to be imitating lines like those of Chaucer's 'Knight's Tale,' ll. 1747 ff., where the stresses fall on boldly alliterative syllables.

29. 'used in the Latin sense, of the brightest, most vivid colouring in general, not of that peculiar tint so called' (Warburton's note on Pope's 'purple year,' 'Spring,' l.28, in his edition, 1751).

30. The practice of inventing them begins at least as early as Chapman's *Homer* (see the list in Professor de Selincourt's *Keats*, 1907 ed., p.577). A list from William Browne occurs *ibid.*, p.579, and from Dryden at p.65 of Mr. Van Doren's *Poetry of John Dryden*, ed. 1931.

31. *Georgics*, III, 286 f.

32. I, 164.

33. *Op. cit.*, II, 148. Dryden is writing late in life, in 1695.

34. Monosyllabic rimes were another means of avoiding burlesque associations: rimes of two or three syllables formed part of the armoury of burlesque writers—they were a feature, for instance, of the Hudibrastic measure. See above, p. 225.

35. It was by these qualifications that rhyme escaped Milton's disdainful charge: 'The jingling sound of like endings.' Dryden considered that Milton turned to blank verse because his own skill in rhyme was clumsy: 'he had neither the ease of doing it, nor the graces of it' (*op. cit.* II, 30). Cf. G. Sewell. *The Whole Works of Mr. John Philips*, 1720, p.xxiii.

36. T. Quayle, *Poetic Diction: A Study of Eighteenth Century Verse*, 1924, p.30.

37. Preface to 'Tales' (*Works*, 1834, IV, 144).

38. *The Course of English Classicism*, 1930, p.98.

39. I. 488.

40. *Ecl.* X, 42.

41. III, 289 f.

42. 'Essay on the Georgics' (*Works of Virgil . . . Translated . . . by . . . Dryden*, ed. 1763, I, 207).

43. *Essays: on Poetry and Music, as they Affect the Mind*, 1778, p.257. Dryden (not *mirabile dictu*) certainly heightens the original, but his fiery additions are not made without generous encouragement from Virgil. Virgil may be more 'figurative,' but Beattie forgets that the figures are often pictures.

44. *Op. cit.*, p. xxv. In the preface to the translation of Virgil by himself and Christopher Pitt, Joseph Warton writes: 'But, alas! . . . what must become of a translator of the Georgics, writing in a language not half so lofty, so sounding, or so elegant as the Latin, incapable of admitting many of its best and boldest figures, and heavily fettered with the Gothick shackles of rhyme!

Is not this endeavouring to imitate a palace of porphyry with flints and bricks?
A poem whose excellence peculiarly consists in the graces of diction is far
more difficult to be translated, than a work where sentiment, or passion, or
imagination, is chiefly displayed. . . . Besides, the meanness of terms of husbandry is concealed and lost in a dead language, and they convey no low or
despicable image to the mind; but the course and common words I was ne-
cessitated to use in the following translation, viz. *plough and sow, wheat, dung,
ashes, horse and cow,* etc. will, I fear, unconquerably disgust many a delicate
reader . . .' (*The Works of Virgil,* 1753, I, vi f.) This passage introduces another subject. Words in a dead language, even when they are realistic, fasten
themselves more lightly than words should to the equivalent objects of the
here and now, and may end by making the objects themselves less real. The
small poets of the eighteenth century did not guard against this enough.
Wordsworth (who is probably speaking of Latin and Greek proses) saw the
danger clearly after he had escaped it:

> . . . . In general terms,
> I was a better judge of thoughts than words,
> Misled as to these latter, not alone
> By common inexperience of youth
> But by the trade in classic niceties,
> Delusion to young Scholars incident
> And old ones also, by that overpriz'd
> And dangerous craft of picking phrases out
> From languages that want the living voice
> To make of them a nature to the heart,
> To tell us what is passion, what is truth,
> What reason, what simplicity and sense.
>
> (*The Prelude,* ed. E. de Selincourt, 1926, p.176
> [the version of 1805-6].)

45. We find Fenton writing as follows: 'I . . . did not like [the word]
Homeric; it has a burlesque sound' (Pope's *Correspondence,* ed. G. Sherburn,
1956, ii. 398).

46. There is an interesting letter from Lady Mary Wortley Montagu to
Pope (*Pope's Correspondence, ed. cit.,* i. 396 ff.) about some Turkish verses
in translation, in the course of which we read: 'I could not forbear retaining
the comparison of her eyes to those of a stag, though perhaps the novelty of
it may give it a burlesque sound in our language' (p.402).

47. *Rambler,* 168. Cf. Beattie, *op. cit.,* pp. 256 ff. for a justification of Pope's
translating Homer's 'swine-herd' as 'swain.' Cf. also Wilde, *The Importance
of Being Earnest,* Act II:

> *Cecily:* . . . When I see a spade I call it a spade.
>
> *Gwendolen* (satirically): I am glad to say I have never seen a spade.
> It is obvious that our social spheres have been widely different.'

In the passage from Johnson there is a ready instance of the way words
shift their category: we now smile at Johnson's word 'risibility,' which was
then a 'serious' word: to us it seems ludicrously pompous. In Johnson's parody
of Robert Potter's translation of Euripides *dun* and *blood-boltered,* both from
Macbeth, are prominent words. Wordsworth consciously made the attempt to
reclaim for serious poetry words that had been burlesque words in the seven-

teenth and eighteenth centuries: see Preface to *Lyrical Ballads*, 1800, para. 7 from end.

48. We can appreciate this linguistic repugnance by examining our own over such a word as *blooming*. It is Saxon, and 'beautiful' (i.e. pleasant to say, having pleasant original associations); it was over-used by eighteenth-century poets and, therefore, vulgarized; it was 'successfully employed in some ludicrous' parody; it even became slang and a euphemistic swear-word; it therefore seems ludicrous whenever it is now met in eighteenth-century poems.

49. *Peri Bathous*, XII.

50. 11. 256 ff.

51. This interest was of long standing, of course: see, e.g. E. M. W. Till-yard, *The Elizabethan World Picture*, 1943, pp. 9 and 29.

52. 'A Paraphrase upon the Psalms,' ed. 1676, pp. 14 and 178.

53. Pope, *Essay on Man*, III, 115 ff.

54. 9th ed., 1737, p.215. Cf. Montaigne, 'Of the use of apparel': 'My opinion is, that even as all plants, trees, living creatures, and whatsoever hath life, is naturally seen furnished with sufficient furniture to defend itself from the injury of all weathers:

> Proptereaque fere res omnes, aut corio sunt,
> Aut seta, aut conchis, aut callo, aut cortice tectae.
> (Luc. I, iv, 932)

> Therefore all things almost we cover'd mark,
> With hide, or hair, or shells, or brawn, or bark.

Even so were we.'

55. I, v, 33.

56. 1604, p.33.

57. II, vi, 57.

58. 1677, p.13.

59. II, 150.

60. Arthur O. Lovejoy, *The Great Chain of Being*, 1936.

61. *State of Innocence*, 1677, p.37.

62. Pope, *Essay on Man*, I, 210.

63. *Op. cit.*, p.9.

64. *Poetic Diction: A Study in Meaning*, 1928, p. 177.

LORD DAVID CECIL

————

The Poetry of Thomas Gray

THIS is an extremely agreeable occasion for me. It is the more so, because I think it might have been an agreeable occasion for Thomas Warton, in whose honour this lecture was founded. Not, I hasten to say, that I imagine he would have wanted to listen to me. Warton lived in the civilized eighteenth century, and so would have been likely to despise the child of a barbarous age like our own. But, whether or not he would have approved of me, Warton would certainly have approved of my subject. In April 1770 he wrote to thank Gray for sending him some notes on the history of English poetry. The letter ended in a tribute to Gray's own work expressed in the rotund strain of compliment characteristic of his period.

> I cannot take my leave [he says], without declaring that my strongest incitement to prosecute the history of English Poetry is the pleasant hope of being approved by you; whose true genius I so justly venerate, and whose genuine poetry has ever given me such sincere pleasure.

To appreciate Gray, then, is an appropriate task for a Warton lecturer. But it is not an easy task. Appreciation of an author, if it is to be profitable, involves more than just making a list of his excellences, taking the reader on a personally-conducted tour, as it were, of his subject's works, stopping to point out outstanding beauties. The critic should interpret as well as exhibit, perceive the relation between particular works in such a way as to discover the general character of the personality that produced them, and to analyse the special compound of

---

From the Warton Lecture on English Poetry, British Academy, 1945. Reprinted by permission of the British Academy, Macmillan & Co., and the author.

233

talent and temperament which gives his writing its individuality. With Gray, this is hard. For one thing, his work is so diverse that it is not easy to see it as the expression of a single personality. It is odd that this should be so; for he wrote very little. There are not more than a dozen or so of his memorable poems. But among this dozen we find light verse and serious verse, reflective and dramatic, a sonnet on the death of a friend, and an ode composed to celebrate the installation of a chancellor of Cambridge University. Further, Gray's poems are composed in a highly conventionalized form which obscures the direct revelation of their author's personality. His figure is separated from us by a veil of literary good manners which blurs its edges and subdues its colour.

All the same, personality and figure are there all right, if we train our eyes to look carefully. The good manners are Gray's special brand of good manners; whether he is being light or serious, personal or public, Gray shows himself as much an individual as Blake or Byron. What, then, is his individuality? As might be expected from the diversity of its expression, it is complex, combining unexpected elements. The first that strikes the critic is the academic. Gray is an outstanding example of the professional man of learning who happened by a chance gift of fortune to be also a poetic artist. No one has ever lived a more intensely academic life. His home background had nothing to offer him: he was a fastidious scholarly type, incongruously born into the Hogarthian world of commercial London. At 9 years old, however, he was sent to Eton: from Eton he proceeded to Cambridge: and at Cambridge—save for two years' tour of the Continent at the age of 24—he remained for the rest of his life. He never married, and never engaged in any work outside the University. For thirty years his life was divided between scholarship and scholarly pleasures; reading in his rooms at Cambridge, going up to London for a concert or, once a year, taking a stately little holiday in some picturesque part of England, where he fastidiously contemplated medieval ruins and sunset lakes. As much as Walter Pater, he represents that peculiar product of the ancient English universities, the scholar-aesthete.

The name Pater, however, suggests a difference. Gray, unlike Pater, lived in the eighteenth century; so he was an eighteenth-century scholar-aesthete. Now this was something very unlike the nineteenth-century type of which Pater is an example. Nineteenth-century aesthetes were spiritual hermits; they fled from the normal world in horror; its interests and its values alike repelled them as barbarous and philistine. Not so their eighteenth-century forebears. For England, in the eighteenth century, was an integrated society in which people agreed to respect each other's interests and united to accept similar standards of value. Often they differed in taste: some liked the town, others liked the country; some were interested in politics, some in hunting, some in learning. But the student did not despise the soldier; the master of foxhounds was proud to quote such Latin tags as he could remember, and the aesthete was not in the least disposed to scorn the avocations of normal active life, or to dismiss its standards as valueless. Certainly Gray was not. Personally, he preferred a life of retirement; but he could admire those who did not; he had, in fact, a certain amount in common with them. Was he not a strong Whig, a full-blooded patriot —he could hardly keep his temper when he thought of the contemptible French—a solid, though broadminded, member of the Church of England, and a believer in the social graces? Donnish provinciality and awkwardness repelled him: and he showed no taste for artistic unconventionality. The people who attracted him were well-bred, well-mannered, and well-dressed. They were also entertaining. For Gray— and this was another difference between him and the Paterian aesthete— had a great deal of humour. His enthusiasm for beauty and romance was always kept rational by the smiling and satirical good sense of his age. Here we come to the second important element in his composition. In addition to being a representative scholar-artist, he was a representative man of the eighteenth-century world.

We have not done with him, though, when we have discovered his typical qualities. Remarkable people are always more than types; they would not be remarkable if they were not. Gray's personality owes its unmistakable flavour to the peculiar bias of his taste, to the peculiar colouring of his temperament. His taste was the expression of his mental life. This, we have seen, was aesthetic: Gray enjoyed things in so far as they appealed to his sense of beauty. 'Beauty' is such a misused, shop-soiled word by now that perhaps I may be allowed to stop for a minute and define in what sense I am using it. It is the ordinary, obvious sense we mean when we say: 'What a beautiful sunset!' 'What a beautiful church!' 'What a beautiful piece of music!' We intend to convey by these exclamations that the object in question appeals to our senses, and, through them, to our imagination. A well-cooked mutton-chop appeals to our senses but not, I fancy, to our imagination; so, however agreeable to the palate, it cannot legitimately be called beautiful. An heroic action appeals to our imagination but not to our senses. It can only be called beautiful metaphorically. When I say that Gray found his chief satisfaction in life in what appealed to his sense of beauty, I do not mean mutton-chops or heroic actions, I mean sunsets and churches and music.

As a matter of fact, he did like all these things. His sensibility was extremely varied. And such other subjects as appealed to him were in some way associated in his mind with aesthetic pleasure. His interest in botany, for instance, came primarily from the fact that he thought plants beautiful. All the same, there was another side to him, only second in importance to his aesthetic sense, namely, his intense feeling for history. The fact that he had spent his life amid the ancient groves and mouldering traceried architecture of Eton and Cambridge, and that his whole education was steeped in the spirit of historic Greece and Rome, made him acutely responsive to the imaginative appeal of past ages.

Such a responsiveness is often regarded as a phenomenon of the Romantic Movement. This has led some people to say that Gray, just because he liked reading Norse sagas and looking at fourteenth-century abbeys, was a romantic before his time. This is all nonsense. It is true that the sense of the past only achieved its full development in the time of the Romantics. Not till Scott wrote the Waverley novels did it show itself capable of stimulating by its own unaided power a new and major form of literature. But it was born earlier. It was the creature of the eighteenth century. Before then people do not seem to have felt it. Shakespeare draws medieval barons and Roman senators alike, as Elizabethan gentlemen; but Pope in his *Eloisa* already shows signs that he feels nunneries and ruins to be romantic. By Gray's time a whole group of persons had grown up who delighted in nothing so much as letting their imaginations luxuriate in dwelling on some past period, in noting the quaintness of its costumes and architecture, and in enjoying the picturesque charm of its archaic tongue. Plays, for the first time, were acted by their producers in what they imagined to be the correct dress of the period in which they were set: authors composed historical novels and mock medieval ballads: scholars edited ancient texts, Horace Walpole built Strawberry Hill.

Why the sense of the past came to birth in the eighteenth century is not certainly known. But I would suggest that the sober rationalism which permeated the general outlook of the age led its more poetic spirits to find contemporary life intolerably prosaic. Their imagination felt constricted by the spectacle of the world of their own time. They therefore sought relief by escaping mentally to the contemplation of other and less rational periods. Since there was no mystery and magic about the coffeehouses and classical architecture of 1750, they looked for them amid the ruins and rusting armour of the age of faith. Academic persons confined to the humdrum security of college life were peculiarly susceptible to this.

Thomas Warton himself felt it, but no one more intensely and more sensitively than Gray. Perpendicular architecture, Elizabethan mansions, medieval illuminated manuscripts alike stirred him to dream and to delight. What wild, mysterious visions arose before his mental eye as he listened to the blind Welsh harpist, Barry, singing the traditional folk-songs of his country! How fascinating it was to walk round the panelled chambers of a Tudor manor-house, tracing the patterns on the blackened carving, noting the picturesque details of dress in the portraits that stared down so uncompromisingly from the walls! In his comic poem, *The Long Story,* he lets his mind play in whimsical fantasy on this taste of his.

> In Britain's Isle, no matter where,
> An ancient pile of building stands:
> The Huntingdons and Hattons there
> Employ'd the power of Fairy hands
>
> To raise the cieling's fretted height,
> Each pannel in achievements cloathing,
> Rich windows that exclude the light,
> And passages, that lead to nothing.
>
> Full oft within the spatious walls,
> When he had fifty winters o'er him,
> My grave Lord-Keeper led the Brawls;
> The Seal, and Maces, danc'd before him.
>
> His bushy beard, and shoe-strings green,
> His high-crown'd hat, and sattin-doublet,
> Mov'd the stout heart of England's Queen,
> Tho' Pope and Spaniard could not trouble it.

When Gray looked at a landscape, immediately, instinctively he peopled it in imagination with the figures of those who had lived there in times past. Here he is writing a letter describing his fancies during a visit to the ruins of Netley Abbey.

In the bosom of the woods (concealed from profane eyes) lie hid the ruins of Netley Abbey; there may be richer and greater houses of religion, but the Abbot is content with his situation. See there, at the top of that hanging meadow, under the shade of those old trees that bend into a half circle about it, he is walking slowly (good man!) and bidding his beads for the souls of his benefactors, interred in that venerable pile that lies beneath him. Beyond it (the meadow still descending) nods a thicket of oaks that mask the building, and have excluded a view too garish and luxuriant for a holy eye; only on either hand they leave an opening to the blue glittering sea. Did you not observe how, as that white sail shot by and was lost, he turned and crossed himself to drive the tempter from him that had thrown that distraction in his way? I should tell you that the ferryman who rowed me, a lusty young fellow, told me that he would not for all the world pass a night at the Abbey, (there were such things near it,) though there was a power of money hid there.

Do you notice in this passage how Gray's aesthetic response to the beauty of the scene mingles inextricably with his response to its historic appeal? His aesthetic emotion was always most intense when it was reinforced by his historic interest, when what was beautiful was also evocative of some vanished age.

Indeed, he always tends to see the contemporary world in relation to its historic past. The Eton College of his Ode lies in the shadow of Windsor's ancestral battlements; the school itself is the place where learning 'still adores her Henry's holy Shade.' Even when he was meditating on the rustic graves in a country churchyard, historic references intrude themselves; village-Hampdens and Miltons, he fancies, may lie buried there: he contrasts the simple funerals of the poor with the pompous obsequies of great persons in some majestic Gothic cathedral

> Where thro' the long-drawn aisle and fretted vault
> The pealing anthem swells the note of praise.

His attitude to literature itself is largely an historian's attitude. Both in *The Bard* and in *The Progress of Poesy* he directs our mental eye to observe the great poets of the past as they file by one by one down the endless corridor of the ages; he sees the development of the art of letters as an historic process. Gray is the first great English writer for whom the imaginative sense of history is an important source of inspiration, the first who consciously cultivates the sense of period.

This inevitably gives an individual colour to his otherwise normal eighteenth-century vision. It is made still more individual by the particular mood in which he surveyed the drama of human existence. This, for all his humour, was predominantly a minor key mood. The circumstances of his early life, an uncongenial home background, and an unhappy family life still further darkened by the shadow of poverty, had made him early aware of the gloomier side of human existence; with the result that his confidence in living was, from the outset of his career, irrevocably damaged. This was why he took up academic life. Shrinking from contact with the rough world, he sought shelter in monastic and solitary seclusion. He found too little stimulus in it to invigorate his vitality. Year after year he idled away his time in aimless study and abortive literary projects—a prey to hypochondria and ennui. True, he had friends whom he loved passionately. But friendship, though it brought him some ecstatic moments, also brought him sorrowful ones. The friendships of the solitary seldom are productive of happiness. If cool, they are not delightful enough to conquer melancholy; if ardent, they are inevitably frustrated of satisfying fulfilment. For they are not founded on a sufficiently stable basis. The friend is liable to drift away to marriage or active life. Conscious of this insecurity the solitary grows suspicious and difficult. Gray was a touchy, uneasy friend, and his intensest friendships generally came to grief. Such experiences did not tend to brighten his spirits. His considered view of life was melancholy: the world was a dangerous place where sorrow is certain and happiness transient. Once more, however, his temperamental outlook was qualified by the age in which he lived. The eighteenth-century point of view was incompatible with that open out-and-out pessimism to which a romantic like Housman could full-bloodedly surrender himself. For one thing, it believed in the golden mean, and disapproved of extremes of any kind. Even if human life was not perfect, it had its good sides: a rational person strove to keep this in mind. Moreover, whatever unpleasantness life on this planet might entail, it had to be lived: and the wise man made the best of it. To give oneself up to lamentation only made things worse.

Nor was it right. The eighteenth century was profoundly moral. The first duty of man, it held, was to pursue virtue; and there was no doubt that suffering, if taken in the right way, was an aid to virtue. Man could learn through it to bear his own sorrows with courage, and to look with sympathy on those of others. Gray's strong religious convictions made him peculiarly conscious of these obligations, with the result that his melancholy was softened, alike by his faith and his good sense. For the most part it was, as he says, a 'white melancholy' which,

> though it seldom laughs or dances nor ever amounts to what one calls Joy or Pleasure, yet is a good easy sort of a state. . . . There is another sort, black indeed, which I have now and then felt that has somewhat in it like Tertullian's rule of faith, *credo quia impossibile est;* for it be-

lieves, nay is sure, of everything that is unlikely, so it be but frightful; and, on the other hand, excludes and shuts its eyes to the most possible hopes, and everything that is pleasurable; from this the Lord deliver us! for none but he and sunshiny weather can do it.

Such, then, was Gray—a typical eighteenth-century scholar-artist with a peculiarly intense response to the imaginative appeal of the past and whose pervading temper was a sober melancholy. His memorable poems—for some are mere craftsman's exercises—are the characteristic expression of such a man. They divide themselves into two or three categories, in accordance with the different aspects of his complex nature. His three long odes are inspired by the historical and aesthetic strain in him. That on the Installation of the Duke of Grafton as Chancellor of Cambridge was, it is true, originally designed as an occasional piece. But in it Gray takes advantage of the occasion to show us in what particular way Cambridge did appeal to his own imagination. As might be expected, this is historical. For him the groves and courts of the University are haunted by the ghosts of its founders, Margaret of Anjou, Edward III, Henry VI, and Henry VIII; and of the great spirits, Milton and Newton, who had studied there. *The Bard* gives Gray's historical imagination greater scope. The last of the Druids prophesies to Edward I the misfortunes that are to overtake his line: in a sort of murky magnificence, names and events heavy with romantic and historic associations pass in pageant before us. *The Progress of Poesy* is less historical, more aesthetic. Though in the second part Gray traces the development of poetic art from Greece to Rome and from Rome to England, this historical motive is made subsidiary to an exposition of what the author considers to be the place of poetry in human life. Like Keats's *Ode on a Grecian Urn,* the *Progress of Poesy* is a meditation about the fundamental significance of art. Not at all the same sort of meditation though. The difference between the Augustan and Romantic attitude to life could not appear more vividly than in the difference between these two poems. There is nothing mystical about Gray's view, no transcendental vision of art as an expression of ultimate spiritual reality, where Truth is the same as Beauty and Beauty the same as Truth. No—poetry to Gray, as to any other sensible eighteenth-century gentleman, was just a pleasure: and the poet so far from being the priest of a mystery was a purveyor of pleasure—'above the great, but,' he is careful to point out, 'far below the good.' But poetry was useful and even educative: a necessary part of the good life, soothing the passions, civilizing the heart and manners, celebrating beauty and virtue, and, above all, providing an alleviation to the inevitable ills of the human lot.

The second category of Gray's poems deals with his personal relation to life: his impressions of experience and the conclusions he drew from them. In one poem, indeed—the sonnet on the death of his friend West— he draws no conclusion: the poem is a simple sigh of lamentation. But, in all the other expressions of this phase of his work, sentiment leads to reflection and reflection to a moral. The Eton College Ode shows Gray surveying the scenes of his youth and observing the unthinking happiness of childhood through the eyes of a disillusioned maturity. With a sad irony he draws his conclusion:

Where ignorance is bliss, 'tis folly to be wise.

The *Ode on the Spring* is inspired by the spectacle of a fine day in early spring, with the buds hastening to open and the insects busily humming. How like the activities of the world of men! says Gray, and hardly more ephemeral. But once more irony steps in—Who is he to condemn? It is true he has chosen to be spectator rather than actor: but he is no wiser than the actors and perhaps enjoys himself less. The unfinished *Ode on Vicissitude* points yet another moral. Though life is a chequer-work of good and ill, sad and happy, we ought not to repine: perhaps without the sadness we should enjoy the intervals of happiness less than we do. The Adversity Ode is sterner in tone. Adversity is a trial sent by God to school us to virtue, if we are strong enough to profit by it. Finally there is the *Elegy*. Here the sight of the graveyard stirs the poet to meditate on the life of man in relation to its inevitable end. Death, he perceives, dwarfs human differences. There is not much to choose between the great and the humble, once they are in the grave. It may be that there never was; it may be that in the obscure graveyard lie persons who but for untoward circumstances would have been as famous as Milton and Hampden. The thought, however, does not sadden him; if circumstances prevented them from achieving great fame, circumstances also saved them from committing great crimes. Yet there is a special pathos in these obscure tombs; the crude inscriptions on the clumsy monuments are so poignant a reminder of the vain longing of all men, however humble, to be loved and to be remembered. This brings Gray round to himself. How does he expect to be remembered? Not as a happy man: he has been sad, obscure, misunderstood. Yet, he reminds himself with his customary balance, there have been alleviations. He has known friendship, loved learning, and attained, in part at least, to virtue. Soberly, but with faith, he resigns himself to the judgement of his God.

This group of poems is all concerned with the same thing, the relation of a sensitive contemplative spirit to the thronging, mysterious, tragic, transient world into which he finds himself thrown. For all their formality of phrase, they are consistently and intensely personal.

There remains the brief and brilliant category of Gray's satirical and humorous verse—*The Long Story, The Ode on a Cat, Hymn to Ignorance*, and the *Impromptu on Lord Holland's House*. Now and again in these poems, more particularly in *The Long Story*, Gray the historian shows his hand; while they all display his scholarly sense of finish. Mainly, however, they reveal Gray the man of the world—Gray the admirer of Pope and the friend of Walpole. In the best eighteenth-century manner he uses his taste and his learning to add wit and grace to the amenities of social life. But they are none the less characteristic for that. As much as pindaric or elegy they contribute essential features to our mental portrait of their author.

Gray's mode of expression is as typical of him as is his choice of themes. His style is pre-eminently an academic style, studied, traditional, highly finished. His standard of finish, indeed, was so high as sometimes to be frustrating. He could take years to complete a brief poem. During the process he sent round fragments to his friends for their advice. Like Mr. James Joyce, though not so publicly, Gray was given to issuing his work while 'in progress'. Sometimes it remained for ever in this unreposeful condition. He never managed to get the *Ode on Vicissitude* finished at all. His choice of forms, too, is a scholar's choice. Sedulously he goes to the best authors for models. He writes the Pindaric Ode—making a more careful attempt than his predecessors had, exactly to follow Pindar—the Horatian Ode, the classical sonnet, and the orthodox elegy, leading up to its final formal epitaph. His diction is a consciously poetic affair; an artificial diction, deliberately created to be an appropriate vehicle for lofty poetry. 'The language of the age,' he stated as an axiom, 'is never the language of poetry.' Certainly his own language was not that of his age—or of any other, for that matter. It is an elaborate compound of the language of those authors whom he most admired: Horace and Virgil, Pope and Dryden, above all, Milton—the youthful Milton who wrote *L'Allegro* and *Lycidas*. For Milton, as the greatest English Master of the artificial style, appealed peculiarly to Gray. Sometimes the influence of one of these poets predominates, sometimes of another, according to which Gray thinks is the best in the kind of verse he is attempting. He follows Pope in satire,

Dryden in declamation, Milton in elegiac and picturesque passages. It was from Milton, incidentally, he learnt the evocative power of proper names:

> Cold is Cadwallo's tongue,
> That hush'd the stormy main:
> Brave Urien sleeps upon his craggy bed:
> Mountains, ye mourn in vain
> Modred, whose magic song
> Made huge Plinlimmon bow his cloud-top'd head.

Nor does he just imitate other authors. He openly quotes them. The Pindaric Odes especially are whispering galleries, murmurous with echoes of dead poets' voices—Shakespeare's, Spenser's, Cowley's. Sometimes he will lift a whole passage; the image of Jove's eagle in the second stanza of *The Progress of Poesy* is transplanted from Pindar's First Pythian. Sometimes he will adapt a phrase: 'ruddy drops that warm my heart' in *The Bard* is a modification of the 'ruddy drops that visit my sad heart' in *Julius Caesar*. Once again, Gray curiously reminds us of a modern author. This device of imbedding other people's phrases in his verse anticipates Mr. T. S. Eliot. Gray's purpose, however, is very different. The quoted phrase is not there to point an ironical contrast as with Mr. Eliot; rather it is inserted to stir the reader's imagination by the literary associations which it evokes. Conscious, as Gray is, of poetry developing in historic process, he wishes to enhance the effect of his own lines by setting astir in the mind memories of those great poets of whom he feels himself the heir.

The trouble about such devices is that they limit the scope of the poem's appeal. Gray's pindarics, like Mr. Eliot's *Waste Land,* can be fully appreciated only by highly educated readers. Indeed, Gray's education was not altogether an advantage to him as a writer. At times his poetry is so clogged with learning as to be obscure. *The Bard* and *The Progress of Poesy* are crowded with allusions that need notes to explain them. While we are painstakingly looking at the notes, our emotional response to the poem grows chilly. In his effort to concentrate his allusion into one polished, pregnant phrase, Gray tends to leave out the facts necessary to make it immediately intelligible:

> The bristled Boar in infant-gore
> Wallows beneath the thorny shade.

To Gray fresh from the libraries of Cambridge this may have seemed lucid enough. But how can the common reader be expected to realize straight away that it refers to Richard III's death at the battle of Bosworth? Like some poets of our own time, Gray seems at moments to forget the difference between a poem and a conundrum.

It is another defect of Gray's academic method—and, it may be added, of his academic temperament—that it involved a certain lack of imaginative heat. Scholars are seldom fiery spirits: Gray's poems are, compared with those of Burns let us say, a touch tepid. This tepidness shows itself in his personifications. Gray is very fond of personifications:

> Warm Charity, the gen'ral Friend,
> With Justice to herself severe,
> And Pity, dropping soft the sadly-pleasing tear.

These personifications are clear and sensible enough. Charity—were she a person—might reasonably be expected to be a friendly one; and Pity to shed tears. But somehow the effect is lifeless. We feel that—having decided to personify these virtues—Gray deliberately, and with the help of his intellect, gets to work to make suitable puppets in which to incarnate them. On the other hand when Keats speaks of

> Joy, whose hand is ever at his lips
> Bidding adieu;

the impression we get is that Joy spontaneously embodied itself in a living figure, which flashed unbidden, and as in a vision, before the poet's mental eye.

Indeed Gray's head is stronger than his fancy or his passions. Always we are aware in his work of the conscious intellect, planning and pruning: seldom does his inspiration take wing to sweep him up into that empyrean where feeling and thought are one. The words clothe the idea beautifully and aptly and in a garment that could only have been devised by a person of the most refined taste and the highest culture. But they clothe it, they do not embody it. For that absolute union of thought and word which is the mark of the very highest poetry of all, we look to Gray in vain. He had not that intensity of inspiration; and, anyway, education had developed his critical spirit too strongly for him to be able completely to let himself go. His poetry, in fact, illustrates perfectly the characteristic limitations of the academic spirit.

But it also reveals, in the highest degree, its characteristic merits. Always it is disciplined by his intellect and refined by his taste. The matter is rational; Gray never talks nonsense; each poem is logically designed, with a beginning, a middle, and an end. Every line and every phrase has its contribution to make to the general effect; so that the whole gives one that particular satisfaction that comes from seeing a problem completely resolved. Even the best lines—and this is a typical beauty of conscious art—are better in their context than when they are lifted from it. Moreover, though Gray fails to achieve the highest triumphs of expression, he maintains a consistently high level of style—better than some greater men do. No doubt it is a style that takes getting used to: artificial styles always do. We must accustom ourselves to the tropes and the antitheses, the abstractions, classical allusions and grandiose periphrases which are his habitual mode of utterance. They are as much a part of it as the garlands and trophies which ornament a piece of baroque architecture; for Gray lived in the baroque period and shared its taste. A poem like *The Progress of Poesy* is like nothing so much as some big decorative painting of the period in which, posed gracefully on an amber-coloured cloud, allegorical figures representing the arts and the passions offer ceremonious homage to the goddesses of Poetry or Beauty:

> Slow melting strains their Queen's approach declare:
> Where'er she turns the Graces homage pay.
> With arms sublime, that float upon the air,
> In gliding state she wins her easy way:
> O'er her warm cheek, and rising bosom, move
> The bloom of young Desire, and purple light of Love.

Does not that recall some radiant, florid ceiling painted by Tiepolo? And it is executed with a similar virtuosity. Gray attempts the most complex and difficult metres. His work is thickly embroidered with image and epigram. But the images and epigrams are appropriate. Every cadence is both musical in itself and an apt echo of the sense:

> Say, has he giv'n in vain the heav'nly Muse?
> Night, and all her sickly dews,
> Her Spectres wan, and Birds of boding cry,
> He gives to range the dreary sky:
> Till down the eastern cliffs afar
> Hyperion's march they spy, and glittering shafts of war.

Once again, I am quoting from *The Progress of Poesy*: for it is in these Pindaric Odes that Gray's virtuosity appears most conspicuously. They are not, however, his most successful works. For in them he is dealing

245

with subject-matter which does reveal his limitations. This is especially true of *The Bard*. Here Gray tries to write dramatically; he addresses us in the person of a medieval druid about to commit suicide. Such a role does not suit him. Gray was excited by reading about druids; but he was not at all like a druid himself. Nor had he the kind of imagination convincingly to impersonate one. He tried very hard—'I felt myself the Bard,' he said—but, alas, the result of all his efforts was only a stagey, if stylish, example of eighteenth-century rhetoric, elaborately decked up with the ornaments of a Strawberry Hill Mock-Gothic. In *The Progress of Poesy* Gray wisely refrains from any attempt at impersonation and the result is far more successful. Indeed, in its way, the poem is a triumph. But a triumph of style rather than substance. The pleasure we get from the work is that given by watching a master-craftsman magnificently displaying his skill in an exercise on a given conventional theme.

No—Gray writes best when he does not try a lofty flight of imagination but, with his feet planted firmly on the earth, comments lightly or gravely on the world he himself knew. Here, once more, he is typical of his period. Eighteenth-century writers are, most of them, not so much concerned with the inward and spiritual as with the social and moral aspects of existence—less with man the solitary soul in relation to the ideal and the visionary, than with man the social animal in relation to the people and the age in which he finds himself. For all he lived a life of retirement, Gray is no exception to his contemporaries. The region of romance and art in which he liked to take refuge was to him a place of pleasant distraction, not the home of a deeper spiritual life, as it was for Blake, for instance. Even when in the *Ode on the Spring* he contrasts his own inactive existence with that of his fellows, his eye is on them; his interest is to see how his life relates to theirs. And the thoughts stirred in him by his contemplations here, as also in his Eton ode, are of the straightforward kind which they could understand. So might any thoughtful person feel on a spring day, or when revisiting their old school. What Johnson said of *The Elegy in a Country Churchyard* is equally true of Gray's other elegiac pieces. 'They abound with sentiments to which every bosom returns an echo.' Indeed Gray's relative lack of originality made him peculiarly able to speak for the common run of mankind. But he spoke for them in words they could not have found for themselves. Poetry, says Pope, should be 'what oft was thought but ne'er so well expressed.' This is not true of all poetry. But it is true of Gray's. The fact that he was an exquisite artist made it possible for him to express the commonplace with an eloquence and a nobility that turn it into immortal poetry. Moreover, his vision is deepened and enriched by his historic sense. His meditations in the churchyard acquire a monumental quality, because they seem to refer to it at any time during its immemorial history: his reflections on his Eton schooldays gain universality from the fact that he perceives his own sojourn there as only an episode in the School's life, and his personal emotions about it as the recurrent emotion of generations of Etonians.

These reflective poems, too, are more moving than the Pindaric Odes. No wonder: they were the product of the deepest emotional crisis of his life. The Pindarics were written in his tranquil middle age; these other poems, all except the *Elegy*, in the later months of 1742; and the *Elegy*, composed a few years later, is a final comment on the same phase of his experience. Two events produced this phase. Gray's prospects were very dark; poverty was forcing him back to take up life at Cambridge at a moment when he felt a strong reaction against it: and the pair of friends who were his chief source of happiness were during this time lost to him. He quarrelled with Walpole, and West died. Under the combined stress of these misfortunes his emotional agitation rose to a pitch which found vent in an unprecedented outburst of poetic activity. Even when inspired by such an impulse, the result is not exactly passionate: but it is heartfelt. The sentiment it expresses has its birth in the very foundations of the poet's nature; it is distilled from the experience of a lifetime. Let me quote the sonnet on the death of West:

> In vain to me the smileing Mornings shine,
>   And redning Phœbus lifts his golden Fire:
> The Birds in vain their amorous Descant joyn;
>   Or chearful Fields resume their green Attire:
> These Ears, alas! for other Notes repine,
>   A different Object do these Eyes require.
> My lonely Anguish melts no Heart, but mine;
>   And in my Breast the imperfect Joys expire.
> Yet Morning smiles the busy Race to chear,
>   And new-born Pleasure brings to happier Men:
> The Fields to all their wonted Tribute bear:
>   To warm their little Loves the Birds complain:
> I fruitless mourn to him, that cannot hear,
>   And weep the more because I weep in vain.

Is not this poignant? Once more, you will remark, its effect is intensified by what I can only call Gray's commonplaceness. It is interesting in this connexion to compare it with a more famous lamentation over the

247

dead, with *Lycidas*. Poetically, of course, it is of a lower order. Gray had nothing like Milton's imaginative and verbal genius. All the same, and just because Gray was not so original a genius, his poem does something that Milton's does not. It expresses exactly what the average person does feel when someone he loves dies.

Nor does its eighteenth-century formality weaken its emotional force. On the contrary, it makes it seem more authentic. Personal feelings of this kind always present peculiar difficulties to a poet; for it is so hard to express them without sentimentality, so hard for the poet not to seem as if he was calculatedly exploiting his private emotions in order to bring tears to the eyes of his readers. The more colloquial and informal the language he uses, the more likely this is to happen. Gray's formality acts as a filter of good-mannered reticence through which his private grief comes to us, purged of any taint of sentimentality or exhibitionism, and with a pathos that seems all the more genuine because it is unemphasized:

> I fruitless mourn to him, that cannot hear,
>   And weep the more because I weep in vain.

In lines like these, as in the more famous *Elegy*, the two dominant strains in Gray serve each to strengthen the effect of the other. The fastidious artist and the eighteenth-century gentleman combine to produce something that is in its way both perfect and profound.

Equally perfect and from similar causes is Gray's lighter verse. Light verse rarely attains classical quality. Either it is so conversational and careless as to be vulgar; or, if the author tries to dignify it by a more stately style, he only succeeds in being pedantically facetious. The writer of light verse walks a narrow path between the abysses of donnish jocularity, on the one hand, and music-hall slanginess, on the other. Gray's curiously compounded nature enabled him to keep to this path unerringly. He is never pedantic, he jests with the elegant ease of a man of fashion. But the solid foundation of scholarly taste, which underlies everything he writes, gives his most frivolous improvisation distinction. Nor do those characteristics of his style which sometimes impede our appreciation of his other work trouble us here. In light verse it does not matter if we are aware of the intellectual process at work. It is right in comedy that the head should rule the heart and fancy. As for Gray's baroque conventionalities of phrase, these, when introduced, as it were, with a smile, enhance his wit by a delightful ironical stylishness:

> The hapless Nymph with wonder saw:
>> A whisker first and then a claw,
>>> With many an ardent wish,
>> She stretch'd in vain to reach the prize.
>> What female heart can gold despise?
>>> What Cat's averse to fish?

'The Cat,' says Dr. Johnson caustically, 'is called a nymph, with some violence both to language and sense.' Perhaps she is. Nevertheless—and one can dare to say so aloud now Dr. Johnson is no longer with us—the effect is charming.

Gray has two masterpieces in this lighter vein; these lines on the Cat, and those on the artificial ruins put up by Lord Holland at Kingsgate. The poem on the Cat is the more exquisite, in its own brief way as enchanting a mixture of wit and prettiness as *The Rape of the Lock* itself. But the bitter brilliance of the other shows that, had he chosen, Gray could equally have rivalled Pope as a satirist in the grand manner:

> OLD and abandon'd by each venal friend
>> Here H\<olland\> took the pious resolution
> To smuggle some few years and strive to mend
>> A broken character and constitution.
> On this congenial spot he fix'd his choice,
>> Earl Godwin trembled for his neighbouring sand,
> Here Seagulls scream and cormorants rejoice,
>> And Mariners tho' shipwreckt dread to land,
> Here reign the blustring north and blighting east,
>> No tree is heard to whisper, bird to sing,
> Yet nature cannot furnish out the feast,
>> Art he invokes new horrors still to bring:
> Now mouldring fanes and battlements arise,
>> Arches and turrets nodding to their fall,
> Unpeopled palaces delude his eyes,
>> And mimick desolation covers all.
> Ah, said the sighing Peer, had Bute been true
>> Nor Shelburn's, Rigby's, Calcraft's friendship vain,
> Far other scenes than these had bless'd our view
>> And realis'd the ruins that we feign.
> Purg'd by the sword and beautifyed by fire,
>> Then had we seen proud London's hated walls,
> Owls might have hooted in St Peters Quire,
>> And foxes stunk and litter'd in St Pauls.

Horace Walpole said that 'humour was Gray's natural and original turn, that he never wrote anything easily but things of Humour.' In view of these poems, it is hard to disagree with him. Nowhere else does Gray's virtuosity seem so effortless; nowhere else does he write with the same spontaneity and gusto. For once Gray seems to be sailing with the wind behind him the whole way. Of all his work, his light verse appears the most inspired.

How far this means that it is also the most precious is a different problem. A very big one too: it opens the whole question as to whether comic art can of its nature be equal in significance to grave art, whether the humorist's views of things is always, comparatively speaking, a superficial view. This takes us into deep waters; too deep to be fathomed in the brief close of a discourse like the present. But the issue is, I suggest, a more doubtful one than those earnest personages, the professional critics of literature, appear for the most part to think.

GEORGE SHERBURN

Fielding's Social Outlook

THE account of Fielding's work here attempted may rightly be condemned as too moralistic; but its view is that Fielding was fundamentally a moralist. If we are to discuss the art of an author, or the
form which he impresses on his material, it seems a necessary preliminary in the case of an intellectual novelist to see how far his opinions
shape his work, both as a whole and as seen in individual episodes. It
would be a mistake to take Fielding very seriously as a systematic
thinker; but only the casual reader can fail to see that his thinking does
shape his stories. *Jonathan Wild* and *Amelia* were obviously conceived
in intellectuality, and even *Tom Jones* and *Joseph Andrews* show their
author as one of the most thoughtful of English novelists.

Apart from his published writings we have little information concerning Fielding's intellectual life. We know that he was a journalist, a
playwright, a lawyer, and a justice of the peace. In his later years he
presided over the busiest police court in London. In his scant leisure
hours he wrote novels. His personality we have to deduce almost entirely from the printed page, and from it actually all that we get is his
opinions, his sympathies, or his prejudices. He shows a curiosity as to
the organization of society as well as to the conduct of private lives,
and it is his opinions in these two fields that are here to be examined.
It is not supposed that Fielding's favorite ideas are original with him
or peculiar to him. The present purpose is to show what those ideas
were and, especially, how they shaped his imaginative work.

His interest in society as an organic whole may first engage our attention. It is easy to conclude that his sympathies lay with the humbler
classes and that he disliked the upper circles, into which he was born

---

From *Philological Quarterly*, January 1956, pp. 1–23. Reprinted by permission
of the publisher and author.

and from which perhaps poverty chiefly separated him. There would be some truth in such a conclusion, but not the whole truth. In his *Covent-Garden Journal,* No. 27, he remarks:

> I do not pretend to say, that the mob have no faults; perhaps they have many. I assert no more than this, that they are in all laudable qualities very greatly superior to those who have hitherto, with much injustice, pretended to look down upon them.[1]

That this apparent praise is somewhat equivocal one can see from another essay (on 'Conversation'), in which he says, 'If men were to be rightly estimated and divided into subordinate classes, according to the superior excellence of their several natures, perhaps the lowest class of either sex would be properly assigned to those two disgracers of the human species, commonly called a beau and a fine lady.'[2] Since the beau and the fine lady are precisely the persons who look down upon the Mob, the merits of that lower class are not so outstanding as the first quotation might indicate.

Fielding's social 'philosophy' is founded upon the concept of a stratified society, such as might constitute a small section of the great scale of being. He believes that all government is based on a principle of subordination and that the duty of all classes of men is to contribute to the good of the Whole. With the rest of his generation he believes that 'All are but parts of one stupendous whole'; and that the parts are mutually dependent: 'nothing stands alone.' In the famous passage in *Jonathan Wild* about 'employing hands' he differentiates sharply between those who employ the labor of others for strictly selfish purposes (men like gangsters or prime ministers) and those who employ hands for the general good.[3] Of the latter examples of rising capitalism he highly approves.

This attitude is seen again in his *Proposal for Making an Effectual Provision for the Poor.* At the outset in this social tract he states fully this basic idea of duty to the Whole, quoting from King Edward VI the view that 'The gentleman ought to labour in the service of his country; the serving-man ought to wait diligently on his master; the artificer ought to labour in his work; the husbandman in tilling the ground; the merchant in passing the tempests; but the vagabonds ought clearly to be banished, as is the superfluous humour of the body'; . . .[4] Fielding develops a further position by asserting the duty of all classes to the Whole. The passage is long, but worth quoting:

Those duties . . . which fall to the higher ranks of men, even in this commonwealth, are by no means of the lightest or easiest kind. The watchings and fatigues, the anxieties and cares which attend the highest stations, render their possessors, in real truth, no proper objects of envy to those in the lowest, whose labours are much less likely to impair the health of their bodies, or to destroy the peace of their minds; are not less consistent with their happiness, and much more consistent with their safety.

It is true, indeed, that in every society where property is established and secured by law, there will be some among the rich whose indolence is superior to the love of wealth and honour, and who will therefore avoid these public duties, for which avarice and ambition will always furnish out a sufficient number of candidates; yet however idle the lives of such may be, it must be observed, first, that they are by no means burdensome to the public, but do support themselves on what the law calls their own; a property acquired by the labour of their ancestors, and often the rewards, or fruits at least, of public services. Secondly, that while they dispose what is their own for the purposes of idleness, (and more especially, perhaps, if for the purposes of luxury,) they may be well called useful members of trading commonwealths, and truly said to contribute to the good of the public.

But with the poor (and such must be in any nation where property is, that is to say, where there are any rich) this is not the case. For having nothing but their labour to bestow on the society, if they withhold this from it, they become useless members; and having nothing but their labour to procure a support for themselves, they must of necessity become burdensome.

On this labour the public hath a right to insist, since this is the only service which the poor can do that society, which in some way or other hath a right to the service of all its members. . . . [5]

In these paragraphs Fielding states the grounds for repressing the appetites of the lower classes for luxury, which are the great causes of the late increase of robbers in the streets of London, and he also states the grounds for his projected reform. He very sensibly proposes that workhouses be built by the county and not by the parish, since parishes are too small to maintain effective institutions. He also proposes that in these workhouses the wilfully idle be compelled to work as prisoners—which name he frankly gives them. Vagabonds must be abolished.

Nowadays Parson Adams, Tom Jones, and Partridge may seem full of the joys of carefree wandering; but when Fielding died the cult of the open road had not yet come into its own. That uncharitable parson, Trulliber, is hardly one of Fielding's sympathetic characters; but, with a sort of dramatic irony, he echoes Fielding's royal economist when he turns Parson Adams away with the remark, 'I know what charity is better than to give to vagabonds.'[6] Fielding's *Provision for the Poor* will be effectual only when the poor are made 'useful members of society'; i.e., when they contribute labor productive of good to the Whole.

Further insight into Fielding's attitude towards the lower classes as well as into his ideas concerning charity may be gathered from his essay found in *The Champion* for 16 February 1739–40. The basic principle here announced concerning charity is at first sight startling: those, he holds, who have never known a happier state than indigence deserve less aid, for they suffer less from poverty than do those who can no longer support 'the character in which they were bred.' If the lowest classes do not really appear in the five groups specified as the properest objects of charity, it is not altogether callousness on Fielding's part. The only poor here condemned are beggars, who are not 'worthy poor' since they do not contribute labor for the good of the Whole. They are a shame, not to the laws, which are adequate, but to the execution of the laws. Fielding then pauses to state his hope of dedicating a whole paper to the provision for the poor: thirteen years later he did just that in an elaborate pamphlet, wherein beggars and idle able-bodied men were to be 'prisoners' in his planned workhouses. The laws were to be enforced. In *The Champion* paper he is not talking of such people, and it is interesting to see how he classifies the unfortunates who have seen better days. The five groups in order of rising importance are:

1. Gentlefolk reduced in circumstances through ill luck or extravagance. (One thinks of the Fielding family and of Billy Booth and his wife Amelia.)

2. Relatives of persons discredited because they opposed ministers of state in the cause of liberty.

3. Persons in 'professions and occupations, who have, by misfortunes and unavoidable accidents, been reduced from an affluency to want.'

4. Able followers of art or science who through envy or ill judgment of mankind suffer undeserved ill fortune and neglect.

5. 'Lastly, and perhaps chiefly,' those imprisoned for debt.[7]

This last class to deserve charity is one to which Fielding recurs more than once, and for which he had an especial sympathy. Here he is advocating an obvious social reform: for the rest of his objects of charity are persons of family, education, or genius. The proletariat hardly appears among them; but such persons as Parson Adams, the St. Albans highwayman whom Tom Jones reforms, Heartfree, and many of the persons in *Amelia* clearly would qualify.

Fielding's central idea, then, concerning the relation of the classes to each other would be the concept of all classes working together for the good of the Whole. A contrasting idea that affects Fielding's imagination is the notion that society as a whole is likely to be merciless towards any individual who is, as we say, out of luck. Joseph Andrews's father, worthy Mr. Wilson, is of the opinion (III. iii) that 'There is a malignity in the nature of man which, when not weeded out, or at least covered by a good education and politeness, delights in making another uneasy or dissatisfied with himself.'[8] Dr. Harrison, benevolist though he is, warns Booth of the dangers of imprudence in this world, 'as the malicious disposition of mankind is too well known, and the cruel pleasure which they take in destroying the reputation of others.'[9] This sort of malice Fielding inconsistently assumes as a normal part of a general human attitude. The imperfect but virtuous individual is continually misjudged or misunderstood, not so much by some one person as by his general social environment. It was, so we are unconvincingly told, 'the universal opinion of all Mr. Allworthy's family that [the boy Tom Jones] was certainly born to be hanged.'[10]

Sarah Fielding in her *David Simple* and elsewhere makes a strong use of similar exhibitions of malicious misjudgments, being particularly keen on the malice of stepmothers towards children. When Henry Fielding was eleven, his mother died, and the six children left were briefly looked after by a shrewish aunt. Presently when General Fielding brought home an Italian stepmother, a reputed papist, this aunt abetted young Harry in impudence towards his stepmother, and in the lawsuit that presently aired the family difficulties the small boy was depicted in a most unfavorable light by his father and his father's servants. Clearly 'the world' might be unfair to a small Tom Jones or a Henry Fielding, or to a writer of political farces and pamphlets, or to an incorruptible successor (as Fielding was) in an established line of 'trading' justices of the peace. Fielding's belief in the malignity of mankind in the abstract had perhaps an empirical as well as a theoretical basis.

Another recurrent attitude towards the relation of the individual to the whole social or cosmic system is the idea that an All-Wise Creator has placed each one of us according to a divine plan, and that it is our duty to fill the 'sphere' assigned to each of us, and to stay in it contentedly—submitting, as Pope put it, 'to be as blest as we can bear.' Failure to stay in one's proper station was a common mistake in conduct in the fiction of the eighteenth century. Fielding more than once uses a variant of this idea. Men appointed to specialized functions, he thinks, are usually admirable when at work in their own skills; but outside their bounded sphere they may exhibit the worst of traits. British officers fighting at Gibraltar are heroic; but the 'city-captains' seen in Fielding's comedies and in London boudoirs are at best idle and at worst effeminate and worthless. At the end of his life during his *Voyage to Lisbon*, Fielding had a chance to study sailors, and of them he says:

> I am convinced that on land there is nothing more idle and dissolute; in their own element, there are no persons near the level of their degree, who live in the constant practice of half so many good qualities. . . . All these good qualities, however, they always leave behind them on shipboard: the sailor out of water is, indeed, as wretched an animal as the fish out of water.[11]

Alongside of this opinion one must put the painful picture of sailors on land given at the beginning of the *Voyage* when Fielding, helpless and dying of dropsy, was carried and hoisted aboard Captain Richard Veale's ship, the *Queen of Portugal*.

> I think [Fielding tells us] upon my entrance into the boat, I presented a spectacle of the highest horror. The total loss of limbs was apparent to all who saw me, and my face contained marks of a most diseased state, if not of death itself. . . . In this condition, I ran the gauntlope (so, I think I may justly call it), through rows of sailors and watermen, few of whom failed of paying their compliments to me, by all manner of insults and jests on my misery. No man who knew me will think I conceived any personal resentment at this behaviour; but it was a lively picture of that cruelty and inhumanity, in the nature of men, which I have often contemplated with concern; and which leads the mind into a train of very uncomfortable and melancholy thoughts. It may be said, that this barbarous custom is peculiar to the English, and of them only to the lowest degree; that it is an excrescence of an uncontroled licentiousness mistaken for liberty, and never shews itself in men who are polished and refined, in such manner as human nature requires, to produce that perfection of which it is susceptible, and to purge away that malevolence of disposition, of which, at our birth, we partake in common with the savage creation.[12]

In a sense the gentleman himself had in Fielding's time a specialized function, a sphere of his own to fill, which in the opinion of Fielding and other writers was not being properly filled. Everywhere Fielding gives a bleak picture of what he called 'the ladder of fashion.' 'The highest life is much the dullest,' he tells us;[13] and one can see that he tolerates Molly Seagrim far more readily than he does Lady Bellaston. One of the harshest of his remarks about high society is found in his Preface to the *Miscellanies,* where he says:

> without considering Newgate as no other than human nature with its mask off, which some very shameless writers have done, a thought which no price should purchase me to entertain, I think we may be excused for suspecting, that the splendid palaces of the great are often no other than Newgate with the mask on.[14]

This remark may well serve to sum up Fielding's prejudice with regard to 'polite' society. He believes in the potentialities of human nature, but he has no faith in the palaces or the activities of 'the great.' On the other hand he cannot tolerate vagabonds, in spite of a burning sense of the unhappiness of the poor.

This attitude towards the extremes of the social spectrum is probably explained in part by the facts of Fielding's own two special functions. As justice of the peace or as social worker (for he really was this last) he was preoccupied with the criminal poor; while as an imaginative writer he was preoccupied with correcting the failings of the literate upperclasses.

With regard to the psychology of the individual moral agent, to which we may now pass, Fielding's central position is not difficult to discern. He is devoted to the portrayal of what he called 'good nature.' It is true that man even apart from his specialized social function may be bad in himself or good in himself. Fielding does not accept any doctrine of the natural goodness of all men. He gives us strong pictures of human malignity in Blifil and Jonathan Wild, but his major concern in his fiction is the dramatization of Good Nature. At times he plays with the idea that this quality is an innate endowment; but he never doubts that good works are the sure manifestation of its presence. The contrasting duality of human nature is illuminated for us in the contrasting sons of Bridget Allworthy. First we may note that Tom Jones's technical illegitimacy serves no moral purpose; it is simply necessary to produce the indispensable plot mystery of his birth, without which there could be no complex weaving of circumstance in the story. We may then go on to observe how neatly Fielding arranges the facts that Jones and Blifil are born of the same mother, that they are brought up in the same healthy en-

vironment, that they are both subjected to the same educational attention from the heavy-handed Thwackum—and that the results in character are antithetical. Fielding's theories of innate predisposition are
obviously illustrated in the fact that one boy turns out to be cold,
calculating, selfish, ambitious—in a word, a villain, who will end as a
Calvinistic Methodist, a type Fielding abhorred. The other lad, Tom
himself, is obviously actuated by the highest innate good nature, that
'glorious lust of doing good,' as Fielding had defined it in an early poem
entitled 'Of Good Nature.' In an even earlier *Champion* essay he had
said, 'Good nature is a delight in the happiness of mankind, and a
concern at their misery, with a desire, as much as possible, to procure
the former, and avert the latter; and this, with a constant regard to
desert.'[15] Tom's juvenile sympathies did not constantly regard desert,
and his true teacher, Allworthy, had to reprove him for his charity
towards the undeserving game-keeper, Black George. Later, when experience has taught the young man his errors—or at least some of them—
Tom concludes his lecture to Nightingale on sexual morality with the
statement: 'Nor would I, to procure pleasure to myself, be knowingly
the cause of misery to any human being.'[16]

This is Tom's—and Fielding's—central position. Benevolence, kindness, good nature—call it what you will—is the essence of virtue. With
this position are contrasted those of Thwackum and Square: Square the
deist prates of the 'natural beauty of virtue' and 'the eternal fitness of
things'[17]—a fitness somewhat skewed when he is caught squatting
behind the curtain in Molly Seagrim's dirty loft. Thwackum, the rationalizing cleric, pays lip service to 'the divine power of grace'; but like
Square has no interest in humble goodness or in charity. Thwackum is
doctrinally akin to Fielding's aversion, the Rev. George Whitefield.
Tom Jones is allowed by Fielding to put up at the Bell Inn, Gloucester,
because the Whitefields who keep it are in no wise tainted by the
notions of their brother the Methodist. Through Parson Adams, Fielding best conveys his view of George Whitefield's supposed reliance on
faith without works. Adams had been Whitefield's admirer as long as
the Methodist had preached against luxury and splendor among the
clergy; 'but,' says the Quixotic parson, 'when he began to call nonsense
and enthusiasm to his aid, and set up the detestable doctrine of faith
against good works, I was his friend no longer; for surely that doctrine
was coined in hell.' On the Day of Doom the Parson expected to hear
such believers (Blifil might be one) cry out, 'Lord it is true I never
obeyed one of thy commandments, yet punish me not, for I believe
them all.'[18]

Tom Jones, like his author, had a fervent belief in good works. It is as a reward for continual kindness that in Tom's darkest hour towards the end of the story such a cloud of character witnesses—the amateur highwayman, Mrs. Miller, her daughter Nancy, Nightingale, Jenny Waters herself, and others—rise up to testify to his good-natured virtue.

While Fielding will have no patience with 'rationalizing divines' who exalt faith against good works, he will assent to the possibility that Tom and Blifil were from birth predestined to virtue and villainy, respectively. In many of his writings Fielding plays with this idea of determinism. He gives a clear indication of his view at the very beginning of his long essay on 'The Knowledge of the Characters of Men.' Men 'even of the same climate, religion, and education,' he tells us, show wide differences from each other such as 'could hardly exist, unless the distinction had some original foundation in nature itself.'

This original difference [he continues] will, I think, alone account for that very early and strong inclination to good or evil, which distinguishes different dispositions in children, in their first infancy; . . . and . . . in persons, who, from the same education, &c., might be thought to have directed nature the same way; yet, among all these, there subsists . . . so manifest and extreme a difference of inclination of character, that almost obliges us, I think, to acknowledge some unacquired original distinction, in the nature or soul of one man, from that of another.[19]

Clearly, it is this idea of violent differences, ranging from good nature to malignity, even in the same household, that Fielding is dramatizing in Tom and Blifil.

The possible influences of environment and education on such native endowment are considered, but not too explicitly. Joseph Andrews, in one of his somewhat surprisingly wise outbursts—this time on the subject of education—touches the matter with a homely analogue:

I remember when I was in the stable, if a young horse was vicious in his nature, no correction would make him otherwise; I take it to be equally the same among men: if a boy be of a mischievous, wicked inclination, no school, though ever so private, will ever make him good; on the contrary, if he be of a righteous temper, you may trust him to London, or wherever else you please—he will be in no danger of being corrupted.[20]

Good nature, 'that amiable quality, which, like the sun, gilds over all our other virtues,'[21] evidently needs not man's adornings, and a really bad nature is quite reprobate. These are strong and extreme positions. Normally Fielding would be content to say that bad education can only corrupt. It is also clear that bad environment is dangerous. 'If he be of a righteous temper, you may trust him to London,' Joseph says; and Joseph, whose Mrs. Potiphar was a widow in Mayfair, knew the dangers of the town. And so, evidently, did Henry Fielding, concerning whose youthful acquaintance with London society we fortunately or unfortunately know nothing. We do know, however, that whenever he writes about London his tone becomes grim, hard, distressing. He could not succeed in high comedy; for he saw nothing comic in high society. Says a 'lady' in one of his plays: 'I know very few people who are ashamed of anything.' [22] In that proposition too many of the 'fine ladies' in his comedies could agree. *Tom Jones,* although written in more exuberant high spirits than almost any novel in English, nevertheless loses its effervescence and verve in its last six books, when the narrative moves to London, to the lodging house, the gaol, the gilded mansion of Lady Bellaston, who was certainly ashamed of nothing; and to events dominated by such persons as the inept and cowardly villain Fellamar, the tawdry Mrs. Fitzpatrick, or so flabby a youth as Nightingale. The effect becomes grim beyond intention.

Except in the case of the tradesman Heartfree, virtue's last-page reward in Fielding's novels is a quiet life in the country. In sly contrast to the celebrated Mrs. Pamela Andrews, half of whose story was 'Pamela in High Life,' Fielding makes Pamela's ex-brother Joseph declare in a final sentence that he will imitate his parents, the Wilsons, in their retirement, 'nor will be prevailed on by any booksellers, or their authors, to make his appearance in high life.' [23] Captain Booth and Amelia gladly quit the town, the scene of so many of their woes, and so, of course, do Tom and Sophia. It is touching to find in the *Journey from this World to the Next* that Fielding represents Anna Boleyn as happy in the country and miserable at court. When her father took her to live in a country house, 'where there was nothing grand or superfluous, but everything neat and agreeable,' she was at first solitary, but, she says,

when I had lived here a little time, I found such a calmness in my mind, and such a difference between this and the restless anxieties I had experienced in a court, that I began to share the tranquillity that visibly appeared in everything around me. I set myself to do works of fancy, and to raise little flower-gardens, with many such innocent rural amusements; which although they are not capable of affording any great pleasure, yet they give that serene turn of mind which I think much preferable to anything else human nature is made susceptible of. I now resolved to spend the rest of

my days here, and that nothing should allure me from that sweet retirement to be again tossed about with tempestuous passions of any kind.[24]

If the fair lady had been merely a character in Fielding, he would have
given her the happy ending that history and life at court made impossible. We may infer that environment can aid the development of
one's nature. Inference must also account for much of any conclusion
reached as to Fielding's notion of the efficacy of education and its
relation to the doctrine of natural goodness. In a late essay he wrote:

> Tho' nature . . . must give the seeds, art may cultivate them. To improve
> or to depress their growth is greatly within the power of education. To
> lay down the proper precept for this purpose, would require a large
> treatise, and such I may possibly publish hereafter.[25]

But he did not, and he is never specific on the subject, though he allows
Parson Adams and Joseph to argue over public vs. private schooling,
and gives us a picture of faulty education as conducted by Thwackum
in *Tom Jones*. Although like his sister Sarah he deprecates the great
aristocratic instrument of education, flogging, he yet seems to think of
education as moral discipline rather than as the acquisition of either
information or skill. The school of experience may or may not be effica-
cious. For Tom Jones it works—at least Fielding pretty certainly thought
Tom acquired prudence and moral wisdom by his contacts with life
on the roads. The inserted histories of Joseph's father, Mr. Wilson, and
the Man of the Hill in *Tom Jones* are examples that make mere experience a dubious teacher.

We shall hardly begin to understand Fielding's psychological doctrines unless we recognize with him a sort of duality of the passions
(as the emotions were in his day called). This duality is bluntly stated
by his sister in one of her stories:

> There appears to be but two grand master passions or movers in the
> human mind, namely, LOVE and PRIDE. And what constitutes the beauty
> or deformity of a man's character, is the choice he makes under which
> banner he determines to enlist himself: but there is a strong distinction
> between different degrees in the same thing, and a mixture of two con-
> traries. Thus a man may be more or less proud, but if PRIDE be his char-
> acteristic, he cannot be a good man. So a man may be more or less
> attracted by love, and rouzed to benevolent actions; but whilst he pre-
> serves LOVE as the characteristic of his mind, he cannot be a bad man.[26]

There is occasional question in Fielding's mind as to whether man is capable of voluntary enlistment under a good or a bad passion or whether some predestined or ruling passion determines his 'character.' There is no doubt in his mind as to the importance of the passions. Like Richard Steele and many others of his general period, he attempts to evaluate the Stoic and the Christian views of man's nature. He would not, with the Stoic, extirpate the passions; but would, with the Christian, emphasize the passions of hope and fear and the related doctrine of rewards and punishments. Like others of his day he talks of a master passion, at times called 'self-love' and at times called simply the dominant or ruling passion. He develops no extensive system of ideas on these subjects, but repeatedly he dramatizes the working of the passions as they contrast in men of good or ill endowment. Note for example, the dramatized contrast between Tom and Blifil in the exquisitely devised little episode concerning the bird that Tom had tamed and given to Sophia. One day the jealous Blifil when in the garden with Sophia

> observing the extreme fondness that she showed for her little bird, desired her to trust it for a moment in his hands. Sophia presently complied . . . and, after some previous caution, delivered him her bird, of which he was no sooner in possession, than he slipped the string from its leg and tossed it into the air.
>
> The foolish animal no sooner perceived itself at liberty, than forgetting all the favors it had received from Sophia, it flew directly from her, and perched on a bough at some distance.

Tom, aglow with kindness, climbs the tree, the bough breaks, he falls into the canal, and is thought to be in danger of drowning. When the excitement is over, Blifil, with finished hypocrisy, explains what happened:

> Indeed, uncle, I am very sorry for what I have done; I have been unhappily the occasion of it all. I had Miss Sophia's bird in my hand, and thinking the poor creature languished for liberty, I own I could not forbear giving it what it desired; for I always thought there was something very cruel in confining anything. It seemed to be against the law of nature, by which everything hath a right to liberty; nay, it is even unchristian, for it is not doing what we would be done by: but if I had imagined Miss Sophia would have been so much concerned at it, I am sure I never would have done it; nay, if I had known what would have happened to the bird itself: for when Master Jones, who climbed up

that tree after it, fell into the water, the bird took a second flight, and presently a nasty hawk carried it away.[27]

For ingenuity and transparency this is admirable. It contributes almost nothing to the advancement of the plot, but it illustrates good nature set off by its foil, and incidentally is an interesting bit of satire on many a sentimental cliché of the time. And it obviously exists to dramatize human motives.

Fielding's most explicit theorizing about the passions is found in his novel, *Amelia*. This, easily the most intellectual of his stories, is really almost a fantasy on the subject of the Stoic and Christian attitudes towards conduct. The plot situation at first sight seems to indicate nothing of this, and from the time of its publication the book has been frequently misunderstood. Fielding devoted more than one essay in his *Covent-Garden Journal* to explanation and defense of what he called his favorite child. Centrally, the novel glorifies the perfect wife; and Amelia, firm as a rock, is the static character against which the storms of adversity beat. Most of the action concerns the unemployment of her husband, Captain Booth, who wants to get back into the army, where he has a rather distinguished record; but commissions had to be purchased (as they did down to 1871), and Booth had neither money nor a patron who would in recognition of the young man's merit provide the purchase money—unless at the price of Amelia's honor. The *personal* aspect of this situation deals with the necessity of curing Booth of psychological flaccidity, the result of his unfortunate belief that men act from their ruling passions, and that moral energy is futile. His ultimate conversion to the Christian point of view solves this difficulty, and there is no reason thereafter to fear that the fortune so happily inherited by Amelia will be dissipated by her husband, who had been economically incompetent only so long as he had no belief in moral struggle. The *social* aspect of the plot deals with the disinclination of more fortunate men of rank and wealth to act from other than selfish passions and to recognize merit (i.e., Booth's merit) disinterestedly. In other words, like Smollett, Dr. Johnson, and many other mid-century authors Fielding was attacking the selfishness, the hardness, of pretending patrons.

The whole psychological theory back of the action, then, rests on the ideas current as to the passions. The Christian religion utilizes the passions; the Stoic scorns them. The first point of view is seen towards the end of the story (Bk. XII, v), where the benevolent Dr. Harrison remarks, 'if men act, as I believe they do, from their passions, it would be fair to conclude that religion to be true which applies immediately to the strongest of these passions, hope and fear; choosing rather to rely on its rewards and punishments than on that native beauty of virtue which some of the ancient philosophers thought proper to recommend to their disciples.' [28] Harrison is Fielding's best embodiment of the Christian or benevolist point of view.

On the other hand, the noble Roman ethic is exhibited in the person of Colonel James.

His mind [Fielding tells us] was formed of those firm materials of which nature formerly hammered out the Stoic, and upon which the sorrows of no man living could make an impression. A man of this temper, who doth not much value danger, will fight for the person he calls his friend, and the man that hath but little value for his money will give it him; but such friendship is never to be absolutely depended on; for, whenever the favorite passion interposes with it, it is sure to subside and vanish into air. Whereas the man whose tender disposition really feels the miseries of another will endeavour to relieve them for his own sake; and in such a mind, friendship will often get the superiority over every other passion.[29]

Here Fielding himself speaks: about 250 pages earlier the less intelligent Booth, blinded by his faulty notions, had characterized James (whom he regarded as his best friend) as 'one of the best natured men in the world'; and he adds:

This worthy man, who had a head and a heart perfectly adequate to every office of friendship, stayed with me almost day and night during my illness; and by strengthening my hopes, raising my spirits, and cheering my thoughts, preserved me from destruction. The behaviour of this man alone is a sufficient proof of my doctrine, that all men act entirely from their passions; for Bob James can never be supposed to act from any motives of virtue or religion, since he constantly laughs at both; and yet his conduct towards me alone demonstrates a degree of goodness which perhaps few of the votaries of either virtue or religion can equal.[30]

Here Booth quite plausibly mistakes casual, selfish kindness for true good will; realistic understanding of James and his type of selfish kindness was one of the hardest lessons Booth had to learn. When James's ruling passion interposed, apparent friendship turned to unscrupulous treachery.

Pope had thought it impossible to determine the specific passion ruling in any mind; and Fielding nowhere indicates any particular passion for Booth; but in the very first paragraph of the novel he comments on the results of Booth's defect—

> the miseries in which men of sense sometimes involve themselves by quitting the directions of Prudence, and following the blind guidance of a predominant passion; in short . . . all the ordinary phenomena which are imputed to Fortune; whom, perhaps, men accuse with no less absurdity in life, than a bad player complains of ill luck at the game of chess. [31]

Booth's 'disadvantageous opinion of Providence' is due to his tendency to place the blame for his misfortunes outside himself. Fielding, with the help of Dr. Barrow's sermons, cures Booth of this trait and sets him again on the right road of moral integrity and struggle for virtue. Fielding always asserts the moral responsibility of the individual; even in *Amelia*, where social conditions loom large, he, unlike some modern novelists, never allows society to become the scapegoat for the individual.

And yet society is bad. In a steady stream of illicit suitors for Amelia's favors, a succession of hard divines and callous noble lords, Fielding exhibits the extreme selfishness of the upper classes, until the gentle Amelia herself, 'a person of calm passions' cries out, 'Good Heavens! . . . what are our great men made of? are they in reality a distinct species from the rest of mankind? are they born without hearts?'[32] Booth's reply, in part, is:

> I have often told you . . . that all men, as well the best as the worst, act alike from the principle of self-love. Where benevolence therefore is the uppermost passion, self-love directs you to gratify it by doing good, and by relieving the distresses of others; for they are then in reality your own. But where ambition, avarice, pride, or any other passion, governs the man and keeps his benevolence down, the miseries of all other men affect him no more than they would a stock or a stone. And thus the man and his statue have often the same degree of feeling or compassion.[33]

This tangle of truth and error proves difficult for Amelia—and for Fielding—to unsnarl. From the few passages here quoted it must be obvious that *Amelia* is a very argumentative novel: enunciation of ethical principles preoccupies the author rather more than plot, character, or dramatic effect.

This preoccupation also existed in *Jonathan Wild*, which is fragmentary and episodic in action, and not too clear in its intellectual skeleton. The whole is given life and apparent movement by the robust irony that marks its method. For our purposes it is interesting as further evidence of Fielding's concern with moral principles, which he attempted to dramatize in effective fable. The ethical pronouncements in *Jonathan Wild* have an accidental interest two hundred years after the fact in that Fielding heaps scorn on a sort of 'great man' whose ideals are courage, power, and ruthlessness. Fielding divides men into three classes: first, the great; for whom the ironic prerequisites are 'a bold heart, a thundering voice, and a steady countenance.'[34] This class includes not merely 'the sackers of towns, the plunderers of provinces, and the conquerors of kingdoms' but more especially the trickster and cheat, whether he be a thief or a prime minister. The whole book has been regarded as a satire on Sir Robert Walpole, the Prime Minister, who was commonly spoken of as 'the great man.' It seems more truly to be directed against the political abuses of the system in which Walpole was deeply involved.

After the great man, we have secondly the good man—typified here by Heartfree, who is the antithesis of both power and ability. He is an Allworthy involved in a tradesman's difficulties that long prove too much for him. But the great man need not always be rogue; nor the good man always inept. There is a third class who combine the best traits of both the great and the good. This class represents, so Fielding tells us,

> the true sublime in human nature. That elevation by which the soul of man, raising and extending itself above the order of this creation, and brightened with a certain ray of divinity, looks down on the condition of mortals. This is indeed a glorious object, on which we can never gaze with too much praise and admiration. A perfect work! the Iliad of Nature! ravishing and astonishing, and which at once fills us with love, wonder, and delight.[35]

This exuberant passage, unusual in Fielding, is important as recognizing an ideal which he admired greatly as embodied in Richardson's *Clarissa*, but which he himself perhaps never attempted unless when he created Amelia, who at times fills a reader with love, wonder, and delight. In general, Fielding's desire to keep fiction within the bounds of the plausible and the probable, kept him near the earth. He deals with the imperfect types of the partly great and the partly good. With regard to the principles of goodness he observes in his prefatory remarks on *Jonathan Wild*: 'This is the doctrine which I have endeavoured to inculcate in this history, confining myself at the same time within the rules of probability.'[36]

In every preface or dedication that he ever wrote Fielding expressed this desire to promote virtue: he had doctrine to state. It is, however, less important to be minute in canvassing the nature of this doctrine than to consider the artistic problem involved—since we do not, if we are wise, go to novelists or playwrights for a system of ethics. The problem is largely one of lively imaginative fusion of diverse elements, such as the moral doctrine (which seems to be the point of departure), and the various circumstances—personality, environment, dramatic action, through which doctrine is expressed. This fusion seems, to present-day readers, at times imperfect, if only because Fielding as commentator will not keep himself off the stage. In *Tom Jones* there are relatively few inorganic details. The story of the Man of the Hill has seemed to some a needless excrescence; but Tom's remarks to this old misanthrope as well as his sermon delivered earlier to the Quaker at Hambrook are Fielding's way of calling attention to Tom's natural wisdom and to the fact that Tom is now rapidly maturing and acquiring prudence. A less fused comment in the story is that designed for the curious episode of Partridge's misconduct with the gypsy woman, arranged by her shameless husband. Here Fielding pauses in order to suggest the superiority of gypsy justice as compared with the commercializing of a wife's virtue seen frequently in the cases of criminal conversation tried in the courts of King George II—and seen in Fielding's *Modern Husband* (1732). The neatly devised gypsy episode would be admirable in a periodical essay, but it adds nothing essential to the tale of *Tom Jones*.

Fielding evidently felt that this sort of comment on the life of his day was a valuable part of his art, and he frequently speaks in his own person in order to include comment. He justifies this intrusion of himself by the example of the Greek tragic chorus; but that sort of infringement on dramatic action, though similar, is on a more subtle imaginative level. The best justification for Fielding's intrusions of himself is their brilliance. His eighteen introductory chapters to the eighteen books of *Tom Jones* are among his most brilliantly written essays. They are footlights illuminating what passes on the stage: we are conscious of their existence as independent of the action of the story, but we enjoy them and profit from their discussions of the problems of narrative art.

It is true, however, that Fielding, unlike the Greek tragic chorus, is frequently an *aloof* spectator of what goes on. At crucial moments he avoids—even shirks, one might say—emotional scenes. He is a comic artist and wit rather than one who loves to depict warmth of emotion. In scenes of emotional elevation he is seldom implicitly and unconsciously *present*. In scenes of comedy tinged with acid he does have this sense of presence. With the lachrymose reconciliation scenes of Colley Cibber's fifth acts in mind we may forgive Fielding for so frequently closing the door on the emotions of his characters. He more than once breaks the illusion by informing us that the pencil of his friend Hogarth alone would do justice to a scene; that the pen of an author cannot. A typical, and not regrettable, case when he does not close the door on the reader may be seen in the episode where Lady Booby brings the heavy artillery of her charms to bear upon Pamela's chaste brother, her footman. In response to her suggestion that under certain circumstances his inclinations might be fired, Joseph replies: 'If they were, I hope I should be able to control them, without suffering them to get the better of my virtue.' At this point both Fielding and Lady Booby strike an attitude:

> You have heard, reader, poets talk of the statue of Surprize; you have heard, likewise, or else you have heard very little, how surprize made one of the sons of Croesus speak, though he was dumb. You have seen the faces, in the eighteen-penny gallery, when, through the trap-door, to soft or no music, Mr. Bridgewater, Mr. William Mills, or some other of ghostly appearance, hath ascended, with a face all pale with powder, and a shirt all bloody with ribbons;—but from none of these, nor from Phidias or Praxitiles, if they should return to life—no, not from the in-imitable pencil of my friend Hogarth, could you receive such an idea of surprize as would have entered in at your eyes had they beheld the Lady Booby when those last words issued out from the lips of Joseph. 'Your virtue!' said the lady, recovering after a silence of two minutes; 'I shall never survive it. Your virtue!' [37]

To condemn this sort of interruption is to indulge in the very sort of eighteenth-century 'rules criticism' which we affect to scorn. The question is not, May this be done? but rather, Is this not well done?

The episode of Sophia's bird is an admirable example of action and utterance fused with setting, persons, and, above all, the moral doctrines involved. Fielding's stories bristle with minute examples equally effective. The Andover coach finds Joseph Andrews robbed, naked, and beaten almost to death, by the side of the road. Prudish ladies cannot tolerate a nude male in the same coach with themselves. An argument ensues, and no one wishing to furnish a great-coat to wrap Joseph in, the young man might have been left to perish, unless, as Fielding tells us, 'the postillion (a lad who hath been since transported for robbing a henroost) had voluntarily stript off a great coat, his only garment, at the same time swearing a great oath (for which he was rebuked by the passengers), "That he would rather ride in his shirt all his life than suffer a fellow-creature to lie in so miserable condition." '[38] Such knife-thrusts of sudden inspiration are not uncommon. The fusion is admirable; the statement of doctrine is made dramatic.

Fusion frequently is attempted by means of witty elaboration, as is most appropriate in a comic artist with an ironic attitude towards life. Jonathan Wild pays an evening visit to Miss Tishy Snap, but on his arrival he

> found only Miss Doshy at home, that young lady being employed alone, in imitation of Penelope, with her thread or worsted, only with this difference, that whereas Penelope unravelled by night what she had knit or wove or spun by day, so what our young heroine unravelled by day she knit again by night. In short, she was mending a pair of blue stockings with red clocks; a circumstance which perhaps we might have omitted, had it not served to show that there are still some ladies of this age who imitate the simplicity of the antients.[39]

The absurdity of this witticism perhaps lends it charm; if you urge that here again Fielding is the intrusive spectator, one may urge that it achieves with economy what James Joyce elaborated in greater detail, namely, the chasm between the epic and the realistic planes of existence. Fielding is at his best, doubtless, in facetious ingenuity rather than in pathetic directness.

He was fascinated by *Don Quixote* and more than once avows his discipleship of Cervantes. On the original titlepage of *Joseph Andrews* he announced that it was written in the manner of *Don Quixote*. There is, however, no readier way of becoming aware of Fielding's limitations than by comparing him with Cervantes. Both men are teachers, satirists, and wits; but the wit of Cervantes was less self-conscious than Fielding's. Sancho Panza's quip, 'We are all as God made us, and many of us much worse,' is beyond Fielding in its simple pungency that was neither biting nor burning. Cervantes has the emotional warmth with which to fuse completely the diverse elements found in a truly rich mind, and this completely fused imaginative richness, though present, is less common in Fielding. He attempts to copy the knight-errant of La Mancha more than once; but look at Sancho Panza sobbing by Don Quixote's death-bed—and sobbing sincerely yet comically—and you see just what Fielding could hardly do:

> 'Alas!' answered *Sancho*, sobbing, 'dear Sir, do not die; but take my counsel, and live many years; for the greatest madness a man can commit in

this life, is, to suffer himself to die, without anybody's killing him, or being brought to his end by any other hand than that of melancholy. Be not lazy, Sir, but get out of bed, and let us be going to the field, dressed like shepherds, as we agreed to do: and who knows, but behind some bush or other we may find the lady *Dulcinea* disenchanted as fine as heart can wish! If you die for grief of being vanquished, lay the blame upon me, and say, you were unhorsed by my not having girted *Rozinante's* saddle as it ought to have been: besides your worship must have read in your book of chivalries, that it is a common thing for one knight to unhorse another, and him, who is vanquished to-day, to become a conqueror to-morrow.'[40]

It is no disgrace not to equal one's master when the master is superlative; but this blend of sincere simplicity with heartbreak and shrewd argumentative effort (for Sancho was of a social class that could imagine no better place to come upon a fine woman than 'behind some bush or other') is in warmth and directness, its lack of self-conscious witticism something that Fielding hardly achieved. On his own comic, ironic level, however, he is brilliant and incisive. A superb example is the scene where Lady Booby makes her major assault on Joseph. She intends to maintain the difference in their social stations and yet be perfectly affectionate and quite clear in her proposals. Consequently she addresses her footman with the somewhat inappropriate but kindly and subordinating appellation of 'child.' She intends to arouse Joseph and yet not involve herself too far until she is sure of Joseph's reaction; consequently she will practise, with seeming carelessness, what Fielding elsewhere calls 'the laying on of hands.' All these implications are present and more too in the following brief passage, in which Lady Booby says, ' "Consider, child," laying her hand carelessly upon his, "you are a handsome young fellow, and might do better; you might make your fortune." '[41] It may be remarked that here again Fielding is the mere spectator. But what a spectator! What insight! What a perfect blend of psychological contrasts, of moral implications, of social satire. What perfect ironic comedy the whole scene is, especially when we remember that the Hogarthian Slipslop, with jealous eyes and enormous heaving breasts, has been drinking it all in—through the key-hole! And with what economy is the effect achieved. Two words, *child* and *carelessly* turn the trick. ' "Consider, child," laying her hand carelessly upon his.'. . .

In such a scene the sense of presence and the robust high spirits so characteristic of Fielding are admirable. It is a mistake to think that his high spirits were gone before he wrote *Amelia*. That novel is less comic than the others because of its subject matter. Even in his later essays and in his last volume, the *Journal of a Voyage to Lisbon,* there are still coruscations of wit and moral comedy. This last work, written, so to speak, with death staring him in the face, was so facetious that its courage and cheerfulness won condemnation from at least one member of the Richardson coterie. Thomas Edwards in a letter to Richardson says: 'That a man, who had led such a life as he had, should trifle in that manner when immediate death was before his eyes, is amazing. From this book I am confirmed in what his other works had fully persuaded me of, that with all his parade of pretences to virtuous and humane affections, the fellow had no heart.'[42]

This is the silly voice of prejudice, designed to please the implacable author of *Pamela.* One must grant, however, that from first to last Fielding was the comic and moral satirist, with less interest in heart-throbs, as such, than had Richardson; he had, however, more interest and more ability in arriving at a rational understanding of man and man's motives. He is intellectual and analytical rather than sentimental in delineations of character; but both as man and as author he did not lack heart. A student of literature is hardly the person to evaluate properly Fielding's distinguished career as justice of the peace in Bow Street or as social reformer, but no reader of his *Proposal for Making an Effectual Provision for the Poor* can fail to recognize its profound understanding and sympathy for the underprivileged. Apparently he once organized a tour of London slums of his day for a group of interested Members of Parliament, who later owned that conditions 'exceeded their imagination.' In reference to such slumming Fielding says:

if we were to make a progress through the outskirts of this town, and look into the habitations of the poor, we should there behold such pictures of human misery as must move the compassion of every heart that deserves the name of human. What, indeed, must be his composition who could see whole families in want of every necessary of life, oppressed with hunger, cold, nakedness, and filth, and with diseases, the certain consequence of all these: what, I say, must be his composition, who could look into such a scene as this, and be affected only in his nostrils?

That such wretchedness as this is so little lamented, arises therefore from its being so little known; but if this be the case with the sufferings of the poor, it is not so with their misdeeds. They starve, and freeze, and rot among themselves; but they beg and steal, and rob among their betters.[43]

This serious, soundly critical attitude towards human misfortunes and weaknesses is present in all of Fielding's best narrative writing. His opinions are sincere convictions, and they everywhere shape his work. He is witty, but seldom, if ever, trifling, and he does not lack sympathy, though his typical attitude towards life is likely to be ironic. His sense of values is just and sure. He is a great creator of character: he *likes* his people, usually, even when they go wrong. He affects a certain aloofness, and his interest in motives and in commenting on actions unfortunately breaks illusion for some readers, but normally he certainly achieves illusion. And above all he writes with a robust and spirited intensity. As has been said, he gives us the open air—never the air of a sick room.

NOTES

1. Fielding's *Works* (ed. W. E. Henley, 1903), xiv, 154. Unless otherwise indicated all references that follow are to this edition, though the texts have been more than once silently corrected by those published in Fielding's own day.

2. xiv, 265.

3. ii, 47–9 (Bk. I, xiv).

4. xiii, 137.

5. xiii, 138–9.

6. i, 192.

7. xv, 205–6.

8. i, 246.

9. vi, 109 (Bk. III, i); and see also *Covent-Garden Journal*, No. 14.

10. iii, 107 (Bk. III, ii).

11. xvi, 273.

12. xvi, 200–1.

13. v, 94 (Bk. XIV, i).

14. xii, 243.

15. xv, 258.

16. v, 108 (Bk. XIV, iv).

17. iii, 114 (Bk. III, iii).

18. i, 96 (Bk. I, xvii).

19. xiv, 281–2.

20. i, 262.

21. xv, 259.

22. xi, 103 (*The Universal Gallant*, Act II).

23. i, 394.

24. ii, 332.

25. xiv, 194 (*The Covent-Garden Journal*, No. 48).

26. *The Cry* (1754), iii, 129–30.

27. iii, 150–52 (Bk. IV, iii).

28. vii, 313 (Bk. XII, v).

29. vii, 90 (Bk. VIII, v).

30. VI, 127 (Bk. III, v).
31. VI, 1-2 (Bk. I, i).
32. VII, 236.
33. VII, 237 (Bk. X, ix).
34. VII, 56.
35. XII, 245.
36. XII, 244.
37. I, 50 (Bk. I, viii).
38. I, 65 Bk. I, xii).
39. II, 61-2 (Bk. II, iii).
40. Translation of Charles Jarvis, second ed. (London, 1749), II, 419-20.
41. I, 49 (Bk. I, viii).
42. *Correspondence of S. Richardson* (1804), I, 125.
43. XIII, 141.

RUFUS D. S. PUTNEY

Laurence Sterne, Apostle of Laughter

'I LAUGH till I cry,' Laurence Sterne wrote David Garrick, 'and in the same tender moment cry till I laugh.' The statement epitomizes his literary career. 'Everything in this world, said my father, is big with jest—and has wit in it, and instruction too—if we can but find it out.' To find it out *Tristram Shandy* was written, but though we laugh often in making the discovery, that novel impresses us with the pathos of life rather than with its comedy. As Sterne approached the end of *A Sentimental Journey,* he wrote to Mrs. James: 'I told you my design in it was to teach us to love the world and our fellow creatures better than we do—so it runs most upon those gentler passions and affections which aid so much to it.' But if the comedy of life ends in pathos, Sterne's delineation of its pathos is comic. To a gay young woman named Hannah, Sterne sent this challenge: 'I have something else for you, which I am fabricating at a great rate, & that is my Journey, which shall make you cry as much as ever it made me laugh—or I'll give up the Business of sentimental writing—& write to the Body.' His hopes were fulfilled beyond his expectations. The echoes of the deluge with which countless Hannahs of both sexes once saturated the pages of *A Sentimental Journey* still drown out the sound of Sterne's laughter.

We are likely to be misled by reading 'sentimentalist' on the label affixed to Laurence Sterne. The term, unless the word be used in its unsentimental eighteenth-century sense, is never appropriate to the writer and only occasionally so to the man. To call Sterne a sentimentalist is to ignore the hard core of comic irony that made him critical of the emotional vagaries of his own life and of his imagined characters.

From *The Age of Johnson: Essays Presented to Chauncey Brewster Tinker* (Yale University Press, 1949), 159–70. Reprinted by permission of the publisher and author.

The reputation for lachrymose sensibility has been fastened unjustly to Sterne by a misunderstanding of *A Sentimental Journey*, fostered by uncritical dependence on the four letters supposed to have been written to Elizabeth Lumley before she became Mrs. Sterne and on the *Journal to Eliza*. Of the two, the letters to his wife are the more damaging because they appear to push back his cardiac instability to 1740 or earlier. Professor Lewis P. Curtis has demonstrated, however, that they could not have been written as we now have them at the date conventionally assigned. Neither the letters nor the *Journal* prove Sterne's excessive sensibility. More manly men than he had tears to shed indiscriminately on real or fictitious woes, and his prompt though somewhat inactive compassion was the result of the hardships and frustrations of his own life. Like Pope and Swift, he was anti-intellectual because he knew that reason often deludes the reasoner and solves only minor problems. He did not subscribe to the philosophical cult of feeling. On the contrary, as Herbert Read has shown, Sterne's sermon, 'The Abuses of Conscience,' insists upon Christian authority as the proper measure of virtue. Man's propensity to self-delusion makes his feelings deceptive guides to right conduct. In his final judgment upon himself Sterne reiterated the fallibility of the emotions. To Mrs. James he wrote in March, 1768, shortly before his death: 'If I die cherish the remembrance of me and forget the follies which you have so often condemn'd—which my heart, not my head betray'd me into.'

Sterne doubtless knew that Mrs. James would more readily forgive the mistakes of the heart than the perversions of the mind, but the self-criticism this passage displays was constant, not unique. Once his effusions of feeling were past, Sterne could and did view his behavior with impartial irony. In 1764 he sent John Hall-Stevenson an account of a love affair identical in all respects to his courtship of Eliza—even to the hemorrhages of the lungs with which he lamented the departures of both ladies:

> I have been for eight weeks smitten with the tenderest passion that ever tender wight underwent. I wish, dear cosin, thou couldest conceive (perhaps thou can'st without my wishing it) how deliciously I canter'd away with it the first month, two up, two down, always upon my hânches along the streets from my hôtel to hers, at first, once—then twice, then three times a day, till at length I was within an ace of setting up my hobby horse in her stable for good and all. I might as well considering how the enemies of the Lord have blasphemed thereupon; the last three weeks we were every hour upon the doleful ditty of parting—and thou mayest concieve, dear cosin, how it alter'd my gaite and air—for I went and

came like any louden'd carl, and did nothing but mix tears, and *Jouer des sentiments* with her from sun-rising even to the setting of the same; and now she is gone to the South of France, and to finish the comedie, I fell ill, and broke a vessel in my lungs and half bled to death. Voila mon Histoire!

Love, as Trim told Uncle Toby, is 'the most serious thing, an please your honour (sometimes) that is in the world.' But not after love has ended. Just as Sterne in this letter laughed at his folly, he mocked in the *Sentimental Journey* the foolish figure he had cut with Eliza Draper.

Though Sterne during the final years of his celebrity often wept to demonstrate the soundness of his heart, he had no faith as a writer in the moral efficacy of tears. In the cathartic effects of laughter he felt complete assurance. 'If 'tis wrote against any thing,—'tis wrote, an' please your worships, against the spleen,' he remarked in volume four of *Tristram Shandy,* 'in order, by a more frequent and a more convulsive elevation and depression of the diaphragm, and the succusations of the intercostal muscles in laughter, to drive the *gall* and other *bitter juices* from the gall bladder, liver and sweet-bread of his majesty's subjects, with all their inimicitious passions which belong to them, down into their duodenums.' His insatiable love of laughter and belief in its worth distinguishes him from Meredith. Otherwise he had the same confidence in the value and healthiness of comedy.

Begun to please himself in the conviction that what he liked the public must also relish, *Tristram Shandy* is one of the funniest of English novels. Sterne's zest for laughter infects every part of the book, characters, style, incidents, satire, and structure. There is an abundance of sentiment as well, but his diffidence in the presence of pathos transmutes sorrow into mirth. Walter and Toby Shandy and Trim are the figures best remembered and loved. The most gracious events are those that take place on Uncle Toby's bowling green where he and Trim re-enact for the good of the nation the victories of English arms abroad, until the Treaty of Utrecht puts an end to glorious war and allows that daughter of Eve, the Widow Wadman, to shatter their masculine Paradise. No less memorable are the scenes at the fireside in Shandy Hall, where the two affectionate but incompatible brothers meet to smoke, to snooze, to talk, and inevitably to vex one another. While Walter 'crucifies Truth' in his impetuous quest for evidence to support his extraordinary hypotheses, benign, sensible, brave, modest, orthodox Uncle Toby finds ample vent for the outrage done his modesty, religion, and common sense in puffing on his pipe or whistling the 'Lillibulero.'

But Walter's patience snaps faster than his pipestems when an inadvertent word sends Toby rushing into discourses on fortifications and ballistics, or when Uncle Toby's naïve questions interrupt Walter's eloquence:

'Tis pity, said my father, that truth can only be on one side, brother *Toby*,—considering what ingenuity these learned men have all shewn in their solutions of noses.—Can noses be dissolved? replied my uncle *Toby*.—

—My father thrust back his chair,—rose up—put on his hat,—took four long strides to the door,—jerked it open,—thrust his head half way out,—shut the door again,—took no notice of the bad hinge,—returned to the table,—pluck'd my mother's thread-paper out of *Slawkenbergius's* book,—went hastily to his bureau,—walk'd slowly back,—twisting my mother's thread-paper about his thumb,—unbutton'd his waistcoat,—threw my mother's thread-paper into the fire,—bit her sattin pin-cushion in two, fill'd his mouth with bran,—confounded it;—but mark!—the oath of confusion was levell'd at my uncle *Toby's* brain,—which was e'en confused enough already,—the curse came charged only with the bran—the bran, may it please your honours,—was no more than powder to the ball.

If Toby, Walter, Trim, and Yorick are Sterne's most praised characters the most neglected is Tristram himself. The chief cause for this neglect has been the identification of Tristram with Sterne, who complained toward the end of his life that 'The world has imagined, because I wrote Tristram Shandy, that I was myself more Shandean than I really ever was.' Tristram, as Edwin Muir some years ago demonstrated, is the projection of a mere fraction of Sterne's personality, not a portrait of the real man. To write *The Life and Opinions of Tristram Shandy, Gent.*, Sterne assumed the character of Tristram as he was later to wear the more subtle disguise of a revamped Yorick to write *A Sentimental Journey*. His imaginative fidelity to these created roles beggars praise, giving unity to the novels and making plausible their eccentricities.

The assumption of Tristram's mind provides also the chief structural device of the book. In the fragment we possess, very little of Tristram's life is narrated, but he was once destined to play a larger part than Sterne's fate allowed him to fulfill. Up to chapter xx of Volume VI, the misadventures of Tristram's life provide the skeleton on which the digressions are hung, and his is the mind so lost in the flux of thought, as explained by Locke's theory of the association of ideas, that each mischance he suffers leads into tangential mazes. What Sterne once designed, after he had given up the notion reported by Stephen

Croft of traveling Tristram all over Europe and returning him home at last a complete English gentleman, can be learned from the first volume:

> But I was begot and born to misfortunes;— . . . so that I was doom'd, by marriage articles, to have my nose squeez'd as flat to my face, as if the destinies had actually spun me without one.
>
> How this event came about,—and what a train of vexatious disappointments, in one stage or other of my life, have pursued me from the mere loss, or rather compression, of this one single member,—shall be laid before the reader all in due time.

This and other passages in the novel make it clear that as he commenced the book Sterne intended to follow Tristram's career into manhood with a series of humiliations and petty disasters.

The abandonment of this scheme in the middle of Volume VI for the interpolation of Uncle Toby's wars, his amour with the Widow Wadman, and Tristram's travels has obscured the structural unity (on the principle of the association of ideas) that prevailed for the first five and a half volumes. All but a few brief and unimportant digressions are connected with the accidents that befall Tristram. Mrs. Shandy's ill-timed question leads to the discussion of the rights of the homunculus, to the date of his conception, and to Walter Shandy's theory of geniture. The date of his birth involves its method, and that brings in the local midwife, whose existence in the neighborhood requires a description of Parson Yorick and his reasons for establishing the old woman in her vocation. Her role in Tristram's misfortunes would be inexplicable, in view of Dr. Slop's proximity, without a knowledge of his mother's marriage settlement. Tristram's name results in an exposition of Walter's theory of names with the history of Aunt Dinah, and Tristram's quasi-logical comment that one cannot be christened before one is born reminds him of the decision of the doctors of the Sorbonne on that subject. While Walter and Toby are awaiting Tristram's birth, they begin a discussion of Mrs. Shandy's reason for rejecting Dr. Slop which cannot be understood until Toby's character has been elucidated. The accident to Tristram's nose in volume three is responsible for the discussion of Walter's theory of the importance of noses with the reasons therefore and an account of his collection of books on the subject. From his favorite work the tale of Slawkenbergius is gleaned. The remainder of the fourth volume follows from the mistake at the christening which reaches its culmination in the ludicrous happenings and talk at the Visitation Dinner. The news of Bobby's death soon after focuses all

Walter's hopes upon Tristram. Hence his father begins writing the Tristra-*pœdia*, upon which he has made considerable progress before Tristram at the age of five suffers his misadventure with the window sash. The arrival of Yorick, Toby, and Trim to explain the defective window not only gives Walter a chance to express his views on circumcision but also provides an audience for the reading of the Tristra-*pœdia*. That introduces the need for a tutor, and Uncle Toby recommends Le Fever's son. Who he is necessitates telling his father's story. The mad rumors about Tristram caused by his last accident make Walter resolve that his son shall be put into breeches, a determination which leads to an account of Walter's researches upon clothes and a description of his beds of justice at which affairs important to the family are decided. Up to this point *Tristram Shandy* is as thoughtfully constructed and as unified as *Tom Jones*.

The probable cause for the alteration in Sterne's design was the clamor against the double entendre and downright indecencies of the second installment. Possibly he also realized that Walter's hypotheses were growing slightly stale. Still the compromise he made was minor. He shifted his subject to the more poignant humor of Uncle Toby's activities, but the consistency of Tristram's character as narrator and consequently the tone and comedy were scrupulously maintained. For Tristram is himself a comic character in whom are blended the diverse strains of the Shandys. From Uncle Toby he inherited pity, from his great Aunt Dinah lasciviousness. His obligations to his father are so great that they require a separate paragraph.

That Tristram would 'neither think nor act like any other man's child' was the conviction to which Walter Shandy was led 'upon his observing a most unaccountable obliquity, (as he call'd it) in my manner of setting up my top, and justifying the principles upon which I had done it, . . . with a thousand other observations he had made upon me.' Never stopping to reflect that his son could be only extraordinary, Walter accounts for Tristram's eccentricities in terms of his favorite theories of geniture, obstetrics, names, noses, and education. In the depiction of father and son Sterne employed his subtlest skill in characterization. Tristram's taste for the oddities of knowledge, his unpredictable attitudes toward persons and things, rival his father's. He has his father's relish also for witty indecencies, and the same irreverence. His representation of Walter's strange opinions is half serious, half playful, for he half believes himself that they explain the idiosyncrasies he enjoys. Besides, he has hypotheses of his own, though like everything else about Tristram when compared to his father, they are diminutive and trifling. Knots, swearing, plackets, buttonholes, chambermaids, chamber pots, and chapters are the sorts of things he theorizes about. Finally, Walter had the zeal or anger (two names for the same quality) to make him a satirist. Uncle Toby's benevolence had eradicated the harshness from Tristram, who thus sums up the difference between himself and his father:

> For my hobby-horse, if you recollect a little, is no way a vicious beast; he has scarce one hair or lineament of the ass [the lower passions in Walter's terminology] about him— 'Tis a sporting little filly-folly which carries you out for the present hour—a maggot, a butter-fly, a picture, a fiddle-stick—an uncle *Toby's* siege—or an *any thing*, which a man makes shift to get astride on, to canter it away from the cares and solicitudes of life— 'Tis as useful a beast as is in the whole creation—nor do I really see how the world could do without it—
>
> —But for my father's ass—oh! mount him—mount him—mount him— (that's three times, is it not?)—mount him not:—'tis a beast concupiscent— and foul befall the man who does not hinder him from kicking.

Some have complained because Sterne's 'filly-folly' did not kick like Walter Shandy's ass. The censure that *Tristram Shandy* lacks high purpose because Sterne undertook no reformations is idle criticism. There is a quantity of sportive satire, although Dr. Burton and the Pope might have detected occasional bitterness, but satire is not what we seek in *Tristram Shandy*. The greatness of the novel and its abiding charm reside in Sterne's humor, that mixture of pathos and wit that sheds its warm glow over the representation of the frailties and foibles as well as the strength of man's nature, matters upon which Sterne was far better informed than most of his critics. More truly than *A Sentimental Journey*, *Tristram* 'teaches us to love the world and our fellow creatures better than we do.'

On the success of *Tristram Shandy* Sterne gambled everything he had—money, his reputation as a clergyman, and his hope of rising in the Church. Friends warned him of his peril in publishing such a book. 'Get your Preferment first Lory,' one said, '& then Write & Welcome.' A note of quiet desperation, induced by forty-six years of obscurity and frustration, pervades his answer, 'But suppose preferment is long acoming (& for aught I know I may not be preferr'd till the Resurrection of the Just) and am all that time in labour—how must I bear my Pains?'

The intoxicating popularity of the novel permitted Sterne to discover what Pope had found before him. 'The greatest advantage I know of being thought a wit by the world,' Pope had said, 'is, that it gives one the greater freedom of playing the fool.' Sterne possessed an impulse to folly that had driven him, while his reputation was merely local, to play the fool agriculturally, politically, clerically, and domestically. Some of the motives for this conduct one should not try to explain. During the years of his fame, however, he deliberately adopted and emphasized his favorite role. 'I wrote,' he told one of his friends, 'not to be fed but to be famous.' To the obscure Yorkshire parson the idea of fame included posthumous reputation if it could be had, but most of all it meant contemporary celebrity, the outward and visible sign of which not infrequently is food of superior quality eaten at the tables of the great. If his book had brought him renown, Sterne resolved that he would whet the appetites of his readers by his life. He therefore undertook to advertise his novel by impersonating the character of Tristram Shandy.

The experiment was only partially successful. He won and kept the friendship of David Garrick, Lord Bathurst, and many more, but the spectacle of a reverend clergyman acting the part of a licentious jester shortly aroused the ire of others. Recovering from the panic that made him present Sterne a purse of guineas as insurance against a lampoon, Bishop Warburton solemnly pronounced him 'an irrecoverable scoundrel.' In and out of print Oliver Goldsmith raged against the man and his work. Whitfield thundered, 'O *Sterne!* thou art scabby, and such is the leprosy of thy mind that it is not to be cured like the leprosy of the body, by dipping nine times in the river Jordan.' The more dignified Dr. Delany was reported to be much offended with 'the man Sterne,' and Dr. Dodd, who was soon to hang for forgery, protested in execrable verse,

> Is it for this you wear the sacred gown,
> To live and write the Shandy of the town?

Sterne could afford to be amused as long as people bought his book, but after 1762 *Tristram Shandy* ceased to pay profits of the size Sterne needed, and the critics began dunning him for his arrears of pathos. A new book was necessary to recoup his literary fortunes without sacrificing, since tears were alien to *Tristram Shandy,* his integrity as an artist. As nearly as can be determined, Sterne conceived A *Sentimental Journey* during the summer of 1766 while he was busy with the last volume of *Shandy.* It was written throughout the summer and fall of 1767.

During that year Sterne suffered a dangerous illness and his love affair with Eliza Draper. Too much effect has been attributed to both in explaining why Sterne, always sentimentally chaste in *Tristram*

Shandy, seems emotionally wanton in *A Sentimental Journey.* He had recovered entirely from the lady and temporarily from the disease by the time he produced most of his book. The exuberant gaiety of his work belies its origin in depression and despair. As for Eliza, she was merely another in the long list of Sterne's sentimental mistresses. They met in January. By February Sterne, following his usual procedure in such cases, had persuaded first himself and then the lady that he was in love. An idealized but essentially accurate description of the beginning of his infatuation can be read in Yorick's description of his enamorment:

> It had ever, as I told the reader, been one of the singular blessings of my life, to be almost every hour of it miserably in love with some one; and my last flame happening to be blown out by a whiff of jealousy on the sudden turn of a corner, I had lighted it up afresh at the pure taper of Eliza but about three months before, swearing as I did it, that it should last me through the whole journey. Why should I dissemble the matter? I had sworn to her eternal fidelity; she had a right to my whole heart; to divide my affections was to lessen them; to expose them, was to risk them: where there is risk, there may be loss.

Six or seven months in affairs of this kind meant eternity to Sterne. Eliza sailed for India in April. By the end of July long gaps appeared in the *Journal,* in which he had vowed he would keep a daily record of his love. On August 4, when he shut up the *Journal* with a lie to Eliza about the date of his wife's homecoming, he had found out what he had just written or soon would write in the drummer's letter to the corporal's wife:

> L'amour n'est *rien* sans sentiment.
> Et le sentiment est encore *moins* sans amour.

Once he had made this discovery Sterne ceased playing at sentiments in the *Journal.*

To write and to laugh were still synonymous for him. He now solved his literary dilemma with a hoax by which he persuaded his contemporaries that the comedy he must write was the pathos they wished to read. He accomplished this by making Yorick weep in order that 'in the same tender moment' he himself might laugh. For Yorick is a dramatically presented comic hero with a heart as erratic as Tristram's head. He is not to be regarded, Edwin Muir and W. B. C. Watkins have shown, as a sympathetic portrait of his creator. Occasionally Sterne's identification of himself with Yorick becomes almost complete. But for the most part the writer records with amused irony the false, ludicrous, or humiliating postures into which Yorick is thrust by his intrepid sensibility. Far from being a manual of sentimental and civilized behavior, as Peter Quennell has lately described the book, *A Sentimental Journey* displays the errors, equivocations, and dilemmas into which Yorick is betrayed by the instability of his heart. For Yorick, unlike the benevolent monsters spawned in imitation of him, runs the full scale of human emotions. He is vain, libidinous, servile, proud, greedy, and fickle as well as humane, faithful, honest, humble, and loving. The gift of his snuffbox mitigates but does not excuse his injustice to the Monk. His somewhat tardy continence scarcely offsets the infidelities to Eliza he commits in spirit. He gives alms to the wrong people and hires a valet for preposterous reasons. Compassion for the master of the dead ass leads him to curse his postilion. He buys the caged starling but does not free it, and purchases popularity with obsequious flattery. He goes, like 'the Knight of the Woeful Countenance,' in quest of a melancholy meeting with Maria, and his pity for her misery ends in concupiscence. At such incongruities Sterne could not help but laugh.

It has been duly noted that Sterne immortalized Eliza by mentioning her name on five occasions in his novel, but I think no one has pointed out the ambiguous role he assigned her in his love comedy as the mistress to whom Yorick could scarcely be true. In two instances her name merely lends the book the piquant impropriety that Jenny had given *Tristram Shandy*. Her other appearances are more amusing. Tormented by his inability to read the Old French fragment, Yorick seeks a remedy for his vexation in correspondence. He writes Eliza, but only as an afterthought. He writes Eugenius first. Elsewhere she is a clog hindering his pursuit of the women that attract him. Commenting on Maria's departing figure, Yorick says,

> Affliction had touch'd her looks with something that was scarcely earthly—still she was feminine, and so much there was about her of all that the heart wishes or the eye looks for in woman, that could the traces be ever worn out of her brain, and those of Eliza out of mine, she should *not only eat of my bread and drink of my own cup*, but Maria should lie in my bosom and be unto me as a daughter.

Earlier, tempted by vision of the joys a visit to Madame de L—— offers, Yorick suddenly remembers Eliza and his vows of constancy. Falling on his knees he swears he 'would not travel to Brussels, unless Eliza went along with me, did the road lead towards heaven,' then wryly adds, 'In transports of this kind the heart, in spite of the understanding, will always say too much.' His fidelity reasserted, Yorick writes gallantly to the lady and hastens on to Paris to expose, risk, and lessen his affections with the beautiful *griset*, the *fille de chambre*, the Marquisina di Fagnani by interpolation, Maria at Moulines, and the lady who shared his room in the Bourbonnois. In the 'Business of sentimental writing' Sterne used Eliza as the symbol of delicate, disinterested, romantic love. In the semiprivate comedy that made him laugh Eliza provides a standard to measure the vagaries of Yorick's heart.

Priesthood was a fortunate accident in the career of Laurence Sterne. Most of the materials for his fiction came from his own far from exemplary life. Yet if he did not practice, he believed sincerely what he preached. Thus his clerical vocation gave him the absolute ethical code that made possible the dispassionate judgment comedy requires. His own behavior after his residence in France in 1762 often resembled Yorick's; his literary account of it is the self-mockery of *A Sentimental Journey*. The disparity between his practice and his professions enriched *Tristram Shandy* in another, less tangible way. Only from the knowledge of his own trials and failures could have come his humorous pity for the frailties of other men. Sterne cannot have added a cubit to the spiritual stature of the Church of England. By making him take thought it added many to his greatness as a writer.

BERTRAND H. BRONSON

The Double Tradition of Dr. Johnson

In a sense so deep as to give most of its meaning to the study of literary history, a great writer is defined not only by his own works but also by what posterity makes of him. What he has meant to the generations between his own and ours is an essential part of what he comes to mean to us. After his death there springs up an eidolon of an author, and it is of this everchanging surrogate, not of the original, that we inevitably form our judgments, and that by so judging we further change. Every such image is an instance of one sort of literary tradition, and, like all tradition, a continuity. Let the losses or gains, the changes, reversals, or accretions be what they may, there can be no second beginning. Every phase of the tradition is an immediate consequence. The original, moreover, is forever inaccessible, and, were it not so, that original would still not be the truth. For the truth is always becoming: the truth of living tradition neither was, nor is, nor shall be, but exists in a continuum. Absolute judgments of a literary figure, therefore, can never possess more than a momentary and private validity, since the eidolon upon which they base themselves is never long the same. Whether consciously or not, we are all necessarily students of tradition in being students of literature. And this would appear to be equally true whether we study the work of a man or a man in his work. It is to this aspect of tradition—not the operative power of tradition which we denominate influence, but something more akin to a transmitted recollection, to a song or ballad—that present attention is invited.

These remarks are to focus in Dr. Johnson, and by implication I have raised the question whether it is possible for two people, or for two generations, to remember and discuss the same Dr. Johnson. The prob-

---

From *ELH, a Journal of English Literary History,* June 1951, pp. 90–106. Reprinted by permission of the publisher and author.

lem of Johnson's identity is further complicated by circumstances almost, if not quite, unique. The uniqueness lies, of course, in the fact that it is possible to 'know' this man, in his habit as he lived, as intimately as we can 'know' his works. The fullness of the biographical record is without parallel for any comparable figure. (Boswell is an exception, but Boswell is incomparable.)

Hence, Johnson has come down to us in a double tradition. Like any other author, he exists for us in his works. But he exists for us also like a character in one of our older novels, and on the same level of objectivity and familiarity. The traditional personality began to be shaped before his death, but became condensed and fully substantiated in Boswell's *Tour* and *Life*. The descent of the two traditions, of the personality and of the author—which we shall differentiate for convenience as the popular and the learned traditions—has proceeded neither with equal stability nor along a parallel track. The popular tradition has been much less affected by the refreshing or contaminating influences of print.

Every student of oral tradition knows that the approved method of procedure is to stop your carrier where you meet him, note the place and date, put questions, get him to talk, and take down his report verbatim. To reach a relatively accurate definition of Johnson as he exists today in popular tradition, one ought to collect as many variants as possible from representative cultural levels and areas, collate and analyze the data, find the common core, trace the deviations and 'sports,' detect the lines of transmission, and establish the norm in the popular mind of the time. The research would be expensive and time-consuming, and I doubt if it has ever been proposed to a Foundation as a proper project for subsidy. Nevertheless, we might learn a good deal from such an investigation about the ways of tradition, the shaping of popular myth, about the nature and component elements of a literary persona abstracted from whatever sources and abraded by the ebb and flow of collective memory. Without it, we can only guess at the state and distribution of the tradition here prefigured.

At its feeblest, the popular tradition is probably little more than an eponym for a crushing reply. In its middling state, it is usually the object of affectionate regard, seldom of opprobrium. What we should doubtless find most frequently in the folk-image would be the ideas of physical bulk, sloppy habits of dress, bad manners, loud voice, witty but weighty speech. There would be a general notion of a man who was always saying quotable things and who had written books that nobody read. In fuller variants, examples of his good things would be cited; and doubtless in the books of Familiar Quotations we should find the likeliest instances of his repartee. Johnson's animal farm would show itself: at the very least, the Cow, the Bull, and the Dog, in those unsuitable postures wherein he delighted to show them for analogical consideration.

The popular image thus faintly and imperfectly suggested would not, we feel sure, have perpetuated itself in the common memory for so long, had Boswell not done his work with such unexampled vividness. But Boswell's image was of a complexity and subtlety far transcending what could be used and carried by the general. Cheap and striking reproduction, enormously simplified, was the need; and the need was supplied, unquestionably, by Macaulay's review of Croker's *Boswell*, in 1831. Macaulay has dropped his seine into Boswell's waters and drawn up nearly all the details that have persisted in later popular variants. He tumbles them headlong into one sprawling sentence:

Everything about him, his coat, his wig, his figure, his face, his scrofula, his St. Vitus's dance, his rolling walk, his blinking eye, the outward signs which too clearly marked his approbation of his dinner, his insatiable appetite for fish-sauce and veal-pie with plums, his inextinguishable thirst for tea, his trick of touching the posts as he walked, his mysterious practice of treasuring up scraps of orange-peel, his morning slumbers, his midnight disputations, his contortions, his mutterings, his gruntings, his puffings, his vigorous, acute, and ready eloquence, his sarcastic wit, his vehemence, his insolence, his fits of tempestuous rage, his queer inmates, old Mr. Levett and blind Mrs. Williams, the cat Hodge and the negro Frank, all are as familiar to us as the objects by which we have been surrounded from childhood.

For every statement of a traditional theme that has the fortune to be written down, there are thousands that go unrecorded. But we have to plot the course of tradition in the individual versions that achieve the accidental permanence of print. Macaulay's essay of 1856 shows variations such as one might note in the rendition of a ballad by the same singer a quarter of a century later. Some parts drop out, others come into stronger prominence: in this case, the later version is softer and more kindly. The variation is so slight, however, as rather to reinforce Macaulay's influence on the popular tradition than to modify it. This second essay, reprinted countless times in school editions, is that which has made it unnecessary for all but the curious and the scholarly-minded ever to read Boswell. 'The old philosopher,' it concludes unforgettably, 'is still among us in the brown coat with the metal buttons and the shirt which ought to be at wash, blinking, puffing, rolling his head, drumming with his fingers, tearing his meat like a tiger, and swallowing his tea in oceans.' The imago is now fixed as firmly as such things can be. (Imago, says the ACD, is 'an idealized concept of a loved one, formed in childhood and retained uncorrected in adult life.')

Carlyle's version, put on paper in 1832 partly to offset Macaulay, preferable in some respects though it is, seems to have had little effect on the popular idea. It is too idiosyncratically conceived and expressed to find familiar residence in the common mind. Carlyle deliberately sets about making a myth, turning the man Johnson into a personified abstraction. Illustrative of the technique is a brief passage describing Johnson as a college student:

> A rugged wild-man of the desert, awakened to the feeling of himself; proud as the proudest, poor as the poorest; stoically shut up, silently enduring the incurable: what a world of blackest gloom, with sun-gleams and pale tearful moon-gleams, and flickerings of a celestial and an infernal splendour, was this that now opened for him! But the weather is wintry; and the toes of the man are looking through his shoes. His muddy features grow of a purple and sea-green colour; a flood of black indignation mantling beneath.

Regarded as a variant in the series, this is too far from the traditional norm: it has been contaminated by the concept of Hero as Man of Letters.

At this point let us turn from the popular to that other branch, which I have called the learned, tradition. What we are to observe is the eidolon, continually remoulded, successively and responsibly viewed in Johnson's works and in the light of all that can be known about him. Every stage of the process is contiguous upon the precedent one; and it is this awareness, and not congruity of opinion, that constitutes the continuity inherent in the idea of tradition.

All description of the learned tradition must falsify by over-simplification. Even to his contemporaries Johnson presented contrary faces; but broadly speaking the man and his works then appeared commensurate, were of a piece, and were great. Separation probably began before the end of the century, and was doubtless hastened by the appearance of Boswell's *Life*. But in 1817 it was still possible for Alexander Chalmers to declare: 'the world has agreed . . . to rank him among the most illustrious writers of any age or nation, and among the benefactors to religion, virtue, and learning.' Of *The Rambler* in particular: 'since the work became popular, every thing in literature or morals, in history or dissertation, is better conceived, and better expressed—conceived with more novelty, and expressed with greater energy.'

In another twenty years, however, the cleavage has become so marked that Macaulay can unquestioningly give the palm to the Johnson in Boswell, a 'far greater' figure than Johnson the author. Says Macaulay:

> His conversation appears to have been quite equal to his writings in matter, and far superior to them in manner. . . . As soon as he took his pen in his hand to write for the public, his style became systematically vicious. . . . It is clear that Johnson himself did not think in the dialect in which he wrote. The expressions which came first to his tongue were simple, energetic, and picturesque. When he wrote for publication, he did his sentences out of English into Johnsonese. (Further:) His whole code of criticism rested on pure assumption. (And again:) The characteristic peculiarity of his intellect was the union of great powers with low prejudices.

The lectures of Thomas Sergeant Perry, published 1882 under the title, *English Literature in the Eighteenth Century,* show us the learned tradition apparently by that time immutably set along the lines forecast by Macaulay. This was authoritative opinion, careful and conscientious, abreast of Continental as well as English and American scholarship. With the confidence of learning and leadership, Perry declared of Johnson: that all his views had been riddled by a later opinion, that *The Rambler* was unreadable, like a petrifaction of Addison and Steele; that, while it might be allowed that the Preface to Shakespeare, though tinged with antique notions, had been serviceable to letters, the influence of the Lives of the Poets could only have been bad. Yet it was not enough to say of him merely that he had encouraged philistinism. 'With all his faults, he is one of the best-loved men in the history of letters, and this is due, not to his writings, but to the faithful record' etc. 'Dr. Johnson's reputation, then, is due to Boswell's book.' So powerful was the tradition by this time that even Leslie Stephen, capable of understanding Johnson and sympathetic to him at many points, deprecates his writing. 'Johnson's sentences,' he writes, 'seem to be contorted, as his gigantic limbs used to twitch, by a kind of mechanical spasmodic action.' 'And yet,' he faintly pleads for *The Rambler,* 'with all its faults, the reader who can plod through its pages will at least feel respect for the author.'

As early as the first decade of the new century there were outspoken protests against the prevailing view. In his historical anthology of English Prose, Henry Craik makes a vigorous attack upon what he calls 'the parody which lives in the popular estimation.' He stands uncompromisingly for Johnson as an author, and declares that, 'in style alone, we may justly claim that he is the vertebrate column of our prose.' Craik brings us back to a view of Johnson surprisingly close to that of Chalmers a century before: 'it is not too much,' he goes on, 'to say that all that is best in English prose since his day is his debtor in respect of not a few of its highest qualities'; and of the *Lives of the Poets* he states his conviction that, 'for vigour and ease and variety of style, for elasticity of confidence, for keenness of sarcasm, for brightnes of humour, the *Lives* hold the first place, absolutely free from competition, amongst all works of English criticism of similar range.'

Taken as a whole, Craik's praise, during the present half-century, and within what I have called the learned tradition, has not yet been reversed. Rather, reinforced immediately by the brilliant essays of Walter Raleigh, it has become in its turn the accepted view, and has been elaborated and refined upon by an impressive and growing number of discriminating scholar-critics.

It is true that tradition is embodied only in its individual instances, is ultimately the sum of these manifestations. There is no instrumentality that will reconcile incommensurables or reduce the prismatic rays of tradition to 'the wide effulgence of a summer noon.' But if we are not to give over our allotted space to a gallery talk among the portraits of Dr. Johnson, we must try to put together some kind of composite that will display his features with the emphases characteristic of our understanding of him. When we look for the points where Johnson's thought seems to focus with maximum intensity, we find them where the currents of his day, whether political, religious, or literary, are threatening to break over into channels leading, as he thought, to mischievous ends. We find them where he is most stoutly engaged in resisting these tendencies. This resistance goes under the name of Johnson's conservatism, and it is by a closer and more sympathetic examination of its character and quality that we find our view of Johnson diverging most sharply from older tradition.

Conservatism is a chameleon term that gets most of its meaning from its surroundings. It can have a negative, a neutral, or a positive cast. It may mean a dogged reluctance to surrender private or group advantage; it may mean a lazy habit of mind that dislikes any change; it may mean a passionate and aggressive determination to preserve the best. Thus, Churchill was heroically conservative in 1942. In 1946, to many, he was a reactionary. So far as we can tell, he and his principles remained unaltered. Conservatism is certainly no genuine opposite to progressivism, unless the latter be carelessly taken as a spirit of innovation. When conservatism is the position of a small minority, it sometimes acquires a radical look. Thus, Rousseau has lately been described—and with justice—as a violent reactionary, sick with nostalgia for an imaginary past where man had lived free and exquisitely uncivilized. barbarously refined.

Of late we have come to perceive more clearly that the spirit that animated Johnson, in his maturity as in his early years, was a positive, not a negative nor a neutral, spirit. The youth of whom he allows us retrospective glimpses in his later conversation was a being very restive under the restraints of his environment, and forward to propose iconoclastic if hypothetical improvements. Between the ages of 25 and 35, he was a violent and outspoken opponent of the government and the reigning house:—a homeless, penniless, dangerous man, keeping questionable company, tramping the streets all night for lack of a lodging or money to pay for one; sustained by political passion, 'brimful of patriotism,' 'resolved to stand by his country' by writing incendiary anti-ministerial pamphlets; the misreporter of Parliamentary debates and, in fact, wanted for questioning by the authorities. Temperamentally intemperate, he was yet less disreputable than would appear, for his passion was supported then and thenceforward by convictions about the bases and structure of society, and of man's obligations to God and his fellow-man which ultimately confirmed his service under the banner of Law.

Macaulay was right when he called him 'as a politician, half ice and half fire'; but Macaulay, it now appears, was quite wrong in the sense he gave to his own remark. For Macaulay thought him, in politics, intellectually apathetic and passionate from unfounded prejudice; and considered that the notorious conversation with Sir Adam Fergusson was enough to demonstrate Johnson's gross and palpable illogicality. For in one breath Johnson could say, 'I would not give half a guinea to live under one form of government rather than another'; and in the next, could turn on his opponent with the outburst, 'Sir, I perceive you are a vile Whig.'

To correct Macaulay, we must look a little more inquiringly into this *volte face*. The scene took place at the Pantheon, where, it will be recalled, Sir Adam 'expressed some apprehension' lest such public amusements might encourage luxury in the populace. Luxury, he declared, 'corrupts a people and destroys the spirit of liberty.' Johnson, as we know, thought that the mass of the common people was in very little immediate danger from over-abundance of material delights, and always protested at their being denied any innocent sweeteners of a bitter existence. 'Luxury,' he said, 'so far as it reaches the poor, will do good

to the race of people; it will strengthen and multiply them.' He therefore put by Sir Adam's philosophical cant with a common-sense answer: 'Sir, I am a great friend to publick amusements; for they
keep people from vice.' Pressed again on the theoretical ground—the
fear that the spirit of liberty would be sapped—he declared, 'Sir, that is
all visionary.' Setting aside the fact that the threat of epidemic luxury
was non-existent, where was the national emergency that demanded
that the nation be kept on the alert to preserve its liberty? No foreign
power was menacing. But Sir Adam, it appeared, was afraid of the
encroachments of the King's Party. Johnson maintained that the average
Briton was likely to feel very little effect in his private life, whatever the
temporary complexion of Parliament. If the country remained peaceful,
even a monarchy in the old sense permitted the normal freedoms of
daily living, which were all that the common subject was aware of.
'Liberty,' he had written some twenty years earlier, 'is, to the lowest rank
of every nation, little more than the choice of working or starving; and
this choice is, I suppose, equally allowed in every country.' If ordinary
men were to be denied amusements lest they grow slack and be unable
to put up resistance to a danger which even if fully realized they would
not feel, what a coil was here! At such a distance from immediate experience, the form of government itself made little difference. 'But, Sir,'
insisted Sir Adam, 'in the British Constitution it is surely of importance
to keep up a spirit in the people, so as to preserve a balance against the
Crown.' JOHNSON:

> 'Sir, I perceive you are a vile Whig. Why all this childish jealousy of the
> power of the crown? The crown has not power enough. When I say
> that all governments are alike, I consider that in no government power
> can be abused long. Mankind will not bear it. If a sovereign oppresses
> his people to a great degree, they will rise and cut off his head. There
> is a remedy in human nature against tyranny, that will keep us safe
> under every form of government.'

Behind Johnson's impatient assertion that the Crown had not power
enough, was the theory, most clearly expressed in *Taxation No Tyranny,*
that the stability of a society rested on the presence in it somewhere of
an impartial, absolute authority, above challenge, to which all contest-
ants could appeal. In the British system, the king was the embodiment
of this principle, the symbol of an ultimate authority, the idea of
decisive right. If, as man, he descended from that high level, his political
defects or perversive influence on the operation of justice and wisdom
in the State—a possibility which Johnson readily admitted—could be

checked or resisted in the persons of his ministers. 'Redress is always to be had against oppression, by punishing the immediate agents.' In effect, then, his subjects would be appealing from him as fallible man to his idea as King infallible. Analogies with the Church are obvious here and need not be developed. Johnson wished that there might be as close an approximation as possible between the king in person and the King as Principle. The Whig effort, on the contrary, was to separate the two by reducing the actual authority of the king and by denying the absolute authority of Sovereignty. Their work, therefore, was ultimately the undermining and destruction of all authority in the State except that of temporary power. Hence Johnson called Whiggism the negation of principle, and declared that the first Whig was the Devil. On the ground of theory, therefore, his retort to Sir Adam involved his whole political philosophy: it was not from pique but from principle. But in the other, the practical, context, he was not inconsistent in saying that the danger of the abuse of power was nothing to a private man, and that the form of government made little difference to the happiness of the individual. His proviso, of course, is essential: that if the actual sovereign grows outrageous, and the abuse becomes enormous, humanity will reestablish its rights by overturning the corrupt system . . . It is impossible to grant the justice here of Macaulay's accusation of an implicit logical dilemma.

Doubtless, there are inconsistencies and paradoxes in the texture of Johnson's thought and speech, and they are no small part of its perennial interest. His sense of moral responsibility has always been recognized. But we see more distinctly today his deep intellectual responsibility as well; and no careful student will now accuse him seriously of setting up thoughtless prejudices in lieu of principles, even where his pronouncements seem to us most cross-grained and perverse.

It is ironically unjust that Johnson should have come to typify, in so many minds, a stubborn resistance to change. The group of whom such a charge could be most fairly made were those inglorious Whigs of his day who were most of all concerned, not to defend principle, but to hold fast to the advantages and emoluments of which they and their friends had become possessed half a century and more ago, and who were motivated in the main by little better than indolent self-interest. They *were* conservative, in a sense that cannot properly be used of Johnson: and he despised them because they were *bottomless*. They were quasi-Tories when in place, but without the underlying philosophy of conservatism, and therefore fundamentally dishonest. He fought them as he fought other kinds of dishonesty, with such tools as he found at hand.

Unquestionably, Johnson's political philosophy was deeply rooted in his religion. The stability of the State, the principle of authority in the State, derived its patent from the Supreme Authority above all states, which governed, however inscrutably, by the moral law adumbrated in the Christian revelation and doctrine. But now, as to our knowledge and understanding of Johnson's religion, it appears to me that we are scarcely more enlightened than were our great-grandparents—if indeed we have not moved farther away from the very possibility of understanding. Nothing of genuine consequence, at any rate, has appeared in print upon the subject. We read the Prayers and Meditations and are moved by the spectacle of Johnson's emotion. We stand respectfully by while he and Boswell discuss theology—or we may prefer to wait outside till they have finished. We read with mild interest and approval the sermons he penned for Dr. Taylor—or more probably we never look at them. We do look, and with sympathetic awe, at the occasional manifestations of his religious terror. But few of us indeed can follow him to the depths of his self-abasement; and those who try are likely to emerge with an untidy little parcel of sciolism insecurely wrapped in pseudo-scientific verbiage. Hypothesis may be tested by experience, but is no substitute for experience. What we seem to observe is a spirit profoundly troubled, not so visibly by religious doubts as by religious convictions. Johnson does not allow us to see him questioning his Maker, but only questioning himself, in order to condemn himself. It may be that this is the only sensible and decent attitude: at any rate, Johnson, in spite of his piety and devotion and genuine religious need, seems very seldom to have received much comfort or happiness from his Christian faith. It is symptomatic that he protested against Blair's assertion that the man 'who does not feel joy in religion is far from the kingdom of heaven.' 'There are many good men,' Johnson insisted, 'whose fear of God predominates over their love.' He admitted to having been a sceptic in early life; but in the years when we know him best seems not often to have been troubled with serious difficulty of that kind. Yet it may be guessed that the act of believing where he could not rationally prove ran counter to his inmost nature. He once wrote: 'None would have recourse to an invisible power, but that all other subjects have eluded their hopes.' He clung to his faith because he was determined to *believe* only because he could not prove, and because he regarded the alternatives of unbelief or agnosticism as doctrines of utter abandoned despair. It seems just to say that he had to believe in the truth of the Christian revelation or lose his sanity; for on that anchor, for him, entirely depended the meaning of existence.

Noting Johnson's extreme habitual scepticism, Macaulay nevertheless charges him with the grossest credulity and downright superstition. 'It is curious,' he writes, 'to observe . . . the contrast between the disdainful manner in which he rejects unauthenticated anecdotes, even when they are consistent with the general laws of nature, and the respectful manner in which he mentions the wildest stories relating to the invisible world.' But the paradox is not a paradox when we understand that it was the sceptical habit of mind, requiring rational demonstration of what he *had* to believe, that drove him to personal investigation of all reports of the supernatural. Not superstition, but the opposite. To the question, Were not the evidences of Christianity sufficient? he replied, 'Yes, but I would have more.'

In fact, Johnson's orthodoxy can be taken as one more evidence of that *un*conservative spirit we divine in him, of the strength of his temperamental bias, to inquire, and try, and prove all things. It was the strait-jacket, or at least the curb and the tight rein, that he felt it necessary to impose upon himself. It was the sign of his self-distrust, a tacit confession of his radical intemperance, the intellectual counterpart of that physical intemperance which so struck Boswell: 'Every thing about his character and manners was forcible and violent; there never was any moderation. . . . He could practise abstinence, but not temperance.'

It is this pervasive sense of what Johnson is keeping in leash, of energy not allowed to run wild, but controlled only by determined and unremitting effort, that makes the man so fascinating. When we look closely, we see that his conservatism vibrates like a taut wire. The immobility that to the casual eye has sometimes appeared to be the mere rigidity of moribund attitudes is now seen to be the precarious triumph of self-government. In days when all fundamental values are subjected to continual challenge, we can look with especial sympathy on one who fought so strenuously not to destroy but to hold fast that which was good.

The spectacle would be interesting even if we found nothing of value in what Johnson was attempting to preserve. But, thanks to Time's whirligig, we now see much that may stead us in our own need, or the challenge of which may serve for measure and clarification of our principles. And nowhere more readily, perhaps, than in confirming literary standards.

Basically, the question of Johnson's value as poet and critic turns on the antinomy of the Particular and the General. It is sufficiently obvious that the nineteenth-century hatred of eighteenth-century poetry was at bottom a hatred of abstraction. Equally clear is the fact that the great triumphs of the nineteenth century were won in important degree by keeping the eye on the object and describing it, however small, however particular, however individualized. By shifting the center of reference from the human race to the human individual, the scale of relative values is violently altered. To move out of the eighteenth century into the nineteenth is an experience like passing from the first book of Gulliver's Travels into the second, where every one is a giant. The Ego becomes the measure of all things.

As Gulliver found out, it is hard to get used to a different scale from the one in which we have been nurtured. The scale of the nineteenth century revealed the strangeness of the world of minutiae and carried with it all the excitements of a voyage into the unknown. The normative values of the eighteenth century were so tame by comparison as hardly to stir the most languid interest. And if the poetry was so dull, it must follow that the criticism supporting that dullness was equally dull, unenlightened, and misguided.

It was only when the celebration of the ego had nearly destroyed any binding frame of general reference and the crowded mass of naturalistic detail had created a scene without perspective, where everything appeared to claim equal importance:—only then did it begin to be asked once more whether individualism was always and invariably good, and whether older ways of conveying truth in art might not have some validity. It became possible to inquire whether the giants of the nineteenth century were really any bigger than the giants of the eighteenth century, or whether perhaps they were after all only giants through a microscope.

Johnson's criticism began to be consulted afresh, and it was found that his judgment of the 'metaphysical' poets had considerable bearing upon the current indigestion. 'If,' he wrote,

> that be considered as wit which is at once natural and new, that which, though not obvious, is, upon its first production, acknowledged to be just; if it be that which he that never found it, wonders how he missed; to wit of this kind the metaphysical poets have seldom risen. Their thoughts are often new, but seldom natural; they are not obvious, but neither are they just, and the reader, far from wondering that he missed them, wonders more frequently by what perverseness of industry they were ever found . . .
>
> . . . they never attempted that comprehension and expanse of thought which at once fills the whole mind, and of which the first effect is sudden astonishment, and the second rational admiration . . . Great thoughts are always general, and consist in positions not limited by exceptions, and in descriptions not descending to minuteness.

This very familiar passage has been quoted, not to compel assent, but because it is a masterly statement of a critical position inveterately and fundamentally hostile to what has proved to be the subsequent course of English poetry, a position to which the dilemma of modern verse has given an urgency quite lacking at its first utterance. It is plain, moreover, that Johnson is not here opposing the unknown because he is afraid of it, nor because he is sentimentally fond of the old and familiar, but because he believes essential values are better achieved by one route than by another.

To defend the eighteenth-century position does not fall within my present purpose. I am the less concerned to do so because it is common knowledge that during the last few decades there has occurred so major a reorientation of critical sympathy and judgment that today it is the Romantics, not their immediate elders, who are most likely to need defense. In sympathetic response, no doubt, to the deeper temper of our generation, a multitude of zealous workers has been laboring in the eighteenth-century vineyard, and this cultivation has quite transformed the quality of the grape. The vintage is a good deal headier than it used to be, and it were not surprising if some of us, soul-hydroptic, were over-exhilarated.

What is at any rate indisputable is the shift in our vision of Johnson which manifests itself when we turn to almost any standard history of English literature written in our time and compare it with those of the previous generation. So far as concerns the 'learned tradition,' the eidolon has been quite re-formed.

But it remains to inquire whether there has been a comparable alteration of the popular image, and whether in fact the work of devoted specialists has made any impact on general opinion. It might be presumed that the literate public at least would be affected; but it appears likely that the folk-image still persists on a far higher level of culture than the specialist would ever dream possible. Even among the teaching profession, almost certainly on the lower levels, and perhaps also at the upper ones where specialization in other areas of literary study has prevented reconsideration, the Macaulayan simulacrum probably yet prevails.

Substance accrues to these suspicions in the shape of two books published within recent years, one entilted *Ursa Major,* by C. E. Vulliamy, the other, *The Conversations of Dr. Johnson,* edited by Raymond Postgate. Mr. Vulliamy has been engaged for more than a decade upon a private crusade against the eighteenth century, in the course of which he has singled out as objects of his special vengeance several of the

Johnsonian circle. Boswell and Mrs. Thrale have each been victimized in a book apiece, and lastly the Bear himself has become the special target of Mr. Vulliamy's hostility. This venomous attack has perhaps received as much critical notice as it deserves, but it demands our attention because it displays in a form somewhat distorted by superior knowledge the old imago suggested by the nickname and promoted by Macaulay. Mr. Vulliamy, doubtless, has read all the relevant material, including the writings of Johnson himself. He declares, in fact, that Johnson is 'only to be appreciated by those who grimly undertake the study of his writings.' His own grim study helps him to the content of a final chapter, in which he illustrates how wrong Johnson was in how many ways. Although he qualifies Macaulay's portrait with added charity for the best of Johnson's prose, he quotes as 'incontrovertibly true' the 'just and simple words' of the 1831 essay: 'The characteristic peculiarity of his intellect was the union of great powers with low prejudices.' Vulliamy concludes that 'Johnson was a bully and a snob,' who hated new ideas as he did immersion in a bath, who stood for convention because it was conventional, and who fascinates the timid because they admire mere pugnacity. He ends his book on the note of satire, with a quoted passage in short couplets concluding as follows:

> For Mr. Johnson won't allow
> That any but himself can know
> The mysteries of high dispute,
> Where noise, not sense, is absolute,
> And every argument is drown'd
> In roaring tides of angry sound.

Yet on this same final page he has already recommended the study of Johnson's writings, albeit grimly, has even promised some rich and unexpected rewards for the pains, has mentioned Johnson's 'sturdy mind' and 'honest virtues,' and declared that he could stand clear of Boswell upon his own merits. *Timeo Danaos.* Such a labefactation of principle who can uphold?

Mr. Postgate's book is a very different kind of work. The body of it, filling 300 pages, consists of Boswell's record of Johnson's conversation, strained out of the *Life* with as little other matter as possible. The operation has an exceptional, if unintended, interest, because it shows as nothing else could do how essentially Boswell's biographical art of disposition and proportion, of anticipatory explanation and skilful high-lighting, of balance and perspective, has contributed to the greatness of his book. But our special and immediate interest lies in Mr. Postgate's introductory matter: a brief preface and a biographical sketch of Johnson up to the time when he met Boswell. The point of view of the sketch is nearly identical with that of Macaulay, who seems in fact to have been under the eye of the author as he wrote. There are the same emphases, the same details, the same judgments: Johnson tore his food at table because he had picked up bad habits while living in filth and misery. His wife was, to quote Macaulay, a 'raddled grandmother.' His *Shakespeare*, to quote Macaulay, 'added nothing to the fame of his abilities and learning.' His *Rambler*, to quote Macaulay, is written in Johnsonese. His 'mind was limited.' 'He was not only a Tory, he was that peculiarly immovable and disastrous Tory who really believes that all forms of government are almost equally bad.' 'His *Dictionary* has long ago been superseded, his *Shakespeare* is never consulted, very few people open the files of *The Rambler*, or *The Idler*, his verse is neglected, *Rasselas* unread, and it is chiefly students who still turn to his *Lives of the Poets*.' . . . 'It is only by his conversations that Johnson is remembered.' We perceive that Mr. Postgate is little better than a vile Whig.

But how can we sufficiently admire the vitality of this folk-image? It captures the imagination of generation after generation; it takes possession of some minds to such an extent that they spend years reading about Johnson and his circle, and even publish their own books on him, and all the while before them looms the same imago, unabashed and incorrigible. It is a humbling spectacle and a chastening one to the specialist. Each of us brings his burnt offering to the altar of truth, and the figure we invoke becomes momentarily visible, obscurely forming and re-forming in the smoke above us, never the same. But the folk-image moves irresistibly onward, almost unaffected by our puny efforts to arrest or divert it.

> We do it wrong, being so majestical,
> To offer it the show of violence;
> For it is, as the air, invulnerable,
> And our vain blows malicious mockery.

WILLIAM R. KEAST

Johnson's Criticism of the Metaphysical Poets[1]

In perhaps none of Johnson's critical writings so much as in the *Life of Cowley* is the modern reader likely to feel that mingling of critical sagacity and wrongheadedness that has always been the burden and despair of Johnson's commentators. It is widely acknowledged that modern criticism of the seventeenth-century poets is heavily indebted to his analysis of metaphysical wit—even if modern critics spurn the inferences which Johnson draws from that analysis; but it is even more widely felt that in dealing with these writers, Johnson's sensitivity failed to keep pace with his analytic powers—that only a man disabled by nature, tradition, or doctrine could be as unperceptive as Johnson seems to be of the beauties of Donne—if not of those of Cowley and Cleveland.

While the *Life of Cowley* has come to be a symbol of the imperviousness of Johnson—and with him, of the eighteenth century—to a state of feeling, a condition of language, and a mode of writing which we now, for whatever reasons, tend to value, certain others of his works, signs of a like incapacity to earlier generations, no longer attract much interest. I do not imagine that a proposal to base this afternoon's discussion on the *Life of Milton* or the *Life of Gray* would have met with much enthusiasm. Yet it was once Johnson's supposed sins against taste and judgment in these, rather than in the *Life of Cowley*, that made his critics storm and his defenders seek cover. The history of Johnson's reputation has yet to be written, but when it is, it will do more than progressively reveal the thought and character of its subject; it will be a miniature history of literary taste and critical theory, recording the

From *ELH, a Journal of English Literary History*, March 1950, pp. 59–70. Reprinted by permission of the publisher and author.

vicissitudes of poetic reputations and the fluctuations of critical doctrine and method. Lacking such a history, we may ask ourselves how far our disappointment with Johnson's treatment of the metaphysical poets reflects genuine deficiencies in Johnson and how far it reflects merely our present conviction that Donne is a greater poet than, say, Gray or even Milton, and our preference for a critical theory that specializes in detailed accounts of metaphorical structure to one that emphasizes the general conditions of literary pleasure.

Our choice of the *Life of Cowley* as the basis for a discussion of Johnson as critic thus implies a judgment, which may not be free of the influence of prejudice and fashion: Johnson thought it the best of the *Lives*; we do not. Our selection of the *Life of Cowley* also seems to express a hope—a hope that we shall be able to give a comprehensive account of Johnson's failure here, a full assemblage of the causes that led him to pronounce as he did upon the metaphysical poets. If we cherish such a hope, I think we are bound to be disappointed—certainly what I am about to say, which is not at all so ambitious as this, will be disappointing. Of the multitude of causes which combine to produce a complex literary judgment, many are buried beyond recovery and many more are but hazardously recoverable, through speculation and conjecture. We can be sure that taste, temperament, education, admired models, ear, habit of mind, and linguistic experience—to mention only a few of the more obvious influences—must have helped to shape Johnson's preferences, as they do our own. But how much? and in what ways? We may speculate about two modes in the use of language, the Augustan and the dramatic-Shakespearean, and about the inhibiting effect of the former on Johnson; but this will not really help us, since Johnson admires and condemns works composed in both these modes, if indeed they are genuine modes. We may conjecture about the temper of the age and its reflection in Johnson's criticism, but this will get us into as many difficulties as it delivers us from, since, among other things, our knowledge of the temper of the age is derived in no small measure from our knowledge of what Johnson wrote.

These and similar questions I shall avoid, although I hope you will not take my silence on them to imply that I do not think them important, or at least entertaining. I should like instead to deal with the more explicit causes of Johnson's judgment on the metaphysical poets: namely, with the assumptions about criticism and poetry which underlie his arguments and control his discussion. Even in so limited an attempt there is a crucial difficulty. Johnson is notably not a literary theorist, by which I mean not that he has no theory of literature but that he never sets it all forth in theoretical fashion in one place. With a few minor exceptions, his criticism is entirely practical—the statement and adjudication of particular cases. His theoretical views are introduced only when needed, and only in such quantity as is needed, for the problem immediately in hand; his general views must often be inferred from the particular lines of argument he devises, or expanded from all too brief assertions. The necessity imposed by this feature of his criticism is that of being careful, as we consider one of his essays, that we do not take the theory which seems to underlie it for the whole of his critical position, or suppose, on the other hand, since the subjects of different essays differ as widely as Cowley from Collins, that the theory fluctuates at random from one to another, or that the assumptions used in the criticism of one species of literary work are uniquely adapted to it and not transferable to works of other kinds. We must read the *Life of Cowley* in relation to the *Rambler,* the *Preface to Shakespeare* and the other *Lives.* Despite this difficulty, however, by centering our attention for a moment on the rational bases for Johnson's judgments in the *Life of Cowley,* and on their relation to the larger body of his criticism, we may be able to recover some of the force which he thought his arguments carried, and perhaps to raise some questions of general interest for literary study.

Johnson's examination of the metaphysical poets, like his criticism in general, is marked by the prominence in it of questions which, if they have not entirely disappeared from modern critical discussion, have been relegated to a position so subordinate as to amount effectively to disappearance. At the same time Johnson fails to give any serious or extended consideration to those questions with which modern critics have been chiefly occupied. Johnson is not much interested in the development and cross-fertilization of metaphor, the structural employment of ambiguity, or the formative use of irony and paradox. His primary concern is with the pleasure which literature is capable of producing. He wants to know chiefly whether poems interest readers, engage their attention, and move them emotionally. The brilliance of his discussion of wit is widely acknowledged, but analysis and discrimination of literary devices are not for him the central business of criticism. Criticism is above all a matter of judgment and evaluation. The true task of the critic is to determine the value of a work on the basis of its permanent power to please and to fix the position in the scale of human ability which the powers of the author merit.

Judgment and taste, Johnson is well aware, are fallible, and the critic deals with an object whose essential character derives from the imagination, a faculty that is limitless in its potentialities for discovery and combination.[2] If he is to render a valid judgment, the critic cannot depend merely on the critical reputation or popular success of a work. He must discover the causes which underlie literary effects.[3] But an adequate explanation of these cannot be found in the rules of art or the examples of past performance: 'the performances of art,' he says, are 'too inconstant and uncertain, to be reduced to any determinate idea'; 'there is therefore scarcely any species of writing, of which we can tell what is its essence, and what are its constituents; every new genius produces some innovation, which, when invented and approved, subverts the rule which the practice of foregoing authors had established.'[4] Johnson's fundamental conviction—to which his spirited defense of Shakespeare's violation of the unities most eloquently testifies—is that no valid poetic criteria can be derived from a consideration of linguistic or technical devices, apart from their function in achieving poetic effects. The only secure basis for critical judgment is not art but nature, for art proceeds from natural powers, uses natural materials, represents natural objects, and appeals to natural desires—and nature, unlike art, is everywhere the same.

Since literature is ordered to the reader—and the prominence of the common reader, not the élite, is a notable feature of Johnson's criticism—it is these natural desires to which the poet must write and from which the critic must reason in estimating the poet's success. Johnson does not think of the reader as one who submits himself to a work in order, after patient study of its verbal structure, to gain understanding; the end of poetry is not the perfection of an object, nor is the end of criticism the disclosure of its inner nature. The work of the poet and the labor of the critic are subordinated to the natural appetite for pleasure from which literature derives its distinctive features and in the satisfaction of which it has its true value. And he insists that the conditions of literary pleasure are twofold. The mind, he says, 'can be captivated only by recollection or by curiosity; by reviving natural sentiments or impressing new appearances of things.'[5] All readers demand, if they are to be attracted and pleased, two qualities in literary works: truth—the ideas that slumber in the heart and the sentiments to which every bosom returns an echo—and novelty—the pleasures of sudden wonder. The two most engaging powers of an author satisfy these demands together—making new things familiar and familiar things new. As one or the other of these qualities is emphasized, the two great poetical effects on which Johnson rests his assessment of the metaphysical poets are produced. The pathetic, the movement of the passions, arises fundamentally from the representation of what is uniform in human experience; the sublime, the stimulation of wonder and admiration, arises basically from the presentation of what is new and hence striking. Johnson does not introduce this division of poetic effects into his discussion of the seventeenth-century poets because they seem to him the effects at which these poets were probably aiming; rather they are for him an exhaustive enumeration of poetic effects—the only fundamental ways in which poets can please—and if the metaphysicals are to be regarded as poets, their success in achieving one or the other of these effects must be the basis of judgment.

Both truth and novelty have their root in human passion. Our emotions are engaged only when we are struck by something new or out of the ordinary—'the pleasures of the mind,' he says, 'imply something sudden and unexpected';[6] 'nothing can strongly strike or affect us, but what is rare or sudden.'[7] And equally our feelings are moved only by what is recognizably human, like ourselves: 'we are affected only as we believe'; 'what I cannot for a moment believe, I cannot for a moment behold with interest or anxiety.'[8] The poet who—unlike the metaphysicals—traces intellectual pleasure to its natural sources in the mind of man, discovers that the passions are so constituted in nature as to permit him to achieve both truth and novelty. The passions are on the one hand few, permanent, and regular in their operations: 'their influence is uniform, and their effects nearly the same in every human breast: a man loves and hates, desires and avoids, exactly like his neighbour; resentment and ambition, avarice and indolence, discover themselves by the same symptoms in minds distant a thousand years from one another.'[9] But the passions, if few, are susceptible of infinite modification: the careful observer sees that the regularity and varied complexity of human life can be brought together, as Johnson joins them in one of the scientific metaphors of which he was so fond: 'It has been discovered by Sir Isaac Newton,' he says,

that the distinct and primogenial colours are only seven; but every eye can witness, that from various mixtures, in various proportions, infinite diversifications of tints may be produced. In like manner, the passions of the mind, which put the world in motion, . . . from whence arise all the pleasures and pains that we see and hear of, if we analyze the mind of man, are very few; but those few agitated and combined, as external causes shall happen to operate, and modified by prevailing opinions and accidental caprices, make such frequent alterations on the surface of life, that the show, while we are busied in delineating it, vanishes from the view, and a new set of objects succeed, doomed to the same shortness of duration with the former . . . the mutability of mankind will always furnish writers with new images.[10]

Johnson's criticism of the metaphysical poets is based on these premises—these poets do not move the passions, because they deal with the remoter feelings and with peripheral situations; they do not evoke wonder, which is akin to surprise, because they are not content to rest in the presentation of striking juxtapositions but must pursue them to the last detail. Johnson develops these general views in the *Life of Cowley* with a high degree of sophistication. His analysis of wit, for example, is conducted with an analytic subtlety not always recognized. Johnson discriminates three meanings of wit, corresponding to the three sources from which poetic effects arise—the language of a poem, its thoughts, and the objects which it represents. The first gives Pope's definition of wit, the second yields the conception of wit as thoughts at once natural and new, and the third gives the famous conception of wit as *discordia concors*. The effect of each kind of wit depends on that which follows it, and the last —the *discordia concors*—is a definition not of metaphysical wit merely, but of all wit, valuable in general, the seventeenth-century poets having merely '*more* than enough,' and yoking the '*most* heterogenous' ideas together 'by *violence*.' And similarly the other premises Johnson uses to criticize the metaphysical poets are not limited in their applicability merely to writers marked by metaphysical wit. The same principles underlie his discussions of poets who are quite un-metaphysical. It is thus not a peculiarity of the metaphysical style that it led Cowley and Donne to miss the sublime by paying too much attention to details; Johnson criticizes Shakespeare's description of Dover Cliff in *King Lear* in precisely the same terms, and he finds Young's poem *The Last Day* languid and unaffecting because a succession of images divides and weakens the general conception.[11] And again, if the metaphysical poets miss the pathetic through their disregard of the uniformity of sentiment which enables us to conceive and excite the pains and pleasures of other minds, so too do many others, among them poets whose language at least has been thought to bring them within the range of Johnson's taste. Like Cowley's, the amorous effusions of Prior are not happy: dictated neither by nature nor by passion and having neither gallantry nor tenderness, they are the work of a man trying to be amorous by dint of study; *Hudibras* is a poem of inexhaustible wit, but most of its effect is now lost, for it is founded not on standing relations and general passions but on those modifications of life and peculiarities of practice which, being the progeny of error and perverseness, must perish with their parents.[12] If the common reader cannot feel the effects of metaphysical poems based on esoteric lore, neither can the reader of Pope's *Imitations of Horace* or West's *Imitations of Spenser*:

> An imitation of Spenser is nothing to a reader, however acute, by whom Spenser has never been perused. . . . The noblest beauties of art are those of which the effect is co-extended with rational nature, or at least with the whole circle of polished life; what is less than this can be only pretty, the plaything of fashion and the amusement of a day.[13]

And so it is with the other items in Johnson's bill against the seventeenth-century poets—each rests on a premise that is brought into play many times elsewhere in Johnson's work, applied with the same result to works superficially very different from the poems of the metaphysicals. But if we cannot find anything peculiar to the metaphysicals in the grounds on which he criticizes them, neither can we arrive at Johnson's conception of poetic excellence by simply taking the contraries of their faults as poetic virtues. Johnson, it is true, seems occasionally to talk as if literary pleasure is to be achieved through the grandeur of generality or the uniform simplicity of primitive qualities; but bear in mind the practical orientation of his criticism that I mentioned earlier. Only so much theory emerges as Johnson needs to decide the case in hand; if he is dealing with a witty or allusive writer like Cowley or Butler, deficiencies can be adequately defined by emphasizing the lack of attention to general passions and large appearances evident in their work. But his criticism is filled with cases of the opposite sort, where the writer, aiming only at general truth, contents himself with the large appearance and the common passions. With these writers Johnson is no less severe, for they too fail to command interest or provide pleasure, and his criticism of them sounds often as if he were recommending a liberal dose of metaphysical subtlety and surprise.

Thus the plays of Nicholas Rowe seldom pierce the breast with pity or terror because they contain no deep search into nature, no accurate discrimination of kindred qualities or nice display of passion in its progress: in them 'all is general and undefined.'[14] Of Young's *Universal Passion*, Johnson says that the poet 'plays, indeed, only on the surface of life; he never penetrates the recesses of the mind, and therefore the whole power of his poetry is exhausted by a single perusal: his conceits please only when they surprise.'[15] And the defect of Dryden's *Eleanora* is that Dryden wrote without exact knowledge: 'the praise being therefore inevitably general fixes no impression on the reader nor excites any tendency to love, nor much desire of imitation.'[16]

From an opposite direction we come at precisely the defect of Cowley —*The Mistress* has no power of seduction; she plays round the head but reaches not the heart; her beauty and absence, her kindness and cruelty, her disdain and inconstancy, produce no correspondence of emotion.[17] The effect is the same; the causes are contrary—Cowley is too learned and particular, Dryden and Young too vulgar and general. Lasting excellence in poetry—the power to please many and please long—arises neither from wit nor sublimity merely, neither from the merely particular nor the merely general. The irregular combinations of fanciful invention may delight awhile, by that novelty of which the common satiety of life sends us all in quest, but uniformity too must tire at last, even though it be uniformity of excellence, for the pleasures of the mind imply something sudden and unexpected; that which elevates must always surprise. A great poem is a composite of qualities which taken alone are evanescent or unaffecting. It must represent the permanent and enduring emotions such as any man, merely because he is a man, has felt and must feel again; it must figure forth an object in which the human imagination can recognize itself. But at the same time it must plumb deeply enough the recesses of the heart and the complexities of human life to seize the attention and hold the interest of the reader with unexpected combinations of the ordinary.

These general principles are not less true for being occasionally employed in the examination or praise of writers and works which it is not the modern fashion to enjoy, nor are they less necessary, in some form of statement, to a comprehensive esthetics, even though their generality —which is in one sense a guarantee against rigidity and dogmatism— makes them difficult to apply in particular cases. But the question remains of the validity of Johnson's judgment on the metaphysical poets themselves, and at the risk of seeming heretical, or of appearing to attempt what Johnson accused Sprat of trying to do—propagate a wonder—I should like to contend briefly for the essential correctness of Johnson's censure of the metaphysical poets. First we must notice that his criticism is by no means unqualified, for if these poets usually fail to please, it is not because they do not have great abilities: 'To write on their plan it was at least necessary to read and think. No man could be born a metaphysical poet.'[18] They have a quality which Johnson prizes beyond most others—originality; and when they err it is not through lack of ability or pains but through a failure of intention—whatever in their work is improper or vicious 'is produced by a voluntary deviation from nature in pursuit of something new and strange, . . . the writers fail to give delight by their desire of exciting admiration.'[19] Nor, again, is Johnson's general criticism of the metaphysical style equivalent to a condemnation of the individual poems of Donne, Cowley and the rest. We do not know what he would have written about those of Donne, but when later in the *Life* he comes to examine Cowley's works individually he gives several of them great praise: the ode on Wit, for example, 'is almost without a rival'; *The Chronicle* is 'a composition unrivalled and alone'; and even of the Pindarics he says that 'those verses are not without a just claim to praise, of which it may be said with truth, that no one but Cowley could have written them.'[20] What Johnson criticizes is the characteristic manner of a school--of 'a race of writers'--which in individual poems may not predominate or may be assimilated to a compelling effect. And who will say that he has not hit off accurately the distinguishing aims and characteristics of this school? There can be little doubt, if we examine the work of Cleveland, Cowley, and the numerous minor imitators of Donne, that it is the manner in which the special distinction of the metaphysical style was thought by them to reside. One must search hard, in these writers, for poems in which genuinely complex states of feeling demand and control a witty or ironic structure. For every *Valediction: Forbidding Mourning* there are a dozen poems like *Fuscara: or the Bee Errant.*

It does not seem likely that anyone not fanatic in his devotion to Cleveland or Cowley will disagree with Johnson's verdict that their poetry is on the whole without any genuine power to interest or move, that it is remarkable chiefly for the extravagance of fancy displayed on every occasion and always in the same way. But can Donne himself be exempted from this charge? Johnson's knowledge of Donne's poetry was curious and extensive; he ranges over the whole corpus of Donne's work except the divine poems, drawing examples of the metaphysical manner from poems rarely read today save by the biographer, the professional critic, and the historian of ideas. And great tracts of Donne's poetry can be read only with difficulty; it is precisely from these much more often than from the smaller body of Donne's work which modern taste has fixed upon as providing the true measure of his talent that Johnson quotes--from the epithalamions, the epicedes, the verse letters, and the Anniversaries; only four of his sixteen quotations, indeed, are from the *Songs and Sonnets.*[21] If we leave aside all consideration of Donne's influence on the development of the language, of his contribution to the sophistication of the lyric, and of his fascinating personal history, how many great poems did he write?--how many that the intelligent common reader, uninstructed by precept and unprejudiced by authority, is likely to read with passion or wonder? I venture to think that they are but few, that they are not to be found primarily among those Johnson quotes, and that the pleasure we take in them does not depend chiefly on the heterogeneity of the elements joined in their metaphors or the distance which naturally separates them.

As a critic Johnson is not without important defects, of which the most serious is not his taste but the absence in his theory of any save a rather general account of literary effects, such as are common alike to all forms of the art. He has no method for isolating the peculiar effects of different species of poetry and for analyzing and judging the means for their production. But this lack—which even modern criticism has made no real progress in supplying—should not obscure the central value of Johnson's example. For he forces upon our attention a concern for the ultimate effects and values of literature—its power to interest and move our emotions—without which the utmost refinement of wit and technique in the poet or of analysis in the critic must prove illusory. He insists, thus, upon a high standard of excellence, and it is no wonder if under it so few works and so few writers win unqualified praise.

'It is not by comparing line with line that the merit of great works is to be estimated,' he says in the *Life of Dryden,*

> but by their general effects and ultimate result. It is easy to note a weak line, and write one more vigorous in its place . . . but what is given to the parts may be subducted from the whole, and the reader may be weary though the critick may commend. Works of imagination excel by their allurement and delight; by their power of attracting and detaining the attention. That book is good in vain which the reader throws away. He only is the master who keeps the mind in pleasing captivity; whose pages are perused with eagerness, and in hope of new pleasure are perused again; and whose conclusion is perceived with an eye of sorrow, such as the traveller casts upon departing day.[22]

NOTES

1. This paper was read before English Group VIII at the 1948 meeting of the Modern Language Association, as part of a symposium on 'Dr. Johnson and the Seventeenth-Century Poets.'

2. See *Rambler* No. 125 (*Works* [Oxford, 1825], III, 93); No. 156 (*ibid.*, p. 239); No. 158 (*ibid.*, p. 249); No. 23 (*ibid.*, II, 116); No. 121 (*ibid.*, III, 76–77).

3. Cf., e. g., *Rambler* No. 92 (*ibid.*, II, 431–32).

4. *Rambler* No. 125 (*ibid.*, III, 93); cf. *Rambler* No. 23 (*ibid.*, II, 115); *Lives of the English Poets*, ed. G. B. Hill (Oxford, 1905), I, 18.

5. *Lives*, I, 458–59.

6. *Ibid.*, p. 59.

7. *Rambler* No. 78 (*Works*, II, 367).

8. *Lives*, III, 438; II, 16; cf. III, 227; III, 235; *Rambler* No. 60 (*Works*, II, 286–288).

9. *Adventurer* No. 95 (*Works*, IV, 81); cf. *Rambler* No. 68 (*ibid.*, II, 322–23).

10. *Adventurer* No. 95 (*ibid.*, IV, 83).

11. *Johnson on Shakespeare*, ed. Raleigh (1931), pp. 158–59; *Lives*, III, 393; cf. Boswell, *Life*, ed. Powell, II, 87; *Rambler* No. 137 (*Works*, III, 147–48).

12. *Lives*, II, 202; I, 213–14.

13. *Ibid.*, III, 247; II, 16.

14. *Ibid.*, II, 76.

15. *Ibid.*, III, 394.

16. *Ibid.*, I, 441–42.

17. *Ibid.*, I, 42.

18. *Ibid.*, I, 21.

19. *Ibid.*, p. 35.

20. *Ibid.*, pp. 36, 37, 48.

21. The quotations from Donne in the *Life of Cowley* are drawn from the following poems (I give page and paragraph numbers to Vol. I of Hill's edition of the *Lives* and page and line numbers to the one-volume Grierson edition of Donne, Oxford, 1933): pp. 23–24, par. 68: 'To the Countesse of Bedford,' pp. 167–68. 21–28; p. 24, par. 69: 'To the Countesse of Bedford,' p. 175. 1–10; p. 24, par. 70: 'To Mr. R. W.,' p. 186. 29–32; p. 26, par. 77: 'A Valediction: of Weeping,' p. 35. 10–18; p. 26, par. 77: 'An Epithalamion, or Marriage Song on the Lady Elizabeth, and Count Palatine,' p. 116. 85–88; pp. 26–27, par. 78: 'Obsequies to the Lord Harrington,' p. 248. 35–40; p. 28, par. 82: 'A Valediction: of my Name, in the Window,' p. 23. 1–4; p. 30, par. 86: 'Elegie on the L. C.' p. 261. 13–16; pp. 30–31, par. 87: 'Ecclogue. 1613. December 26,' pp. 117–18. 23–32; p. 31, par. 90: 'To the Countesse of Bedford,' p. 173. 43–47; p. 31, par. 91: 'To Mr. B. B.,' p. 188. 10–14; pp. 31–32, par. 92: 'The Second Anniversarie,' p. 232. 173–84; p. 32, par. 94: 'Twicknam Garden,' p. 27. 19–22; p. 32, par. 95: 'Elegie VIII,' p. 81. 1–7; p. 33, par. 98: 'Obsequies to the Lord Harrington.' p. 247. 15–25; p. 34, par. 100: 'A Valediction: Forbidding Mourning,' p. 45. 21–36.

22. *Lives*, I, 454.

NORTHROP FRYE

Towards Defining an Age of Sensibility

THE period of English literature which covers roughly the second half of the eighteenth century is one which has always suffered from not having a clear historical or functional label applied to it. I call it here the age of sensibility, which is not intended to be anything but a label. This period has the 'Augustan' age on one side of it and the 'Romantic' movement on the other, and it is usually approached transitionally, as a period of reaction against Pope and anticipation of Wordsworth. The chaos that results from treating this period, or any other, in terms of reaction has been well described by Professor Crane in a recent article in the Toronto Quarterly.° What we do is to set up, as the logical expression of Augustanism, some impossibly pedantic view of following rules and repressing feelings, which nobody could ever have held, and then treat any symptom of freedom or emotion as a departure from this. Our students are thus graduated with a vague notion that the age of sensibility was the time when poetry moved from a reptilian Classicism, all cold and dry reason, to a mammalian Romanticism, all warm and wet feeling.

As for the term 'pre-romantic,' that, as a term for the age itself, has the peculiar demerit of committing us to anachronism before we start, and imposing a false teleology on everything we study. Not only did the 'pre-romantics' not know that the Romantic movement was going to succeed them, but there has probably never been a case on record of a poet's having regarded a later poet's work as the fulfilment of his own.

° R. S. Crane, 'On Writing the History of English Criticism, 1650–1800,' *University of Toronto Quarterly*, July 1953, pp. 376–91.

From *ELH, a Journal of English Literary History*, June 1956, pp. 144–52. Reprinted by permission of the publisher and author.

However, I do not care about terminology, only about appreciation for an extraordinarily interesting period of English literature, and the first stage in renewing that appreciation seems to me the gaining of a clear sense of what it is in itself.

Some languages use verb-tenses to express, not time, but the difference between completed and continuous action. And in the history of literature we become aware, not only of periods, but of a recurrent opposition of two views of literature. These two views are the Aristotelian and the Longinian, the aesthetic and the psychological, the view of literature as product and the view of literature as process. In our day we have acquired a good deal of respect for literature as process, notably in prose fiction. The stream of consciousness gets careful treatment in our criticism, and when we compare Arnold Bennett and Virginia Woolf on the subject of Mrs. Brown we generally take the side of Virginia Woolf. So it seems that our age ought to feel a close kinship with the prose fiction of the age of sensibility, when the sense of literature as process was brought to a peculiarly exquisite perfection by Sterne, and in lesser degree by Richardson and Boswell.

All the great story-tellers, including the Augustan ones, have a strong sense of literature as a finished product. The suspense is thrown forward until it reaches the end, and is based on our confidence that the author knows what is coming next. A story-teller does not break his illusion by talking to the reader as Fielding does, because we know from the start that we are listening to Fielding telling a story—that is, Johnson's arguments about illusion in drama apply equally well to prose fiction of Fielding's kind. But when we turn to *Tristram Shandy* we not only read the book but watch the author at work writing it: at any moment the house of Walter Shandy may vanish and be replaced by the author's study. This does break the illusion, or would if there were any illusion to break, but here we are not being led into a story, but into the process of writing a story: we wonder, not what is coming next, but what the author will think of next.

Sterne is, of course, an unusually pure example of a process-writer, but even in Richardson we find many of the same characteristics. Johnson's well-known remark that if you read Richardson for the story you would hang yourself indicates that Richardson is not interested in a plot with a quick-march rhythm. Richardson does not throw the suspense forward, but keeps the emotion at a continuous present. Readers of *Pamela* have become so fascinated by watching the sheets of Pamela's manuscript spawning and secreting all over her master's house, even into the recesses of her clothes, as she fends off assault with one hand

and writes about it with the other, that they sometimes overlook the reason for an apparently clumsy device. The reason is, of course, to give the impression of literature as process, as created on the spot out of the events it describes. And in the very beginning of *Boswell in London* we can see the boy of twenty-one already practising the art of writing as a continuous process from experience. When he writes of his adventure with Louisa he may be writing several days after the event, but he does not use his later knowledge.

In poetry the sense of literature as a finished product normally expresses itself in some kind of regularly recurring metre, the general pattern of which is established as soon as possible. In listening to Pope's couplets we have a sense of continually fulfilled expectation which is the opposite of obviousness: a sense that eighteenth-century music also often gives us. Such a technique demands a clear statement of what sound-patterns we may expect. We hear at once the full ring of the rhyming couplet, and all other sound-patterns are kept to a minimum. In such a line as:

> And strains from hard-bound brains eight lines a year,

the extra assonance is a deliberate discord, expressing the difficulties of constipated genius. Similarly with the alliteration in:

> Great Cibber's brazen, brainless brothers stand,

and the fact that these are deliberate discords used for parody indicates that they are normally not present. Johnson's disapproval of such devices in serious contexts is written all over the *Lives of the Poets*.

When we turn from Pope to the age of sensibility, we get something of the same kind of shock that we get when we turn from Tennyson or Matthew Arnold to Hopkins. Our ears are assaulted by unpredictable assonances, alliterations, inter-rhymings and echolalia:

> Mie love ys dedde,
> Gon to hys death-bedde . . .

> With brede ethereal wove,
> O'erhang his wavy bed . . .

> The couthy cracks begin whan supper's o'er,
> The cheering bicker gars them glibly gash .

> But a pebble of the brook
> Warbled out these metres meet . . .

In many of the best-known poems of the period, in Smart's *Song to David*, in Chatterton's elegies, in Burns's songs and Blake's lyrics, even in some of the Wesley hymns, we find a delight in refrain for refrain's sake. Sometimes, naturally, we can see the appropriate literary influences helping to shape the form, such as the incremental repetition of the ballad, or Old Norse alliteration in *The Fatal Sisters*. And whatever may be thought of the poetic value of the Ossianic poems, most estimates of that value parrot Wordsworth, and Wordsworth's criticisms of Ossian's imagery are quite beside the point. The vague generalized imagery of Ossian, like the mysterious resonant names and the fixed epithets, are part of a deliberate and well unified scheme. *Fingal* and *Temora* are long poems for the same reason that *Clarissa* is a long novel: not because there is a complicated story to be told, as in *Tom Jones* or an epic of Southey, but because the emotion is being maintained at a continuous present by various devices of repetition.

The reason for these intensified sound-patterns, is, once again, an interest in the poetic process as distinct from the product. In the composing of poetry, where rhyme is as important as reason, there is a primary stage in which words are linked by sound rather than sense. From the point of view of sense this stage is merely free or uncontrolled association, and in the way it operates it is very like the dream. Again like the dream, it has to meet a censor-principle, and shape itself into intelligible patterns. Where the emphasis is on the communicated product, the qualities of consciousness take the lead: a regular metre, clarity of syntax, epigram and wit, repetition of sense in antithesis and balance rather than of sound. Swift speaks with admiration of Pope's ability to get more 'sense' into one couplet than he can into six: concentration of sense for him is clearly a major criterion of poetry. Where the emphasis is on the original process, the qualities of subconscious association take the lead, and the poetry becomes hypnotically repetitive, oracular, incantatory, dreamlike and in the original sense of the word charming. The response to it includes a subconscious factor, the surrendering to a spell. In Ossian, who carries this tendency further than anyone else, the aim is not concentration of sense but diffusion of sense, hence Johnson's remark that anybody could write like Ossian if he would abandon his mind to it. Literature as product may take a lyrical form, as it does in the sublime ode about which Professor Maclean has written so well, but it is also the conception of literature that makes the longer continuous poem possible. Literature as process, being based on an irregular and unpredictable coincidence of sound-patterns, tends to seek the brief or even the fragmentary utterance, in other words to centre itself on the lyric, which accounts for the feeling of a sudden emergence of a lyrical impulse in the age of sensibility.

The 'pre-romantic' approach to this period sees it as developing a conception of the creative imagination, which became the basis of Romanticism. This is true, but the Romantics tended to see the poem as the *product* of the creative imagination, thus reverting in at least one respect to the Augustan attitude. For the Augustan, art is posterior to nature because nature is the art of God; for the Romantic, art is prior to nature because God is an artist; one deals in physical and the other in biological analogies, as Professor Abrams' *Mirror and the Lamp* has shown. But for the Romantic poet the poem is still an artefact: in Coleridge's terms, a secondary or productive imagination has been imposed on a primary imaginative process. So, different as it is from Augustan poetry, Romantic poetry is like it in being a conservative rhetoric, and in being founded on relatively regular metrical schemes. Poe's rejection of the continuous poem does not express anything very central in Romanticism itself, as nearly every major Romantic poet composed poems of considerable, sometimes immense, length. Poe's theory is closer to the practice of the age of sensibility before him and the *symbolistes* after him.

In the age of sensibility most of the long poems, of course, simply carry on with standard continuous metres, or exploit the greater degree of intensified recurrent sound afforded by stanzaic forms, notably the Spenserian. But sometimes the peculiar problems of making associative poetry continuous were faced in a more experimental way, experiments largely ignored by the Romantics. Oracular poetry in a long form often tends to become a series of utterances, irregular in rhythm but strongly marked off one from the other. We notice in Whitman, for instance, that the end of every line has a strong pause—for when the rhythm is variable there is no point in a run-on line. Sometimes this oracular rhythm takes on at least a typographical resemblance to prose, as it does in Rimbaud's *Saison en Enfer,* or, more frequently, to a discontinuous blend of prose and verse in which the sentence, the paragraph and the line are much the same unit. The chief literary influence for this rhythm has always been the translated Bible, which took on a new impetus in the age of sensibility; and if we study carefully the rhythm of Ossian, of Smart's *Jubilate Agno* and of the Blake Prophecies, we can see three very different but equally logical developments of this semi-Biblical rhythm.

Where there is a strong sense of literature as aesthetic product, there is also a sense of its detachment from the spectator. Aristotle's theory of catharsis describes how this works for tragedy: pity and fear are detached from the beholder by being directed towards objects. Where there is a sense of literature as process, pity and fear become states of mind without objects, moods which are common to the work of art and the reader, and which bind them together psychologically instead of separating them aesthetically.

Fear without an object, as a condition of mind prior to being afraid of anything, is called *Angst* or anxiety, a somewhat narrow term for what may be almost anything between pleasure and pain. In the general area of pleasure comes the eighteenth-century conception of the sublime, where qualities of austerity, gloom, grandeur, melancholy or even menace are a source of romantic or penseroso feelings. The appeal of Ossian to his time on this basis needs no comment. From here we move through the graveyard poets, the Gothic-horror novelists and the writers of tragic ballads to such *fleurs du mal* as Cowper's *Castaway* and Blake's Golden Chapel poem in the Rossetti MS.

Pity without an object has never to my knowledge been given a name, but it expresses itself as an imaginative animism, or treating everything in nature as though it had human feelings or qualities. At one end of its range is the apocalyptic exultation of all nature bursting into human life that we have in Smart's *Song to David* and the ninth Night of *The Four Zoas*. Next comes an imaginative sympathy with the kind of folklore that peoples the countryside with elemental spirits, such as we have in Collins, Fergusson, Burns and the Wartons. Next we have the curiously intense awareness of the animal world which (except for some poems of D. H. Lawrence) is unrivalled in this period, and is expressed in some of its best realized writing: in Burns's *To a Mouse*, in Cowper's exquisite snail poem, in Smart's superb lines on his cat Geoffrey, in the famous starling and ass episodes in Sterne, in the opening of Blake's *Auguries of Innocence*. Finally comes the sense of sympathy with man himself, the sense that no one can afford to be indifferent to the fate of anyone else, which underlies the protests against slavery and misery in Cowper, in Crabbe and in Blake's *Songs of Experience*.

This concentration on the primitive process of writing is projected in two directions, into nature and into history. The appropriate natural setting for much of the poetry of sensibility is nature at one of the two poles of process, creation and decay. The poet is attracted by the ruinous and the mephitic, or by the primeval and 'unspoiled'—a picturesque subtly but perceptibly different from the Romantic picturesque. The projection into history assumes that the psychological progress of the poet from lyrical through epic to dramatic presentations, discussed by Stephen at the end of Joyce's *Portrait,* must be the historical progress of literature as well. Even as late as the preface to Victor Hugo's *Cromwell* this assumption persists. The Ossian and Rowley poems are not simple hoaxes: they are pseudepigrapha, like the Book of Enoch, and like it they take what is psychologically primitive, the oracular process of composition, and project it as something historically primitive.

The poetry of process is oracular, and the medium of the oracle is often in an ecstatic or trance-like state: autonomous voices seem to speak through him, and as he is concerned to utter rather than to address, he is turned away from his listener, so to speak, in a state of rapt self-communion. The free association of words, in which sound is prior to sense, is often a literary way of representing insanity. In Rimbaud's terrifyingly accurate phrase, poetry of the associative or oracular type requires a 'dérèglement de tous les sens.' Hence the qualities that make a man an oracular poet are often the qualities that work against, and sometimes destroy, his social personality. Far more than the time of Rimbaud and Verlaine is this period of literature a period of the *poète maudit.* The list of poets over whom the shadows of mental breakdown fell is far too long to be coincidence. The much publicized death of Chatterton is certainly one of the personal tragedies of the age, but an easier one to take than the kind of agony which is expressed with an almost definitive poignancy by Smart in *Jubilate Agno:*

> For in my nature I quested for beauty, but God, God, hath sent me to sea for pearls.

It is characteristic of the age of sensibility that this personal or biographical aspect of it should be so closely connected with its central technical feature. The basis of poetic language is the metaphor, and the metaphor, in its radical form, is a statement of identity: 'this is that.' In all our ordinary experience the metaphor is non-literal: nobody but a savage or a lunatic can take metaphor literally. For Classical or Augustan critics the metaphor is a condensed simile: its real or common-sense basis is likeness, not identity, and when it obliterates the sense of likeness it becomes barbaric. In Johnson's strictures on the music and water metaphor of Gray's *Bard* we can see what intellectual abysses, for him, would open up if metaphors ever passed beyond the stage of resemblance. For the Romantic critic, the identification in the metaphor is ideal: two images are identified within the mind of the creating poet.

But where metaphor is conceived as part of an oracular and half-ecstatic process, there is a direct identification in which the poet himself is involved. To use another phrase of Rimbaud's, the poet feels not 'je pense,' but 'on me pense.' In the age of sensibility some of the identifications involving the poet seem manic, like Blake's with Druidic bards or Smart's with Hebrew prophets, or depressive, like Cowper's with a scapegoat figure, a stricken deer or castaway, or merely bizarre, like Macpherson's with Ossian or Chatterton's with Rowley. But it is in this psychological self-identification that the central 'primitive' quality of this age really emerges. In Collins's *Ode on the Poetical Character,* in Smart's *Jubilate Agno,* and in Blake's *Four Zoas,* it attains its greatest intensity and completeness.

In these three poems, especially the last two, God, the poet's soul and nature are brought into a white-hot fusion of identity, an imaginative fiery furnace in which the reader may, if he chooses, make a fourth. All three poems are of the greatest complexity, yet the emotion on which they are founded is of a simplicity and directness that English literature has rarely attained again. With the 1800 edition of *Lyrical Ballads,* secondary imagination and recollection in tranquillity took over English poetry and dominated it until the end of the nineteenth century. The primitivism of Blake and Smart revived in France with Rimbaud and Gérard de Nerval, but even this development had become conservative by the time its influence reached England, and only in a few poems of Dylan Thomas, and those perhaps not his best, does the older tradition revive. But contemporary poetry is still deeply concerned with the problems and techniques of the age of sensibility, and while the latter's resemblance to our time is not a merit in it, it is a logical enough reason for re-examining it with fresh eyes.

ARTHUR O. LOVEJOY

Optimism and Romanticism

THE purpose of this paper is, first, to attempt to correct a still rather widely prevalent error concerning the logical import and the usual emotional temper of eighteenth-century optimism, and, second, to point out that the significance in the history of ideas of the multiplication and the popularity of theodicies in the first half of that century consisted less in the tendency of these arguments to diffuse optimistic views of the nature of reality than in their tendency to procure acceptance for certain new ideas of the nature of the good, which the logical exigencies of the optimistic argument involved—ideas pregnant with important consequences for both ethics and aesthetics, since they were to be among the most distinctive elements in what perhaps best deserves to be named 'Romanticism.'

The common thesis of eighteenth-century optimists was, as every schoolboy knows, the proposition that this is the best of possible worlds; and this fact, together with the connotation which the term 'optimism' has come to assume in popular usage, has given rise to the belief that the adherents of this doctrine must have been exuberantly cheerful persons, fatuously blind to the realities of human experience and of human nature, or insensible to all the pain and frustration and conflict which are manifest through the entire range of sentient life. Yet there was in fact nothing in the optimist's creed which logically required him either to blink or to belittle the facts which we ordinarily call evil. So far from asserting the unreality of evils, the philosophical optimist in

---

From *Publications of the Modern Language Association*, December 1927, pp. 921–45. Reprinted by permission of the publisher, of the Harvard University Press, and of the author.

the eighteenth century was chiefly occupied in demonstrating their necessity. To assert that this is the best of possible worlds implies nothing as to the absolute goodness of this world; it implies only that any other world which is metaphysically capable of existence would be worse. The reasoning of the optimist was directed less tò showing how much of what men commonly reckon good there is in the world of reality than to showing how little of it there is in the world of possibility—in that eternal logical order which contains the Ideal of all things possible and compossible, which the mind of God was conceived to have contemplated 'before the creation,' and by the necessities of which, ineluctable even to Omnipotence, his creative power was restricted.

At bottom, indeed, optimism had much in common with that Manichean dualism, against Bayle's defense of which so many of the theodicies were directed. Optimism too, as Leibniz acknowledged, had its two antagonistic 'principles.' The rôle of the 'evil principle' was simply assigned to the divine reason, which imposed singular impediments upon the benevolent intentions of the divine will. The very ills which Bayle had argued must be attributed to the interference of a species of extraneous Anti-God, for whose existence and hostility to the good no rational explanation could be given, were by the optimist attributed to a necessity inhering in the nature of things; and it was questionable whether this was not the less cheerful view of the two. For it was possible to hope that in the fullness of time the Devil might be put under foot, and believers in revealed religion were assured that he would be; but logical necessities are eternal, and the evils which arise from them must therefore be perpetual. Thus eighteenth-century optimism not only had affinities with the dualism to which it was supposed to be antithetic, but the arguments of its advocates at times sounded strangely like those of the pessimist—a type by no means unknown in the period.[1] The moral was different, but the view of the concrete facts of experience was sometimes very much the same; since it was the optimist's contention that evil—and a great deal of it—is involved in the general constitution of things, he found it to his purpose to dilate, on occasion, upon the magnitude of the sum of evil and upon the depth and breadth of its penetration into life. It is thus, for example, that Soame Jenyns, in one of the typical theodicies of the middle of the century, seeks to persuade us of the admirable rationality of the cosmic plan:

> I am persuaded that there is something in the abstract nature of pain conducive to pleasure; that the sufferings of individuals are absolutely

necessary to universal happiness. . . . Scarce one instance, I believe, can be produced of the acquisition of pleasure or convenience by any creatures, which is not purchased by the previous or consequential sufferings of themselves or others. Over what mountains of slain is every empire rolled up to the summit of prosperity and luxury, and what new scenes of desolation attend its fall. To what infinite toil of men, and other animals, is every flourishing city indebted for all the conveniences and enjoyments of life, and what vice and misery do those very equipments introduce. . . . The pleasures annexed to the preservation of ourselves are both preceded and followed by numberless sufferings; preceded by massacres and tortures of various animals preparatory to a feast, and followed by as many diseases lying wait in every dish to pour forth vengeance on their destroyers.[2]

This gloomy rhetoric was perfectly consistent in principle with optimism, and it manifested at least one natural tendency of the champions of that doctrine; for the more numerous and monstrous the evils to be explained, the greater was the triumph when the author of a theodicy explained them.

The argument, indeed, in some of its more naïve expressions tends to beget in the reader a certain pity for an embarrassed Creator, infinitely well-meaning, but tragically hampered by 'necessities in the nature of things' in his efforts to make a good world. What could be more pathetic than the position in which—as Soame Jenyns authoritatively informs us—Omnipotence found itself when contemplating the creation of mankind?

> Our difficulties arise from our forgetting how many difficulties Omnipotence has to contend with: in the present instance it is obliged either to afflict innocence or be the cause of wickedness; it has no other option.[3]

In short the writings of the optimists afforded abundant ground for Voltaire's exclamation:

> Vous criez "Tout est bien" d'une voix lamentable!

Voltaire's chief complaint of these philosophers in the *Poem on the Lisbon Disaster* was not, as has often been supposed, that they were too indecently cheerful, that their view of the reality of evil was superficial; his complaint was that they were too depressing, that they made the actual evils we experience appear worse by representing them as inevitable and inherent in the permanent structure of the universe.[4]

Non, ne présentez plus à mon coeur agité
Ces immuables lois de la nécessité!

An evil unexplained seemed to Voltaire more endurable than the same evil explained, when the explanation consisted in showing that from all eternity the avoidance of just that evil had been, and through all eternity the avoidance of others like it would be, logically inconceivable. In this his own feeling, and his assumption about the psychology of the emotions in other men, was precisely opposite to that of Spinoza, who believed that everything becomes endurable when we once see clearly that it could never have been otherwise, that it is truly rooted in the eternal world of Ideas: *quatenus mens res omnes ut necessarias intelligit, eatenus minus ab affectibus patitur.*[5] Though most of the optimistic writers of the eighteenth century were less thorough-going or less frank in their cosmical determinism than Spinoza, such philosophic consolation as they offered was at bottom the same as his. It was an essentially intellectual consolation; the mood that it was usually designed to produce was that of reasoned acquiescence in the inevitable, based upon a conviction that its inevitableness was of the nature of *logical* necessity, and was due to no arbitrary caprice; or, at a higher pitch, a devout willingness to be damned—that is, to be as much damned as one was—for the better demonstration of the reasonableness of the scheme of things. Whether confronted with physical or moral evils, wrote Pope, 'to reason well is to submit'; and again:

> Know thy own point; this kind, this due degree,
> Of blindness, weakness, Heaven bestows on thee.
> Submit!

It is, of course, true that the optimistic writers were eager to show how good comes out of evil; but the point which it was indispensable for them to establish was that it could come in no other way. It is true, also, that they were wont, when they reached the height of their argument, to discourse with eloquence on the perfection of the Universal System as a whole; but that perfection in no way implied either the happiness or the excellence of the finite parts of the system. On the contrary, the fundamental and characteristic premise of the usual proof of optimism was the proposition that the perfection of the whole depends upon, indeed, consists in, the existence of every possible degree of imperfection in the parts. Voltaire, once more, summarized the argument not altogether unjustly when he wrote:

Vous composerez dans ce chaos fatal
Des malheurs de chaque être un bonheur général.

The essence of the optimist's enterprise was to find the evidence of the 'goodness' of the universe, not in the paucity but rather in the multiplicity of what to the unphilosophic mind appeared to be evils. And it was also from this central paradox of optimism that those ulterior implications followed which were to help to generate the 'Romantic' view of life and of art.

All this can best be shown by an analysis of the argument in its logical sequence, as it is set forth in the earliest and, perhaps, when its indirect influence is also considered, the most influential, of eighteenth-century theodicies—the *De origine mali* (1702) of William King, then Bishop of Derry, afterwards Archbishop of Dublin. The original Latin work does not appear to have had wide currency; but in 1731 an English version appeared,[6] with copious additions, partly extracts from King's posthumous papers, partly original notes 'tending to vindicate the author's principles against the objections of Bayle, Leibnitz, the author of a Philosophical Inquiry concerning Human Liberty, and others,' by the translator, Edmund Law, subsequently bishop of Carlisle. The translation went through five editions during Law's lifetime;[7] and it seems to have been much read and discussed. Law was a figure of importance in his day, being the spokesman of 'the most latitudinarian position' in the Anglican theology of the time;[8] and his academic dignities as Master of Peterhouse and Knightbridge Professor of Moral Philosophy at Cambridge in the 1750's and 60's doubtless increased the range of his influence. There can hardly be much doubt that it was largely from the original work of King that Pope derived, directly or through Bolingbroke, the conceptions which, re-arranged with curious incoherency, served for his vindication of optimism in the First Epistle of the *Essay on Man*.[9]

It can by no means be said that King begins his reflection on the subject by putting on rose-tinted spectacles. He recognizes from the outset all the facts which seem most incompatible with an optimistic view: the 'perpetual war between the elements, between animals, between men'; 'the errors, miseries and vices' which are 'the contant companions of human life from its infancy'; the prosperity of the wicked and the suffering of the righteous. There are 'troops of miseries marching through human life.' And King is innocent of the amazing superficiality of Milton's theodicy; while he, too, assumes the freedom of the will, he sees clearly that this assumption can touch only a fraction of the problem. Not all evils are 'external, or acquired by our choice'; many of them 'proceed from the constitution of Nature itself.'[10] The dualistic doctorine of Bayle, while it, too, has the advantage of 'acquitting God of all manner of blame,' is philosophically an 'absurd hypothesis.' King, in short, is to attribute evil, not—at least not primarily nor chiefly—either to the mysterious perversity of man's will or to the machinations of the Devil; he is to show its *necessity* from a consideration of the nature of deity itself. His undertaking is nothing less than that of facing all the evils of existence and showing them to be 'not only consistent with infinite wisdom, goodness and power, but necessarily resulting from them.'[11]

The traditional division of evils into three classes—evils of limitation or imperfection, 'natural' evils, and moral evils—provides the general scheme of the argument, which is, in brief, that there could not conceivably have been any creation at all without the first sort of evil; and that all of the second sort, at least, follow with strict logical necessity from the first. Even Omnipotence could not create its own double; if any beings other than God were to exist they must in the nature of the case be differentiated from him through the 'evil of defect'—and, as is assumed, be differentiated from one another by the diversity of their defects. Evil, in short, is primarily privation; and privation is involved in the very concept of all beings except one. This Law puts in the terms of Aristotelian and Scholastic philosophy in his summary of King's 'scheme':

> All creatures are necessarily imperfect, and at an infinite distance from the perfection of the Deity, and if a negative principle were admitted, such as the Privation of the Peripatetics, it might be said that every created being consists of existence and non-existence, for it is nothing in respect both of those perfections which it wants, and of those which others have. And this . . . mixture of non-entity in the constitution of created beings is the necessary principle of all natural evils, and of a possibility of moral ones.[12]

In other words, in King's own phrase, 'a creature is descended from God, a most perfect Father; but from Nothing as its Mother, which is Imperfection.' And the virtually dualistic character of this conception is shown by the fact that the inferior parent, in spite of the purely negative rôle which appeared to be implied by her name, was conceived to be responsible for many seemingly highly positive peculiarities of the offspring. This, however, was felt to be an unobjectionable dualism, partly because the second or evil principle was *called* 'Nothing,' and partly because its existence as a factor in the world, and the effects of it, could be regarded as logically necessary and not as a mysterious accident.

But the significant issue did not lie in this simple, almost tautological piece of reasoning. Doubtless, if the Absolute Being was not to remain forever in the solitude of his own perfection, the prime evil of limitation or imperfection must characterize whatever other beings he brought forth. But that evil was not thereby justified unless it were shown, or assumed, that the creation of such other, necessarily defective beings is itself a good. This crucial assumption King unhesitatingly makes, as well as a further assumption which seems far from self-evident. Even if it were granted that it is good that *some* beings other than God, some finite and imperfect natures, should exist, would it not (some might ask) have been less irrational that only the highest grade of imperfection should be generated—as had, indeed, been originally the case, according to an account of the creation supported by a considerable weight of authority in the theological tradition of Christianity, and comparatively recently revived by Milton.[13] If God could be supposed to need company—which it seemed philosophically a paradox and was theologically a heresy to admit—should it not at least have been good company, a *civitas dei* composed wholly of pure spirits? King saw no way of achieving a satisfactory theodicy unless this latter question were answered (again with the support of many ancient and medieval writers) in the negative. It was requisite to show that not only imperfection in general, but every one of the observable concrete imperfections of the actual world, ought to have been created; and this could not be shown unless it were laid down as a premise that it is inherently and absolutely good that *every* kind of thing (however far down in the scale of possibles) should actually be, so far as its existence is logically conceivable, *i.e.*, involves no contradiction.

This proposition then—expressed in theological terminology—was the essential thesis in the argument for optimism propounded by King and Law. There is inherent in the divine essence as an element in God's perfection a special attribute of 'goodness,' which makes it necessary that all other and less excellent essences down to the very lowest—so far as they are severally and jointly possible—shall have actual existence after their kind.

God might, indeed, have refrained from creating, and continued alone, self-sufficient and perfect to all eternity; but his infinite Goodness would by no means allow it; this obliged him to produce external things; which things, since they could not possibly be perfect, the Divine Goodness preferred imperfect ones to none at all. Imperfection, then, arose from the infinity of Divine Goodness.[14]

And, thus committed by his own nature to the impartation of actual being to *some* imperfect essences, God could not refuse the boon of existence to any:

If you say, God might have omitted the more imperfect beings, I grant it, and if that had been best, he would undoubtedly have done it. But it is the part of infinite Goodness to choose the very best; from thence it proceeds, therefore, that the more imperfect beings have existence; for it was agreeable to that, not to omit the very least good that could be produced. Finite goodness might possibly have been exhausted in creating the greater beings, but infinite extends to all. . . . There must then be many, perhaps infinite, degrees of perfection in the divine works. . . . It was better not to give some so great a degree of happiness as their natures might receive, than that a whole species of being should be wanting to the world.[15]

Not only must all possible *species* enjoy existence, but, adds King's editor, 'from the observation that there is no manner of chasm or void, no link deficient in this great Chain of Being, and the reason of it, it will appear extremely probable also that every distinct order, every class or species, is as full as the nature of it would permit, or [Law devoutly but, upon his own principles, tautologically adds] as God saw proper.'

The foundation, then, of the argument for optimism was a very old conception, than which few, I think, have affected Western thought more profoundly or at more diverse points—but which has been so little recognized or connectedly studied by historians that it has received no appropriate name. I shall call it the principle of plenitude. It is the assumption that a good or rational universe must be a *plenum formarum,* that every Platonic Idea has—subject only to the law of contradiction, to the limitations of logical impossibility and incompossibility—a valid claim to existence, that if a single such claim remained avoidably unrealized the world would be *eo ipso* shown to be, not merely incomplete, but irrational and therefore evil, and that the entire series of other essences whose necessary actualization is thus implied by the assumption of the perfection of the divine essence must constitute a minutely graded hierarchy, a *continuum* of forms from highest to lowest, of which any two adjacent members differ only infinitesimally. The conception takes its start in a famous passage of the *Timæus*;[16] it is the essential principle of the dialectic of Neoplatonic emanationism;[17] it had been used by Abelard in the twelfth century as the basis at once for a proof of cosmical determinism similar to Spinoza's, and of optimism similar to that of King and his eighteenth-century successors;[18] it had played a great part in the system of Thomas Aquinas, though accompanied by ingenious distinctions and elusive modifications designed to rid it of its heterodox consequences;[19] and in the seventeenth century it had been a favorite theme of some of the English Platonists. On the other hand it, or the rationalistic premises on which it rested, had been rejected, as inconsistent with the freedom of the divine will, by a slightly less long line of philosophers and theologians, notably by Peter Lombard in the famous compend which was for centuries the chief textbook of students of theology,[20] and by Duns Scotus and his followers; and it had been not only conspicuously absent from, but plainly contradicted by, the cosmogony and theodicy of Milton, who in this matter is a continuer rather of the Scotist than the Thomist tradition. Since the principle of plenitude had received expression from hundreds of writers before King, its utilization by later optimists is no evidence that they derived it from him. Nevertheless, for reasons already indicated, the probability remains that it was because of the reiteration and elaboration of the principle in the *De origine mali* that Pope gave the fundamental place, in his own argument for the thesis that whatever is, is right, to the premise that, in the 'best of systems possible,'

> All must full or not coherent be,
> And all that rises, rise in due degree.

For the purposes of a theodicy, the principle of plenitude served most directly and obviously as an 'explanation' of the 'evil of defect.' The limitations of each species of creature, which define its place in the scale, are indispensable to that infinite differentiation of things in which the 'fullness' of the universe consists, and are therefore necessary to the realization of the greatest of goods. Man, therefore, cannot rationally complain because he lacks many endowments and means of enjoyment which might conceivably have been granted him. In Law's words:

> From the supposition of a Scale of Being, gradually descending from perfection to nonentity, and complete in every intermediate rank and

degree, we shall soon see the absurdity of such questions as these, Why was not man made more perfect? Why are not his faculties equal to those of angels? Since this is only asking why he was not placed in a different class of beings, when at the same time all other classes are supposed to be full.[21]

It was, in short, 'necessary that the creature should fill the station wherein it was, or none at all.' If he were anywhere else, he would not be the same entity; and if he did not exist at all, there would a gap in the series, and the perfection of the creation would thereby be destroyed. Undeniably these distinguishing deficiencies 'bring many inconveniences on the persons whose lot it is to fill that part of the universe which requires a creature of such an imperfect nature.' For example, a man has no wings, a perfection granted to birds.

> 'Tis plain that in his present circumstances he cannot have them, and that the use of them would be very mischievous to society; and yet the want of them necessarily exposes us to many inconveniences. . . . A thousand instances may be given where the evil of imperfection necessarily subjects us to disappointment of appetite, and several other natural evils, which yet are all necessary for the common good.[22]

To this particular form of purely logical consolation Pope recurs repeatedly, with fairly evident dependence upon King. In a 'full' system 'there must be, somewhere, such a rank as Man'; and the occupant of that rank cannot rationally desire the distinctive attributes of those below or those above him in the scale.[23]

> Why has not man a microscopic eye?
> For this plain reason, man is not a fly.

And

> On superior powers
> Were we to press, inferior might on ours;
> Or in the full creation leave a void,
> Where, one step broken, the great scale's destroyed.[24]

But if the principle of plenitude had been applicable only for the explanation of the 'metaphysical' evil of limitation or particularity, it would not have carried the optimist far towards his goal. Most of the things we call evil hardly appear to be adequately describable as mere deficiencies. Even a Platonistic philosopher with a toothache will probably find it difficult to persuade himself that his pain is a wholly negative thing, a metaphysical vacuum consisting merely in the absence of some conceivable positive good. King was therefore forced to use some ingenuity—or rather, to utilize the ingenuity of his many precursors—in order to exhibit the numerous train of 'natural' evils as equally necessary implications of the same fundamental principle. He seeks to do this, in the first place, on the ground that in a really 'full' universe there must be opposition. Creatures necessarily crowd upon, restrict, and therefore come into conflict with, one another. This necessity appears in its primary form in the motion of matter. It was theoretically possible for God to have so disposed matter that it would move 'uniformly and all together, either in a direct line or in a circle and the contrariety of motions by that means be prevented.' But a material system so simple and harmonious must also, we are assured, have been barren and useless.

> Such a motion therefore was to be excited in it as would separate it into parts, make it fluid, and render it an habitation for animals. But that could not be without contrariety of motion, as any one that thinks of it at all will perceive. And if this be once admitted in matter, there necessarily follows a division and disparity of parts, clashing and opposition, comminution, concretion and repulsion, and all those evils which we behold in generation and corruption. . . . The mutual clashing of these concretions could therefore not be avoided, and as they strike upon one another a concussion of the parts and a separation from each other would be necessarily produced, . . . [i.e.] corruption.[25]

And since man's place in the Scale of Being is that of a creature partly material, partly spiritual, he is necessarily involved in, and unhappily affected by, these collisions of matter. The preoccupation of the optimists with the notion of the 'fullness' of the organic world sometimes led them (by a natural confusion of ideas) to draw an almost Darwinian or Malthusian picture of a Nature over-crowded with aspirants for life and consequently given over to a ubiquitous struggle for existence. King assures us that there is something like a housing-problem even in Heaven.

> If you ask why God does not immediately transplant men into heaven, since 'tis plain they are capable of that happier state; or why he confines them so long . . . on the earth as in a darksome prison, . . . I answer, Because the Heavens are already furnished with inhabitants, and cannot with convenience admit of new ones, till some of the present possessors depart to a better state, or make room some other way for these to change their condition.[26]

329

Into the further naïve reasonings by which King seeks to deduce the genesis of 'pain, uneasiness and dread of death,' and indirectly of the other emotions by which man is tormented, we need not enter. It suffices to quote the concise genealogy of woes in which he sums up his reasons for holding this to be the best of possible worlds:

> Behold how evils spring from and multiply upon each other, while infinite Goodness still urges the Deity to do the very best. This moved him to give existence to creatures, which cannot exist without imperfections and inequality. This excited him to create matter, and to put it in motion, which is necessarily attended with separation and dissolution, generation and corruption. This persuaded him to couple souls with bodies, and to give them mutual affections, whence proceeded pain and sorrow, hatred and fear, with the rest of the passions. Yet all of them are necessary.[27]

Such an argument for optimism closely resembles, and might easily be substituted for, some of the formulas in which primitive Buddhism summed up the creed of pessimism.

The author of the most popular English theodicy of the mid-nineteenth century found, as everyone remembers, peculiar difficulty in the spectacle of 'Nature red in tooth and claw with ravin'—in the universal conflict, the daily and hourly cruelties and little, dumb tragedies, which are hidden behind the surface-beauty of every field and wood. But to the typical eighteenth-century writer of a theodicy, even these aspects of Nature gave little trouble. He was no more blind to them than Tennyson; but his universal solvent, the principle of plenitude, served him here as elsewhere. Doubtless, King granted, God could have made a world free from these horrors, simply by refraining from creating carnivorous and predacious animals. But this, again, would have meant a world less full of life.

> A being that has life is (*caeteris paribus*) preferable to one that has not; God, therefore, animated that machine which furnishes out provision for the more perfect animals; which was both graciously and providently done: for by this means he gained so much life to the world as there is in those animals which are food for others; for by this means they themselves enjoy some kind of life, and are of service also to the rest. . . . Matter, which is fit for the nourishment of man, is also capable of life; if therefore God had denied it life, he had omitted a degree of good which might have been produced without any impediment to his principal design, which does not seem very agreeable to infinite goodness. 'Tis

better, therefore, that it should be endowed with life for a time, though 'tis to be devoured afterwards, than to continue totally stupid and unactive. . . . Let us not be surprised, then, at the universal war as it were among animals, . . . or that the strong devour the weaker.[28]

The application of this to the special case of domesticated animals reared for slaughter, which furnished Pope with the theme for some characteristic and detestable lines, was also made by King. Man

> Feasts the animal he dooms his feast,
> And, till he ends the being, makes it blest.

Undeniably the carnivora were among the antecedently possible kinds of creatures; and if the excellence of Nature or its Author consists quite simply in having as many kinds as possible, nothing more need be said in justification of the existence of such animals; in the words of another contemporary divine, quoted with admiration by Law, 'it is evident that by this means there is room for more whole species of creatures than there otherwise would be, and that the variety of the creation is thereby very much enlarged and the goodness of its Author displayed.'[29] The tendency of the theodicies to promote belief in the blessedness of sheer multitude, the all-importance of having an abundance of 'different natures' in the world, at whatever cost, could hardly be better illustrated.

But even if the criterion of the goodness of the universe were assumed to consist, not solely in the diversity of creatures, but in the quantity of the *joie de vivre* it contains, the creation of beasts of prey could still, according to a further argument of King's, be justified. 'Animals are of such a nature as to delight in action, or in the exercise of their faculties, nor can we have any other notion of happiness even in God himself.' But among the pleasurable activities conceivable before the creation were those which might attach to the procuring of food by predatory creatures. Why, then, should these intense and positive pleasures be lacking, merely that feebler kinds might be spared the transitory pains of being pursued and eaten? Clearly, since 'the infinite Power of God was able to produce animals of such capacities,' his 'infinite Goodness' may 'be conceived to have almost compelled him not to refuse or envy (them) the benefit of life.' 'If you insist,' says the archbishop genially to a supposititious critic, 'that a lion might have been made without teeth or claws, a viper without venom; I grant it, as a knife without an edge; but then they would have been of quite another species [i.e., there would have been a missing link in the Chain of

Being], and have had neither the nature, nor use, nor genius, which they now enjoy.' As for the lion's victim, if it were a rational animal it doubtless would, or at all events should, rejoice as does its Maker in the thought of the agreeable exercise which it is affording the 'genius' of the lion. If the victim be not endowed with reason, or be too mean-spirited to take a large philosophical view of the matter, the consoling insight into the higher meaning of its sufferings is still, through the happy ordering of things, left to be enjoyed vicariously by optimistic archbishops.[30]

Plainly this amiable and devout ecclesiastic had, in the course of his endeavor to justify God's ways to men, been driven not only to a conception of God but also to a conception of ultimate values which came somewhat strangely from a Christian teacher. Though King would, of course, have said that his God was a God of love, the term must necessarily have had for him an unusual sense. The God of the *De origine mali* loved abundance and variety of life more than he loved peace and concord among his creatures and more than he desired their exemption from pain. He loved lions, in short, as well as lambs; and loving lions, he wished them to behave in accordance with the 'nature,' or Platonic Idea, of a lion, which implies devouring lambs and not lying down with them. And in these preferences the 'goodness' of God was assumed to be most clearly manifested—'goodness' thus coming to mean a delight in fullness and diversity of finite being, rather than in harmony and happiness. King and his editor seem only occasionally and confusedly aware how deeply their argument has involved them in such a radical transvaluation of values; they waver between this and the more conventional conception of 'divine goodness,' and for the most part touch but lightly upon the more paradoxical implications of their premises. Yet they at times betray some uneasy feeling of the incongruity between these premises and certain traditional elements of Christian belief. It was, for example, a part of that belief that in the earthly paradise before the Fall, and also in the celestial paradise which awaits the elect, most of the evils which these theologians were zealously proving to be 'necessary,' because required by the 'divine goodness,' were in fact absent. It seemed, therefore, difficult to avoid the awkward dilemma that either the paradisaical state is not good, or else a good 'system' does not, after all, require quite so much evil and so many degrees of imperfection as the authors of the theodicies conceived. King meets this difficulty but lamely; he is, in fact, driven to suggest that the felicity of our first parents in Eden has probably been somewhat exaggerated: 'it doth not appear that Adam in Paradise was altogether without pain or passion,' but rather 'that he was only secured from such pains as might cause his death, and that for a time, till removed to a better place.'[31]

The outcome of King's reasoning (so far as it was consistently carried through) is not, of course, surprising. He who attempts a theodicy without first shutting his eyes to a large range of the facts of experience, must necessarily take for the object of his piety the God of Things as They Are; and since things as they are include the whole countless troop of natural ills, it became necessary so to transform the conception of the good as to make it possible to argue that these ills are—not, indeed, goods, considered by themselves—but implicates of some supreme good, in the realization of which the essential nature of deity is most truly manifested. The principle of plenitude, taken as a species of value-theory, was a natural, if not the necessary, result of this enforced revision of the notion of good. Certainly that which the Author of Nature as it is chiefly values could not, on empirical grounds, be supposed to be identical with those things which men have commonly set their hearts upon and have pictured to themselves in their dreams of paradise. Stated in its most general terms, the paradox underlying all these singular implications of the optimist's reasoning is the assumption which is of the essence of the principle of plenitude itself—that *the desirability of a thing's existence bears no relation to its excellence*.

King's further reflections upon the problem of evil do not concern us here, since the conception of the Chain of Being does not much figure in them. It might, indeed, and with more consistency, have done so. For the sort of evil not dealt with by King upon the principles already indicated, namely, moral evil, might naturally have been regarded as a special case of the 'evil of defect.' A creature having the specific degree of blindness and weakness appropriate to man's place in the scale, and at the same time subject to the passions which King had represented as necessarily inseparable from our psychophysical constitution, could hardly fail, it would seem, to make frequent 'wrong elections.' So much, indeed, King is constrained to admit; there are many errors of conduct which are due to our ignorance and necessary imperfection, and these are to be classed among the 'natural evils' and explained in the same manner as others of that class. But there remains a residuum of 'moral evil' not so explicable, but due to a 'depraved will.' On this theme King for the most part repeats the familiar arguments. Bolingbroke did not follow the archbishop in this, but derived the necessity of moral evil directly from the principle of plenitude. If men had been so constituted as to follow always the ethical 'law of nature, . . . the moral state of mankind would have been paradisaical, but it would not have been human.

We should not have been the creatures we were designed to be, and a gap would have been left in the order of created intelligences.'[32] In this application of the principle, the antinomian implications of which are sufficiently obvious, Bolingbroke had been anticipated by so saintly a philosopher as Spinoza:

> To those who ask, Why has not God created all men such as to be directed solely by the guidance of reason, I reply only that it is because he had no lack of material wherewith to create all things, from the very highest to the very lowest grade of perfection, or, more properly speaking, because the laws of his nature were so ample as to suffice for the production of everything that can be conceived by an infinite intellect.[33]

This was carrying a step farther the argument which Pope was to versify: since the best of systems must be as 'full' as possible,

> Then in the scale of reasoning life, 'tis plain,
> There must be somewhere such a rank as—

not man only, but also, among men, the fool and the evil-doer.

The theodicy of Leibniz was in most essentials the same as that of his English precursor;[34] and in summarizing with approval the main argument of the archbishop's *bel ouvrage, plein de savoir et d'élégance,* Leibniz significantly accentuated the theological paradox contained in it:

> Why, someone asks, did not God refrain from creating things altogether. The author well replies that the abundance of God's goodness is the reason. He wished to communicate himself, even at the expense of that delicacy which our imaginations ascribe to him, when we assume that imperfections shock him. Thus he preferred that the imperfect should exist, rather than nothing.[35]

This emphasis upon the implication that the Creator of the actual world cannot be supposed to be a 'delicate' or squeamish God, caring only for perfection—and that, in fact, he would, if more nicely selective in his act of creation, have thereby shown himself the less divine—illustrates clearly the tendency of the optimistic argument to generate a new conception of that in which the goodness of things in general consists. And in developing the theory of value thus implicit in optimism, the German philosopher is franker, more ardent, and more cheerful, than the Anglican theologian. Some analogies in human life to the standards of valuation which the optimists had applied in explaining the supposed purpose of the deity in the creation are not obscurely suggested by Leibniz.

> Wisdom requires variety *(la sagesse doit varier)*. To multiply exclusively the same thing, however noble it be, would be a superfluity; it would be a kind of poverty. To have a thousand well-bound copies of Vergil in your library; to sing only airs from the opera of Cadmus and Hermione; to break all your porcelain in order to have only golden cups; to have all your buttons made of diamonds; to eat only partridges and to drink only the wine of Hungary or of Shiraz—could any one call this reasonable? [36]

Something very similar to this had, in point of fact, been regarded as the essence of reasonableness both by neo-classical æsthetic theorists and by a multitude of influential moralists. It would scarcely have seemed evident to the former that two copies of Vergil are of less value than one copy *plus* a copy of the worst epic ever written—still less that a reading of the first followed by a reading of the second is preferable to two readings of Vergil. And the apparent object of the endeavor of most ethical teaching had been to produce a close approach to uniformity in human character and behavior, and in men's political and social institutions. The desire for variety—or for change, the temporal form of it—had rather commonly been conceived to be a non-rational, indeed a pathological, idiosyncrasy of human creatures. But Leibniz not only gave it a sort of cosmic dignity by attributing it to God himself, but also represented it as the very summit of rationality.

The ethically significant consequence which is most plainly drawn from this by Leibniz is that neither what is commonly called moral goodness, nor pleasure, is the most important thing in the world. Both hedonism, in short, and an abstract moralism (such, for example, as Kant and Fichte were afterwards to express) were equally contrary to the value-theory implicit in the principle of plenitude. Virtue and happiness both, of course, have their place in the scale of values; but if it were the highest place, it is inconceivable that God would have made the kind of a world he has made.

> The moral or physical good or evil of rational creatures does not infinitely transcend the good or evil which is purely metaphysical, that is to say, the good which consists in the perfection of the other creatures.

... No substance is either absolutely precious or absolutely contemptible in the sight of God. It is certain that God attaches more importance to a man than to a lion, but I do not know that we can be sure that he prefers one man to the entire species of lions.[37]

To this thesis Leibniz reverts again and again throughout the *Theodicy*:

(It is) a false maxim that the happiness of rational creatures is the sole purpose of God. If that had been so, there would, perhaps, have been neither sin nor unhappiness, not even as concomitants. God would have chosen a set of possibles from which all evils were excluded. But he would in that case have fallen short of what is due to the universe, that is, what is due to himself. . . . It is true that one can imagine possible worlds without sin and without suffering, just as one can invent romances about Utopias or Sévarambes; but these worlds would be much inferior to ours. I cannot show this in detail; you must infer it, as I do, *ab effectu*, since this world, as it is, is the world God chose. . . . Virtue is the noblest quality of created things, but it is not the only good quality of creatures. There is an infinite number of others that attract the inclination of God; it is from all these inclinations together that the greatest possible sum of good results; and there would be less good than there is if there were nothing but virtue, if only rational creatures existed. . . . Midas was less rich when he possessed only gold.[38]

To this is added the trite æsthetic argument for the indispensability of contrast in the production of beauty in a work of art, and, indeed, in the mere physical pleasure of the gustatory sense:

Sweet things become insipid if we eat nothing else; sharp, tart and even bitter things must be combined with them so as to stimulate the taste. He who has not tasted bitter things does not deserve sweet, and, indeed, will not appreciate them.

Thus the argument for optimism represented the Cosmic Artist as cramming his canvas with diversified detail to the last infinitesimal fraction of an inch; as caring far more for fullness and variety of content than for simplicity and perfection of form; and as seeking this richness of coloring and abundance of contrast even at the cost of disharmony, irregularity, and what to us appears confusion. For there is much truth, says Leibniz, in 'the fine principle of St. Bernard: *ordinatissimum est, minus interdum ordinate fieri aliquid.*'

The word 'Romanticism,' I have suggested in an earlier paper, ought to be used in the plural or with the indefinite article; there is a formidably large collection of distinct, seemingly unrelated, and even opposed, ideas or tendencies to which the name has been applied by different writers, and since none has taken the precaution of obtaining copyright for the term, it can hardly be said that one of the current uses is more authorized than another.[39] Nevertheless, if one were to select from among these meanings that one which would do most to clarify the history of ideas, the criteria to be applied are not difficult to formulate. It is usually agreed that 'Romanticism' should designate a thing which, if it did not originate, at all events became far more explicit and potent, in the later eighteenth century, and was essentially antithetic to the tendencies of thought and taste dominant in the earlier part of that century and in the preceding one. 'Romanticism' *par excellence,* then, should be that change in ruling presuppositions, occurring in the period in question, which is at once the most profound, the most completely and significantly opposed to the preconceptions alike of the ruling philosophy of the Enlightenment and of the neo-classical æsthetics, the most fruitful of revolutionary consequences, and from which the greatest number of other 'Romanticisms' can be seen to derive. If the same innovation can be shown to have been fundamental in the program of those German writers who first introduced the term 'romantic' into the vocabulary of philosophy and literary criticism, it would be still better entitled to be considered the prime Romanticism.

There is one manifest change in fundamental conceptions which meets all these criteria. For two centuries the thought of the Western world and, above all, the efforts made during those centuries for improvement and correction in beliefs, in institutions, and in art, had been, in the main, dominated by the assumption that, in each phase of human activity, excellence consists in conforming as nearly as possible to a standard conceived as universal, static, uncomplicated, uniform for every rational being. Rationality and uniformity were, indeed, commonly assumed to be inseparable notions, and there was a marked tendency to define the rational simply as that which is found to be actually universal in the human mind. 'Nature' was the word oftenest used to designate such a standard of excellence; and the amazing proposition endlessly reiterated by seventeenth- and the early eighteenth-century writers was that nature 'is everywhere the same.' The norm, then, whether of truth or of beauty, was simple and invariant. In religion the champions of deism, the religion of nature, sought to bring men back to the simple creed which could be supposed (in Leslie Stephen's phrase) to be literally catholic, *i.e.*, to have been understood and accepted *semper, ubique et ab omnibus*. Ethics was summed up in the law of nature, of which universality was the distinguishing mark:

> La morale uniforme en tout temps, en tout lieu.

Political philosophy, in so far as it rested upon the notion of natural rights, was concerned only with that which is generic in man; and it tended on the whole, though not without important exceptions, to set up a uniform scheme of government as the ideal for all peoples. In the æsthetics of literature the high neo-classical dogma demanded that the subject-matter and emotional content of a drama or epic should be limited to that which is universal in human experience and capable of appealing equally to all men in all times and all lands. It was their supposed greater universality, both in content and in appeal, which constituted the essence of the superiority attributed to the classical models. In every domain, in short, the program of improvement or reform was one of simplification, standardization, the avoidance of the particular, the elimination of local variations and individual diversities supposed to have arisen through some strange and unhappy aberration from the uniformity of the 'natural' order.[40]

There has, in the entire history of thought, been hardly any change in standards of value more profound and more momentous than that which came when the contrary principle began widely to prevail—when it came to be believed that in many, if not all, phases of human activity, not only are there diverse excellences, but that diversity itself is of the essence of excellence; and that of art, in particular, the objective is neither the attainment of some ideal perfection of form in a small number of fixed *genres*, nor, on the other hand, the gratification of that least common denominator of æsthetic susceptibility which is shared by mankind in all ages, but rather the fullest possible expression of the abundance of differentness that there is, actually or potentially, in nature and human nature, and—for the function of the artist in relation to his public—the evocation of capacities for understanding, sympathy, and enjoyment, which are latent in most men, and perhaps never capable of universalization. These assumptions, though assuredly not the only important, are plainly the one *common*, factor in a score of otherwise diverse tendencies which, by one or another critic or historian, have been termed 'Romantic': the immense multiplication of *genres* and of verse-forms; the admission of the æsthetic legitimacy of the *genre mixte*; the *goût de la nuance*; the naturalization in art of the 'grotesque';

the quest for local color; the endeavor to reconstruct in imagination the *distinctive* inner life of peoples remote in space or in cultural condition; the *étalage du moi*; the demand for particularized fidelity in landscape-description; the revulsion against simplicity; the distrust of universal formulas in politics; the æsthetic antipathy to standardization; the apotheosis of the 'concrete universal' in metaphysics; sentimentalism about 'the glory of the imperfect'; the cultivation of personal, national and racial idiosyncrasy; the general high valuation (wholly foreign to most earlier periods) of originality, and the usually futile and absurd self-conscious pursuit of that attribute. It is, however, of no great consequence whether or not we apply to this transformation of current assumptions about value the name of 'Romanticism'; what it is essential to remember is that the transformation has taken place and that it, perhaps, more than any other one thing distinguishes, both for better and worse, the prevailing assumptions of the thought of the nineteenth and of our own century from those of the preceding period in the intellectual history of the West.

Now the historical thesis which I here suggest—space is not available for the full proof of it [41]—is that the general transition from universalism to what may be called diversitarianism in the normative provinces of thought was promoted—by no means solely, but perhaps chiefly—by the emphasis and reiteration given to the principle of plenitude in the arguments of the eighteenth-century defenders of optimism, in the course of the controversy in which so considerable a part of the religious interest and intellectual energy of that age was absorbed. These subtle philosophers and grave divines, and poets like Pope and Haller who popularized their reasonings, rested their assertion of the goodness of the universe ultimately upon the same ground as Stevenson's child in the nursery:

> The world is so full of a number of things.

This did not, it is true, necessarily make them 'as happy as kings.' That was a matter of individual temperament; and in point of fact most of them had not the child's robust delight in the sheer diversity and multiplicity of things. They were often men whose natural taste or training would have inclined them rather to prefer a somewhat thin, simple and exclusive universe. The philosophers of optimism were not, in short, as a rule of a Romantic disposition; and what they were desirous of proving was that reality is rational through and through, that every fact of existence, however unpleasant, is grounded in some reason as clear and evident as an axiom of mathematics. But in the exigencies of their argument to this ambitious conclusion, they found themselves constrained to attribute to the Divine Reason a conception of the good extremely different from that which had been most current among men, and especially among philosophers; and they were thus led, often against their original temper and intention, to impress upon the minds of their generation a revolutionary and paradoxical theory of the criterion of all value, which may be summed up in the words of a highly Romantic and optimistic lover of paradox in our own day:

> One thing alone is needful: Everything.
> The rest is vanity of vanities.

NOTES

1. See, for an example, the writer's paper 'Rousseau's Pessimist,' *Mod. Lang. Notes*, XXXVIII (1924), 449; and for an earlier one, Prior's *Solomon* (1718), a poetical elaboration of the thesis that 'the pleasures of life do not compensate our miseries; age steals upon us unawares; and death, as the only cure of our ills, ought to be expected, not feared.'

2. *A Free Inquiry into the Nature and Origin of Evil* (1757), 60–2. Jenyns for the most part merely puts into clear and concise form the arguments of King, Leibniz and Pope; but he differs from these in unequivocally and emphatically rejecting the freedomist solution of the problem of moral evil. His book had a considerable vogue, went into numerous editions, and was translated into French.

3. *Ibid.*, 104, where the curious reader may, if he will, find why this option was 'necessary,' and how 'Infinite Wisdom' made the best of it.

4. Voltaire, however, is arguing in the poem against two distinct and essentially opposed types of theodicy: the philosophical and necessitarian type, which endeavored to explain such a thing as the Lisbon earthquake as

l'effet des éternelles lois

Qui d'un Dieu libre et bón nécessitent le choix,

and the theological and indeterminist type, which saw in such catastrophes special interpositions of deity in punishment of men's free choice of moral evil. The reasonings aimed at these two opposite objectives Voltaire confusingly runs together.

5. *Ethica*, V., Prop. 6.

6. *An Essay on the Origin of Evil by Dr. William King, translated from the Latin with Notes and a Dissertation concerning the Principle and Criterion of Virtue and of the Passions; By Edmund Law, M. A., Fellow of Christ College in Cambridge.* I quote from the second edition, Lond., 1732, here referred to as 'Essay.'

7. The dates are 1731, 1732, 1739, 1758, 1781.

8. Stephen, *English Thought*, p. 406.

9. Bolingbroke in the *Fragments* quotes King frequently and with respect; he recognizes in him the one theologian who 'saw plainly' the truth of the thesis which Bolingbroke devotes scores of pages to developing and defending, *viz.*, that man is not the final cause of the creation; and his own argument for optimism, though less methodically stated, follows in great part the same line as King's.

10. *Essay*, I, 103.

11. *Ibid.*, 109–113.

12. *Ibid.*, XIX. This argument remained as the usual starting point of a numerous series of subsequent theodicies, some of which have a place in literature: *e. g.*, Victor Hugo still thought it needful to devote a number of lines to the exposition of it in *Les Contemplations* ('Ce que dit la Bouche d'Ombre,' 350 ff.).

13. See the patristic authorities cited by Sumner in his tr. of Milton's *Christian Doctrine*, 187, n. 4. The view adopted by Milton, however, was of dubious orthodoxy. It had been rejected by Thomas Aquinas, *Summa Theol.*, I, q. 61, a. 3; and by Dante, *Paradiso* XXIX, 37.

14. King, *op. cit.*, I, 116 f. For the same conception of the Scale of Being and its necessary completeness in a well-ordered universe, *cf.* Bolingbroke, *Fragments* (*Works*, 1809, VIII, 173, 183, 186, 192, 218 f., 232, 363, 364–5).

15. *Op. cit.*, 137f, 129–131f, 156. Both King and Law fell into curious waverings, and in the end into self-contradiction, when the question was raised whether the number of degrees in the scale of being is actually infinite. Into this it is unnecessary to enter here.

16. *Timaeus*, 29.

17. Cf., *e. g.*, Plotinus, Enn. V, 4, 1; IV, 86.

18. *Introd. ad Theologiam*, III; in *Migne, Patrol. Lat.*, CLXXVIII, cols. 1093–1101.

19. *Summa contra Gentiles*, I, 75; II, 45; II, 68; II, 71.

20. *Liber Sent.*, I, 442.

21. *Essay* I, 131. The argument may already be found in Plotinus, *Enn.* III, 2, 11.

22. *Op. cit.*, 137.

23. For the same argument in Bolingbroke, see *Fragments* (*Works*, 1809 ed., VIII, 233, 287, 363, 364–5).

24. *Essay on Man*, Ep. I, 48, 193–4, 241–4.

25. *Essay*, I, 147–8; *cf. Essay on Man*, I: 169:

> But all subsists by elemental Strife,
> And passions are the elements of life.

26. *Ibid.*, I, 134.

27. *Ibid.*, I, 176. The argument for the necessity of natural evils based upon the principle of plenitude is supplemented by that drawn from the indispensability of uniform general laws; *e. g.* I, 150–3, 196–7; *cf. Essay on Man*, I, 145 ff. This part of King's reasoning does not fall within the theme of the present paper.

28. *Ibid.*, I, 184–5.

29. J. Clarke, *Discourse concerning Natural Evil*, 1719; the same argument in Plotinus, *Enn.* III, 211. Goldsmith, among others, was still repeating it later in the eighteenth century; v. his *Essays* (1767), 132.

30. It is only fair to add that King is equally ready to view as 'necessary,' and consequently to approve and justify, specific evils less remote from archiepiscopal experience, such as 'gout, one of the most tormenting diseases that attend us'— by which, in fact, this resolute optimist was cruelly harassed for nearly half a century, and from an attack of which, according to his biographer, he died. (See Sir C. S. King's volume, 1906, p. 14 and *passim*). Gout, the archbishop observes, in a sportsmanlike if not wholly edifying vein, has compensations which, on the whole, outweigh its pains: 'Who would not rather endure it than lose the pleasure of feeling? Most men are sensible that eating certain meats, and indulging ourselves in the use of several drinks, will bring it; and yet we see this doth not deter us from them, and we think it more tolerable to endure the gout, than lose the pleasure that plentiful eating and drinking yields us.' (I., 177). Why it was 'necessary' *a priori* that these pleasures should be purchasable only at that price remains, in the end, somewhat obscure.

31. *Essay*, I, 176; *cf.* also 148–9.

32. *Fragments or Minutes of Essays*, Sec. XVI.

33. *Ethics*, I, *ad. fin.*

34. There is no question of any influence of King upon Leibniz or of Leibniz upon King. Though the *Théodicée* was not published until 1710, eight years after the *De origine mali*, the greater part of it was written between 1697 and the beginning of 1705; and the ideas it contains had long been familiar to Leibniz. Cf. Gerhardt's preface to Leibniz's *Philosophische Schriften*, vol. VI, 3–10.

35. 'Remarques sur le livre sur l'origine du mal publié depuis peu en Angleterre,' appended to the *Théodicée; Philos. Schriften*, VI, 400, ff. Leibniz observes that he is in agreement with King 'only in respect to half of the subject,' the disagreement relates chiefly to King's chapter on liberty and necessity, which (quite inconsistently with the implications of his argument for optimism) asserts that God exercised a *liberum arbitrium indifferentiae* in creating the world.

36. *Théodicée,* § 124.

37. *Théodicée,* § 118.

38. *Ibid.,* §§120, 10, 124; *cf* also 213.

39. On the ambiguities of the term, *cf.* the writer's 'The Discrimination of Romanticisms,' *PMLA,* XXXIX (1924), 299 ff.

40. A part of Milton's argument in the *Areopagitica* is perhaps the most remarkable seventeenth-century exception to this universalism.

41. The rôle of the principle of plenitude, as it had been presented by the optimistic writers, in bringing about this transition may most clearly be seen in Schiller's *Philosophische Briefe,* especially the *Theosophie des Julius* and the concluding letter; in the passages in the *Athenaeum* in which Friedrich Schlegel developed the conception of *romantische Poesie* (on which see the writer's papers, *Mod. Lang. Notes,* 1916 and 1917); and in Schleiermacher's *Reden* (especially II and V) and *Monologen.* I cite only the following: 'So ist mir aufgegangen, was jetzt meine höchste Anschauung ist, es ist mir klar geworden, dass jeder Mensch auf eigne Art die Menschheit darstellen soll, in einer eignen Mischung ihrer Elemente, damit auf jede Weise sie sich offenbare, und wirklich werde in der Fülle der Unendlichkeit alles was aus ihrem Schosse hervorgehen kann . . . . Allein nur schwer und spät gelangt der Mensch zum vollen Bewusstein seiner Eigentümlichkeit; nicht immer wagt ers drauf hinzusehn, und richtet lieber das Auge auf den Gemeinbesitz der Menschheit, den er so liebend und so dankbar festhält; er zweifelt oft, ob er sich als ein eignes Wesen wieder aus ihm ausscheiden soll . . . . Das eigenste Bestreben der Natur wird oftmals nicht bemerkt, und wenn am deutlichsten sich ihre Schranken offenbaren, gleitet an der Scharfen Ecke das Auge allzuleicht vorbei, und hält nur das Allgemeine fest, wo eben in der Verneinung sich das Eigne zeigt.' (*Monologen,* ed. Schiele, 1914, p. 30).

SELECTIVE INDEX

Abelard, Peter, 327
Abercromby, David, 43, 57
Abrams, Meyer, 315
Addison, Joseph, viii, 15-18, 84, 87, 117, 144-57, 224, 289; *Freeholder*, 145; 'Pleasures of the Imagination,' 195, 198, 200-201, 204-5, 210; *Spectator*, 16-17, 46, 56, 61, 65; *Tatler*, 87
Akenside, Mark, 195, 199, 208; *Pleasures of Imagination*, 181, 194, 200-205
Allen, Ralph, 65
Anne, Queen of England, viii, ix, 8-9, 30, 98, 105, 135
Aquinas, Thomas, 327, 341
Arbuthnot, Dr. John, 6-8, 12, 84, 95, 132, 136; John Bull papers, 93; as satirist, 10-11, 19, 81
Aristotle, 57, 74-5, 151, 215, 312, 316, 324
Arnold, Matthew, as critic, 22, 132-3, 141, 151, 155, 216, 229; as poet, 219-20, 313
Astell, Mary (?), *Bart'lemy Fair*, 45, 60
Atterbury, Francis, Bishop of Rochester, 56, 61
Auden, W. H., 39
Augustus Caesar, 34, 224

Bacon, Francis, 56, 69ff., 114, 161
Barfield, Owen, 228
Barrow, Dr. Isaac, 265
Barry (Welsh harpist), 237
Bathurst, Allen Bathurst, 1st Earl, 66, 281
Baxter, Richard, 78
Bayle, Pierre, 320, 323-4
Beattie, James, 224, 230

Beddoes, Thomas L., 141
Beerbohm, Max, 220
Bennett, Arnold, 312
Bentley, Richard, 152
Bergson, Henri, 219
Bernard, Saint, of Clairvaux, 336
Bethel, Slingsby, 106
Biggs, Noah, 72
Blackmore, Sir Richard, 198, 228
Blackwall, Anthony, 43
Blair, Dr. Hugh, 294
Blake, William, 192, 212, 234, 246, 314-18
Blount, Martha, 63
Blount, Teresa, 66
Boileau-Despréaux, Nicolas, 18, 57, 154
Boleyn, Anne, 260
Bolingbroke, Henry St. John, Lord, 66, 84, 116; as politician, 8-10, 12, 65; as philosopher, 5-6, 323, 333-4, 341
Boswell, James, *Life of Johnson*, 286-9, 294-5, 298, 312; *London Journal*, 313; *Tour*, 286
Bouhours, Dominique, 61
Boulter, Hugh, Archbishop of Armagh, 108-9
Boyle, Robert, 54, 56, 71, 78-82, 152
Braddon, Laurence, 105
Brewster, Sir Francis, 104
Brooke, Henry, 13
Broome, William, 65, 67
Brown, John (*Estimate*), 13-14, 20
Browne, Sir Thomas, 153
Browning, Robert, 212, 216
Buckingham, John Sheffield, Duke of, 43
Buckingham, Duchess of, 65
Buerdsell, James, 46
Bunyan, John, 220

Burke, Edmund, vii, 15, 17; *The Sublime and Beautiful*, 154, 197, 199, 204-8

Burlington, Richard Boyle, 3rd Earl of, 65, 140

Burnet, Thomas, 153-4

Burns, Robert, 181, 187-93, 244, 314, 316

Burton, Dr. John, 280

Butler, Samuel, 225, 305-6

Byron, George Gordon, Lord, 132, 158, 212, 234

Campe, Johann Heinrich, 168-9

Carlyle, Thomas, 165, 288

Cary, John, 107

Caryll, John, 67

Casaubon, Meric, 75, 76

Cawthorn, James, 195

Cervantes, *Don Quixote*, 158, 269-70, 283

Chain of Being, 117, 119, 228, 319-36, 342

Chalmers, Alexander, 288, 290

Chanson de Roland, 151

Chapman, John, 145

Charles II, 49, 50, 59, 71

Charleton, Walter, 44

Chatterton, Thomas, **Rowley poems,** 154, 314, 317-18

Chesterfield, Philip Dormer Stanhope, 4th Earl of, 149

'Chevy Chase', ballad, 150-51

Child, Sir Josiah, 104, 107

Churchill, Sir Winston, 290

Cibber, Colley, 28, 29, 33, 38, 268

Cicero, 86, 87, 94

Clarke, Dr. Samuel, 45

Claude Lorrain, 223

Clerke, Timothy, 81

Cleveland, John, 300, 308

Coke, Roger, 106

Coleridge, Samuel Taylor, as critic, 36, 212, 216-17, 220, 315; as poet, 180, 218, 229

Collins, William, 302, 316, 318

Comenius, Johann Amos, 72, 161

Congreve, William, 65, 140

Conington, John, 178

Cotton, Charles, 141, **225**

Cowley, Abraham, 47, 141, 151, 243, 300-310

Cowper, William, viii, 133, 186, 193, 220, 316, 318

Crabbe, George, 222, 316

Craik, Henry, 289-90

Crane, Ronald, S., 311

Croft, Stephen, 277-8

Croker, John Wilson, 287

Cromwell, Henry, 65

Cromwell, Oliver, 71

Crowne, John, 140

Cumberland, William, Duke of, 138

Curll, Edmund, 62, 63

Curtis, Lewis P. 275

Darwin, Charles, 329

Davenant, Charles, 104-5, 110

Davenant, Sir William, *Gondibert*, 56, 227

Defoe, Daniel, 104, 158-79

De la Mare, Walter, 176

Delany, Dr. Patrick, 281

Demosthenes, 86, 89

Dennis, John, 27-8, 58, 229

Derham, William, 227-8

Descartes, René, 71, 73, 77-81, 114, 116, 122, 126

Dibelius, Wilhelm, 175

Dickens, Charles, 175

Dodd, Dr. William, 281

Dodsley, Robert, 181

Donne, John, 23-6, 47, 300-301, 305, 308-9

Draper, Eliza, 275-6, 281-4

Dryden, John, viii, 44, 47, 214, 309; as critic, 43, 57-8, 86, 154, 222, 229-30; as dramatist, 145, 227-8; as poet, 21-3, 25, 216, 221, 224, 242-3, 306-7

Duns (Joannes) Scotus, 327

Dury, John, 72

Dyer, John, 194

Economic man, idea of, 160, 170-76

Edward VI, 252

Edwards, Thomas, 271

Eliot, T. S., 21, 37, 39, 122, 243
Emerson, Ralph W., 76
Empson, William, 42, 218
Erasmus, 152

Farquhar, George, 140
Faulkner, George, 96, 97
Faust, 158
Fenton, Elijah, 231
Fergusson, Sir Adam, 291-3
Fergusson, Robert, 189, 190, 316
Fichte, Johann Gottlieb, 335
Fielding, General Edmund, 255
Fielding, Henry, 13, 15, 34, 36, 65, 251-73, 279, 312, 314
Fielding, Sarah, 255, 261
Flecknoe, Richard, 54
Ford, Charles, 96

Galileo, 114
Garrick, David, 274, 281
Garth, Samuel, 61
Gassendi, Pierre, 73, 76
Gawain and the Green Knight, 150
Gay, John, 6, 8, 11, 12, 16, 19, 36, 65, 84, 225; personality and works, 130-43
Genres, theory of, 213-17, 338
George II, viii, 33, 34
Gilbert, William, 69, 70
Glanvill, Joseph, 55, 74, 78, 79
Glover, Richard, 13
Godwin, William, 15
Goldsmith, Oliver, 223, 281, 342
Gothicism, 150-52, 246, 316
Grafton, Augustus Henry Fitzroy, 3rd Duke of, 240
Gray, Thomas, 5, 143, 180, 221, 233-50, 301, 314, 317
Gunning, Peter, Bishop of Chichester, 75

Hall, John, 72
Hall, Thomas, 75
Haller, Albrecht von, 339
Hampden, John, 238, 241

Hannah, (friend of Sterne), 274
Hanson, John, 227
Harris, James, 16
Harte, Walter, 200
Hayward, John, 96
Hazlitt, William, 186-7, 220-21
Heckscher, Eli F., 110
Herrick, Robert, 133
Hill, Aaron, 66, 200
Hill, G. Birkbeck, 11
Hobbes, Thomas, 6-7, 17, 53, 74, 77-9
Hogarth, William, 13, 268
Holland, Henry Fox, First Baron, 249
Homer, 27, 43, 86, 214-15
Hopkins, Gerard Manley, 313
Horace, 34, 43, 133, 151, 242
Housman, A. E., 239
Howard, Sir Robert, 143
Hugo, Victor, 317, 341

James, William, 18
James, Mrs. William (friend of Sterne), 274-5
Jenyns, Soame, 320-21, 341
Jervas, Charles, 65
Johnson, Esther (Stella), 5, 85, 91, 92, 148
Johnson, James, 190
Johnson, Samuel (chief discussions, 285-310), vii, viii, ix, 5, 15, 155, 181, 231, 263; *Dictionary*, 184, 222, 299; *Idler*, 299; *Lives of the Poets*, 11-14, 22, 130-33, 140-41, 184, 186, 246, 249, 289-90, 296, 299, 300-310, 313, 317; *London*, 11, 13; *Marmor*, 14; *Prayers*, 294; *Preface to Shakespeare*, 225, 289, 299, 302-3, 312; quoted, 3, 17, 149, 181-2, 314; *Rambler*, 288-9, 299, 302; *Rasselas*, 299; sermons, 294; *Taxation No Tyranny*, 292-3
Jonson, Ben, 86
Joyce, James, 242, 269, 317
Juvenal, 138

Kant, Immanuel, 335
Keats, John, 132, 212, 214, 220, 222, 229, 240, 244

Kent, William, 65
King, Dr. William, Archbishop of Dublin, *De Origine Mali,* 323ff.
King, Dr. William (Principal of St. Mary's Hall), 13
Kneller, Sir Godfrey, 65

Labor, dignity of, 160, 163-70, 178, 223
Lamartine, Alphonse de, 133
La Rochefoucauld, François de, 6-8, 15, 48, 54-6
Law, Edmund, 323 ff.
Law, William, viii, 148
Lawrence, D. H., 316
Leavis, F. R., 22, 32
Le Bossu, René, 151
Lecky, W. E. H., 14
Le Clerc, Jean, 45
Leibnitz, Gottfried Wilhelm, 320, 323, 334-6, 343
Lejay, Paul, 178
Lepell, Mary (Lady Hervey), 64
Lewis, C. S., 38
Locke, John, 52, 56, 59, 152, 161, 199, 206-7, 277
Lombard, Peter, 327
Lovejoy, A. O., 228
Lumley, Elizabeth (Mrs. Sterne), 275

Macaulay, Thomas Babington, 154, 287ff.
Machiavelli, Niccolo, 74
McKenzie, Henry, 188
Maclean, Norman, 314
Macpherson, James (*Ossian*), 154, 314-18
Malebranche, Nicholas, 44, 152
Malherbe, François de, 215
Malinowski, Bronislaw, 159, 174
Mallet (or Mallett), David, 13, 198
Malory, Thomas, 156
Malthus, Thomas Robert, 329
Mandelso, J. Albert de, 167
Mandeville, Bernard, 6, 7, 16-17, 104, 163

Marlborough, Sarah, Duchess of, 65, 145
Marx, Karl, 164-5, 171, 175
Melmoth, William, 229
Mercantilism, 102-11
Meredith, George, 276
Metaphors, neoclassic use of, 22-3, 26-39, 317-18
Metaphysical poetry, 21, 23-6, 32, 39, 300-310
Milton, John, 142, 145, 216, 238, 240-43, 343; imitation of, 38, 183-4, 189, 228, 243; as poet, 26-7, 38, 230, 248, 301; theodicy, 324-5, 327, 341
Mock-heroic, 36-9
Montagu, Lady Mary Wortley, 66, 67, 231
Montaigne, Michel de, 46, 232
More, Henry, 78, 79
More, Sir Thomas, *Utopia,* 152, 166, 169
Morris, William, 164, 170
Mozart, ix
Muir, Edwin, 277, 282
Murry, Middleton, 40
Myths, 34, 36, 158-60, 164, 165, 168, 172, 174, 178

Nature, attitude towards, viii, 70, 76, 135, 151, 153, 160, 182, 185-7, 217ff., 337
Nerval, Gérard de, 318
Newcastle, Margaret Cavendish, Duchess of, 44, 54
Newcastle, Thomas Pelham-Holles, Duke of, 108
Newman, John Henry, 219
Newton, Sir Isaac, 81, 82, 114, 122, 240, 304; influence of *Opticks,* 194-211
Nourisson, Paul, 161
Nugent, Robert, 13

Oldmixon, John, 43, 61
Optimism, vii-ix, 114-17, 129, 170, 319-36, 339-40, 342-3
Ormond, James Butler, 2nd Duke

of, 10

Orrery, John Boyle, 5th Earl of, 66, 84, 88, 149

Ovid, 34, 150, 151

Oxford, Edward Harley, 2nd Earl of, 64

Oxford, Robert Harley, 1st Earl of, 8-10, 65, 98

Parker, Samuel, 46

Parnell, Thomas, 10, 65

Pascal, Blaise de, 117, 119, 155, 175

Pater, Walter, 217, 234-5

Percy, Thomas, 153

Perry, Thomas Sergeant, 289

Petty, Sir William, 72, 103

Petyt, William, 103-4, 106

Philips, John, 225

Pindarics, 242-3, 245, 308

Pitt, Christopher, 194, 230

Pitt, William (the elder), 13, 14

The Plain Dealer, 46

Plato, 5, 87, 169, 326-8, 332

Plenitude, doctrine of, 326-36, 339, 342-3

Plessis, Frédéric, 178

Poe, Edgar Allan, 315

Politics, ix, 8-10, 12-15, 99-100, 122-4, 145-6, 266, 290-95

Pope, Alexander (chief discussions, 21-67), mentioned, viii, 12-13, 16, 95, 130, 132, 152, 154, 156, 181, 221, 225, 242, 275, 280, 311, 339; personality, 3-4, 62ff., 144-5; poetic art, ix, 21-41, 84, 140, 199, 212, 214, 222, 313-14; religion, 147; as satirist, 3, 8, 19, 68, 81, 146; *Art of Sinking in Poetry*, 67; Correspondence, 6, 10-11, 62-7, 115-16, 131; *Donne's Satires Versified*, 25-6, 30; *Dunciad*, vii, 12, 24, 27-33, 36-9, 67, 144, 152, 208-9, 216; *Eloisa*, 24, 31, 147, 236; *Essay on Criticism*, 32, 33, 42-59, 181, 214, 246, 305; *Essay on Man*, 5, 29, 31, 33, 117, 147, 153, 322-3, 327-8, 331, 339, 341-2; Homer translation, 27, 65-6, 214-15, 217, 229;

Moral Essays and *Horatian Imitations*, 13, 14, 18, 24, 26, 28-36, 306; *Pastorals*, 186, 219-20; *Rape of the Lock*, 30-32, 36-7, 64, 249; *Unfortunate Lady*, 23, 25; *Windsor Forest*, 24, 29, 31, 186

Postgate, Raymond, 297-9

Potter, Robert, 231

Pre-romaticism, use of term, 39, 311, 315

Primitivism, 162, 164, 166, 316-17

Prior, Matthew, 5, 10, 141, 305, 341

Progress, idea of, viii, 69, 72, 114

Pultenay, William, Earl of Bath, 84

Puns, use of, 30-32, 39

Purcell, Henry, ix

Queensberry, Catherine, Duchess of, 131-2; Charles Douglas, 3rd Duke of, 139

Quennell, Peter, 283

Quintana, Ricardo, 6

Rabelais, François, 144, 152

Raleigh, Sir Walter, 153, 228, 290

Ralph, James, 229

Ramsay, Allan, 188, 190

Rapin, René, 229

Ravenscroft, Edward, 140

Read, Herbert, 275

Reason, attitudes towards, vii, 5, 77, 80-83, 114, 116, 120-22, 126, 201, 208, 337, 339-40

Remarques on the Humours of the Town, 54

Ricardo, David, 171

Richards, I. A., 143

Richardson, Samuel, *Clarissa*, 184, 266, 314; *Pamela*, 188, 260, 271, 312

Richter, Jean Paul, 11

Rimbaud, Jean Arthur, 315, 317-18

Ritson, Joseph, 153

Rochester, John Wilmot, 2nd Earl of, 149

Romanticism, viii, 151, 153, 180, 236, 240, 311, 315, 319, 323, 337-40

Rothschild (Nathaniel Mayer Victor), Baron, 95
Rousseau, Jean Jacques, 15, 162-3, 169, 175, 291; *Émile*, 160-61, 164
Rowe, Nicholas, 306
Royal Society, 70ff., 114, 122
Ruskin, John, 175, 223
Rymer, Thomas, 229

Saint-Hyacinthe, H. Cordonnier de, 161
Saintsbury, George, 141
Sandys, George, 226
Savage, Richard, 194
Scaliger, 151
Schiller, Johann Christoph Friedrich von, 343
Schlegel, Friedrich, 343
Schleiermacher, Friedrich, 343
Science, attitude towards, 68-83, 100, 114, 122, 123-4, 152, 194ff.
Scott, Sir Walter, 153, 236
Scriblerus Club, 8-11
Selkirk, Alexander, 167, 174
Sewell, George, 225
Shadwell, Thomas, 81
Shaftesbury, Anthony Ashley Cooper, 3rd Earl of, viii, 16-17, 45-6, 56, 201
Shakespeare, William, 33, 147, 153, 189, 192, 236, 243, 244, 303; *Hamlet*, 3, 113, 150; *King Lear*, 3, 118, 127, 305; *Macbeth*, 225; *Timon of Athens*, 116
Shelley, Percy B., 132, 142, 212, 219, 225, 229
Shenstone, William, 36, 188, 219, 221
Sherburn, George, 66
Sheridan, Thomas, 18, 91-5
Shiels, Robert, 184
Sitwell, Edith, 132
Smart, Christopher, viii, 314-18
Smiles, Samuel, 165
Smith, Adam, 163, 171
Smith, D. Nichol, 7
Smollett, Tobias, 188, 263
Socrates, 5-6
Songs, 18th-century, 190-93

South, Robert, 71-2
Southey, Robert, 217, 229, 314
Southwell, Thomas Southwell, 2nd Baron, 149
Spence, Ferrand, 45
Spence, Joseph, 49, 66, 214
Spenser, Edmund, 147, 213, 214, 219, 243, 306
Speroni degli Alvarotti (Sperone), 86
Spinoza, Benedict de, 322, 327, 334
Sprat, Thomas, 74, 76, 80, 307
Stanhope, George, Dean of Canterbury, 54
Steele, Sir Richard, 16, 146, 150, 262, 289; *The Conscious Lovers*, 15; *The Guardian*, 65; *The Tatler*, 17, 46, 58, 85
Stella, *see* Johnson, Esther
Stephen, Leslie, 3, 289, 337-8
Sterne, Laurence, 274-84, 312; works, 188, 274ff., 316
Stevenson, John Hall, 275, 283
Stevenson, Robert Louis, 339
Stoicism, 126, 155-6, 166, 176, 263-5
Stubbe, Henry, 75, 76
Sublime, The, 144, 153-4, 195-211
Swift, Jonathan (chief discussions, 84-129), correspondence, 11, 63, 67; mentioned, vii, viii, 16, 22, 130-32, 147, 153, 156, 275, 314; personality, 4-5, 144; prose style, 84-101; religion, 115, 147-9; as satirist, 3, 6-12, 19, 33, 61, 68, 81, 100, 112ff., 146, 148-9, 152, 225; *Answer to the Craftsman*, 109; *Drapier's Letters*, 10; *Examiner*, 85, 93; *Gulliver's Travels*, vii, 5, 10, 16, 18, 85, 96-8, 101, 112-29, 144, 148, 296; *Intelligencer*, 87, 93, 106, 111; *A Letter of Advice to a Young Poet* (?), 96; *Maxims Controlled*, 102-3, 106; *Miscellanies*, 95-6; *Modest Proposal*, 33, 102-11; *Sermons*, 88-92, 148; *Tale of a Tub*, 5-6, 46, 86, 93; other works, 9, 46, 86, 93-4, 96, 105, 110, 148
Sylvester, Joshua (*Du Bartas*), 213, 227
Symbols, neoclassic use of, 38-9

Tawney, R. H., 166, 172
Taylor, Dr. John, 294
Temple, Sir William, 52, 152
Tennyson, Alfred, 212, 220, 313, 330
Thackeray, William Makepeace, 125
Theobald, Lewis, 28, 38, 145, 152
Thomas, Dylan, 318
Thomson, James, 13, 180-88; *The Seasons*, 181ff., 195ff., 205, 208, 218, 221, 223, 225-6
Thornhill, Sir James, 194
Thrale, Hester Lynch, 298
Tickell, Thomas, 18
Tiepolo, Giovanni Battista, 245
Tillotson, Geoffrey, 21, 42
Tillotson, John, Archbishop of Canterbury, 84, 88
Troeltsch, Ernst, 166
Twain, Mark (Samuel Clemens), 17

Van Doren, Mark, 40
Van Effen, Justus, 161
Vauvenargues, Marquis de, 15
Veale, Capt. Richard, 256
Verlaine, Paul, 317
Viner, Jacob, 110
Vines, Sherard, 223
Virgil, 34, 37, 43, 86, 214, 242, 335; *Aeneid*, 37; *Georgics*, 177-8, 219ff.
Vives, Joannes Ludovicus, 152
Vogüé, Eugene de, 175
Voltaire (François Marie Arouet de), viii, 20, 321-2, 341
Vulliamy, C. E., 297-8

Wallis, John, 71-2, 78, 83
Walmoden, Amalie Sophie, Countess of Yarmouth, 33
Walpole, Horace, 154, 242, 247 250; Strawberry Hill, 236, 246
Walpole, Sir Robert, 12-14, 266

Walsh, William, 47, 57
Warburton, William, 61, 281
Ward, Ned, 133
Warton, Joseph, 13, 14, 16, 20, 131, 153, 223, 230, 316
Warton, Thomas, 153, 233, 237, 316
Warwick, Edward Henry Rich, 7th Earl of, 146
Watkins, W. B. C., 282
Watson, James, 190
Watts, Isaac, viii, 193
Weber, Max, 166, 169, 171, 173
Webster, John, 72
Welsted, Leonard, 54, 57
Wesley, John and Samuel, viii, 193, 314
West, Gilbert, 306
West, Richard, 247
White, Gilbert, 221
Whitefield, Rev. George, 258, 281
Whitman, Walt, 315
The Whole Duty of Man, 61
Wilde, Oscar, 231
Wilkinson, L. P., 178
William III, 50
Wimsatt, W. K. Jr., 22
Wit, 21, 24-5, 42-61, 150, 305
Wood, William, 88-9
Woolf, Virginia, 159, 312
Wordsworth, William, 76, 153, 180, 311; as critic, 141-2, 183-4, 212, 214-17, 231, 314, 318; as poet, 186-7, 218
Wotton, Sir. Henry, 18
Wycherley, William, 47-50, 54, 56, 59, 61, 65, 145

Young, Edward, 199, 305-7

Zeugma, 30, 32

Galaxy Books for the Discriminating Reader

ABRAMS, Meyer H.   ENGLISH ROMANTIC POETS   GB35
AQUINAS, St. Thomas   PHILOSOPHICAL TEXTS selected and translated by
  Thomas Gilby   GB29
BARKER, Ernest   REFLECTIONS ON GOVERNMENT   GB15
BERLIN, Isaiah   KARL MARX   GB25
BOWRA, C. M.   ANCIENT GREEK LITERATURE   GB30
BRUUN, Geoffrey   NINETEENTH-CENTURY EUROPEAN CIVILIZATION   GB36
CLARK, George   EARLY MODERN EUROPE   GB37
CLIFFORD, James L.   EIGHTEENTH-CENTURY ENGLISH LITERATURE   GB23
COCHRANE, Charles Norris   CHRISTIANITY AND CLASSICAL CULTURE   GB7
COLLINGWOOD, R. G.   THE IDEA OF HISTORY   GB1
COLLINGWOOD, R. G.   THE IDEA OF NATURE   GB31
COLLINGWOOD, R. G.   THE PRINCIPLES OF ART   GB11
CRUICKSHANK, John   ALBERT CAMUS AND THE LITERATURE OF REVOLT   GB43
DIXON, W. Macneile   THE HUMAN SITUATION   GB12
EVANS-WENTZ, W. Y.   THE TIBETAN BOOK OF THE DEAD   GB39
FEIDELSON and BRODTKORB   INTERPRETATIONS OF AMERICAN LITERATURE   GB26
GEROULD, Gordon Hall   THE BALLAD OF TRADITION   GB8
GRIERSON, Herbert J. C.   METAPHYSICAL LYRICS AND POEMS OF THE
  SEVENTEENTH CENTURY   GB19
HEILER, Friedrich   PRAYER translated by Samuel McComb   GB16
HERKLOTS, H. G. G.   HOW OUR BIBLE CAME TO US   GB4
HIGHET, Gilbert   THE CLASSICAL TRADITION   GB5
HOMER   THE ODYSSEY OF HOMER translated by T. E. Shaw   GB2
LEWIS, C. S.   THE ALLEGORY OF LOVE   GB17
MALINOWSKI, Bronislaw   A SCIENTIFIC THEORY OF CULTURE   GB40
MATTHIESSEN, F. O.   THE ACHIEVEMENT OF T. S. ELIOT *third edition*   GB22
MILLS, C. Wright   THE POWER ELITE   GB20
MILLS, C. Wright   WHITE COLLAR   GB3
MULLER, Herbert J.   THE USES OF THE PAST   GB9
MURRAY, Gilbert   THE RISE OF THE GREEK EPIC   GB41
OTTO, Rudolph   THE IDEA OF THE HOLY   GB14
RADHAKRISHNAN, S.   EASTERN RELIGIONS AND WESTERN THOUGHT   GB27
ROBERTS, David E.   EXISTENTIALISM AND RELIGIOUS BELIEF edited by
  Roger Hazelton   GB28
ROSTOVTZEFF, M.   ROME   GB42
RUSSELL, Bertrand   THE PROBLEMS OF PHILOSOPHY   GB21
SHAPIRO, Harry L.   MAN, CULTURE, AND SOCIETY   GB32
THUCYDIDES   A HISTORY OF THE PELOPONNESIAN WAR edited in translation
  by R. W. Livingstone   GB33
TILLICH, Paul   LOVE, POWER, AND JUSTICE   GB38
TURBERVILLE, A. S.   ENGLISH MEN AND MANNERS IN THE EIGHTEENTH CENTUPY   GB10
WAGENKNECHT, Edward   CHAUCER   GB24
WEBER, Max   FROM MAX WEBER: ESSAYS IN SOCIOLOGY translated and edited
  by H. H. Gerth and C. Wright Mills   GB13
WHITEHEAD, Alfred North   AN INTRODUCTION TO MATHEMATICS   GB18
WOODWARD, C. Vann   THE STRANGE CAREER OF JIM CROW   GB6
YOUNG, J. Z.   DOUBT AND CERTAINTY IN SCIENCE   GB34